A THEORY OF SENTIENCE

A Theory of Sentience

AUSTEN CLARK

OXFORD

UNIVERSITY PRESS

OXFORD

UNIVERSITY PRESS

Great Clarendon Street, Oxford OX2 6DP

Oxford University Press is a department of the University of Oxford.
It furthers the University's objective of excellence in research, scholarship,
and education by publishing worldwide in

Oxford New York

Athens Auckland Bangkok Bogotá Buenos Aires Calcutta
Cape Town Chennai Dar es Salaam Delhi Florence Hong Kong Istanbul
Karachi Kuala Lumpur Madrid Melbourne Mexico City Mumbai
Nairobi Paris São Paulo Singapore Taipei Tokyo Toronto Warsaw

with associated companies in Berlin Ibadan

Oxford is a registered trade mark of Oxford University Press
in the UK and in certain other countries

Published in the United States
by Oxford University Press Inc., New York

© Austen Clark 2000

British Library Cataloguing in Publication Data

Data available

Library of Congress Cataloging-in-publication Data
Clark, Austen.
A theory of sentience/Austin Clark.
Includes bibliographical references.
1. Senses and sensation. 2. Perception (Philosophy) I. Title.
BD214.C535 2000   152.1--dc21   99-59001

ISBN 0-19-823851-7

1 3 5 7 9 10 8 6 4 2

Typeset in Times by
Cambrian Typesetters, Frimley, Surrey

Printed in Great Britain
on acid-free paper by
Biddles Ltd
Guildford and King's Lynn

PREFACE

CONSCIOUSNESS without sentience is conceivable, but ghastly to contemplate. There you are, sitting quietly in your chair, thinking hard about some philosophical problem, eyes closed, brow furrowed. Perhaps your concentration is so good that you will not notice as we gradually remove all of your capacities of sensation. First you are rendered blind and deaf. It is fortunate that your eyes are closed, since it may postpone the disturbing discovery that you have lost your sense of sight. Similarly the absence of auditory stimulation might actually improve the clarity of your thoughts. Taste and smell next vanish without a trace. No more alluring odours or tart tastes, but you try to keep the distractions of food out of the study anyway. We proceed to eliminate your sensitivity to pain and to temperature. Perhaps even this could be managed without disturbing your concentration—you have no aches or chills at the moment, so notice no change—but at some point in the final excisions, of touch and the remaining bodily senses, you are bound to notice that something is happening to you. You must lose all sense of bodily attitude, so that you can no longer tell whether you are sitting or standing. All of your limbs come to feel as if anaesthetized. You lose all sense of the direction of gravity and of your body pressing into the chair. Finally you lose all tactile sensitivity, so that you can no longer feel yourself touching anything at all. In fact the loss is somewhat more radical: you could no longer feel yourself to have any locatable bodily boundaries or position. To you there would cease to be any sensible distinction between regions that are you and regions that are not. One might say that in the end you feel utterly disembodied, but in truth you feel nothing at all.

In these dire straits Descartes would offer you his congratulations: you are now, at last, ready to think clearly and distinctly. No more distractions! And indeed, it is conceivable that you continue thinking. Absent all clamour from the senses, you might make remarkable progress on the philosophical problem that had been troubling you; but it would be impossible to communicate your results, or in any way to sense the existence of other human beings who might care to hear them. You would of course be spared all bodily pain, but if one had a choice in the matter, one might in the end choose to feel some pain rather than feel nothing.

Sentience is then an important part, but still only a part, of consciousness. Generally sensation is placed at the very bottom of the various hierarchies of complexity leading up to the summit of self-conscious mental states. In one simple sense of the word 'conscious', any animal that is awake and has some sensation is conscious. If it can see, hear, feel, or in some way sense something of its surroundings, then it is conscious. Such 'creature consciousness' is phylogenetically widespread, extending as far and as wide as the receipt of the capacity to sense. Those receipts are now spread far and wide indeed. The initial endowments precede the birth of our species, and indeed precede the entire class of mammalia. These capacities have an ancient ancestry. So it is not surprising to find a kinship between our colour vision and the colour vision of fish, or between our eyes and the eyes of a frog. Some of the basic architecture of bodily sensation may be common to all vertebrates, elaborations on a common plan laid down hundreds of millions of years ago. Plans for spines were being laid at roughly the same time.

In this book I offer what with reservations can be called a 'theory' of sentience. My title is actually an attempt simultaneously to acknowledge two books that I admire: George Pitcher's *A Theory of Perception* and Wallace Matson's *Sentience*. Cross-breeding gives us *A Theory of Sentience*. Let us hope it manifests hybrid vigour. I admire the systematic character of Pitcher's theory of the intentional content of perception, but also want to accommodate details of the simpler endowments granted to us by raw feeling. Indeed one theme will be that sentience is not exactly perception; the intentionality of sensation differs from the intentionality of thought. Sensing does not employ sentences, and sensory states are not beliefs. We are endowed with systems of mental representation of different kinds. But then it is incumbent upon us to spell out the differences at some level of detail. Developments since Pitcher's book have made more details available. This project bears on debates both old and on-going about the intentionality of sensation. Are sensory states intentional states? Or are they merely pseudo-intentional, or for that matter, non-intentional? I think these questions can be sensibly addressed only if one provides a systematic account of how sensing represents—an account of the system of sensory representation—and that is what this book tries to do.

Its subject-matter should be identified without imposing a dichotomy between sensation and perception, or between sensory and perceptual processes. Psychologists have largely abandoned such dichotomies, and I propose to follow suit. Instead of talking about 'visual sensation', followed after some *n* stages by 'visual perception', followed after *m* stages by 'cognition', and finally, if one is lucky, followed by a few clear and distinct ideas, we now have something of a tangled hierarchy or semi-ordering of processes, some of which are 'early' and others of which are 'late'. 'Early vision' is generally taken to include processes in the visual nervous system from transduction up to and including tertiary visual association areas in the neocortex. Those areas have considerable traffic both up and down—indeed, some collateral influences descend to the retina—but almost all the traffic is in some sense clearly visual. Whereas beyond the tertiary association areas one finds polysensory traffic, inputs from multiple modalities, and outputs to speech and motor regions. Taking 'early vision' as a paradigm, by 'sensory process' I mean processes in the modality in question from transduction up to and including tertiary association areas in the neocortex. That is what this book is about. This identification is not an a priori definition, but I will argue that models of those processes are in fact models of what people have been talking about all along when they talk about 'sensation'.

The other reservation to be noted about my title is that the 'theory' the book proposes is a *philosophical* theory. It is not itself a theory of sensation or an attempt to account for sensory capacities. Although I certainly hope that it is consistent with what we know about sensory systems, it is not meant to compete with empirical accounts produced by psychologists, neuroscientists, psychophysiologists, or ethologists. It is instead an account of how those *accounts* might hang together. I propose a tentative road map, a view of how various scattered pieces of our intellectual and scientific landscape might fit together. Such a road map is what we need when we stumble into conceptual problems. There are some big ones lurking out there, in the nether regions around raw feeling, and the goal of this project is to grapple with some of them.

The central one might be put simply: how is sensation *possible*? How can a merely material nervous system—if that is what we have—produce the alluring or tangy phenomenology of sense? Most descriptions of the mystery of the mind–body problem sooner or later get to this question. While insentient thought has its own deeply puzzling features, sensory phenomena invariably grab the spotlight in such presentations. One summons up an artful display of vivid colour or wretched pain. After a drum roll, the philosopher steps out from the backdrop, points dramatically, and asks: How could neurons produce *that*? The audience gasps appreciatively. This philosophical puzzle would largely be resolved if one could provide a *possible* account: an account that is internally consistent, consistent with what is known about sensory systems, and that could in principle explain how a merely material nervous system yields the phenomenology of sense. As Sellars urged, the goal is to achieve a synoptic view: an account of how all the different pieces of the landscape *could* fit together in a plausible way.

Once one sees how a solution is possible, the problem of determining which solution is the actual one is no longer specifically philosophical. It no longer generates the conceptual perplexity, the vertiginous feeling, that is the hallmark of a philosophical problem. So just when the things get interesting to the experimentalist, the philosopher loses interest. I hope this genesis explains some features of the account that will undoubtedly prove irksome to anyone who performs experiments or collects data. To an experimentalist such a philosophical 'theory' will seem by turns schematic and speculative, alternately straining at what seem to be conceptual minutiae, ignoring vast tracts of laboriously acquired empirical detail, and then in the next moment leaping, without so much as a fare-thee-well, far beyond the bounds of what is currently known. Such antics can be breathtaking. But the philosophical goal is to reach a synoptic view, a view of how things might hang together, and attempts to reach it must have this quirky character.

I was prompted to start writing these pages by a question from David Rosenthal, who over lunch at the Track Nine Diner in West Willington, Connecticut, asked me: why not write another book? Why not, indeed? I could not think of a good argument. As will be obvious to the reader, the process turned out to be great fun. It helped that Mark Emmert, Provost and later Chancellor of the University of Connecticut, had instituted Provost's Research Fellowships, one of which made it possible for me to devote a semester entirely to writing. It helped even more to have an outstanding group of good-humoured and acute colleagues in the Department of Philosophy at Storrs. I particularly want to thank Crawford Elder, Ruth Millikan, and John Troyer for their extensive (and, as we say, pains-taking) comments on the manuscript, and for their enthusiasm about the project. I also received very helpful comments and queries on parts of the argument from Don Baxter, Scott Lehmann, and Sam Wheeler. Graduate students Dan Blair, Jim Phelps, Karl Stocker, Weimin Sun, and Virgil Whitmyer made a seminar on sentience which I taught in the fall of 1997 a challenge and a delight, and I thank them for all their comments too. Although we have been trying to keep the attractions of the Department of Philosophy at Storrs a secret, I am afraid I must break our code of silence and acknowledge publicly that it is a wonderful place. From further afield I received very thorough and helpful comments on the proposal and the eventual manuscript from Justin Broackes, Larry Hardin, Lawrence Marks, and Evan Thompson. I am grateful to David Rosenthal not only for his comments but also for introducing me to Peter Ross, who sent lengthy and stimulating comments from afar. Rick Grush did too. To all these people I give thanks; their pages of comments and suggestions filled a fat notebook, and although I have by no means answered all the objections therein, working through them has improved the final result considerably. Finally, I would like to thank Peter Momtchiloff for once again providing his expert editorial guidance; he shepherded *Sensory Qualities* to completion without a hitch, and as an author it is restful to be able to trust his services again. I am grateful to Robert Ritter, who took on the project as assistant editor at Oxford University Press, and to Laurien Berkeley, who did the copy-editing.

A.C.

Willington, Connecticut
August 1999

ACKNOWLEDGEMENTS

Parts of Chapter 3 are based on parts of my 'Three varieties of visual field', *Philosophical Psychology*, 9/4 (Dec. 1996), 477–95, and used by permission of Carfax Publishing Limited (PO Box 25, Abingdon, Oxfordshire OX14 3UE). Parts of Chapter 5 are based on parts of 'True theories, false colors', published in the *Philosophy of Science* PSA Supplemental Issue (Oct. 1996), 143–50, copyright by the Philosophy of Science Association, and used by permission. Other portions of the text have been presented in talks at the CUNY Graduate Center, the John B. Pierce Laboratory at Yale University, the University of Pennsylvania, the University of Connecticut, and at conferences in Cleveland, Ischia, Los Angeles, and San Francisco.

CONTENTS

Contents

1

Quality Space

THERE is more to sentience than sensory qualities. Even if there comes a day when all the conceptual tangles wrapped around the qualities of sensory experience have been resolved, the job of understanding sentience would still be only half done. Lurking beyond the thickets of qualia lies another problem that is just as big and nasty. So even after those thickets are cleared, philosophers still could not rest; they would still have work to do. They would still have gainful employment. To make this case I need to explain (in this chapter) how one might come to understand the qualities of sensory experience, and then (in the next) show that even when that task is done there are aspects of sentience that remain untouched.

1.1 FOUR ASSAYS OF QUALITY

A *quality space* is an ordering of the qualities presented by a sensory modality in which relative similarities among those qualities are represented by their relative distances. Qualities that are relatively similar to one another are closer to one another than are qualities that are relatively less similar. The machinery required to derive such multidimensional orders is rather elaborate (see Clark 1993*b*), so it is easy to lose track of what the end-product will do for us, and why we might want some. Let us start then with a synopsis of the scope and limits of quality space.

The label itself turns out to be ambiguous. It helps to distinguish two different senses in which one might describe the 'qualities of experience'. As in so much of contemporary philosophy of mind, the distinction can be traced back to some prominent discussions by Wilfrid Sellars (1963: 93–4, 192–3), who noted the difference between ascribing a property to something experienced—something seen, felt, or heard, for example—and ascribing a property to the experiencing of it. Sellars urged that predicates such as 'red', 'square', 'loud', 'smooth', 'sweet', and 'cold' are in their initial and paradigm uses ascribed to the objects seen, heard, felt, tasted, or touched. The logical subjects of these predicates are, in the manifest image, physical objects, physically in front of the sense organs. A 'sensation of red' is first and foremost a sensation of an *object* that is red; 'red' characterizes the thing seen, not the seeing of it. But Sellars noted that once we have acquired the notion of a sense impression—which is not something seen, but instead a seeing of something—these predicates can acquire a second, distinct use.

Imagine, he suggests, that the notion of a sense impression is introduced as a theoretical term in an explicit theory. To do any work for us these hypothetical entities must be endowed with properties that allow them to play the appropriate role in the generation of perceptual episodes. What properties? Sellars suggested that they are constructed by analogy with the sensed qualities themselves. Our initial analogical model for a sense impression of a red triangle is precisely: a red triangular wafer. Clearly we cannot attribute 'red' to the sense impression in the same sense in which we attribute it to the wafer. So, Sellars suggests, we limit the application of the analogy to those structural patterns of resemblance and difference found among the colours. We invent 'counterpart properties' red*, green*, and so on, whose relations of resemblance and difference to one another are structurally similar to those found among the colours of objects, but which can be attributed to sense impressions. A sensation *of* a red apple is not itself red; instead it has some counterpart property, red*, in virtue of which the apple in front of the eyes *looks* red.

This distinction is not original with Sellars; it is clearly related to Thomas Reid's distinction of two different senses in which one can speak of the properties of 'ideas'. And the distinction has been noted, in various guises, by many authors since Sellars. An etymologically memorable and hence useful terminology is provided by Galen Strawson (1989). He distinguishes between 'phenomenal' properties and 'qualitative' properties, and I shall adopt this terminology. Phenomenal properties are all those that characterize how things appear. They are attributed to things in front of the sense organs. If the apple one spots, picks, and bites looks red, feels cold, and tastes sweet, then red, cold, and sweet are phenomenal properties. They characterize aspects of the appearance of the apple. Those appearances depend in part upon internal states of whoever happens to be apple-picking: upon the 'sense impressions', 'sensations', or 'experiences' of the apple-picker. Qualitative properties are properties of such internal states, in virtue of which things out there, dangling in front of one's grasping fingers, appear as they do. So the sense impression of the apple has a 'red qualitative character': a character in virtue of which the apple *looks* red. One might also use the Sellarsian notation: red*. The qualitative property is a property of an internal state in virtue of which something else—the apple at one's fingertips—has a phenomenal property: it looks red.

The proposed technical distinction uses the words 'phenomenal' and 'qualitative' in two of their accepted senses, but one must immediately acknowledge that those same words are used in other contexts in entirely different ways. Sensation being such an interesting subject to our species, we have evolved an extraordinarily intricate and flexible terminology for signalling, classifying, characterizing, analysing, describing, savouring, and stimulating it. So, for example, it is possible to find natural language usages that invert the proposed technical distinction: we speak of the 'phenomenal character' of experience and use 'phenomenally red' and similar locutions to ascribe properties to some mental states. Conversely, we speak of the red colour and sweet taste of the apple as obvious examples of the qualities of sensation. Even the philosopher's technical term 'qualia' is ambiguous between what I have called phenomenal properties and qualitative properties. C. I. Lewis (1929) used the term in both senses, for example. The redness of the red patch is for many philosophers the paradigm example of a quale; yet to the innocent eye it appears to be attributed to something out there in front of the eyes. Smooth, cold, and sweet are other qualia crowding in as one hefts the apple into biting range; yet they too characterize how the thing in the hand appears.

Some theoreticians identify qualia with what I have called 'phenomenal properties', and the going hypothesis is that these are properties represented by one's sensory experiences (Lycan 1996; Tye 1995). Yet qualia are typically thought to be properties of mental states, not of apples; one would be considered lunatic if one tried to resolve their problematic character by a careful study of arboreal botany. Qualia at least provide one subject properly studied in (and perhaps confined to) the halls of philosophy of mind. Theoreticians favouring this usage speak of qualia or qualitative character as properties ascribed to mental states (see Shoemaker 1990, 1994*a,b*). On one version, qualitative character consists of those properties of mental states in virtue of which they represent phenomenal properties (Harman 1990); on another, qualitative character is independent of the representational properties of mental states, but is accessible via introspection (Block 1990, 1995). The debate is further confused by the fact that the term 'qualia' itself has become invested and infested with theoretical commitments, so that to many participants the question of whether qualia exist is now synonymous with the question of whether intrinsic, non-intentional, introspectible properties of mental states exist (see Dennett 1988). Hence, sadly, the term 'qualia' can no longer be used as a neutral term describing a problem; now it entails a commitment to one kind of solution. This ruins the word for my purposes; the neutral term 'qualitative properties', introduced above, should not be assumed to have any of the defining characteristics of the now infamous 'qualia'.[1]

---

[1] Likewise any use I make of the words 'quale' or 'qualia' in what follows should be interpreted in the old-fashioned sense of C. I. Lewis, James, and Goodman; not as the infamous new 'strange qualia' (Lycan 1996: 110).

Like 'qualia', the label 'quality space' is ambiguous. The properties whose order it presents might be phenomenal properties, or they might be qualitative properties. In the former sense quality space is an ordering of the qualities that things appear to have; in the latter it is an ordering of properties of sensation, in virtue of which things out there appear as they do.

The distinction between phenomenal and qualitative properties helps to clarify the status of quality space. In fact the manufacturing process that yields this product has at least four distinct stages, or four different interpretations for the 'qualities' thereby spaced: (*a*) stimulus classes; (*b*) phenomenal properties; (*c*) qualitative properties; and (*d*) psycho-physical properties. Stimulus classes are used as the entering wedge to identify phenomenal properties, but, as will be seen, those properties cannot be defined in terms of stimulus parameters. And qualitative properties, if all goes well, ultimately are identified with neural ones. The crucial step is the step from (*b*) to (*c*), from phenomenal properties to qualitative ones; and this is genuinely a change in subject-matter, as the properties have distinct logical subjects. But let us trace the genesis of the product.

1.1.1 Classes of Stimuli

It is important to recognize from the outset that the occupants of quality space are not stimuli, but rather the qualities that stimuli present. In any ordering of hues, orange is between red and yellow (it is a binary combination of the two), but this ordering is not an ordering of stimuli. It has nothing to do with the fact that a 600 nanometre wavelength is between 580 and 620. In fact there may be no stimulus metric in terms of which an arbitrary stimulus for orange is 'between' arbitrary stimuli for red and yellow respectively. Physically disparate stimuli may all present the same hue quality. Metamers, or combinations of wavelengths that have the same effect on the visual system, will do so. Even though orange is between red and yellow, there is no determinate sense to the suggestion that all the metamers that present orange are somehow 'between' all those metamers that present red and all those that present yellow.

A stimulus is best considered an occasion, a particular episode of irritation of transducer surfaces. The various ambient energies involved can differ physically even though all those episodes appear the same to the creature suffering the irritations. The ordering of qualities does not order that hotchpotch of varieties of ambient physical energies. Relations of matching and discriminability are instead used to order the qualities that those stimuli present.

Matching is the simplest of such relations, since its relata are particular stimuli—particular occasions. But even matching has its subtleties. For example, in colour vision the relation has not just two terms—stimuli x and y match—but at least eight: stimulus x matches stimulus y for observer O in state of adaptation A under ambient illumination I viewed with surround S at angle α with angular subtense β. Change any of these terms, and the match is disturbed. Such profligate relativism provides a second reason to deny that the ordering provided by quality space is an ordering of stimuli. Physically the 'same' stimulus might on a second occasion present a different quality. If the observer's state of adaptation or the ambient illumination are changed sufficiently, it will do so. Flood the field with red light for a while, and a second presentation of that 'same' packet of ambient energies will look distinctly greenish.

Occasions being so fleeting, a science can get under way only if some scheme of classification can be devised under which one can recognize something repeatable in the flux. The notion already mooted, of generating a second instance of an event which is physically the 'same', provides one route. To the extent that one can develop instruments to control and repeatedly generate new instances of the 'same' packet of ambient energies, one can start to experiment. In practice within psycho-physics a 'stimulus' is a class of such occasions: physically controllable and repeatable instances of the 'same' packet of photons to the eye, compression waves to the ear, gases to the nose, and so on.

It is only after one can begin to manipulate such classes of occasions that one can begin to assess the more complicated relations of discriminability. We need these more complicated notions to cope with the otherwise disconcerting variability in responses to a forced-choice task. Present the 'same' pair of stimuli to an observer repeatedly, and sometimes they will be judged to match, sometimes not. One must assess whether that *distribution* of responses differs from one produced by chance alone. Such assessment is invariably statistical, requiring repeated trials. It follows that the terms for the relations of discriminability are classes of stimuli: occasions collected by the underlying physics of the ambient energies. Other workable terms for similarity have at least this minimal complexity: they too relate classes of stimuli. For example, triadic relations of relative similarity (x is more similar to y than to z) are unworkable if the terms are restricted to single, unrepeatable occasions. In comparing relative similarities of three colour patches, one may typically first compare x to y, and then compare x to z; but if x is allowed to range only over occasions, this second comparison is not a comparison of the 'same' x as found in the first.

Given some particular classes of repeatable stimuli that look orange, red, and yellow, one might be able to devise some physical interpretation for the claim that 'orange is between red and yellow' in stimulus terms.

Unfortunately, tomorrow one is likely to find other, disparate classes of stimuli that are metamers for those used yesterday, and which fail to satisfy those physical relations. Furthermore, the stimuli used yesterday might today present different qualities, since today it is overcast, or we are testing a different observer, or we finished repainting the walls of the shop. Relationships between the qualities cannot be cashed out directly in stimulus terms, and attempts to define 'orange' in stimulus terms are doomed to failure.

To the question 'What are the occupants of quality space?' the natural answer is 'qualities', and what these considerations show is that while we might be able to *label* a point in quality space with some stimulus specification—some class of stimuli which happened to present that quality—we cannot *identify* the quality with that class. A finite class of occasions might help to pick out the quality, but it cannot be used to define the identity of that quality. So from the very beginning, the relations of matching, discriminability, and relative similarity among classes of stimuli are used to order something other than those stimuli themselves. Discriminations among stimuli serve to order the qualities that the stimuli present.

How this works still seems like magic. It is not magic, but it is still wondrous to behold. Order emerges from indifference, to use Nelson Goodman's apt phrase (Goodman 1972: 423–36). In appearance we find structure. The various similarity relations—matching, discriminability, and relative similarity—have formal features that generate the order of qualities. Matching, for example, is non-transitive; x might be judged to match y, and y z, but the differences accumulating between x and z might be sufficient to reject a match between them. An ordering of qualities that respects the principle that more similar qualities should be placed closer to one another than less similar ones is obliged to put the quality presented by y between those presented by x and by z. Other more direct methods and more powerful inferences are possible; if you hunger for such, you can find satiation in *Sensory Qualities* (Clark 1993*b*).

The various similarity relations holding among classes of stimuli are used to order the qualities that those stimuli present. It follows that the relations among the qualities themselves are at some remove from relations among stimuli. The occupants of a quality space for colours will be, not packets of photons, but colour qualities: red, yellow, green, blue, orange, and so on. In such an ordering we find orange between red and yellow. This fact is at some remove from relations that we can state in stimulus terms. It does not imply that one packet of photons is 'between' two other packets. The relations of discriminability and relative similarity that suffice to place orange between red and yellow are not relations among the qualities themselves. One does not discriminate the quality orange from the quality red; instead discrimination always has as its terms classes of stimuli. What sort of fact is it that orange is between red and yellow? It is not directly about discriminations. Perhaps it could be called a *structural* fact. It is a fact about properties of the relationships of discriminability, matching, and so on holding among classes of stimuli that present the qualities in question.

Another implication of this somewhat indirect relationship between points in a quality space and particular stimuli should be mentioned. Attempts to order the qualities presented by stimuli are perforce limited to those stimuli used in the attempt. A quality space is always an ordering of qualities presented by a particular gamut or sample of stimuli; it depicts the order within that population, but foreign stimuli may follow other laws. In the lab one seeks occasions that are precisely controlled and replicable, and so coloured lights might always be presented through a reduction tube, and surface colours will always be presented as patches of a fixed size and angle, under constant ambient illumination, with neutral surrounds, and using procedures to ensure that the subject between trials returns to a neutral state of adaptation. A lab whose results change when it repaints its walls would not have its grants renewed. With a particular gamut of such stimuli we might find a colour space of just three dimensions: hue, saturation, and brightness. But these three dimensions will undoubtedly prove inadequate to describe the dimensions of variation in visual appearance found in a larger and more diverse sample of naturally occurring stimuli. Brown is found nowhere in such a space, for example, as its appearance depends critically on the presence of a bright surround. Even the number of dimensions of the quality space will depend upon the sample chosen. Glossy surfaces, reflections, translucency, transparency, shadows, and mists all require dimensions of variation in appearance beyond the three sufficient for coloured surfaces or lights presented in the lab.

1.1.2 Properties of Appearance

Now to pull some strands together. The science can start only after it forms classes of repeatable stimulus occasions. These classes might be used to label or identify a point in quality space, but these points are not identical to any such collection of occasions. The occupants of quality space are not stimuli. Instead they are something distinct: the qualities those stimuli present. These are, precisely, phenomenal properties, or properties of appearance. Matching, discriminability, and relative similarity do not proceed along any straightforward physical metric, but instead along a metric of similarity of appearance. Two stimuli match because they look the same, sound the same, taste the same, and so on. So in this first interpretation of quality space, the qualities that are its occupants are phenomenal properties. The dimensions of hue, saturation, and brightness are dimensions that suffice to order the variations in appearance among precisely controlled coloured lights in a reduction tube, or two degree coloured patches in a neutral surround. (Technically the dimension called 'brightness' for coloured lights is called 'lightness' for coloured surfaces.) Those variables describe how the stimuli *look*. Similarities and differences in those appearances can be captured with three independent terms. They delimit the gamut of phenomenal properties presented by that population. Granted, as soon as we loose the strictures of the lab, and consider some naturally occurring stimuli, we must be prepared for some additional complexities. Three dimensions prove inadequate to describe a reflection of the blue sky seen in a brown mud puddle, for example. But whatever dimensions we add will still be dimensions of variation in appearance: dimensions that order phenomenal properties.

On this interpretation a colour 'quality space' is very close to a colour order system. One way to reveal the variation in colour appearance is to construct a gamut of stimuli that present varying appearances, and then physically order the stimuli in such a way that stimuli that are close to one another present qualities that are relatively similar to one another. Colour sample systems are the best example, but arrays of tuning forks provide an auditory version. With the colour sample system one attempts to print pages whose inked patches are such that two patches are relatively close to one another on the page only if they look relatively similar in colour. The enterprise is by no means trivial; it requires sophisticated understanding of the chemistry of inks and dyes and of the rules of their combination. Even when it is successful it should be clear that the colour quality presented by a particular patch cannot be defined by the particular combination of inks that happen to present it.

1.1.3 Qualitative Properties

If we had to stop after printing an array of colour patches, the project would be relatively uninteresting, at least to psychologists and philosophers. But the plot thickens: these arrays of colour patches serve as something like illuminated manuscripts, revealing some of the secular mysteries of vision. Study of the dimensions of variation in phenomenal appearance provides surprisingly potent insights into what must be going on inside a creature's visual apparatus.

A paradigm example of this sort of reasoning was provided by Thomas Young in 1801. The premiss was a fact long known about colour mixing and matching: that the appearance of any coloured light can be matched by mixing and adjusting the intensities of just three distinct 'primaries'. The primaries had only to meet the requirement that no one of them could be matched by any combination of intensities of the other two. So three dimensions suffice to describe the variation possible in the appearances of coloured lights. What Young inferred from this was the trichromatic character of human colour vision: that there are at least three, and probably no more than three, distinct types of colour sensitive receptors ('particles') in the retina (see Boring 1942: 111). These we now identify as three classes of cones. Young recognized that there might be more than three, but that the facts of colour-mixing and -matching required only three. More than three would crowd the retina unnecessarily, so Young plumped, parsimoniously, for the minimum required.

Qualitative properties are properties of the internal states of the creature—those sensory states without which the creature would not see (or sense) what it sees (or senses). To revert to Sellarsian terminology: a sense impression of red is endowed with some property in virtue of which that sense impression is an impression of red, and not of some other colour. This property is not redness, exactly, but it is tied, by an analogous structure of resemblances and differences, to colour properties—to those properties *of which* the sense impression is a sense impression. The sense impression has the qualitative character red*, and in virtue of being red*, is a sense impression *of* red, and not (say) of blue.

What this manœuvre requires (and what Young recognized in 1801) is that the structure of similarities and differences among the qualitative properties of sensation must be sufficient to account for the structure of similarities and differences among phenomenal properties. By no means can there be *less* structure among qualitative properties than among the phenomenal ones, since such a finding would render miraculous the creature's capacities to discriminate. There could be more structure, but it is unparsimonious to suppose so. In technical, information-theoretic terms, the channel between transducer irritations and the eventual muscle twitches that indicate a discrimination has some capacity that can be measured in bits. More discriminations require more bits. If anywhere within this channel there are intermediary states that throw away information, conflate incoming Ps with incoming Qs, then such information can never reliably be regained, and the channel capacity of the whole must suffer. Sensory states are intermediary states within such a channel. Hence the information content of those sensory states must at least match that of the discriminations. And so there must be at least as much structure among the similarities and differences of qualitative properties as there is among phenomenal ones.

So now, if this reasoning is sound, 'quality space' receives a second interpretation. It tells us not just about the similarities and differences among the properties of appearance. It also tells us something about properties of the creature's states of mind. That order is now an ordering of the qualitative properties of sensation.

Qualitative properties are not properties of the things seen, heard, felt, or tasted, nor are they properties that characterize how those things appear. Instead they are properties of states of mind that help to explain why things appear as they do. So knowledge of them is not 'knowledge by acquaintance', or at any rate it is not knowledge that might be confirmed in some relatively direct fashion by looking, listening, or touching, no matter how carefully. Instead it is closer to 'knowledge by description' (see Shoemaker 1994*b*: 310). We make inferences about what the qualitative character of sensations must be in order to explain aspects of our relatively direct acquaintance with how things look. It is gratifying to note that other authors have come to similar conclusions on independent grounds. Dretske (1995: 41–4, 53) describes knowledge of the qualitative character of sensations as 'displaced perception'. By attending carefully to the variations in shades among inked patches of paper in front of one's eyes, one can come to appreciate something about the variations in qualitative character among visual states that are found somewhere behind those eyes. The array of colour patches—the colour sample system—allows indirect perception of the qualitative character of one's own visual states. In such fashion this illuminated manuscript casts light into the workings of one's own visual apparatus.

Suppose Otto is looking at colour patches in a lab, and the patches and conditions are controlled in such a way that the variations in appearance of the patches can be described in just three dimensions: hue, saturation, and lightness. Otto sees a red patch. Now we propose that colours have locations in a colour quality space. If Otto sees the redness of the patch, must he therefore see it as a location in colour quality space? Boghossian and Velleman (1991), considering this question, say

either one already sees colors in terms of their locations in a space of co-determinates—in which case, the appearance of one color alludes to the others—or one doesn't yet see colors in terms of their locations in color space—in which case, their appearances furnish no grounds for drawing the similarities and differences constitutive of such a space. (Boghossian and Velleman 1991: 104)

They quite rightly attack the first alternative, on the grounds that the appearance of a particular shade of red does not imply that there exist neighbouring shades that are yellower or bluer. So we are left with the other alternative, and the problem of understanding what locations in colour quality space have to do with seeing a particular colour. As they say, 'If one doesn't already see colors under characterizations locating them in such a space, then one sees nothing on the basis of which locations could be assigned to them' (Boghossian and Velleman 1991: 104).

But notice what happens to this argument if one can distinguish between phenomenal properties and qualitative properties. The appearance presented to Otto by a particular red patch has a particular location within the order of phenomenal properties, but it need not present itself *as* having that location. To describe the gamut of colour appearances presented to Otto while he participates in our experiment, we require three dimensions of variation in colour appearance. The patch 'has' a location in the sense that it has some determinate value in each of those three dimensions. Otto can discriminate this patch from others we present him in the lab, and if we simply try to catalogue his discriminatory abilities in the domain of surface colours, we find we need three dimensions—three variables—to *describe* the data. Hence to describe a particular appearance of a particular patch, we must give some determinate value for each of those three dimensions. Otto need not see that particular shade *as* having those three 'coordinates', but if he does see that particular shade, he sees the shade that *has* those coordinates—the one that occupies that particular place within the order of phenomenal qualities. That is all it means to say that the appearance has a location; it need not be a content carried in the appearance itself.

Furthermore, the distinction between phenomenal and qualitative properties opens the possibility that Boghossian and Velleman deny. Appearances might furnish grounds for assigning a perceptual state a location within quality space even though that location is no part of the appearance itself. What is going on in Otto when he sees the red patch? He is in some sensory state S in virtue of which the patch looks as it does. We attribute qualitative properties to the internal state S. For S to have that particular qualitative character is for it (for example) to have a property in virtue of which the stimulus appears to have a particular hue, a property in virtue of which the stimulus appears to have a particular saturation, and a property in virtue of which it appears to have a particular brightness. Call these three properties 'differentiative' (see Clark 1993*b*: 70 ff.); what they help to differentiate are things in front of the eyes. If S varied in any of its three differentiative properties, the stimulus would look to have a different hue, or saturation, or brightness. That is all it means to say that S has a location in colour quality space.

If we require three dimensions to describe Otto's capacities to discriminate, then qualitative states within Otto must also have at least three independent dimensions of variation. If there were less, his discriminations would suffer, since the channel capacity would fall. A switch with just four wires cannot connect six people. It cannot happen. But we do not need to suppose that Otto can detect these states or these capacities within himself, or that he is even aware that he has such keen discrimination of the patches in front of his eyes. His own qualitative states never trot across the field of view. Perhaps, if he has read Shoemaker and Dretske, he can perceive them indirectly, but even then he must stay alert, and pay attention to these distinctions.

1.1.4 Psycho-Physical Properties

There is one more step before our product is complete and we can send it out the door. We must find a neurophysiological interpretation for the dimensions of variation in qualitative properties.

Colour vision is one modality in which one can readily anticipate making this step. It has not yet been made; identifications are at best tentative, and the data are confusing. But the 'opponent process' theory has with good reason become something of the 'standard model' in colour vision, and it yields a sketch of how these identifications are likely to proceed.

To say that there are three dimensions of variation in qualitative character does not say which three. It could be any three, as long as they are independent of one another. Various coordinate schemes could carry the information required. A Cartesian system of orthogonal axes is possible. The hue, saturation, brightness system treats hue as an angular coordinate, saturation as a radius, and brightness as a vertical distance. When we seek a psychophysical interpretation for our quality space, we seek to know how those dimensions of variation in qualitative states are actually registered by the nervous system. In a sense it is only after this is done that qualitative properties have been identified. Until then, we know at best that there are some k distinct dimensions of variation in the qualitative character of states in the given modality, but we do not know what those dimensions are.

The answer turns out to be quite surprising. Colours of a given brightness are not registered by separate coordinates of hue and saturation; the latter are *not* the differentiative properties on which chromatic discriminations actually proceed. Instead the gamut is described by two 'opponent' axes. One axis registers where the colour is in a series from yellow through grey to blue, and the other where it is in a series from red through grey to green. Both opponent axes carry information about both hue and saturation, but mathematically the result is the same: they describe a plane. The pair of coordinates yields a unique position in the two-dimensional order of hues and saturations of a given brightness. But no a priori theorist would ever have guessed that this specification actually proceeds with one coordinate for yellow–blue and another for red–green.

The simplest model that accounts for the trichromatic character of colour vision would be one in which chromatic systems use just three independent primaries (such as red, green, and cyan), as do printers and televisions. To pair red with green in one channel, and yellow with blue in another, seems inelegant and inefficient. The Young–Helmholtz model denied the existence of opponent processes, and of the counter-intuitive pairings of red with green and yellow with blue. But nature here trumps our intuitions: colour vision is trichromatic, but the actual axes on which discriminations turn are provided by opponent processes. Each such axis has distinct 'unitary' hue qualities at opposite ends. Those two hues are complements. Red cancels green, and yellow does blue. Mixtures of them yield some point in the achromatic scale from white to black. Such chromatic cancellation gives the theory its 'opponent' character.

We should think of red as the end-point in a series which derives from the series-generating relationship 'is redder than'. At the opposite pole of this relationship is the quality *green*. Even though we have no term in a natural language for this order-generating relation, red–green is one of the axes of variation along which the visual nervous system actually makes its discriminations. So too for yellow–blue and white–black.

1.2 THE STRUCTURE OF APPEARANCE

The moral of the story is that we might be surprised when we discover which dimensions of variation in phenomenal appearance are actually registered by the nervous system. How is it possible to be surprised by such facts? How can elements of the structure of appearance be hidden from us in this way?

It helps to return to the question of how to characterize the relations between qualities—between the occupants of quality space. Consider the fact that in an ordering of hues, any appearance of orange is found between those of red and yellow. This is not a straightforward physical fact: the various stimuli that appear to be orange (or red or yellow) form a heterogeneous physical collection. Logic forbids us from mentioning any stimulus specification in a definition of these phenomenal properties, since it is logically possible that any such stimulus could present a different quality. It could look different. Tomorrow it might.

The fact that orange is between red and yellow is not a straightforward physical fact. I shall dub it a fact of 'qualitative structure'. That structure is generated by relations of discriminability, matching, and relative similarity among classes of stimuli; the relations between qualities are consequences of that structure. I shall also use the term 'qualitative similarities' to encompass the relations among qualities. So, for example, it is a fact about qualitative similarities that places orange between red and yellow. This is not a fact that could be confirmed in any single discrimination trial or matching task. Similarities among qualities are at some remove from the relations of discriminability, matching, and relative similarity that hold among stimuli. A sensory system can register similarities between instances of orange and of red, but the qualities themselves are not objects of discrimination. Otto can sense instances that appear orange, but the quality orange could not fit within his field of view.

There are good reasons to think that all the facts that could be mentioned in defining a particular qualitative term are found among such facts of qualitative structure. The first reason is that only such structural properties generalize across individuals. Stimulus specifications do not. Differences in colour perception, even among those with 'normal' colour vision, can be demonstrated in various ways. The simplest is to pick monochromatic primaries— lights of just one wavelength—and have observers attempt to match some intermediate stimulus by mixing the primaries in different proportions. The proportions may differ vividly.[2] A mixture that matches the target for Otto may not for Sally. So if we are attempting to define the name of the hue presented by that intermediate stimulus, we cannot name what matches for Otto or for Sally.

More dramatic demonstrations are available once percipients know some hue names. Given an array of greenish Munsell chips, and the instruction 'pick the chip that to you presents a unitary green—not at all yellowish and not at all bluish', an individual will manage to pick one chip, and will reliably pick that same chip again on repeated occasions. But different individuals will (reliably) pick different chips (see Hurvich 1981: 223). The differences are readily perceptible to anyone involved in the test: Otto's chip may look noticeably bluish to Sally, while hers will seem yellowish to Otto.

These differences present a problem. Given the variations in normal colour vision, we cannot identify colour kinds with classes of stimuli. The class that presents aqua to Otto may not do for Sally. What then generalizes? Why do we even think that two different people are sometimes presented with the same aqua quale? What we find is that while the exact stimuli needed to make a match vary somewhat from person to person, there is an identifiable pattern of relations that generalizes from person to person. The structure of relations generalizes, even if the particular relata do not.

---

[2] The 'Nagel anomaloscope' presents observers with a split field, in half of which is a stimulus of 589 nm. In the other half is a mixture of 535 nm and 670 nm light, whose relative intensities are adjusted by the observer until they match the 589 nm stimulus. That ratio is commonly used to assess various colour vision anomalies. But even in the range of ratios considered 'normal', some observers will completely reject matches made by others. See Hurvich (1981: 227, 230).

The point can be put in simple logical terms. Consider just those with 'normal' colour vision: the non-anomalous trichromats. One might expect to be able to generalize across those people at least with propositions of the form:

> There is a stimulus y perceived by every person z as a green that is not at all yellowish and not at all bluish.

This hope is dashed, even among those with normal discriminations. Instead we need to say something of the form:

> For every person z there is a stimulus y perceived by z as a green that is not at all yellowish and not at all bluish.

Once we identify such 'unitary' hues for an individual, we can state a great deal about the colour perceptions of *that* individual in terms of those hues. For example, suppose we find that to Otto wavelength mixture x presents unitary blue, and mixture y presents unitary yellow. Then for Otto x and y are complements: some combination of them will yield achromatic white. But that same pair may not be complements for Sally (even though she too has 'normal' colour vision). To Sally x may appear to be a slightly greenish blue, and y a slightly greenish yellow. Their combination will always appear somewhat greenish to Sally, no matter how she adjusts their relative intensities. So it is false to say

> There are wavelength spectra x and y such that, for any person z, x combined with y yields an achromatic white for z

but true that

> For any person z there are wavelength mixtures x and y such that x combined with y yields an achromatic white for z.

The structure generalizes, but the particular stimuli occupying a particular place in the structure vary somewhat from person to person.

Even if colour discriminations were identical across a population, one could not define a particular colour term by the stimuli that happen to present it. Suppose we say that a thing looks red if it presents the same colour as geranium petals. One problem is paradigm existence: if this is to be true by definition, it implies that geranium petals must exist if anything in the universe looks red. But geraniums might not have evolved, even though we still paint our fire trucks red. Secondly, treating the identification as an analysis would imply that geranium petals must be red. But that too seems a contingent matter: they might have evolved to be yellow instead.

A simple conclusion follows: if we are to define a term for a qualitative property (a 'qualitative term'), we cannot mention any stimuli. We can mention only the structural properties that give the quale its place in the quality space. 'Orange' cannot be defined as 'the colour of ripe oranges' or in any similar way, no matter how sophisticated. It can only be defined as something like 'the colour midway between red and yellow, and more similar to either than to turquoise'. The terms 'red', 'yellow', and 'turquoise' would all receive similar analyses.

For any particular observer, the qualitative property 'orange' corresponds to a place in the colour quality space, which can be indicated, picked out, or tagged by a sample of stimuli. But as soon as we change observers (or the illumination, or the state of adaptation of the observer, or any other member of the eight-term matching relation mentioned in Section 1.1.1), those stimulus pointers may point to the wrong quality. We must somehow identify *corresponding* places in the colour quality spaces of other individuals, but this cannot be done by listing stimuli. Only a structure description will do. The problem is analogous to identifying, in the skeleton or anatomy of different people, which parts are the femur or the nose. These parts are rarely shaped identically in any two people, so one could not identify the femur or the nose with any specific configuration of bone or tissue. Fortunately, the pattern of relations that they bear to other parts of the person generalizes in a rough (homologous) fashion. We pick the corresponding place in a homologous (not identical) pattern of relations.

The implication is that we cannot treat stimulus characterization as any part of the *analysis* of qualitative terms. If we try to define a particular qualitative term, the only sorts of facts we can mention are facts about the similarities of the given quality to others. And all the essential properties that we might think of are encompassed in that structure. So, for example, no particular stimulus is such that it must look orange, but anything that does look orange presents an appearance that must be somewhat reddish and somewhat yellowish. Anything that presents that particular quality presents a quality that must stand in particular relations of qualitative similarity to red and to yellow. Otherwise it is not orange. Orange could not more closely resemble turquoise than it does red.

One can think of these structural facts as 'geometrically intrinsic' properties of the colour quality space. Intrinsic properties are properties that a geometer confined to its surface could discover; they are all facts of structure. If your goal is to define a particular qualitative term, then all the essential properties you might need (and more besides) will be found in this list. Extrinsic facts require a coordinate scheme defined independently of the surface itself. The fact that a particular stimulus happens to present a particular quality is extrinsic to the geometry of the space itself. So, as implied by the analogy, it has nothing essential to do with that quality.

Previously I described the contrast between intrinsic and extrinsic properties in terms of the difference between 'distal' and 'proximal' functional roles (Clark 1993*b*: 201–2), but the latter terminology now seems wrong. As just seen, the causes of sensations of orange add nothing essential to and cannot be mentioned in any analysis of the qualitative property that those sensations instantiate. We are also unlikely to find any set of effects that is unique to having had a sensation of orange, and in terms of which the qualitative property might be defined. What makes orange orange is not a fact about the consequences of seeing something as orange. If we bundle those causal relations together as a 'functional role'—a job that signals of orange serve within the psychological economy of the creature—then there does not seem to be any particular functional role that sensations of orange invariably and distinctively perform. Whatever orange signals could just as well have been signalled by turquoise. If defined by their jobs, these employees are truly interchangeable.

Talk of 'distal' and 'proximal' functional roles was based on Ned Block's distinction between 'long-arm' and 'short-arm' roles. Block defined 'long-arm' functional roles as ones that 'reach out into the world of things' and 'short-arm' functional roles as ones that are 'purely internal' (Block 1990: 70). He asked:

Why can't the functionalist identify intentional contents with long-arm functional states and qualitative content with short-arm functional states? The result would be a kind of 'dualist' or 'two factor' version of functionalism. My response: perhaps such a two factor theory is workable, but the burden of proof is on the functionalist to tell us what the short-arm functional states might be. (Block 1990: 70)

One might think of the short-arm roles as all and only those that define the place of a qualitative property in its quality space, but for the fact that the latter are not functional roles at all. Just as there is no particular stimulus unique to orange, so there is no particular causal consequence that is unique to sensing orange. The box in the flow chart to be labelled 'sensations of orange' cannot be identified by its causal relations to other boxes. Instead those contents are to be identified by the relations of qualitative similarity that define the intrinsic spacing of qualities.

If we are looking for a 'functional definition' then conventional wisdom presumes that we are looking for a definition in terms of a theory whose root relation is '. . . causes . . .'. One identifies nodes in a causal network, or boxes in a functional flow chart model, and specifies causal relations between the inputs and outputs of the boxes. Such a theory is converted into a 'Ramsey sentence', which provides a higher-order description of a structure of relations. (To make a Ramsey sentence, replace each theoretical term with an existentially quantified variable whose values are specified solely by the relations they bear to the values of other such variables. See the Appendix for details.) In a conventional 'functional definition', the relations providing the structure are causal. Particular clauses of the Ramsey sentence (particular 'Ramsey functional correlates') are then used to define particular theoretical terms. Each is assigned a job.

But facts of qualitative structure cannot be assimilated to this model. The root relations that define this structure are not causal ones; they are relations of qualitative similarity. Rather than accept a theory that requires us to specify some particular 'causal niche' that is always and only occupied by sensations of orange, we should abandon the theory (see Levine 1995). There is no 'causal niche' filled characteristically and uniquely by sensations of orange. But a relational structure can be built up using relations other than 'causes'. I suggest that if our goal is to describe qualitative character, the root relations will be those of qualitative similarity.

We should think of the definiens for a qualitative term as a *qualitative niche*. The niche for orange is provided by the structural facts that place it between red and yellow. That is where orange belongs; that is its proper home. When we attempt to define a qualitative term we should confine ourselves to those structural properties that locate the given quality in its quality space. Describe the relations of qualitative similarity among the occupants, but mention no stimuli. So 'orange' could at best be defined as something like 'a reddish yellow, equally similar to red as to yellow, complementary to turquoise, more similar to red or to yellow than it is to turquoise', and so on. Each of the other qualitative terms would receive an equally enigmatic treatment. Clearly this regimen can succeed only if it is utterly methodical: one must form the Ramsey sentence for the entire structure of qualitative relations, and associate each particular term with a particular Ramsey correlate.

Of course it is unlikely that any term in a natural language has as part of its language-meaning a structure description of this sort sufficiently rich to determine its extension. But there are much simpler ways the term might latch onto its extension. Any creature that could use the term natively to report its sensory episodes is endowed with the sense of qualitative similarity that such structure descriptions *describe*. So all that creature needs is a few presentations of paradigm and foil, and a reference-fixing ceremony of the form 'orange is any colour more similar to this (paradigm) than to those (foils)' will succeed admirably. We do not need to describe the relations of qualitative similarity satisfied by the quality, since we can *sense* their instances.

1.3 INTRINSIC VERSUS RELATIONAL

A consequence of this account is that qualitative character is a relational affair. Qualitative properties seem to be intrinsic properties, but they are not.

When one sees a patch of orange, the experience seems to involve an intrinsic monadic quale: the quale orange. But this experience is an illusion. The facts in virtue of which that experience is an experience of orange, and not of some other quality, are all relational facts.

Of course when one has an experience as of something orange, one need not have an experience as of something related in such-and-such a way to other things red and yellow. Qualitative content may be relational even though it is not invariably experienced as relational. Analogously, weight is a relational property even though it seems intrinsic to the loads one might carry. It seems outlandish to suggest that one could change the weight of a sack of groceries without disturbing a single atom of its contents. Nevertheless, the facts in virtue of which the sack weighs what it does are relational facts about mass and distance. The sack is somewhat lighter at high tide, and if aliens stole the core of our planet they would make all of our groceries lighter. Similarly, the facts in virtue of which a sensation has the particular qualitative character it has are all relational facts.

This suggestion is a 'psycho-functional' hypothesis and not an 'analytic' definition (see Block 1980). It is not derived from analysis of our ordinary concepts. A psycho-functionalist believes that many of the putative necessary truths that one derives from analysis of those concepts are, in the end, neither necessary nor true. Instead empirical inquiry is to be given the task of discovering the 'real essence' of our psychological states. The theory describing that nature may contradict smaller or larger portions of our ordinary conceptual scheme yet still, on the whole, be the best theory going. Perhaps it is part of our ordinary conceptual framework that qualia are intrinsic. And perhaps that part is a portion of our folk inheritance that we must renounce. Empirical inquiry suggests that the facts of qualitative character have at root a relational form.

The most dramatic illustration uses the blandest qualia imaginable: those had when looking at a 'grey scale', or array of non-chromatic stimuli ranging from white through the various greys to black. Such non-chromatic colour qualia turn out to be just as mysterious as the chromatic varieties. Suppose that one perceives a patch somewhere in the middle of the series as a middling grey. In virtue of what are two sensations both sensations of this particular phenomenal property—the appearance of a middling grey?

In 1948 Hans Wallach performed a simple experiment that suggested a surprising answer to this question. He projected a circle of light onto a screen, and set up a second projector that could surround that circle with an annulus, whose luminance could be controlled independently. Wallach found that the apparent brightness of the centre disc could be changed without touching the projector that sent light into it. He had only to change the brightness of the surround; the brighter it was, the darker the centre appeared. In other words, the same fixed luminance reflecting off the centre circle on the screen could be made to appear as any one of many different shades of grey. He performed a second experiment in which the observer was confronted with two such centre–surround displays at different luminance levels. The observer could adjust the intensity of light in the disc in one of the displays, and was told to adjust it until the centre discs in both displays looked to be the same grey. One centre spot might be reflecting up to ten times as much light as the other. Nevertheless, it could be made to appear the same grey as the other if it bore the same ratio to the luminance of its surround. So the facts that make something appear grey are relational in form: that its luminance stands in a certain ratio to the luminance of its surround. This ratio principle holds over a large range of intensities.[3]

What appears to be an intrinsic property of the centre patch in fact registers a relation between luminance levels of the centre and the surround. That central grey certainly looks as if it is a monadic property, ensconced in the centre, independent of its surroundings. Just like the weight of the sack of groceries, the grey of the patch seems to be intrinsic to the patch, but it is not. It depends on relations among luminance levels. Note that the latter in turn may or may not be relational in form; the claim should not be taken to imply that *all* of the facts on which the greyness of the patch depends are relational in form. Greyness depends on relations of luminance levels, but perhaps physicists and metaphysicians will ultimately tell us that luminance levels are intrinsic properties. Analogously, while weight depends on facts about the relations of mass and distance, the latter facts may or may not ultimately have a relational character. Perhaps the mass of the cheese one purchased is an intrinsic property of that cheese. Its ultimate metaphysical status can be left for others to resolve. Whatever that resolution, it is clear that mass and weight are different properties: even if the sack becomes weightless, it still has mass. It is also clear that the sack weighs what it does in virtue of relational facts about mass. Similarly, luminance and lightness are distinct properties, and lightness depends on relations among luminance levels.

This finding did not surprise those who had absorbed the principles of the opponent process theory of vision; all the surprises are already contained within that theory. Ewald Hering's model for an opponent process was a group of opposing muscles; he thought the chromatic quality presented by a stimulus was essentially the *resultant* of opposing forces within the visual

---

[3] Wallach's experiment was careful enough that he detected slight deviations from the ratio principle: sometimes the setting for the disc in the less intense pair was somewhat lower than predicted by an exact ratio, sometimes higher. And high intensities could make the centre disc appear luminous (Wallach 1948: 317). These deviations from perfect brightness constancy later became targets for independent investigation.

system. Green pushes one way, and red pulls the other. One could cancel green by adding red. This is a very odd and counter-intuitive theory, and over a century passed before experimenters took it seriously. Now the evidence is quite strong in its favour; it seems to be the truth about how we perceive colours.

Hering argued in 1878 that the quale black is in fact a relational property. The 'resting-point' for the visual system is a middling grey, neither black, nor white, nor of any hue. To nudge the system out of its neutral resting-point, it must be pushed or pulled in one or another direction. Physiologically it has three axes, and it can be activated or inhibited along each such axis. But it followed, said Hering, that one could not see black unless one added inhibition somewhere else. That is, you cannot see black unless you can also see white. In fact one must be able to see white somewhere else at the same time. Otherwise, no black.

Wallach confirmed this prediction. The only way to get the centre circle to look black is to turn up the intensity of the surround until that surround looks white. If the surround is some middling grey, then so is the centre. You need the bright white surround, creating lots of inhibition, to get the centre to look black. Some ordinary experiences can confirm this. In the complete absence of light, what sensory quality is apparent when you open your eyes? The interior of even the darkest room does not look as black as the interior of a filled inkwell seen in daylight. Dark indeed it is—we use the term partly to designate luminance levels—but the quality appearing before one's eyes does not match the blackness of the inkwell when one turns on the lights. To get black, you must add luminance, create inhibition, to push the opponent process in the appropriate direction. Hering called the dark grey that you see in the complete absence of light 'brain grey': it corresponds to the resting-point of the opponent process.

A simpler example is described by C. L. Hardin (1988: 24). When a television set is off, the screen always appears to be some shade of grey. But with the television turned on, one can see on the screen surfaces that appear to be black: the black hat of the villain, or black oil gushing from the Oklahoma oil well. The appearance is created by *adding* luminance to other portions of the screen. Even high technology cannot produce a raster gun that subtracts photons. So how is it that we get the appearance of black by adding light? It makes sense only if black is not just the absence of light, but a quality produced when an opponent system is inhibited, or pushed below its baseline.

So the appearance of black is a relational affair, even though it appears to be intrinsic. The same moral holds for hues. Orange is a resultant of activation in two opponent processes. It has a red component and a yellow component in the same way that a north-easterly heading has a northerly component and an easterly one. Just as one cannot head north-easterly unless one can also travel easterly, so one cannot see orange unless one can also see red. The hypothesis is, admittedly, outlandish, implausible, perhaps even conceptually incoherent. Analysis of our ordinary concepts would never lead to such a bizarre position. Its only virtue is that it seems to be true. As Joseph Levine has quite reasonably written, 'it certainly seemed possible that someone could experience a sensation with a reddish quality even if they were incapable of experiencing sensations of other chromatic types' (Levine 1995: 286). I agree. It does seem possible. Our intuitions yield not the slightest murmur of complaint at the prospect. But alas, our intuitions have once again led us astray. Even though it seems possible, it is not. A person incapable of seeing green could not see red. The best available theory implies that it cannot happen. Levine goes on to say: 'I think we could take this to an extreme and imagine someone whose entire visual experience involved just one hue, and that one was qualitatively similar to the one involved in my experiences of type Q_R. Why shouldn't this be (at least conceptually) possible?' (Levine 1995: 286). Indeed, it is conceptually possible: nothing in our ordinary concepts forbids it. Nevertheless, it cannot happen. That one could not see red if one lacked the capacity also to see green by no means follows from analysis of our ordinary concepts. It follows from a theoretical account—based on opponent process theory—of colour vision. Such theories always yield an indissoluble mix of new claims and new concepts, and this one will indeed force us to revise some of our pre-theoretic notions.

To the complaint that 'this method does not explain the *intrinsic* nature of a colour experience' (Chalmers 1996: 235), my response is 'Guilty as charged, Your Honour'. There is no such nature to be explained. Not only is there no intrinsic nature to colour experience, but given what we know about vertebrate sensory physiology, it is difficult to see how intrinsic properties could account for the qualitative character of any sensory experience.

The difficulty derives from the opening gambit made by every vertebrate sensory system so far studied: transduction. At the outermost afferent ends of any such system we find transducers, which are just specialized cells devoted to converting energy of one sort into another sort. In vertebrates the other sort is always a difference in electric potential energy: differences in ion concentration across a neural membrane. Many varieties of stimulus energy are rendered into such differences. Sensory systems convert electromagnetic energy, compression waves in the air, thermal energy, mechanical distortion, etc., into differences in electric charge across the membrane of neurons. In a human about 70 per cent of all transducers are visual, which may explain why visual examples so dominate the literature.

Now for each transducer of a given kind there is some stimulus that is the optimal stimulator for that transducer. Of all the stimuli out there it is the sort that is most likely to make the transducer shriek with joy. For example, the short-wavelength cones in your retina are most likely to respond when bombarded with photons whose wavelength is roughly 430 nanometres (nm). But although this is the optimal stimulator, others will do. If we bombard the same cones with light of 480 nm, they will respond, but less readily, less happily, at perhaps half the rate. Simply ramp up the intensity of the 480 nm stimulus, double the number of photons, and the two stimuli will become indistinguishable. The cones respond identically to 430 nm light or to more intense stimulation at 480. We cannot treat them as 'wavelength detectors'. They conflate wavelength and intensity.

The problem is that transducers are 'broadly tuned' or 'broad-band'. So how can one use a cell that conflates wavelength and intensity to discriminate among wavelengths? The answer is that one cannot use a cell to do this, but if one had two such cells, whose optimal wavelengths differed somewhat, and one could compare their outputs, one could begin to separate variations in wavelength from variations in intensity. After transduction one of the next moves in a sensory system is invariably a comparison of results. As Russell and Karen De Valois said, 'This mode of operation, with broadly tuned receptors feeding into neural circuits that compare and contrast the outputs of different receptors to extract specific information, seems to be general to all sensory systems' (De Valois and De Valois 1975: 121). They go on to say 'it is the comparison of the excitatory and inhibitory inputs at each synaptic level which forms the very basis of the information processing that takes place in sensory systems' (De Valois and De Valois 1975: 125).

If that is the basis, then we are limited in the choice of structures we can build on top of it. Even if we imagine that some receptor is stimulated by packets of intrinsic red, any such receptor could be stimulated to respond by other, unprivileged packets as well. Within a synapse or two, to sort out the jumble, the nervous system must resort to comparing the responses of its different constituents. At that point we must abandon the pretence that it is detecting or registering intrinsic properties; instead we find the beginnings of a relentless process of comparison. Thereafter the sensory system transacts its business in relational terms alone.

Perhaps this is the reason such systems seem appallingly insensitive to absolute intensities, and tend instead to favour ratios and relations. While Wallach could vary the intensity of illumination falling on his centre disc by a factor of roughly one to a thousand, normal photopic vision copes with a gamut of intensities a thousand times wider, from one to a million (Schiffman 1982: 179). Yet Wallach's centre disc still appeared the same shade of grey, as long as it stood in roughly the same ratio of luminance to its surround. So in

nervous system terms, that apparently intrinsic shade of grey does not register a monadic property or a particular level of luminance intensity. Instead it
registers a relation between the luminance of the patch and the luminance of
its surround: a relation that might obtain anywhere within a rather large gamut
of absolute intensities. Opponent process theory suggests that the same moral
should be applied to the chromatic colours: what seems to be bright monadic
red can be cancelled by green. Like a positive charge, a heavy weight, or a
northerly heading, the hue quality is at root relational.

The claim that qualitative character is intrinsic also runs foul of the facts of
qualitative structure. If these were intrinsic properties, then no necessity
would attach to any of the relations of qualitative similarity. If orange were a
monadic property, then it need not be composed of red and yellow. And the
resemblances among colours would be contingent consequences of the
monads in question. Monadic properties as distinct existences cannot imply or
necessitate any of their relations. So, on this line, orange is the property that
it is; that it appears to resemble red and yellow is a contingent by-product of
the funny way our vision works. If our vision worked in a different way,
perhaps orange—that very same monadic property—could appear most
closely to resemble blue or green. If you find this consequence jarring, then
you feel the strong tug of resemblance among the hue qualities. The relations
among them are not mere accidents; what appear to be monadic qualities
derive from a relational root.

1.4 FOUR REFUTATIONS

Any account of qualia immediately faces a barrage of a priori objections.
While any stratagem for deflecting such projectiles is to be commended, it is
particularly valuable to find an account that provides a coherent defence
against a large number of them simultaneously. In this section I pick four of
the most famous objections and show how this account has the resources to
answer all four.

1.4.1 *Spectrum Inversion*

To imagine spectrum inversion is to imagine a new mapping from stimuli to
the colour qualities they present. Suppose Otto and Sally are spectrum-
inverted relative to one another. If inversion is to preserve 'functional isomor-
phism', then all the judgements of matching and relative similarity made by
Otto must be made as well by Sally. This implies a rather strong and surprising condition on colour quality space: to be invertible, it must manifest some

variety of symmetry. There must be at least two distinct assignments of stimuli to colour qualities that preserve all the relations of qualitative similarity among the colours that those stimuli present. Otherwise in some region or other Otto will find two classes of stimuli to be relatively similar that Sally does not, and the game is up.

Since it is a biological product, it would be remarkable if the colour quality space had the structure of any of the Platonic solids. That is to say, it seems overwhelmingly likely that the colour quality space is asymmetrical. It is a lumpy, anisotropic, asymmetrical ovoid. These asymmetries will also give the clues needed to hook the structure up with neural hardware.

Human colour quality space is not isotropic; in some parts of the spectrum it is much easier to discriminate wavelength differences than in other parts (see Boynton 1979: 256, 281; Hurvich 1981: 296). So using physical coordinates, the space will vary in 'density'. We add other constraints. In moonlight we are all monochromats, but as rosy-fingered dawn approaches, reds and greens become visible first, followed by yellows and blues.[4] The red–green process has a lower threshold, and wakes up before the yellow–blue process (see Hurvich 1981: 72). Hence at the dark end of the colour ovoid, hues start bumping out in the red and green directions before much happens in the way of yellow or blue. We can note other asymmetries. Some hues can become more saturated—less similar to white—than others. The most saturated yellow still seems more similar to white than does the most saturated red. (If saturation is a radius, the most saturated red will be further away from the achromatic centre of the hue 'circle' than will be the most saturated yellow.) The 'colour solid' is not a Platonic solid. It is a lumpy product of our biology.[5] So even though it is conceivable that there be a systematic inversion, in fact any such inversion would be detectable.

Nevertheless, the mere thought experiment causes considerable consternation in the camp of analytic functionalists, who attempt to define the meanings of our ordinary qualitative terms by appeal to causal or functional roles.

---

[4] This is the 'Bezold–Brücke' phenomenon. The apparent brightness of hues changes as illumination changes. Although red may be the first visible hue, yellow soon makes an appearance, and can eventually surpass red in apparent brightness. The yellow–blue process requires more illumination to get going in the morning, but then accelerates more quickly. See Hurvich (1981: 72–4).

[5] Two other asymmetries are worth noting. The first is that hues presented by a given package of wavelengths typically shift as luminance increases, but there are exceptions, called 'invariant hues'. An interesting identity statement (that *can* be explained) is: the invariant hues = the unitary hues (Hurvich 1981: 73). The combination of curved and straight hue contours at different illuminations provides an asymmetry. Secondly, red–green and yellow–blue processes are not equally or symmetrically distributed across the retina. Yellow–blue discriminations fail for very small objects, even though objects of that size can be seen as red or green. This is called 'small field tritanopia' (Hurvich 1981: 21, 162).

Quality Space

According to the analytic functionalist, two instances of the same qualitative character are instances of that same character because they share a functional role. They have the same job; they perform the same causal duties. But it is conceivable that what looks red to you looks green to me, so that the functional role served by sensations of red in you is played by sensations of green in me. Hence what makes your sensation of red a sensation of red is not its functional role, and functional accounts fail as an analysis of qualitative character.

The account proposed above agrees that the facts in virtue of which a sensation has a particular qualitative character are all relational in form. But the relation at work is not '. . . causes . . .', but rather those relations of qualitative similarity that give the particular quale its place in the spacing of qualities. If your aim is to *define* a particular qualitative term, the only facts you could mention are such facts of qualitative structure. One must acknowledge that the results are meagre. Try it. Lay out the surgical implements, roll up your sleeves, then perform conceptual analysis on the word 'red'. There is scant stuffing to unpack; the attempt terminates with shocking abruptness. As William Lycan (1996: 80) has noted, analysis yields slim pickings in the domain of colour perception, and indeed in any sensory domain. Perhaps this is because much of the semantics of these terms is implicit in the operation of sensory mechanisms. We cannot *describe* the extension of the term; instead we point to a few samples and hope that our interlocutor shares our sense of what matches what. If analysis yields anything at all, it will yield only facts intrinsic to the geometry of the quality space—those that a geometer confined to its surface could discover. These are facts about the structure of relationships which the qualities bear to one another. Such analyses do not and cannot mention any stimuli.

If that is our concept of red, we can explain why spectrum inversion is conceptually possible. No conceptual rule is violated if we suppose that what looks green to you looks red to me. Inversion leaves unaltered the structure of relationships in which the various colour qualities stand. Red is still the complement of green, orange is still between red and yellow, and so on. What changes is merely that new stimuli come to present those qualities. The structural facts are unperturbed by an inversion. So contemplation of it does not cause any squawk of protest from our concepts.

It follows that this account does not deny the conceptual possibility that the stimuli presenting a given quale might all change. It is conceivable that the causal consequences of having a sensation with a particular qualitative character might all change as well. Since it is not a causal fact that places orange between red and yellow, the account remains indifferent to the job changes a quale may undergo in the course of its career. It is still the same old orange, but now activated by different events out at the periphery, and having different effects within. The same old orange moves into a new office and is given a new job. What makes it the same old orange is that it still stands in just the same place in the structure of qualitative similarities.

The only sort of inversion that the structural account need fear would be one in which (allegedly) the same quale is moved to a different place in the structure of relations to other qualities. For example, if the quale orange could come most closely to resemble blue or green, or if it could cease to have a reddish component and a yellowish component, even while remaining the same quale, then the facts of qualitative structure would not suffice to fix qualitative character. But this thought experiment is a very different beast from the one loosed upon the analytic functionalists, and it is much more difficult to manage successfully. Frankly I find it impossible to conceive of the envisioned state of affairs. If the quale is still orange, it could not lack a reddish component, and it could not more closely resemble blue than it does yellow. To move the quality into a new, greenish-blue neighbourhood, we must either change its character—so that it flies new colours—or change the constitution of the relations of qualitative similarity and difference that it bears to its neighbours. One or the other must give, yet this thought experiment requires both to be fixed even as the move is consummated.

The relations that generate the structure are not causal but qualitative. Even if the stimuli presenting the quale orange were to change, and the job or functional role of sensations of orange were also to change, we could still apply the same techniques of analysis to the discriminations of our hapless observer, determine that the same structure of qualitative relations obtains, and identify within that structure the same old orange, now with new stimulants and a brilliant new career. We could congratulate our old friend—good old orange!—on its successful move to a new office. The structure description associated with a given qualitative term describes a qualitative niche, not a causal one.

1.4.2 *What it is Like to be a Bat*

Although the analysis of discriminations can yield a structural definite description for a given qualitative character, it is implausible to think that such a description is part of the meaning of any word of a natural language. There is no synonymy between 'orange' and 'a reddish yellow, equally similar to red as to . . .', even though the two may have the same extension. The words we have for sensory qualities cannot readily be associated with conditions true of all and only the stimuli that present them. As noted, 'conceptual analysis' of such words disgorges little. Perhaps we get some paltry description of orange (e.g. that it is a colour, that it is a reddish yellow, etc.), but such descriptions fail to determine the extension of the term.

Fortunately our sensory systems themselves can furnish the wherewithal to connect a term to its extension. The structural definite description attempts to describe the relations of qualitative similarity that obtain among the qualities. If one is endowed with the modality in question, there is no need to describe those similarities, since one can *sense* them. Instead of trying to cobble together a description using the relatively immature faculties of linguistic representation, one can achieve the same end by activating the ancient and well-honed machinery of sentience itself.

Perhaps the semantics of qualitative terms is in large part implicit in the operations of mechanisms of sensory discrimination. A search for semantic regularities takes us in short order out of the civilized realm of rules and conventions and into the jungle of pre-linguistic psychological capacities. Perhaps the best way to understand what the average English-speaking human means by 'orange' is to possess the sensory capacities of the average human, and then look at enough samples so that one can discern the gamut that falls within 'orange', and the gamut that falls without. A language-learner has nothing more than this to work with, so it must be enough. More formally, one needs a shared sense of qualitative similarity—those capacities of discrimination, matching, and relative similarity that order the qualities in a given sensory modality—and presentation of a sufficient number of para-digms and foils (samples within and without the extension of the term) so that one learns the correct use of the term. Any term in any natural language for any sensory quality could be learned in this fashion.

If we knock out one or another of these two conditions, we get one or the other of two big thought experiments. The first is Thomas Nagel's 'What is it like to be a bat?' (1979). The basic difficulty posed by the echolocating bat, according to Nagel, is that echolocation presents the bat with experiences that have a particular qualitative character, and we humans cannot form concepts adequate to describe that character. Why can't humans form such concepts? This sensory modality is radically unlike any of our own: 'bat sonar, though clearly a form of perception, is not similar in its operation to any sense that we possess, and there is no reason to suppose that it is subjectively like anything we can experience or imagine' (Nagel 1979: 168). The bat has an alien structure of qualitative similarities—of what resembles what. Not only can the bat detect stimuli that we cannot, but it will discriminate stimuli that to us are indiscriminable (such as two minutely different locations of a flut-tering moth), and it will fail to discriminate stimuli that to us are readily discriminable (such as the colour of the moths). This yields a structure of qualitative similarities and differences for which we can find no analogue.

To understand what it is like to be a bat chasing a moth is to understand the structure of qualitative similarities operative in the bat. Put another way, we need to understand what classes of experiences would be qualitatively identical *for the bat*. The problem is precisely that bat echolocation has a qualitative structure that is alien to us. In it stimuli x and y resemble one another, where for us they do not. So mentioning x does not help us at all to understand what it is like to experience y. We cannot imagine what it is like, in the sense that our paradigms and our sense of qualitative similarity cannot get us to the point where for us (like the bat) x and y are qualitatively similar. We would need to acquire the bat's quality space.

Nagel goes on to define 'subjective facts' as facts that embody a particular point of view. I suggest that this talk of 'points of view' is another way of asking whose sense of similarity is germane. To experience things from the bat's point of view is to experience the resemblances that the *bat* experiences; to have *its* quality space. This is why, to adopt that point of view, we must imagine radical changes in our own mental structure; the entire constellation of similarities and differences must change.

By hypothesis the bat operates with an alien structure of qualitative similarities. We *cannot* sense the matches that it does. Allow me to mangle Wittgenstein. If the bat had words for its qualia, we could not learn them. More precisely, we could not learn successfully to apply the words in direct, first-person fashion. To be sure, with measuring instruments and calculators of sufficient speed and capacity, we could simulate the sensory system of the bat, and laboriously calculate the parameters for the application of a given term. Reading the meter, we could then apply the word. But *our* internal meters—our sensory systems—are just not built that way, and the calculations do not correspond to anything going on within our nervous systems, so without those instruments and calculators we would be at a loss. In that sense we *could not* learn the words for bat qualia.

Now if 'to know what it is like' to be a bat is not just a matter of know-how, or of knowledge by acquaintance, then it requires that one make some judgement. That in turn requires that one deploy concepts (or at least terms). But by the preceding, humans could not learn to use the needed terms. It follows that there is a sense in which we cannot know what it is like to be a bat. We could not natively deploy the concepts that a bat might use to describe its qualia. We do not share the structure of qualitative similarities on which those concepts rely.

So we can agree with many of the premisses, and assign an agreeable interpretation to many of Nagel's claims about our abilities to form concepts of alien minds. For example, he says: 'We are forced, I think, to conclude that all these creatures have specific experiences which cannot be represented by

any mental concepts of which we could have first-person understanding'
(Nagel 1986: 24). If by 'have first-person understanding' Nagel means
'acquire the ability natively to deploy' or 'have the capacity for direct and
unstudied observational use', then I agree. But this does not show that there
is some alien *concept* whose content is of a different order from objective
concepts. The reason we could not have 'first-person understanding' of the
concepts of phenomenal experience of an alien mind is simply that we do not
have the same structure of qualitative similarities as the alien mind, the same
quality space. As Nagel says, 'our structure does not permit us to operate with
concepts of the requisite type' (Nagel 1979: 171). Since use of the terms relies
on native abilities to sense similarities among stimuli, if we lack such abilities, we cannot pick out the extension of the term without our instruments.

But I think this admission is a harmless one; it does not entail that there is
some metaphysical fact which is perpetually beyond our comprehension.
Nagel goes on to argue that there are 'subjective' facts accessible *only* from
that subject's point of view (Nagel 1979: 172). Only a bat or something sufficiently similar to a bat could form the concepts necessary to understand what
it is like to be a bat. This last inference is the problematic one.[6] Granted, we
cannot be bats, nor could we learn first-person terms for bat qualia. But we
can still study the similarities that structure the bat's quality space. The
subject-matter of sensory resemblance is not one that is accessible *only* from
one point of view; it can be studied in the various halls of psychology, physiology, and neuroscience (see Section 3.6). In studying those similarities we
are studying the very same facts as are accessible to the bat from the bat's
point of view.

1.4.3 The Knowledge Argument

Frank Jackson's 'knowledge argument' is a variant of Nagel's worries. It
again adopts the perspective of someone studying a sensory modality without
enjoying its use. But instead of concentrating on an alien modality—one
structured by resemblances that we do not share—here the modality is one
that the student possesses, but has never exercised. Mary, the brilliant neuro-
physiologist, knows every physical fact there is to know about human colour
vision, about the reflectances of surfaces, about the wavelength composition
of light, and so on. But she has never seen any colours. One day she is let out

---

  [6] The critical move is from the claim that some facts 'embody' a point of view to the claim
that some facts are accessible *only* from that point of view. This in turn relies on the suggestion
that 'experience does not have, in addition to its subjective character, an objective character that
can be apprehended from many different points of view' (Nagel 1979: 173). This latter premiss
is unsupported. For a powerful reply to 'subjective facts', see esp. Lycan (1996: 45–68).

of her room, and sees red for the first time. She learns *what it is like* to see red, and what it has been like all along for all the people living their lives outside the room. But by hypothesis she already knew all the physical facts there were to know. Hence knowing what it is like to see red is knowing something other than a physical fact.

There have been many different responses to this argument (see Van Gulick 1993). The general principle is to admit that Mary would learn something, but then urge that because the word 'know' is ambiguous, accepting the premiss that Mary learns something does not entail that Mary learns some non-physical fact. For example, Lawrence Nemirow and David Lewis have argued that what she learns is know-how rather than knowledge that. She learns a new ability to place herself, at will, in a state representative of the experience (see D. Lewis 1990). This involves skills of imagination, memory, and recognition. Learning a new skill is consistent with her prior knowledge of all the facts. So even though she already knew everything (in one sense), she can still learn something.

One worry about the Nemirow–Lewis line is that what happens when Mary is let out of the room does not seem akin to what happens when you learn a new skill like juggling or bird-watching. Granted, thereafter she has various new abilities, but they all seem to be consequent upon a judgement, of the form '*that's* red', whose content cannot be identified with a cluster of skills. And the transmission seems remarkably abrupt. Does what she learns take practice? Not all the knowledge gained seems to be know-how.

I have argued that qualitative terms have an essential indexical component. To engage the mechanisms allowing unstudied direct observational use of the term, one must have some actual historical episode of a successful demonstrative identification. Otherwise even a well-honed sense of qualitative similarity will not enable you to identify any of its terms—to pick out any instances of a quality. When Mary steps out of the room, she makes her first successful demonstrative identification of a colour. The content of this identification is expressed, naturally enough, with a demonstrative: something to the effect of 'so *that's* red!'.

Why can't Mary in her room learn what she learns when she steps outside it? One explanation is that what she learns is a non-physical fact. But there is a simple alternative. In her achromatic chamber Mary cannot demonstratively identify *any* colour. This is not because colours are non-physical properties, but simply because no actual samples are present. So no matter what text or other transmissions are sent into the room, we could not make it possible for her to identify a colour demonstratively.

Now even within her room Mary would be able to calculate the verdict of a particular observer outside the room who is presented with a particular colour patch and queried whether or not it is red. Suppose our observer is Otto. By hypothesis she knows the reflectance properties of the patch, the character of the ambient illumination, the densities of the various classes of cones in Otto's eyes, and their state of adaptation. To make it interesting, perhaps the illumination is provided by energy-saving fluorescent lights with some prominent spectral lines (which give them a skewed colour-rendering), and Otto has been sitting in the sun reading, while wearing pink sunglasses. Nevertheless, Mary could calculate the product of ambient and reflectance spectra, obtain the resulting absorptions in Otto's three classes of cones, adjust for his adaptation state, and finish with something like a colorimetric coordinate for that stimulus occasion. Then since she knows Otto's past track record of verdicts *re* 'red?' for stimuli with just those coordinates, she could calculate the probability that Otto will assent. She could even calculate its distance in quality space from those occasions that Otto took to be paradigms of red. But even though she could complete such inferences, Mary would still be unable to say, just by looking at them herself, which objects are red. When she ascribes 'red', she must always proceed by inference and calculation. For her 'red' is not an observation term; its reference is always assisted, never direct.[7]

Suppose we let Mary out of the room, confront her with a novel stimulus, ask her whether it looks red, and set the clock ticking. She starts madly scribbling away to calculate reflectance efficiencies, wavelength spectra, and the effects on her retina, but before she is done her time runs out. Then we tell her: 'that's *red*'. She learns: 'ah, so *that's* red'. Perhaps she could not have made this judgement prior to her release, not because red is a non-physical property, but simply because demonstrative identification requires an actual sample.

Second trial. We confront her with a stimulus which is a metamer to the previous one; it reflects a very different spectrum, but that spectrum has the same effect on Mary's cones. We set the clock ticking. She glances at it and says immediately, 'that's red too'.

The demonstrative episode has given Mary new abilities. She can now rely on her built-in sense of qualitative similarity, instead of calculating the eventual verdict. We have fired up the ancient engines; for the first time, the juices start flowing through Mary's chromatic systems. 'Red' soon becomes an observation term; she can apply it in an unstudied, first-person fashion. The

---

[7] Mary, before she leaves her black-and-white room, can *refer* to red, and can deduce the conditions under which the term applies. But her reference is assisted, laborious, and inferential in ways that the normal use is not. Her use of the word 'red' before she steps out of the room is essentially that of a theoretical term. It is also analogous to the use she might make of a term she has coined for the qualia of a *bat*.

baptism gave Mary her bearings in quality space; now she has a touchstone for application of the term. Like the Nemirow–Lewis line, this account agrees that Mary learns something new when she leaves the room, and that she gains know-how. But on this account those abilities derive from a successful demonstrative identification. So, parting company with Nemirow and Lewis, and agreeing with Lycan (1996) and Van Gulick (1993), Mary does learn something in addition to a skill. In her a sensory system of representation gets fired up for the first time. The sample activates what for Mary is a new way of representing states of affairs in front of her sense organs, and this new way of representing gives her new skills.

Perhaps an analogy would be helpful. We need some domain in which one could learn everything propositional there is to learn, yet still be totally at sea until a successful demonstrative identification has been made. Fortunately, there is a delightful analogy to be had: the Ozma problem (see Gardner 1991). This is roughly the problem of defining 'left' and 'right'. These terms are part of a family (including clockwise and counter-clockwise, east and west, north pole and south pole), any one of which can be defined in terms of the others, but all of which seem to rely ultimately on some successful demonstrative identification. In particular, suppose we begin receiving transmissions from a planet on the far side of the galaxy (so far away that no stars are mutually observable, or at least we cannot tell from the descriptions that they are mutually observable). The aliens have terms 'lana' and 'rana', which we know mean left and right, but we don't know which is which. Similarly they also have rotational terms kana-wise and counter-kana wise, directions eana and wana, planetary poles nana and sana, and we know that these stand for one or the other of our cognate notions, but we don't know which is which.

The Ozma problem is: can you think of any possible transmission that would allow an unambiguous translation of these terms? We might learn that if on their planet you face the sun at sunrise, you are looking towards eana, but unfortunately their planet might be rotating in the reverse direction from ours, so 'eana' is west, not east. We do not know whether 'kana-wise' means clockwise or counter-clockwise. We learn that if you curl the fingers of your lana hand, they are curled kana-wise, but 'lana' might be the right hand, so 'kana-wise' would be counter-clockwise. They could transmit pictures, but we don't know if they normally scan them from left to right or from right to left (and of course there is no way for them to tell us). So perhaps we're printing all their negatives backwards; or, to use the correct printer's term, *flopped*. Call their planet 'Flopped Earth'. (By the way, it is called the 'Ozma' problem because Oz was flopped: the planet (and clocks) rotated the wrong way; the sun rose in the west, which was called 'east', and so on.)

You learn the latitude and longitude of the visitor's centre on Flopped

Earth, and boldly volunteer to fly there under suspended animation. You awake many centuries later after your NASA rocket malfunctions and crash-lands. You are about to step out of your rocket. Which way should you start walking to head to the visitor's centre?

I submit that your position is precisely analogous to that of Mary when she is about to step out of her black-and-white room. You have a mass of propositional knowledge but an inability to employ the terms demonstratively. But all it would take is meeting a native who would say, '*This* is your lana hand. *That* is your rana hand.' Or even more simply, the native need simply point in the correct direction ('The visitor's centre is *that* way'). From your knowledge of the latitude and longitude you could then deduce, 'Ah, so "nana" is the south pole, "eana" is east, and "kana" is clockwise.' All the terms would lock in place and you would know how to orient yourself.

You have learned something, but you have not learned some funny new fact. In a sense you already knew all the facts—anything which could be conveyed linguistically was already in that packet of transmissions. But those transmissions did not suffice to fix the reference of 'lana' and 'rana'. A successful demonstrative identification finally does the job. You learn something to the effect of 'the lana hand is *this* hand'. Such learning is not learning some spooky new kind of fact.

Analogously, Mary does learn something when she steps out of the room, but she does not learn a new non-physical fact. She learns a second, demonstrative, route to the identification of properties with which she is already professionally acquainted. She can then *use* her inborn faculties of perceptual resemblance, rather than merely mention them in her calculations. This gives her the abilities to use colour terms demonstratively and as observation terms. But the indexical element is essential to that function of the terms. It is therefore not surprising that Mary must actually confront a sample and proceed through the baptism of demonstrative identification before she can use the terms in the normal way.

Like Mary, given enough time once you had arrived on the planet, you could probably *deduce* the correct application of the various terms from what you know. You face the sun at sunrise and then can yourself complete the demonstrative identification 'eana is *that* way'. Similarly, if Mary knew all the physical facts, she could presumably deduce on her own that the first coloured object she encounters is red and not green. Deduction of the appropriate labels to apply is not the issue. Unstudied first-person use of the terms requires actual confrontation with a sample.

Use of our qualitative terms relies essentially on a shared sense of qualitative similarity, and on some successful demonstrative identifications. Nagel's worries about 'what is it like to be a bat?;' are illustrative of what happens if we do not share a sense of qualitative similarity. Jackson's worries about Mary in the achromatic chamber show the need for successful demonstrative identifications. We could not successfully deploy first-person terms for bat qualia because their sense of resemblance is so radically different from our own. Mary could not make first-person observational use of colour terms because she has never made a successful demonstrative identification of any colour. Both are necessary.

1.4.4 The Explanatory Gap

Finally we come to an objection that can be formulated without use of modal notions, counterfactual conditionals, odd locutions, begged questions, or bluster. This least objectionable and most difficult of objections is Joseph Levine's 'explanatory gap'. It is difficult in part because answering it requires that one provide a successful explanation, and all parties admit that such explanations are nowhere in sight. So here, in something of a role-reversal, the respondent is forced to take off on a flight of fancy.

Levine's objection does not deny the truth of identity statements that, for example, identify a sensation of red with a particular state of the brain. The problem, Levine says, is not that these identities are false, but that they are inexplicable. In many other domains, physical science both establishes identity claims (heat is the motion of molecules, water is H_2O) and yields full and satisfying explanations of the identities. The explanations provide what Levine calls a 'bottom-up necessitation' for the identity statements. Such necessitation is a matter of ruling out alternatives; it does not require any necessary truths to be lodged within the explanans, but instead a derivation of the identity from the contingent physics and chemistry that we know. One shows that denying the identity is inconsistent with the physical story conjoined with an ordinary understanding of the words 'water' or 'heat'. But it is difficult to see how such an explanation could be given for identities of the form 'sensing redly = brain process squiggle-squiggle', where 'squiggle-squiggle' is the technical name for the process in question. The explanatory gap is encountered in attempts to explain identities of this form.

How do we explain identities in other domains? Levine suggests that we have some pre-theoretic understanding of what stuff water is, or of what heat does. In a 'quasi-analytic' stage of the proceedings, one analyses the essential features of these notions, and identifies a particular causal niche for each. Water is the substance that quenches our thirst; flows as the predominant ingredient in all inland springs, streams, and rivers; freezes into ice; condenses into clouds and falls from the sky as rain and snow; and so on. Heat is the common property of most things that can burn the skin, turn water into steam, cook our food, and so on. We identify each by identifying a causal role; water or heat is whatever occupies that role. As Levine puts it: 'our very concept of water is of a substance that plays such and such a causal role' (Levine 1993: 131).

But then when we turn to physical science and the world as it happens to be constituted, we find that there is just one thing that fills that role. It is just H_2O that quenches our thirst, flows in inland streams and rivers, freezes into ice, and so on; and it is the kinetic energy of molecules that burns the skin, boils water, cooks our food. We identify the physical occupant of the given role. From such an identification we can *derive* the identity statement. It is implied by the conjunction of the quasi-analytic description and the physical story. Suppose that there are various superficial macro properties by which we identify something as water. While it is perfectly conceivable that something other than H_2O manifest those properties, Levine suggests that if we take the physical story as a premiss—if we 'keep our chemistry constant'—then there is a sense in which it is inconceivable that H_2O fail to manifest those properties. 'There is an apparent necessity that flows from the reduction of water to H_2O, a kind of necessity that is missing from the reduction of' sensations of red to brain process squiggle-squiggle (Levine 1993: 128). If the identity can be derived from the physical story and our quasi-analytic description of a causal niche, then indeed we can rule out any other alternatives, and so we achieve a 'bottom-up necessitation' even though none of the sentences employed are necessary truths.

According to Levine this approach will fail to explain why a sensation with a particular qualitative character ('sensing redly', for example) is identical to a particular brain state. There is nothing about sensing redly that necessitates its identity with that particular brain state rather than some other one. Or, given the brain state in question, it seems equally conceivable that that very brain state be a state of sensing greenly, and not redly. The identities seem to be arbitrary and inexplicable. As John Locke put it: 'the *Ideas* of sensible secondary Qualities, which we have in our Minds, can, by us, be no way deduced from Bodily Causes, nor any correspondence or connexion be found between them and those primary Qualities which (Experience shews us) produce them in us' (Locke 1975: IV. iii. 28). To understand the connection, Locke says, 'we are fain to quit our Reason, go beyond our Ideas, and attribute it wholly to the good Pleasure of our Maker' (IV. iii. 6); the particular connections are attributed to 'the arbitrary Determination of that All-wise Agent, who has made them to be, and to operate as they do, in a way wholly above our weak Understandings to conceive' (IV. iii. 13).

The objection is formidable; many of its premises must be granted. First we should acknowledge that current science has yet to confirm any precise mind–brain identities of the sort envisioned. Even in colour science such identifications have yet to be secured. Secondly, it follows that currently we lack any explanations for such identities, and speculation about their form is just that. So all sides agree that an explanatory gap exists today. Thirdly, analysis of the meanings of ordinary language terms for red, green, and so on seems unlikely to provide the wherewithal for any variety of 'bottom-up necessitation'. In this domain there is little grist for the conceptual analysis mill; returns are paltry. For 'red' we cannot describe a uniquely identifying causal role, as we might with 'water' or 'heat'. It is unlikely that any analysans we produce for the natural language term 'red' even manages uniquely to identify its extension. From what was said above, this is only to be expected, since that semantics is largely embodied instead in the reliable operation of mechanisms of sensory discrimination. (This is why it follows that nothing in those ordinary concepts forbids spectrum inversion; the latter is 'conceivable'.) Fourthly, if we must close the gap using just these resources, it is very hard to imagine how it might be closed. Nothing in our ordinary concept of 'red' or 'green' seems sufficient to pin sensations of red or of green to particular brain states. So, in those terms, the association between sensations of red and brain process squiggle-squiggle seems indeed an arbitrary determination, wholly above our weak understandings to conceive.

If we have to close the gap in just the way that Levine proposes, it seems unlikely that it could ever be closed. But perhaps there is another way. Instead of analysing the words, we could embark on an empirical analysis of the qualities themselves. That is, analyse the mechanisms of discrimination whose reliable operation underwrites any successful application of those words. The construction and analysis of quality space *replaces* the analysis of concepts. It can serve a similar role in the closing of the gap as does conceptual analysis, but in this domain it will not provide us with a 'causal niche' occupied uniquely by a particular qualitative property. Instead we identify a 'qualitative niche': a place in the structure of qualities. The structure derives not from relations of cause and effect, but from relations of relative similarity, matching, and discriminability. We should also deny that the resulting structural definite description, whatever it is, is any analysis of the meaning of the words 'red' or 'green'. It identifies the 'real essence' of those qualities, but the structural definite description is not something that anyone who knows the language knows.

To close the explanatory gap, the world must be such that there is one best way that the spacing of qualities could be implemented in the nervous systems with which we are endowed. But here the asymmetries in the human colour quality space, noted in the reply to spectrum inversion, come to our

rescue.[8] Once we have discerned the lumpy, asymmetric, anisotropic structure of that space, and we have detailed the home-grown capacities of our
sensory nervous systems, we will see that there is just one best way to fit the
two together.

With these different resources employed in this different way, it is at least
conceivable that the explanatory gap can be closed. We could logically derive
the identities in question from the conjunction of completed neuroscience
and—not completed analysis, but—completed quality space. So I claim that
we can conceive of a conceptual scheme and of empirical details under which
it would be inconceivable that sensing redly be anything other than brain
process squiggle-squiggle. Here is one such story. Sensing redly is conceptu-
alized as a state with a particular qualitative character. That qualitative character is a particular place in a quality space: a qualitative niche, identified by
facts of qualitative structure. Only that quality could combine with yellow to
give orange, could cancel green, and so on. We form a structural definite
description, identifying this niche. Future neuroscience confirms Paul
Churchland's bold conjecture (1986, 1989: 102, 1995: 21–7) that a quality
space is a vector space of activation patterns in particular populations of
neurons. Such-and-such an activation pattern in that vector space fills just the
qualitative niche needed for sensations of red. That activation pattern is brain
process squiggle-squiggle. Ergo, sensing redly = brain process squiggle-
squiggle. How could it be anything else?

Formal details for this flight of fancy are presented in the Appendix. Of
course it is still just a schema; actually producing such an explanation
requires the scheme to be fleshed out empirically on both sides of the identity
sign. Undoubtedly it will not happen in this way. But just seeing how it *might*
be done relieves some of the distressing vacancy of the explanatory gap.

---

[8] A logically analogous asymmetry—a failure in parity in the decay of cobalt 60 atoms—
plays a similar role in solving the Ozma problem. Gardner (1991: 94) suggests the following
transmission: 'Cool the atoms of cobalt-60 to near absolute zero. Line up their nuclear axes with
a powerful magnetic field. Count the number of electrons flung out by the two ends of the axes.
The end that flings out the most electrons is the end that we call "south".' Just as with the colour
solid, this asymmetry would allow us to fix the reference of the word 'left', but it is not part of
the *meaning* of the word. Analysis would not reveal it.

2

Qualities and their Places

THE machinery for analysing sensory qualities and producing a multidimensional ordering of their similarities—a 'quality space'—seems relatively well developed and robust. Now I propose to throw a wooden shoe into the works.

2.1 THE APPEARANCE OF SPACE

The opening gambit is an innocent one: suppose we want to catalogue *all* of the dimensions of variation in phenomenal appearance in a given sensory modality. What will such a catalogue include?

A quality space is an ordering of the qualities presented by some sample of stimuli, and so must be relativized to the sample presented. The laboratory regimen obliges one to choose a sample that can be well controlled, eliminating as much noise as possible, so one tends naturally to use mixtures of wavelengths presented in an optical viewfinder, or standardized colour samples presented in carefully controlled viewing conditions. With such stimulus samples we have learned that there are three dimensions of variation in the appearances of colour, as (for example) hue, saturation, and brightness.

But a model that suggests that hue, saturation, and brightness exhaust the dimensions of variation in visual appearance would be true only in a world in which there is one sentient subject, confined to a pitch-black room, allowed to see just one visible point, whose colour qualities are varied in just those three ways. Add even a second point, or such vagaries as ambient illumination, a surround, shadows, glossy surfaces, mists, or reflections, and one quickly sees that even after the questions about chromatic sensory qualities have been answered, there is more work to do. Colours appear to characterize surfaces or volumes, which have relative locations, shapes, and arguably depths as well; and these locations, shapes, and depths are all as much characteristics of how things appear as are colours themselves. Phenomena such as occluding contours, glossiness, reflections, depth, translucency, and shadows enormously increase the complexity of the account. In any catalogue of the visible qualities, hue, saturation, and brightness are barely sufficient for a one-point world; depths and relative locations have yet to be plumbed.

Arguably every sensory modality presents appearances that have some spatial character. Suppose you wake up in the middle of the night in a dolorous state. An ache, cramp, or sprain seems to fill the afflicted body part, while sciatic pain, if that is your allotment, shoots alarmingly from one place to another. You open your eyes, and even in the dark, vision presents appearances that have a voluminous character:

We do not see a black surface like a wall in front of us, but a space filled with darkness, and even when we succeed in seeing this darkness as terminated by a black wall there still remains in front of this wall the dark space. . . . If I look into a dark box I find it *filled* with darkness, and this is seen not merely as the dark-coloured sides of walls of the box. (Ewald Hering, quoted in James 1890*b*: 137)

If you get up and walk barefoot across the room, you feel the textures and temperatures of those portions of the external world lying out there beyond your toes. With warm feet you can still feel the cold floor as something cold, outside of you. Other modalities contribute to the nightmare. Even without touching it you can feel the oppressive heat of the stove, radiating from the corner. Perhaps as you shuffle along you hear a solitary siren wailing in the distance. Even smells have enough spatial character to be tracked. Consider how hunger might prompt you to follow your nose into the kitchen. Watch a dog sniffing excitedly along a game trail and there can be little doubt that to it smells indicate a direction, and perhaps even a time. Deer went that-a-way, not-so-long-ago.

William James was the master at describing the 'voluminous' character of many sensory experiences, and his catalogue is still unsurpassed:

We call the reverberations of a thunderstorm more voluminous than the squeaking of a slate-pencil; the entrance into a warm bath gives our skin a more massive feeling than the prick of a pin; a little neuralgic pain, fine as a cobweb, in the face, seems less extensive than the heavy soreness of a boil or the vast discomfort of a colic or a lumbago; and a solitary star looks smaller than the noonday sky. (James 1890*b*: 134)

That sensory appearance has these spatial characteristics can come to seem as mysterious as the existence of sentience itself. That one feels an ache or a pain is for the materialist mysterious enough: what sort of property of a state of the nervous system, if any, could be such as to endow its unlucky host with that kind of experience? Yet the late-night wonder is that these qualities also appear as if spread out in space, filling a volume. How could any state of the nervous system be such as to make that discomfiting quality appear *where* it does?

I think the mystery of these spatial attributes has a particularly compelling form in the case of audition. That we have the capacity to detect the direction of sounds was first demonstrated by the Italian physicist Giovanni Venturi in 1796 (see Murch 1973: 206). He blindfolded subjects, sat them in an open field, and asked them to hold their heads still. He then walked around, piping an occasional note on a flute, and asked them to point in the direction of the sound. Even with more sophisticated methods, errors in localization are surprisingly low. In the best-discriminated regions, at azimuth zero, altitude zero (directly in front of the nose), we get errors averaging just two to three degrees horizontally and four to nine degrees vertically (Carlile 1996: 14). Errors in regions lateral and posterior reach a maximum of about fifteen degrees. That is about the angle occupied by a fist and extended thumb when held out at arm's length, so even the largest errors are surprisingly small.

We sense both auditory direction and depth. Late at night one can detect not only the direction in which a siren is travelling, but something of its distance. Somehow one hears a loud siren in the distance *as* a loud siren, far away. When you think about it, this feat is quite remarkable. After all, a less energetic source of sound nearby—a television in the next room perhaps, tuned to a police drama—could produce compression waves that transmit to your eardrums the same amount of energy in the same frequencies. Sometimes one is indeed confused by such stimuli: one might hear the ringing of the hero's telephone as a ringing of one's own. Yet typically one parses the energy of compression waves into separate components of loudness and distance. You hear the loud siren *as* a loud siren far away, not as a softer one hurtling about in the adjacent room.

Spatial perception is an intriguing and mysterious subject. The mystery is that it is possible at all. Your auditory sensations are utterly dependent on events within your cochlear nucleus, inside your inner ear. But what you hear seems to happen out there in space. How is this possible? How can you auditorily locate sounds outside your skin, given that *all* your auditory experience is dependent upon events inside your cochlear nucleus? I think we are here asking for a psychological model, and indeed there are various accounts of the cues used by the nervous system to manage this remarkable feat.

Auditory localization was long thought impossible, on two grounds: first that sounds have no shape, and second that unlike the eyes or the skin the ears do not employ arrays of receptors spread out in space (see Boring 1942: 381–2). It took a while for psychologists to recognize that the differing locations of the two ears alone might do the trick. Unless the source of the sounds is directly ahead of you or behind you, the compression waves will strike one eardrum with greater intensity than the other, and the system uses those intensity differences to help determine auditory direction. More importantly, because one ear is slightly further away from the source than the other, there will also be slight differences in the *phase* of the sounds at the two ears. The waves crest at one ear at a slightly different time than they do at the other. The auditory system actually picks up these tiny time differences—differences on the order of microseconds—and uses them as cues for azimuth. Given a known distance between the ears and a known time difference, it is a matter of trigonometry to compute the difference in distances from left ear to source and from right ear to source. Presumably the mechanisms that yield auditory azimuth from phase differences reliably employ those trigonometric equations, even though their host had conscious access to them only briefly, dimly, and unreliably, during trigonometry class.

The spatial order intrinsic to sounds has some peculiarities, however. At best the cues yield a ratio of the distance from left ear to source and from right ear to source. Imagine a triangle whose base is the interaural axis—the line between the two ears—and whose third vertex is the source of the sound. If there is a point in front of you that satisfies that ratio, there is also one behind you that satisfies the same ratio. Just flip the triangle over. In fact subjects often make such front–back reversals, pointing behind themselves when the sound is actually presented in front (and conversely). They will, however, point more or less precisely at the reversed spot, so that (for example) a sound thirty degrees in front of the interaural axis will sometimes be localized as thirty degrees behind it (and conversely), with an average error of roughly fifteen degrees in either case. The two points have the same distances to both ears, so are liable to be confused (see Gulick *et al.* 1989: 320; Boring 1942: 384).

I am sure you have experienced such auditory spatial illusions. Telephones in offices open to a hall provide a nice example. Standing in the hall, it is sometimes easy to be fooled into thinking yours is the one ringing. Quite often this is a front–back reversal. The rings are brief enough, and the hall smothers enough other cues, that it sounds as if a telephone up the hall is ringing, when in fact it is one down the hall. You rush to your door, only to discover at the next ring that your auditory system led you astray.

2.2 SOME BRAIN–MIND MYSTERIES

Some of the mysteries of spatial localization are best revealed from the *brain's* point of view. I think of these as 'brain–mind' puzzles, since they start with the brain as a given and try to explain how a mind could arise therein. They provide a respite from the philosopher's preoccupation with the mind's point of view. By no means will they all be solved by the end of this chapter, or even by the end of the book; but it is useful to post a list of them some-where, both to define terms and to keep us humble.

The first is the 'Convergence' dilemma. Here is how Davida Teller (citing Barlow 1972) poses it: 'If two or more neurons are to act jointly to determine a perceptual state, must their outputs necessarily converge upon a successive neuron whose state uniquely determines the perceptual state?' (Teller 1984: 1244). For example, if one is touched in two different places at once, one can typically register that there are two such places, and which two they are. Must the outputs of the receptors responsive to those touches therefore converge on some neuron somewhere in the nervous system? It is a 'dilemma' in the sense that both answers seem unacceptable. Requiring such convergence would require lots of neurons whose only job would be to register combinations of activity among other neurons. But without such convergence it is difficult to see how some joint effects could be produced.

Ernst Weber did some of the first experiments testing such 'two point' thresholds in 1834 (Boring 1942: 476). A person is lightly touched with the points of a compass which is either fully closed or opened to varying degrees. Can subjects detect whether they were touched once or twice, and how far apart must the points be spread in order reliably to yield the latter? Weber found that the distances varied enormously at different parts of the body. On the lips and fingertips, even the smallest separation could often be detected, while on the back, compass points spread as far as two centimetres are often felt as one. (If we map such spatial discrimination thresholds isotropically, so that points equally distant are always equally likely to be discriminated, we get the rather disturbing image of humankind known as the 'sensory homunculus', which has large hands, enormous lips, and gargantuan geni-talia.) Now in order to sense that one has been touched at two points, sepa-rated by a distance, must there be some neuron upon which effects of the distinct skin receptors eventually converge? It seems one cannot have a sensa-tion of two points at a distance unless the signal from one is somehow related to the signal of the other. The problem is understanding how a *pattern* could have effects sufficient to allow localization if there is no convergence.

The *reductio ad absurdum* lurking in the background of the convergence dilemma is the dreaded 'grandmother cell'. If we must have a cell on which the effects of two or more sensory neurons converge if those neurons are to have a joint effect, then for each particular object that you can discriminate on the basis of its distinctive combination of features, there must be at least one neuron whose activities are devoted to the recognition of that object. Hence, your 'grandmother cell' is the cell that fires if and only if you see, hear, or otherwise sensibly discriminate your grandmother. It is your own personal grandmother detector. The problem is not the grandmother cell *per se*—one could wire up one such neuron—but the sheer size of the extended family to which it would belong: not only one cell for each family member, but one for every other person and every other particular object you have ever encountered or will encounter, as well as one for each discriminably different combination of sensible features in objects you could discriminate. The resulting combinatorial explosion would tax even the large numbers of neurons we possess; and in any case dedicating one neuron per potentially discriminable object seems an inefficient use of that multitude.

The alternative is to allow that a particular object might be represented by activity in several different parts of the brain. Grandmother is registered, not by one neuron, but by the joint activity of a set of neurons. Those neurons might be found in different parts of the nervous system. With this we reach a second, more recent, and better-known brain–mind problem: the 'binding problem'. There are several different versions, but phrased most generally this is the problem of how activation of a set of neurons could serve to represent one thing. How can activity of the many serve to represent one? Somehow the system must treat activity across that perhaps scattered set as representing one thing; those activities are somehow 'bound' together. The 'one thing' their joint activity represents need not be an ordinary physical object, but might be one line, one shape, or anything else the system treats as one. So even the representation of a sequence of overlapping receptive fields as an oriented line, or the recognition of the shape of a letter of the alphabet, involve versions of binding (see Crick and Koch 1997: 284; Sajda and Finkel 1995: 268).

But the most exciting kind of binding is that involved in the perception of combinations of sensory features: colour, shape, motion, texture, and so on. This is called 'property binding' or 'feature integration' (Treisman 1996: 171). Suppose, for example, that there is just one red triangle in a display that includes squares and triangles that are red or green. The target cannot be identified by colour alone or by shape alone; to pick it out one must perceive one thing as both red and triangular. The task demands a 'binding' of colour and shape. This demand is more daunting than it may appear. Colours and shapes are registered by different portions of visual neuroanatomy; they are found in different 'feature maps', to use a term that will become prominent in what follows.

What neuroscientists mean by a 'feature' is roughly a 'sensory quality': some determinate value of a dimension of variation in phenomenal appearance. Some areas of cortex are called 'feature maps' for two reasons: first, that all the cells of some identifiable kind in that region respond to some particular dimension of variation in phenomenal appearance (and states of the cells are states registering those variations); and, secondly, that those cells are arranged in roughly topographical (here, retinotopic) order, so that adjacency relations are more or less respected. Cells next to one another in the retina typically project to cells next to one another in the lateral geniculate, which in turn usually project to cells next to one another in striate (or primary visual) cortex (area V1). So cells in V1 are in that sense a 'map' of retinal receptors. This is by no means a road map, nor is it a strict topological mapping, since there are many tears and discontinuities in the projection. The most prominent one is that retinal cells in both eyes are divided down the midline, and cells in the right hemifield of both retinas project to the right cortex, while those in the left half of both retinas project to the left cortex. The retinal image is of course inverted by the lens of the eye; and a twist in the fibre bundles also inverts lateral–midline relations, so that the most lateral regions of visual perimetry are sent to the midline portions of V1 and conversely. Finally, the mapping is not isotropic; areas better populated with receptors are better represented in the cortex, even if this stretches or compresses the spatial metric proportionately.

How common are these feature maps? In vertebrate sensory physiology they seem to be everywhere. You will not go far wrong if you summarize the neuroscience in a series of headlines: Layered Topographical Distributed Feature Maps (see Arbib 1972, 1989, 1995). In fact typically there are many feature maps per modality; in vision one has separate maps for hue, lightness, local motion, shape, spatial frequency, retinal disparity, and so on. Even within 'one' dimension of variation in phenomenal appearance such as colour, one finds multiple feature maps at different levels within the neuroanatomical hierarchy: blob cells in V1, thin stripes in V2, projections to V4, and so on (Davidoff 1991: 20–5). By one count, in the macaque monkey we have now identified thirty-two distinct visual areas (see Felleman and Van Essen 1991). Thirty-two! Either the design works or Mother Nature is a wastrel.

A colour feature map might register that something is red, and a shape feature map that something is triangular, but to solve the feature integration problem we need somehow to register that both properties are properties of one thing: that something is both red and triangular. This requires 'binding' the activity in the colour feature map with that of the shape. A similar binding problem can be generated across any of the permutations among features: colour with texture, shape with motion, motion with texture, and so on.

One strong piece of evidence for the reality of feature integration is the intriguing and otherwise unexpected phenomenon of 'illusory conjunction'. Under time pressure, 'errors in synthesis' can take place. In a display of blue Xs, green Ts, and red Os, for example, subjects might sometimes seem to see a red X or a green O. With brief displays and particular task demands, this can happen in as many as one out of every three trials.

The subjects made these conjunction errors much more often than they reported a colour or shape that was not present in the display, which suggests that the errors reflect genuine exchanges of properties rather than simply misperceptions of a single object. Many of these errors appear to be real illusions, so convincing that subjects demand to see the display again to convince themselves that the errors were indeed mistakes. (Treisman 1986: 100)

One or another feature is literally misplaced: green and 'O' are seen as characterizing the same place, when in fact no place in the array is both. The error is something other than misperceiving the character of any feature in the scene (see Prinzmetal 1995); the features present in the scene may all be correctly perceived. But some are mislocated or misplaced. These illusions should alert us to the possibility of sensory misidentification—of error in the mechanisms of spatial discrimination.

   Although the neuroanatomical details may be disorienting, philosophers may nevertheless recognize the feature integration problem, but under a different name. Frank Jackson (1977: 65) called it the 'Many Properties' problem. The set-up is slightly more complicated, but it involves the same challenge of identifying an object by its unique combination of features. The task is to discriminate between scenes such as the following:

   Scene 1: red square next to green triangle
   Scene 2: red triangle next to green square.

A creature equipped merely with the capacity to discriminate squares from triangles and red from green will fail the test, since both scenes contain all four. Instead the creature must divvy up the features appropriately, and perceive that Scene 1 contains something that is both red and square, while Scene 2 does not. In this way Jackson's problem is a version of the binding problem.

   Some of the mystery of the two-point threshold is wrapped up in issues of convergence and binding: of how the nervous system manages to represent two points as two, and how one might discriminate among pairs of stimuli with differing combinations of features. But part of the mystery remains centred on the spatial character of the experience. How does one manage to feel the touch *there*, at that particular point? I will call this aspect of the puzzle the 'Unlabelled Meter Reading' problem, in honour of Robert Boynton:

Imagine yourself locked up in the LGN [lateral geniculate nucleus], surrounded by meters indicating the frequency of spike activity in a million neural units there. Would you be able to deduce the color of an external stimulus on the basis of changes in the readings of those meters? Surely not, unless they were organized, grouped, and tagged in some reasonable way. No certain conclusion could be drawn from the sampling of two units, one from each side of 560 nm. Only if large populations of them were sampled could any deductions be made. (Boynton 1979: 236–7)

The image is a charming one, and it points to a general problem in neurosensory engineering. Even if we think of a sensory system as yielding up a set of 'meter readings', it is difficult to see how one could provide any groups, tags, or labels that would tell it what those meter readings are readings *about*. Our homunculus should be provided with a million *unlabelled* meters, and his deductions must proceed from those alone. Suppose, for example, that you have volunteered to sit in as a homunculus in the post-central gyrus. There you sit, watching a million or so meter readings of voltages across neural membranes. These membranes happen to belong to somaesthetic nerves, and the readings in fact indicate such things as distortion of Pacinian corpuscles and other receptors scattered throughout the skin, muscles, and joints. But unfortunately no meter is labelled. Could you determine *where* the events recorded by those meters are occurring? Suppose that suddenly some 10,000 or so meters hit their maxima, needles all jumping into the red zones, indicating that receptors in the vicinity are being *crushed*. Alarums! Massive bodily damage is being suffered, somewhere, and it is your job to steer the vessel out of harm's way and stem the devastation. What orders should you issue to the pre-central gyrus, to move which member? (We imagine a million levers, also unlabelled, corresponding to a million muscle fibres you might cause to twitch.) Think fast! A wrong move, or a move too long delayed, may send your boat to the bottom.

What makes Unlabelled Meter Reading a puzzle is not so much that the meters are all unlabelled, but that it does not seem possible for the nervous system ever to provide them any labels. A neuron deep in the cortex may be stimulated by neurons in the thalamus, which are stimulated by neurons in the spinal cord, which are stimulated by sensory nerves, which sum the responses of a number of transducers. The 'meter readings' up in the cortex are in some sense 'about' happenings amongst the transducers—or at least when you feel the crushing pain, that is where it seems to be—but it is hard to see how the nervous system could establish that those are the regions that the meter readings register. Consider: the cell up in the cortex would need to register not only that the cells impinging on its dendrites are firing, but also which are the cells impinging on *those* cells, and more particularly, where *their* dendrites are. It would need to register the locations of the receptive fields at the outermost afferent ends of the nervous system: the receptive fields of the cells that fire the cells that fire the cells that . . . fire it. And given the principle of univariance, all it can register are the events impinging on its own dendrites. To 'label' those meters, cells at the centre need somehow to determine the distal locations of the causes of cells firing at the periphery.

They need access to the inputs of their inputs, but are perforce confined to their own inputs.

The feat seems impossible, but the nervous system of every sentient species manages it in every waking moment, and in real time too. This is probably a good sign that the question is ill posed. In some respects it clearly is ill posed: neurons, for example, do not 'know', and do not need to know, anything. A meter might serve as an indicator for remote events—pressures deep in the reactor vessel, say—even though the information we receive on the meter itself is insufficient for us to determine which events they are (see Dretske 1995: 23–7). Still, the late-night pain seems to have a frightfully determinate location, and the sensation of having cold feet is distinctly of feet, and not (say) of elbows; so there are cases in which central events provide not only a set of readings about distal events, but also an indication as to where those events are located.

Why should the stimulation of two spatially separated tactile receptors on the skin lead to a *perception* of spatial separation? It is important to see that there is a *problem* here. The mere spatial separation of receptors is not sufficient to explain how one comes to have the *sensation* of two points separated in space. James (1890*b*: 169) says: 'A sensitive surface which has to be excited in all its parts at once can yield nothing but a sense of undivided largeness.' But why should it yield even that? How is it that the stimulation of spatially extended receptors gives a sensation of spatial extension? The spatial order of sensation is by no means *anatomically* intrinsic, although the density of receptors does play a causal role in the metric of that order. (Thresholds of spatial discrimination are smallest in areas where receptors are most dense.) The problem is to assess, from the centre, the location of events at the periphery. But how does this central neuron indicate that there is a disturbance *out there*? And why should the host *feel* something going on out there?

The puzzle has engendered odd doctrines in both psychology and philosophy: the psychological theories of 'local sign', and the philosophical theories of 'projection'.

The psychological theories of 'local sign' provided various mechanisms to solve this puzzle. One solution is to suppose that the peripheral regions in effect do have labels, and that those labels play a role in subsequent sensory processing. Lotze introduced the term 'local sign' to serve this purpose:

Since the spatial specification of a sensory element is independent of its qualitative content (so that at different moments very different sensations can fill the same places in our picture of space), each stimulation must have a characteristic peculiarity, given it by the point in the nervous system at which it occurs. We shall call this its *local sign* . . . we can only characterize them generally as physical nervous processes, one for every place in the nervous system, consistently associated with the variable nervous process that is the basis for the qualitative content of the changing sensations that arise at the same place. (Lotze 1852, cited in Herrnstein and Boring 1965: 136)

The idea was that points that could be felt as distinct must have distinct local signs, to account for the capacity to discriminate among them. A given point always has the same local sign, even as the qualities sensed at that point change. As William James described it:

different points of the surface shall differ in the quality of their immanent sensibility, that is, that each shall carry its special local-sign. . . . The local-signs are indispensable; two points which have the same local-sign will always be felt as the same point. We do not judge them two unless we have discerned their sensations to be different. (James 1890*b*: 167)

So if in Weber's experiment the two points on the back were felt as one, then on this account they carry the same local sign. But it soon became evident that different accounts of how 'local signs' work were possible. For example, some thought these signs were conscious (Wundt), while others argued that local signs were provided by physiological mechanisms inaccessible to consciousness (Külpe). Some thought the local signs had purely intensive variations (Lotze), while others assigned them qualitative ones (Wundt). And the question of whether these local signs were in some sense 'intrinsically' spatial (as Hering proposed), or whether a spatial meaning for local signs had to be learned, was the main focus of the lengthy nineteenth-century debate between nativists and empiricists. With such a variety of theories the term 'local sign' itself became something of a functional term, standing for whatever does the job of discriminating and localizing places.

Local sign theories solve our Unlabelled Meter Reading dilemma by proposing that nerves 'carry' a local sign. The signal carries an indicator of its own origins, like a broadcast from New York that starts 'Live, from New York . . .'. But instead of 'New York' we have some neural token, for which I will again use the technical term 'squiggle-squiggle', giving us 'Live, from squiggle-squiggle . . .'. The debates can then be cast as questions about squiggle-squiggle. Is it a pattern of intensive variation, or a simple quality? Is it accessible to consciousness or not? Is it intrinsically spatial, or must its spatial reference be learned? Of course 'carrying' a local sign only works if the sign can be interpreted. The homunculus trapped inside is not appreciably better off when he learns that a given meter should be labelled 'squiggle-squiggle'. He needs to learn the reference of the label, and in this task the same problems recur as the local sign theory was invented to solve. The resulting logical contortions are instructive. James, for example, finds an 'insuperable logical difficulty' in the notion that each sensation has an inherent spatial quality:

No single *quale* of sensation can, by itself, amount to a consciousness of *position*. Suppose no feeling but that of a single point ever to be awakened. Could that possibly be the feeling of any special *whereness* or *thereness*? Certainly not. *Only when a second point is felt to arise can the first one acquire a determination of up, down, right, or left, and these determinations are all relative to that second point*. . . . This is as much to say that position has nothing intrinsic about it; and that, although a feeling of absolute bigness may, *a feeling of place cannot possibly form an immanent element in any single isolated sensation.* (James 1890*b*: 154)

But in one sense this seems plainly wrong. Late at night the solitary siren still sounds as if it is out *there*, in one particular direction, all by itself. One need not add a second siren in order to localize the first one.

The nineteenth-century debate is enormously interesting because of its chaotic mix of conceptual and empirical questions. As in any interesting debate, half the confusion lies in how to frame the questions. The very terminology of 'local sign' was a source of confusion; it suggests that we answer a question about spatial relations with a theory about properties. If we think of 'local sign' as whatever it is that accounts for capacities of spatial discrimination, then perhaps local signs will be neither local nor signs. The other moral to draw for now is that there are indeed rival psychological accounts of these capacities; the theory that there are consciously accessible spatial qualia was one of many.

Philosophers too have a magical answer to the question of how states of cells deep in the cortex manage to present an appearance of something in front of the eyes: they 'project' the appearance there. If there is any lingering doubt that the perception of spatial relations is a mysterious and confusing subject, one need only examine philosophical accounts of 'projection' to be convinced. The root idea is well described by Sydney Shoemaker:

in our perceptual experience we in some sense project what are in fact nonintentional features of our experiences, i.e., qualia, onto the states of affairs that these represent. So when I revel in the blue of the sky the quality to which I am responding aesthetically is really a feature of my experience, which I mistakenly take to be instantiated in front of me. When I taste the wine I project the qualia of my experience onto my tongue and palate. And when I feel pain I project the qualia of my sensation into my back or foot or tooth. (Shoemaker 1990: 113–14)

There are many variants of 'projective' theories. As a description of appearance—of how things seem—projection can be cast in unexceptionable form: sensory qualities such as colours, tastes, and pains appear to characterize regions or volumes of space. Or, to use the formulation I prefer: among the dimensions of variation in phenomenal appearance, we must include some spatial characteristics. But usually a projective account is more than this: it is an attempt also to *explain* these appearances. The fundamental idea is that thcrc are qualities of states of mind, and a relationship of 'projection', and that colours, pains, and tastes appear to characterize regions of space in front of the sense organs *because* qualities of mind are projected onto those regions.

The analogy underlying the projection relation is optical, and in some ways dates back to Ptolemy's 'visual solid angles'. An after-image provides the paradigm example. If you are dazzled by a photographer's flashbulb, you seem to see a relatively distinct outline of the bulb, whose colour changes rapidly as the after-image fades. The colour appears to characterize a particular region of your visual field. Interestingly, the apparent *size* of the after-image depends on the distance of the surface that those colours appear to characterize. If you direct the affected portion of your eyeball at a nearby wall, the colours appear to characterize a relatively small region; whereas if you lift your gaze to a more distant surface, the after-image looks larger. Its apparent size depends on how far away it appears to be. The quantification of this relationship was one of the first quantitative laws in psychology (Emmert's law, 1881). The after-image always occupies the same 'visual solid angle' (it fills the same number of degrees of azimuth and altitude, because it is defined by an area of retinal bleaching), but the apparent size of the region filling that angle is proportional to its apparent distance. This projective relation is (strictly) optical: the size is just the distance times the tangent of the visual angle. Exactly the same relation holds between the size of an image projected onto a movie screen and the distance between the projector and the screen. The relation is 'projection' also because the colours that appear to occupy that region are generated internally, and 'projected' outwards. The projective theorist suggests that all appearances of colour are to be explained in the same way as the colours of after-images; and, more generally, that a similar account applies to tastes, pains, and other sensory qualities.

Shoemaker (1990) has usefully distinguished between two major classes of projective theory: the 'literal' and the 'figurative'. A literal projectivist thinks that the properties that appear to characterize regions of space in front of the sense organs *are* the properties of states of mind whose projection accounts for those appearances. The blue that appears to characterize the dome of the heavens in daytime is, on this view, the very same property as a property of sensation. A 'figurative' projectivist defines the 'projection' relation somewhat more loosely, and denies any identity between the property of appearance and the property of sensation whose projection accounts for that appearance. They are related; in fact the relation is precisely the one earlier characterized as holding between 'phenomenal' properties and 'qualitative' ones, or between manifest colours and the 'counterpart' properties of sense impressions (Section 1.1). The figurative projectivist explains the spatial character of experience by positing projection from the qualitative properties of sensation to corresponding phenomenal ones, the latter characterizing regions of space in or around the body of the sentient organism.

By this reckoning many theorists are projectivists of one stripe of another. In the course of his career Sellars manifested many stripes, but his concluding stance in the Carus lectures is clearly projectivist:

> the volume of pink of which we are aware does not present itself to us as a sensory state of ourselves—even though, at the end of a long (and familiar) story, that is what it turns out to be. . . . Rather, it presents itself to us *as*—we are aware of it *as*—over *there*, in physical space, cheek by jowl with other objects . . . (Sellars 1981*b*: 68)

The pink that appears to be out there, cheek by jowl with other objects, is at the end of the story a state of ourselves. Literal projectivism entails that sensory qualities are literally misplaced; what appear to be properties of distal objects are in fact properties of one's own sensory states. Somewhat more recently Brian O'Shaughnessy and Thomas Baldwin have formulated sophisticated versions of projective accounts:

> it seems that the bodily sensation must be projected onto the limb, where to be 'projected' is for a psychological item to be experienced *as* inhabiting something that lies without the mind of the experiencer. It seems that the place of the sensation must be the place it is experienced to be, that place being of necessity a part of the body. As the after-image is projected onto whatever physical item occupies its sector of the visual field—and items in physical space projectively sustain visual sensations when eyes are open—so the bodily sensation is projected onto the one physical landscape capable of sustaining it, viz. the animal body that is veridically given to the awareness of its owner. (O'Shaughnessy 1980: 178–9)

Interestingly, this projective relation is given conditions of satisfaction. It can succeed or fail:

> The location of a bodily sensation is and can never be anything but the real point on the presently existing body part of its owner at which it really and not merely seemingly is experienced to be. Accordingly, if the body part is not there, or if the sensation fails to successfully 'project' onto an existing body part and is hence not really experienced *at* any body part, then in the sense under consideration the sensation has *no* location. (O'Shaughnessy 1980: 181)

And how does one tell whether a sensation does or does not 'successfully project'?

> We proceed as follows. We line up point sensation and corresponding point in physical space by managing to trace a regular causal link between the two. . . . Thus, we manage to systematically correlate sensuous colour and movement at that . . . part of

the visual field with visible colour and movement lying in the required direction in physical space. (O'Shaughnessy 1980: 191)

Although the optical analogy is once again beguiling, there is no coordinate scheme within which one could 'line up' both visual sensations and points of physical space. Such 'lining up' is in fact a matter of tracing a causal link from a physical region to a portion of the retina, and then to some 'corresponding' visual sensation.

With a direction of fit and conditions of satisfaction, projection is endowed with some of the hallmarks of intentionality. The various causal conditions on this relation determine whether or not a sensation successfully projects. The sensation of a tomato projects red onto the surface of the tomato if and only if the sensation refers to the surface of the tomato, and represents it as being red. A sensation 'fails successfully to project' if and only if it fails to *refer*. Indeed the spatial character of sensation is closely allied both to projection and to the apparent reference or aboutness of these states. Consider the example of using one's warm feet to feel the cold floor. The cold appears to be located at points outside the skin, underneath one's feet. On a projectivist account, some quality of sensation is projected out there, into extra-dermal regions. The same phenomenon can be described intentionally: the thermal sensation is about a region of space outside the skin, and it characterizes that region as having a particular feature. This link is very clear in O'Shaughnessy:

in either successful case, sensations that are seemingly of some something—round red object (in sight)—paining big toe at end of leg (in feeling)—manage veridically both to bring something to awareness (sun, toe), *and* to land successfully projectively onto that projective sustainer (sun, toe). In short, we become aware of the contents of space and of individual points on our body, through projecting these brain-located phenomena onto the unique items that can support them, viz. the physical world, and one's body. (O'Shaughnessy 1980: 179)

To invoke such notions as successful projection, veridical awareness, awareness of contents, or the uniqueness of items that can support projection, one must drink deep from the wells of intentionality. These states have contents, truth conditions, reference, direction of fit, and normative conditions of success or failure. Projection is just the sensory form of aboutness or intentionality; the root source for both is that the sensations appear to characterize regions of space. As O'Shaughnessy (1980: 180) says, 'each bodily sensation is either merely putatively or else actually of a body part'.

Thomas Baldwin makes explicit this link between a projective theory of sensory content and the intentionality of sensation. His projection is, fundamentally, reference:

sense experience incorporates a reference to regions within the subject's egocentric sensory space—which is just a region of physical space organized from the subject's 'point of view' (or point of hearing, smelling, etc.)—and that the sensory quality which identifies the type of an experience is given as 'projected' into the region of space referred to in the experience. (Baldwin 1992: 184–5)

This reference is not to appearances, but 'to a region of real, physical space' (Baldwin 1992: 186). Sensory qualities are 'given as' or 'appear to be' qualities of regions of that space, because sensation refers to those regions. Baldwin urges that sensory experience 'attains' a primitive intentionality because sensory qualities are projected in this fashion.

This parallel is no accident: projection is a species of intentionality. Our barefoot insomniac, walking across the cold floor, feels the cold floor beneath the feet, or the heat radiating from the corner stove. These 'sensations of the cold floor' or 'of the hot stove' are best read as sensations *about* the cold floor or about the hot stove. Call it 'projection' if you will, but it is no more (or less) mysterious than *reference*. The place to which sensation 'projects' is the region it is about. 'Projection' for the philosopher (like 'local sign' for the nineteenth-century psychologist) is a functional label, for whatever does that job, and I will argue that what fills the job description—what accounts for the intentionality of sensation—is nothing more or less than our capacity for spatial discrimination.

2.3 SPATIAL QUALIA

Suppose we admit that any complete catalogue of the properties of appearance must include spatial properties and relations. Along with hue, saturation, and brightness we need at least visual azimuth, altitude, and depth. The next step is to argue that any account of the organization of sentience must treat the spatial dimensions of appearance in a rather different way than it does the others. In particular, the model we use to understand qualities such as hue, saturation, or brightness does not work when applied to visual locations. Although visible hue and visible depth both characterize how things appear, they play different roles in the organization of sentience. The same is true of auditory qualities and auditory locations, tactile qualities and tactile locations, and so on. Even at the level of mere appearance we are obliged to distinguish between qualities and their locations. In this section I will describe some of the difficulties that erupt when one attempts to apply the same model to visible locations as to visible hues.

Initially the study of visual spatial discrimination seems perfectly to mimic that of visual chromatic discrimination. The same methods of analysis apply.

We first determine the number of dimensions of independent variation required to describe the data, and then attempt to isolate the actual axes along which the visual nervous system registers those variations. The mere fact that one can make discriminations in three dimensions does not dictate the choice of a coordinate scheme; one might use Cartesian coordinates or polar ones, for example, and the choice of axes is open. In visual perimetry terms, the fixation point (the point on which both eyes are focused) provides the origin, and the position of a visible point in the frontal plane is described by horizontal and vertical visual angles away from that origin. (These are what I have been calling the azimuth and altitude: hereafter θ and ϕ.) Depth along that ray, Berkeley fashion, gives the third dimension. But other coordinate schemes are equally workable, and indeed there is good evidence that the visual system uses different coordinate schemes at different levels (see Section 5.6). The visual perimetry scheme is 'retinocentric' because the fixation point always falls onto the same place (the fovea) in both retinas, and visual angles away from that point translate directly into retinal locales at greater or lesser angles from the fovea. But if the task is to heft a visibly tempting apple into biting range, the retinocentric map yields few clues. There is no way to trace a trail on that map from apple to mouth. It helps to have a sequence of 'egocentric' maps that identify that visual location along axes defined by various bodily parts (see Grush, forthcoming). As the eyes can swivel about in their sockets, the fixation point can be at varying angles relative to the head; a 'head-centred' map performs the needed coordinate translations and describes the position of a point relative to the sagittal and horizontal planes of the skull itself. Similarly, with a head that can rotate on the neck, further translations are required to derive the position of that tempting red patch relative to the sagittal and horizontal planes defined by the shoulders and spine. Finally, 'allocentric' schemes proceed independently of bodily coordinates altogether, using such prominent axes as provided by the tug of gravity or the visual horizon, or less obvious ones such as the 'centroid' and 'slope' of things seen (see O'Keefe 1993).

So far the case seems exactly parallel to discovering that chromatic discriminations proceed in three independent dimensions, and then that the visual system actually registers those dimensions along the counter-intuitive axes of red–green, yellow–blue, and white–black. Section 1.1.4 argued that whenever one sees something of a particular colour, the corresponding visual state has qualitative properties defined by relative position within those three dimensions. They help to explain why the thing one sees looks as it does. Suppose we establish to our satisfaction that visual spatial discrimination is three-dimensional, and that at some level of visual processing it is registered by visual azimuth, altitude, and depth. Should we likewise think of the visual state as having qualitative properties corresponding to the spatial dimensions of azimuth, altitude, and depth?

Under this hypothesis, visual perception presents not only a panoply of chromatic qualia, but a well-organized array of spatial ones as well. Points that appear distinct will have distinct triplets of spatial qualia, and neighbouring points will have neighbourly qualia.[1] To use the terminology of the previous section, the particular triplet of spatial qualia associated with a particular visible point is that point's qualitative local sign. We posit these spatial qualitative properties to explain why that point appears *where* it does. The resulting array of spatial qualia is, per hypothesis, presented whenever visual perception takes place, no matter what one sees. Indeed, while depths can vary, qualia corresponding to coordinates θ and ϕ, describing the frontal plane, would never vary at all, except for the rare circumstance in which one suffers a scotoma or some other visual field defect. Furthermore, to account for Hering's experience of voluminous blackness, filling space, we must suppose that the same array of spatial qualia can sometimes occur unaccompanied by any chromatic ones other than black. Otherwise, no voluminousness.

While clearly we must somehow explain spatial discrimination, there is something unsettling about explaining it in this fashion. The first qualm can be put as follows. It implies that in any normal visual perception, a particular triplet of spatial qualitative properties can occur only once. Since these properties describe the apparent location of a point, the model cannot allow there to exist two distinct simultaneous instances of that particular spatial quale. Each triplet is a singularity.[2] Why? In every other dimension of qualitative variation, it is possible to sense multiple simultaneous instances of any particular value. Red, as a sensory quality, can have multiple instances. It is scattered here and there. Whereas spatial qualia—posited to account for the hereness and thereness—are forbidden multiple instantiation. What prevents disjoint points within visual perimetry from sometimes sporting the same spatial qualia? In Hering's experience every point in the volume presented the quale black. Why couldn't every point within the volume present the same

---

[1] One immediate complication is that peripheral vision is colour-blind. As one proceeds outwards from the fixation point one loses first red–green, then yellow–blue, leaving only white–black (Hurvich 1981: 21). Another complication: points away from the fixation point present differing azimuths and altitudes to the two eyes. They require two triplets of coordinates, one triplet for each eye. The spatial appearance of a double image, for example, cannot be described with just three dimensions; it requires more. I suppress these complications in what follows; the simple-minded model has problems enough.

[2] If we require m dimensions of spatial qualitative variation, then each such m-tuple is unique. By a 'particular spatial quale' I mean just such an m-tuple: a specification of a value for each of the m dimensions of spatial qualitative variation.

spatial quale? The result would be a volume filled with the qualia of one point.

Some other odd implications follow. Sometimes nothing red is visible. That particular quality has, at that moment, no instances. If this ever happened with spatial qualitative properties, however, the result would be pathological. Suppose there were an interval during which a particular swath of spatial qualitative properties, defining a visual solid angle centred on (θ, ϕ), happened not to occur. The spatial qualitative properties are uninstantiated during that interval. The result would be something of a 'super blindspot'. In a normal blindspot, there is a portion of visual perimetry within which nothing is seen. But loss of spatial qualia must eliminate the appearance of space. So in a super blindspot, not only does one see nothing in that portion of visual perimetry, but there can no longer appear to be a region within which one sees nothing. In that sense, the blindspot itself disappears: the very space in which it exists is not instantiated.

Even worse implications follow. On this account, the place at the centre of the visual field appears to be there because it causes a state with the appropriate place *quale*. But sometimes, alas, things are not as they seem. Something that is not 'really' red might occasionally 'look' red: it causes a visual state with the same qualitative properties as does something that is red. Generalizing the approach, we must allow for the possibility that places might likewise cause states with inappropriate spatial qualia. A place that is not at the centre of the visual field might appear to be there. It causes a state that sports the appropriate spatial qualia. We might have several contenders simultaneously. How disconcerting. One would be obliged to test whether or not visual field places really are where they appear to be. Is that the centre of my visual field, or does it merely appear to be there? Please proceed gingerly! Until such tests are complete, picking up a pencil, turning a knob, or grasping a coffee cup would be activities fraught with peril.

These qualms all arise from the same indigestible implication: that during any normal visual perception, each particular spatial quale must occur exactly once. Whereas your typical quality can have several instances, or none at all. This is our first clue. The problem with spatial qualia, I will suggest, is that they are not qualities. Instead the role they serve is closer to that of singular terms. Similarly, qualitative local signs are not qualities; if they are signs at all, they should be assimilated not to predicates, but to names.

Of course qualms are not arguments, and indigestibility does not invariably flag falsehood. One might simply endorse additional theoretical postulates to the effect that spatial qualitative properties happen to differ in these ways from other kinds. After all, we noted various classes of possible theories that postulate local signs, but differ over their properties. Perhaps we simply

endorse the bold conjecture that in every sensory episode in which a particular spatial quale occurs, it must occur exactly once. For my purposes the
important point is not whether or not we call the results 'qualia', but that we
acknowledge these peculiarities in their behaviour. Even at the level of
sensory appearance we find a distinction—however labelled—between
sensory qualities and the places that those qualities appear to characterize.

2.4 APPEARANCES PARTITIONED

Now for a second clue. Spatial qualitative properties, if they exist, have
another disconcerting feature: they seem to have little if any qualitative character. Even though we can discriminate the locations of stimuli, differences
that are merely differences in location yield scant difference in the quality of
sensation. Upon inspection, in controlled conditions, those differences seem
to vanish altogether.

Here is a simple illustration. Suppose you agree to participate in an experiment by a latter-day Giovanni. You are blindfolded like the eighteenth-
century participants. This Giovanni, however, has instruments that can
reliably produce pure brief tones—beeps, cheeps, or clicks. As he moves
about, you are asked two questions: have the auditory qualities of the tone
changed at all, and: where is it now? I submit that you could answer these two
questions separately. In a slight variant, one can imagine hearing two simultaneous beeps or clicks in different locations. Out in the woods one might
hear two apparently identical bird cheeps, one off to the left and one overhead. Perhaps they sound exactly the same, and the only thing that appears to
differentiate the cheeps is their location. If this is possible, then the difference
in apparent location does not preclude the possibility that the cheeps themselves sound identical. It follows in turn that whatever properties of sensation
account for differences in apparent location, those properties of sensation are
not among those counted when we consider the question of whether those two
sensations are qualitatively identical. The cheeps differ merely in apparent
location; this difference is not counted a qualitative difference. We treat pitch
and place in very different ways. I will call this the 'partition' argument.[3]

Qualitatively the same A flat or red spot can be presented on the left side or
the right. The timbre and pitch of the note need not change simply because one
turns one's head. Similarly, red on the left side need not differ qualitatively

---

[3] Ernst Weber produced a variant of it in 1846. His example: two watches whose ticking
noises could not be discriminated from one another. With the watches placed on either side of
the head, one hears two distinct instances of qualitatively the same ticking. See Boring (1942:
383).

from red on the right. If it did, a split-field test could not show that the two stimuli present the same quality. Even as the apparent border between the two halves of the field vanished, one would have to say, 'No, they are not the same colour, since one has a definite leftish quality, and the other rightish.' The alternative to this bizarre testimony is to admit that sensations of the two halves of the field could become qualitatively indiscernible. In this way the qualitative character of purely spatial differences dwindles to nothing.

Two presentations might differ *only* in apparent location, as with the two qualitatively identical cheeps, one heard overhead and one to the left. This possibility arises in any sensory modality in which it is possible to have two distinct, simultaneous, qualitatively identical presentations. You hear two qualitatively identical cheeps, you see two qualitatively identical red spots, you feel two qualitatively identical pinpricks. Any such modality presents a *manifold* of appearances, differentiated spatially. We could not distinguish two qualitatively identical presentations *as* two unless presentations in that modality have a spatial character.

To allow for the possibility of such manifolds, we must partition the dimensions of variation in appearance into two kinds, or two categories: those that count when we consider the question of whether the two presentations are qualitatively identical, and those that do not. Spatial discriminations fall into the latter category. Pairs of bird cheeps, pinpricks, or red spots may yield qualitatively identical sensations even though the cheeps, pricks, or spots differ in location. So even though those cheeps, pricks, and spots are, in virtue of their differing locations, discriminable from one another, those differences in location do not perturb qualitative identity. Instead the capacities of spatial discrimination serve a different role. They make it possible to discriminate the two qualitatively identical items *as* two. Both kinds of dimensions of variation in appearance are necessary if one is ever to have the experience of two distinct but qualitatively identical presentations.

Distant solitary sounds provide a dramatic example of this partition in action. The loud siren in the distance is heard as a loud siren in the distance, even though, as noted, a less energetic source nearby could transmit an equivalent amount of energy to one's eardrums. The activity at those transducers is a resultant of two factors: the intensity of the source of the sound and the distance to it. Yet somehow, remarkably, you manage to hear the sound as a sound of a particular loudness at a particular distance.

The feat is repeated in other modalities. In vision one sees objects of a particular size at a particular distance, even though various combinations of sizes and distances could equally stimulate the same solid visual angle. The 'moon illusion' furnishes a wonderful example. Often the moon 'looks larger' when seen at the horizon than at the zenith, even though it fills the same visual solid angle at both locations. The textbook explanation is that when the moon is on the horizon, objects along it provide more clues to lunar distance, so the moon looks further away, and so it must look larger. George Pitcher asked the right question about this illusion: 'What can the moon's looking larger to us when it is near the horizon than when it is near the zenith *consist in*? What is the nature of that perceptual state? It cannot consist in the moon's subtending a larger visual angle in our visual field, because it demonstrably does not' (Pitcher 1971: 70). It is a very good question, because the constant two-dimensional visual angle cannot account for the varying apparent size. Pitcher suggests that the moon's looking larger consists in our having an immediate impulse to *believe* that the moon is larger. But if we are allowed a third spatial dimension, to give us an appearance of size at a depth—a visual analogue to loudness at a distance—an alternative is possible. Perhaps the moon looks like a large body far away, as opposed to a smaller one nearby, even though both would subtend the same visual angle.

Typically one manages to parse the energy of compression waves into separate components of loudness and distance. You hear the loud siren as a loud siren, far away, as opposed to a faint one in the next room. More generally, the source of stimulation is in various modalities typically perceived as a source *of* a particular intensity *at* a particular distance. 'Parse' is not quite the right verb; better is 'partition', as in partitioning the variance (of transducer energies) into separate components (of loudness and distance). Recall the statistical notion of analysis of variance. Members of a population vary in some attribute of interest. If we know that those members belong to two distinct groups, we can treat the overall variation from person to person as a resultant of two components: the variation within groups, and the variation between groups. You can look at the proportion of variation that each explains and ask whether the 'between group' variation is 'statistically significant'. Similarly, I suggest, the variation in phenomenal appearance in a sensory modality is partitioned into two components: variation in location, and variation in the qualities at those locations.

To respect this partition, we need two different kinds of place-holders in any schema describing the contents of sensory experience. It cannot be collapsed to a univariate form. We cannot capture those contents by substituting different qualities Q in a schema of the form

appearance of qualities Q.

Instead we need two place-holders:

appearance *of* qualities Q *at* region R.

Here Q and R are place-holders to be filled in by qualitative and spatial dimensions respectively. The two play different roles, which cannot be interchanged.

But with both in place we get, at last, a schema adequate to report the contents of sensation. So, for example, one hears the siren as a sound *of* a particular loudness *at* a particular distance. The moon is seen (both at the zenith and the horizon) as a body of a particular size at a particular distance, even though those differing combinations yield the same visual solid angle.

The solitary character of the late-night siren is also revealing. Even though there are no other auditory points of reference, and auditory space is otherwise empty, the siren nevertheless appears to have a particular, perhaps vaguely identifiable, location. A sound with the same qualities could occur at a different place, and in this sense, apparent location is not given by the addition of other qualities to the ones already present. There seems to be nothing analysable in the quality of the tone that makes it a tone from here rather than there. But the single tone certainly seems to have a location. In fact silence provides an equally good example. After a building collapses you might be called upon to determine if you can hear anything underneath the rubble. Do you hear anything down there? You might listen intently, and hear nothing *there*.

One way to put the conclusion thus far is that the characterization of appearance seems to require reference to phenomenal individuals: the regions or volumes at which qualities seem to be located. If we lose such identification, we cannot adequately characterize the facts of sensible appearance. We need two distinct place-holders in the schema

appearance *of* quality Q *at* region R,

and the two place-holders serve different roles. The next stage of the argument will be to spell out those differences; as already hinted, I shall argue that the terms that fill out the R slot have a function similar to that of singular terms. But before moving on it is worth examining one other attempt to collapse the partition just erected.

That attempt is the adverbial theory. Its goal is to eliminate all putative reference to properties of sensation, and to treat all such characterizations as adverbial characterizations of manners of sensing. So instead of a 'sensation of red', we have a process of sensing, characterized adverbially: a 'redly sensing'. But how do we handle the spatial characteristics of sensory appearance? They too must be rendered into adverbs. Instead of

sensation of red at the left corner

we need something of the form

redly left-cornerly sensing.

In effect the adverbial theory tries to describe the contents of sensation in a schema with just one kind of place-holder, but it is a place to be filled with adverbs rather than qualia. Our partition is collapsed, and all the dimensions of variation in appearance are treated the same way: adverbially. This strategy leads the theorist into considerable difficulties, and in the end I think the theory does not succeed. Michael Tye (1989) had developed the most sophisticated version of the adverbial approach (before abandoning it), and his difficulties with the spatial characteristics of appearance prove instructive.

Suppose we call upon Otto again. Otto can see the difference between a red square next to a green triangle and a green square next to a red triangle. We must endow Otto with resources sufficient for this remarkable feat of discrimination. The traditional solution is to posit locations in Otto's visual field and say that both redness and squareness characterize the same place therein, while redness and triangularity characterize different places. Perhaps the red square is to the left of the green triangle. The problem that Frank Jackson (1977) points out with this is that visual field locations are just as much mental objects as were sense-data. The adverbialist must treat 'leftness' adverbially, like redness. As a first try the tableau is rendered: Otto senses redly squarely to-the-left-ly and greenly triangularly to-the-right-ly. Jackson (1977: 65) points out that this too won't work; such a conjunction would be equivalent to sensing redly and triangularly and to-the-right-ly and squarely and greenly and to-the-left-ly. Our scenes would be indiscriminable. We have found the birthplace of the 'Many Properties' problem.

Tye (1989: 80–4) attempts to solve it by creating an adverbial operator that modifies the other manners of sensing ('redly', 'greenly', and so on), and prefixing the result with an existential quantifier. We get the form:

There is a region x such that I sense redly at-x-ly.

We use distinct variables in these operators to pick out distinct places. Otto's feat might be cast as

There are regions x and y such that Otto senses redly squarely at-x-ly and greenly triangularly at-y-ly.

Spatial differences are registered as adverbial differences: differences in manners of sensing, with discrete manners captured by discrete quantified variables.

Can this apparatus solve the Many Properties problem? Can it represent a successful binding? I shall argue that it cannot. The problem can be demonstrated using an even simpler example. Consider the difference between a scene that contains a red square and another scene that contains something red and something square, but nothing that is both. If Otto's mind ran on the principles enunciated above, could it grasp this distinction? One might think that both feats could be represented. Otto senses a red square if there are regions *x* and *y* such that Otto senses redly at-*x*-ly and squarely at-*y*-ly and region *x* = region *y*. The red place is the square place; ergo, that place is occupied by a red square. Whereas he has the scattered impression of red here and square there—but nothing that is both—if there are regions *x* and *y* such that Otto senses redly at-*x*-ly and squarely at-*y*-ly and *x* is not identical to *y*.

But these formulations are ambiguous. Is the identity clause within the scope of the description of what Otto senses, or not? The simpler interpretation is to treat it as outside the scope of the verb. That is:

> Otto senses something both red and square $\equiv$ There are regions *x* and *y* such that ($x = y$) and (Otto senses redly at-*x*-ly and squarely at-*y*-ly).
>
> Otto senses something red and something else that is square $\equiv$ There are regions *x* and *y* such that ($x \neq y$) and (Otto senses redly at-*x*-ly and squarely at-*y*-ly).

But the former does not guarantee that Otto senses a red square. Not only must the red place be the square place, but Otto must sense their identity. Otherwise he will not sense red as characterizing something that is also square. A counter-example to the analysis is provided by any case in which Otto senses *x* as red and *y* as square, and in fact they are in the same place, but Otto does not perceive them as such.

Although the mere possibility of such a counter-example defeats the analysis, it takes a bit more work to produce a real one. Perhaps we can set up a beam-splitter and half-mirrors in such a way that through the eyepiece, a red surface of indeterminate shape appears to be in one place, and a non-chromatic square in another, though in fact both the red and the square are in the same place. When one sees something through a window, and at the same time a reflection in the window, the things one sees appear to be at different depths and different places. At dusk one might see the square outline of a building outside, while at the same time the bright lights indoors produce a reflection in the window of some red surface behind you. Perhaps with our optical apparatus something similar could be done with the colour and shape of one red square.

The analysis of the second situation is even more obviously flawed. It is wrong about the conditions under which one fails to sense a red square. Any instance of a 'false conjunction' (Section 2.2) provides a counter-example.[4] Suppose the appearance of a red square is a false conjunction. In the display, there is a red place and there is a square place, but they are different places: there is no red square. Otto senses redly at-*x*-ly and squarely at-*y*-ly, and they

---

[4] If a false conjunction is a false positive, false negatives are also possible: red squares not perceived as such, whose features are not successfully 'conjoined', even though in fact they characterize the same place. These would also provide counter-examples to the analysis of the first sentence.

are different places, but he perceives them as the same place. He will attest to seeing a red square in the display, but he is wrong. The analysis would forbid such an illusion from occurring.

The alternative is to assert the identity or non-identity of places within the description of what Otto senses:

> Otto senses something both red and square $\equiv$ There are regions x and y such that (Otto senses redly at-x-ly and squarely at-y-ly and $(x = y)$).

> Otto senses something red and something else that is square $\equiv$ There are regions x and y such that (Otto senses redly at-x-ly and squarely at-y-ly and $(x \neq y)$).

I think something like this is necessary, but both of these formulations violate the adverbial canon. We have Otto sensing facts: that x is identical to y or is not identical to y. For this version of the adverbial theory to succeed, these must be translated into adverbs. The task seems impossible.[5] Sensing 'at-x-ly at-y-ly' won't do, since those constructions are predicate operators, and in an identity statement we have no predicates to operate upon. Perhaps we can dodge the problem by using just one variable in the first sentence; but it seems irresolvable in the second sentence. Otto must sense red in a different place than the square, and the adverbial analysis cannot capture that difference. The difference between those 'different places' is a *numeric* difference, not just a qualitative one.

In short, the adverbial theorist is faced with a dilemma. To distinguish our two episodes we need to know whether or not the red and the square are sensed at the same place. Putting an identity statement outside the context of 'Otto senses . . .' does not guarantee that he senses the two places as the same. Denying it does not guarantee he senses a difference. Quantifiers and identity statements outside that context do not individuate what lies within. It seems that we need an apparatus of identification within the content of sensation itself. We cannot construct such an apparatus using only adverbs.[6]

---

[5] Tye's solution (1989: 118–20) is to add a combinatory operator that maps two predicate operators into one that expresses their coincidence. So the coincidence of 'red' with 'square' yields 'red-with-square', and Otto senses red-with-square-ly at x-ly. We also need another operator to express spatial separation (Tye 1989: 122–4), so that Otto can sense two disjoint instances of the same feature. These manœuvres require us to create distinct predicates for each possible distinct *combination* of visible features. The entire structure of coincidence, overlap, and distinction among features visible at a time is, on this account, captured by rather arduous compounding operations on our predicates.

[6] If we are sufficiently prolix with predicate operators, though, perhaps we can. Quine shows how six predicate functors suffice to 'explain variables away' (Quine 1966; Burgess and Rosen 1997: 184–8). If we add a predicate operator for each of these six functors, the resulting construction can eliminate variables altogether. It faces the same objection mentioned in the previous note: before adverbializing we must in effect generate a new predicate for every possible combination of features. That's a lot of predicates. (I thank Dan Blair for these references.)

In these struggles one can see some consequences of attempting to abolish the partition between the qualities of appearance and the places at which those qualities appear. The 'placing' component serves an individuative role, which adverbs cannot provide. So I agree with Lycan (1996: 71, 180); these adverbial manœuvres do not succeed in eliminating what seems to be reference to phenomenal individuals: the places and volumes apparent in sensory experience.

2.5 TIES THAT BIND

Developments thus far have suggested that we partition dimensions of variation in appearance into two kinds, qualitative and spatial; that only the former bear on qualitative identity; and that to describe the content of sensory experience we need a two place schema such as

appearance of quality Q at region R

in which the two place-holders serve irreducibly different roles. But what are the differences in those roles? Enough of qualms and clues; we need some sort of argument. Presumably those differences, whatever they are, prevent the collapse of the partition, and prevent us from treating all variation in appearance as variation in the qualities presented; but what are they?

It helps to return to the binding problem introduced in Section 2.2, and in particular, to the Many Properties version of it. Suppose we are trying to choose between two rather garish schemes of interior decoration. One is

matte red next to glossy green

while the alternative is

glossy red next to matte green.

The fact that we can distinguish between the two schemes shows that our visual system can solve the Many Properties problem. Both scenes involve two textures and two colours, and so the simple capacities to discriminate textures or colours separately would not render the scenes discriminable from one another. Instead one must detect the overlap or co-instantiation of features: that the first scene contains something that is both matte and red, while the second contains something that is both glossy and red. The features of texture and colour are 'integrated', are perceived as features of one thing; to use the neuroscience term, there is a 'binding' of matte and red in the first scene, and of glossy and red in the second. Only the particular combinations (or bindings) of features differentiate the two scenes from one another.

What makes binding possible? Careful consideration of this question will reveal the formal differences between the qualitative characteristics of sensory experience and the spatial ones.

Suppose that textures and colours are registered in different feature maps within the visual nervous system. A 'texture map' registers that something is matte, and a colour map that something is red. The conclusion we seek is that something is both matte and red. Formally, listing the contributions of our feature maps as premises, we have:

(1) Something is matte.
(2) Something is red.
_____

Something is both matte and red.

As any philosopher will quickly tell you, this inference is not valid. To make the inference truth-preserving, we must ensure that the matte thing is the red thing, or at least that there is some overlap between matte and red. Formally, using 'a' and 'b' as names for whatever is sensed as matte or red respectively, we need to add a third premiss:

(1) a is matte.
(2) b is red.
(3) $a = b$.
_____

Something is both matte and red.

Now we have a valid inference, but to get it some variant of the third premiss is essential. Unless we can identify the subject-matter of the first premiss with that of the second, we cannot logically secure the conclusion.

Such identification may be partial. That is, we do not need the matte portion and the red portion of the scene to be perfectly coincident, or identical, as long as there is some overlap. If 'a' names the matte portion, and 'b' the red, then it suffices that some part of a = a part of b. This variant of the third premiss suffices to get to the conclusion that something is both matte and red. But notice that there is still an underlying identity required. We need something matte such that the very same thing is red.

Now according to the feature integration model, and all the work on the binding problem which has followed from it, what makes it possible to bind matte and red together is that they are both features *of the same place-time*. As Treisman and Gelade put it:

We assume that the visual scene is initially coded along a number of separable dimensions, such as color, orientation, spatial frequency, brightness, direction of movement. In order to recombine these separate representations and to ensure the correct synthesis of features for each object in a complex display, stimulus locations are processed serially with focal attention. Any features which are present in the same central 'fixation' of attention are combined to form a single object. Thus focal attention provides the 'glue' which integrates the initially separable features into unitary objects. (Treisman and Gelade 1980: 98)

In a more recent statement, Treisman (1996: 171) says that property-binding is mediated by a serial scan of spatial areas, 'conjoining the features that each contains and excluding features from adjacent areas'. Features scanned are bound together because at the time of scanning they characterize the same place. Identity of place-times drives the bindings: what gets bound to the matte feature is whatever other feature is at the same spatio-temporal location. The system must in one way or another detect that coincidence of locations in order for binding to proceed successfully. Treisman's model includes a 'master map' of locations, whose job is to ensure that such coincidence can be detected readily. When it goes wrong, we get 'false conjunctions'.

With this we can make our schema a bit more realistic. A texture map registers the locations of texture features, and similarly for a colour map. The two premisses might be rendered

(1) ((matte) (here))
(2) ((red) (there))

where the 'here' and 'there' are stand-ins for whatever capacities are employed to identify the place-times that are matte or red respectively. To achieve the binding of matte to red, to get to the perception of something that is both matte and red, the same form of suppressed premiss is necessary, namely

(3) here = there

or perhaps a partial identification—an overlap of regions:

(3) some place here = a place there.

Without one or another identity, feature integration fails. The premisses would fail to show that there is something that is both matte and red.

The schema helps to explain our earlier difficulties in trying to treat the spatial character of sensory experience as just another species of qualia (Section 2.3). Suppose we cast 'here' and 'there' not as spatial identifiers, but as spatial qualitative attributes: something like 'hitherness' and 'thitherness'. These attributes are to be conjoined to the other features found in the scene. Our first interior decorator scheme would yield

(matte & red & hither & green & glossy & thither)

while the second presents

(glossy & red & hither & matte & green & thither).

Unfortunately, the two conjunctions are precisely equivalent. If we treat the spatial character of experience in this way, we lose the capacity to distinguish between the two scenes. As Quine (1992: 29) puts it, 'conjunction is too loose'. We must somehow focus the attribution of qualities: we need matte and red in one place, and green and glossy in another, distinct place. If places are reduced merely to dimensions of qualitative variation, this focusing becomes impossible, and feature integration disintegrates. Since we can readily discriminate between the two scenes, such a collapse of our partition cannot be allowed. Even in appearance we make a distinction between qualities and the places at which they appear.

Although our conclusion describes a conjunction of features, the logic that gets us there is *not* conjunction. It is predication. Consider the difference between the conjunction of 'Lo, a pebble' and 'Lo, blue', and the form 'Lo, a blue pebble'. As Quine says,

The conjunction is fulfilled so long as the stimulation shows each of the component observation sentences to be fulfilled somewhere in the scene—thus a white pebble here, a blue flower over there. On the other hand the predication focuses the two fulfillments, requiring them to coincide or amply overlap. The blue must encompass the pebble. It may also extend beyond; the construction is not symmetric. (Quine 1992: 4)

'Pebble' is not exactly a feature, but the logic is impeccable. To get something that is both blue and a pebble, we must identify some blue place as the same place occupied by the pebble. This cannot be done with general terms and conjunction. We require some capacity to identify and discriminate the subject-matters of the general terms: to detect whether or not this one is the same as that one.

Property binding can be characterized as a grouping process: its result somehow is to associate, focus, bind, or group together a collection of features (see Sajda and Finkel 1995: 268). Confronted by the conjunction

(red & matte & hither & green & glossy & thither)

one's overwhelming temptation is to try to leap directly into the mind, and stick in some parentheses to indicate grouping. One would like to tell the homunculus directly that (red & matte & hither) go together, as do (green & glossy & thither). Or we might invent nesting operations among our features, so that some can modify others. Perhaps we have (redly (matte)) and (glossily (green)).

While grouping is indeed the goal, it cannot be secured with such devices. The commutative and associative properties of conjunction assure that such parentheses have no semantic significance. To get the desired grouping, a logical operation of a different order is required. What constitutes the needed group is a common subject-matter: that those features are all features *of* one thing. The groups are groups of predicates true *of* the same subject; boundaries between the groups are boundaries between the distinct things *to which* the features are attributed.

We have stumbled onto a profound formal difference between features and bindings: while features are general terms, open to multiple instantiation, binding requires singular terms, the picking-out of places. The work of binding is the work of identifying the subject-matters of the various feature maps. It is not conjunction, but rather joint predication. This map and that map map the same territory. If such identification relies on spatial discrimination, it is not a process of attributing additional features, or of adding more qualities or descriptive clauses to the already fulsome list. Even if we postulate a 'master map' of locations, that map clearly is not another feature map like all the others. Instead its job is to help identify the subject-matter of one feature map with that of another. Some place occupied by feature F = a place occupied by feature G. Such identities drive the bindings. We cannot express them with an apparatus confined to sensory qualities—general terms. We require a distinct logical function, like that served by a singular term: a capacity to identify that which the qualities qualify. So within sentience itself we find capacities that fill two distinct logical functions. One is predicative: the capacity to sense red (or any other feature) both here and there. The other is referential: the capacity to identify the place that is red as the place that is matte.

Suppose you are out in the woods again, listening to the birds sing. You hear two birds cheeping merrily at the same time, one overhead and one to your left. If auditory sensation were a pure flux of qualia, its content would be of the form

(cheep) (cheep-cheep),

where the 'cheep' and 'cheep-cheep' are technical names for the given qualities of auditory sensation. If the argument thus far is correct, such a form is inadequate to represent the content of acts of sense. One would be unable to distinguish that auditory scene from

(cheep-cheep) (cheep);

that is, from a scene in which the same two auditory qualities switch places. Conjunctions of qualities 'C & D' and 'D & C' are equivalent. Instead we partition variation in phenomenal appearance into two components: variation in locations, and variation in qualities at those locations. So auditory sensing would have something of the form

((cheep) (here)) ((cheep-cheep) (there)),

where the 'here' and 'there' represent this second component of variation: variation in the apparent location of the auditory qualities. Capturing the content requires not only predicates but singular terms, 'a' and 'b', as names of places. So

((cheep) (here)) ((cheep-cheep) (there))

would have a form akin to 'Ca & Db'. Our singular terms 'here' and 'there' are place-holders for the efforts of mechanisms of spatial discrimination: they identify *where* those features appear to be.

With two kinds of term we can represent independent variations in apparent place and apparent quality. The bird overhead and the bird to your left might swap places, and in the next moment one might hear a merry

((cheep-cheep) (here)) ((cheep) (there)).

But now we can distinguish the two scenes: the latter yields 'Da & Cb'. With this separately partitioned component of variation in apparent location, we might also simultaneously enjoy two qualitatively identical cheeps, indistinguishable in their auditory qualities, at two distinct places:

((cheep) (here)) ((cheep) (there))

('Ca & Cb'). At last we have the machinery to attack the partition problem, and to distinguish the various cheeps, clicks, pinpricks, and red spots that bedevil us. Moments later, the same apparent auditory locations might be occupied by shockingly distinct features,

((quack) (here)) ((quack-quack) (there)),

whose symbolization is left as an exercise for the reader. The differences among these various combinations are impossible to represent under the regimen of purely qualitative variations.

We need two *kinds* of term: two place-holders with different roles in the schema 'appearance of quality Q at region R'. These identify a location and attribute qualities to that location.[7] The two roles cannot be collapsed or interchanged. Finally in this section we see why. The existence of the partition and the formal difference between the two orders can be derived from the conditions

---

[7] As will be argued in Ch. 3, these 'regions' and 'locations' should be understood to possess temporal coordinates. They are best conceived as place-times: spatio-temporal regions, or locations in space-time.

necessary to solve the Many Properties problem. To solve that problem we must have the capacity to distinguish between sensory qualities and the places at which they appear, and we must assign different formal roles to the two kinds of place-holder. We manifestly can solve the Many Properties problem. So the conditions necessary for its solution must obtain.

The idea that the spatial and qualitative attributes of sensory experience play different roles is by no means new. Here, for example, is the source for my term 'formal difference', Rudolf Carnap:

The constructional separation of the visual field order and the order of colors depends upon a formal difference between the two orders: it is impossible that in a single experience two different colors should appear at the same visual field place, but two visual field places can very well have the same color. Because of this formal difference, it is possible that the visual field order and the spatial order which results from it, but not the color order, can serve as the principle of individuation for reality. (Carnap 1967: 170)

He says that the orders of colour and of place serve altogether different roles in the construction of knowledge:

One of the two determinations, the location sign, serves as the foundation of the 'principle of individuation'. It determines a preliminary ordering of places, upon which the spatial ordering ultimately rests. That this function can be fulfilled by only one of the determinations is due precisely to that formal property of place identity through which we have separated it from color identity, namely, that non-identical, place-identical qualities cannot occur in the same experience. (Carnap 1967: 145–6)

In this passage one can recognize the outlines of our first clue (Section 2.3). In fact most of the complaints one could raise about either passage are terminological. The 'location sign' (local sign) has already raised our hackles, and 'visual field place' will do so in Chapter 3. Terminological quibbles aside, Carnap's conclusion that spatio-temporal and qualitative determinables serve different roles in the construction of knowledge is right on target. But what exactly is the difference in these two roles? I have suggested, with Carnap, that it is akin to the difference between reference and predication; but can the kinship be delineated precisely?

Any account with the requisite generality to answer that question must perforce be rather abstract. Here is an approach suggested by Sir Peter Strawson's seminal work on the distinction between subjects and predicates. On what basis do we classify a term as one or the other? The problem becomes rather intricate, because general terms, which serve as prototypical predicates, can so readily slide over into the subject slot. Granted, the spot is red, but we can also talk about the redness of the spot, and proceed to say things about it: redness is a colour, colour is a visible quality, and so on. So how do we differentiate between subjects and predicates? Strawson (1963: 168–75) suggests examining the 'ties' or pairings between particular instances. The same subject term might be found paired with many different predicates: the spot is red, hot, sharp, painful. The same predicate term can be paired with many different subjects: that spot is red, but so is this other one, as well as this patch and that one. Furthermore, consider what Strawson calls the 'attributional ties' between subjects and the particular instances of properties that characterize them. That very spot is tied to a particular instance of red, a particular instance of warmth, and so on. Finally, the particular instances of the properties of the spot might in turn be tied to different predicates: the red of the spot is bright and is highly saturated; the warmth of the spot is intense but not voluminous, and so on.

Examine all of these pairings, and we can extract what Strawson calls 'collecting principles' that govern how instances of one kind of term are tied to instances of the other. The fundamental idea is that subjects and predicates do not enter into these collecting principles in exactly the same way. To one subject term we can attach many different predicates: Socrates is a mammal and is a man; is happy and is wise. To one predicate we can attach many subjects: both Socrates and Xantippe are mammals; Socrates and Aristotle are wise. To one subject term we can attach many different instances of predicates. Socrates 'collects' many particular instances of breathing, talking, and smiling, as well as instances of all the other predicates that ever characterize him. But particular instances of predicates each collect only one subject term. The particular smile of Socrates can collect only Socrates; the smile of Xantippe, only Xantippe. Even though there are many different instances of the smile of Socrates, they are never tied to any subject other than Socrates. This many–one collecting principle provides an asymmetry in our pairings.

An even more potent asymmetry is described in later works. Strawson notes that there is 'a certain asymmetry which particulars and general characters have relative to each other, in respect, as I put it, of the possession of incompatibility ranges and involvement ranges. General characters typically have such ranges in relation to particulars, particulars cannot have them in relation to general characters' (Strawson 1974: 126). An 'incompatibility group' is described as follows. If a general characteristic out of such a range is exemplified by a particular, then other general characteristics out of that same range cannot be exemplified by the same particular (see Elder 1996*b*, *d*). But there are no such incompatibility groups of particulars *vis-à-vis* general characteristics. That a particular exemplifies a general characteristic does not rule out the possibility that others do too. The asymmetry in involvement groups is similar: 'for many a general character there is another general character such that any particular which exemplifies the first must exemplify the second or vice versa; but there is no pair of particulars so related that every general character the first exemplifies must be exemplified by the second or vice versa' (Strawson 1974: 126). Another way to put this: general characteristics come in ranges of incompatibility groups and involvement groups *vis-à-vis* particulars, but there are no such groups among particulars *vis-à-vis* general characteristics (Strawson 1974: 18–19).

All we know are the pairings of one term with another, and whether those pairings are one–many, many–one, one–one, many–many. We would like to know the difference between subjects and predicates, and which terms are which. Strawson's collecting principles provide a route from one to the other. Subjects and predicates cannot enter the various pairings in exactly equivalent ways. The asymmetries in collecting principles give us the wherewithal to determine which are subjects and which are predicates.

I suggest that similar collecting principles apply to sensory pairings of place-times and features. The same patch can be both red and glossy, smooth and warm. The same red can be found in many simultaneous patches, as can glossiness, smoothness, or warmth. But to this particular instance of red we can tie exactly one place-time. And if that one place-time is red, it cannot also be green. This pairing, recall, is what makes binding possible: to that particular instance of red we 'bind' whatever other features characterize the place-time it occupies. Without the many–one character of this collecting principle (many features, one place-time), it would not be possible to sense that same place-time as red, glossy, smooth, and warm: to sense it as characterized by multiple features.

Our two kinds of term—our two kinds of place-holder, or two kinds of dimensions of variation in sensory appearance—can thus be differentiated from one another by the asymmetry in the collecting principles that govern their association. They enter into ties with one another, but not in exactly the same way. The differences justify the claim that we have terms of two different kinds, serving logically distinct functions within the organization of sentience.

I have suggested that the difference between spatio-temporal and qualitative attributes of sensory content is akin to the difference between reference and predication. Now for a speculative postscript: perhaps this similarity is no accident. It is more than skin-deep. Perhaps it is familial. If in fact similar collecting principles apply to pairings of place-times and features as to subjects and predicates, then the two phenomena may be related to one another, and the linguistic phenomena of reference and predication may have ancestors in our sensory systems. Nature tends to copy solutions that work, and if aeons ago the ancestors of our visual system (for example) managed to solve the Many Properties problem, it would not be entirely surprising to find that later linguistic systems simply copied their solution. If this were so, then the distinction between reference and predication reflects an even deeper and older architectural feature of the neural organization of our sensory systems. Even at a purely sensory level our minds operate with principles of collection between one and many that are strikingly similar to those later found in language, and found there to distinguish reference and predication. Perhaps the latter distinction rests on the primal distinction between one place-time and many features: the primal distinction on which binding itself depends.

2.6 FEATURE-PLACING INTRODUCED

What the preceding arguments show is that we must treat variation in appearance as having two distinct components: variation in apparent location, and variation in phenomenal qualities at those locations. Such a partition would explain why we use, and need to use, two place-holders in the schema

appearance of quality Q at region R

since the two sorts cannot be fused. A two-way analysis of variance cannot be mapped onto a one-way. The first member of each ordered pair is a sensory quality, to be analysed and understood using the previously developed account of quality space. The second member is a stand-in for the capacities of spatio-temporal discrimination in virtue of which the sensory quality appears *where* it appears. Both are needed, and the second component functions differently from the first. A distinctive role for phenomenal locations has been suggested: they serve to focus the attributions of qualities, allowing us to distinguish one scene from another in which the same qualities are present, but rearranged. With that second component in place we have the wherewithal to launch a simple scheme of mental representation.

Here is the general hypothesis. Sensing proceeds by picking out place-times and characterizing qualities that appear at those place-times. It is a primitive variety of mental representation—probably the most primitive variety. Mechanisms to account for the spatial character of sensory experience have a referential or proto-referential function. They function something like singular terms. Mechanisms that serve to characterize the qualities that appear at those locations have a predicative or proto-predicative function. These proto-predicates are just determinate values along the various dimensions of qualitative variation in the modality in question. Such features or sensory qualities can have multiple simultaneous instances: they serve as characterizing universals or general terms.

The distinction between the spatio-temporal and qualitative components of variation in phenomenal appearance mimics the distinction between reference and predication. But the latter are linguistic phenomena, and we are talking about their sensory analogues. For this reason I will sometimes, as above, use the label 'proto-referential' for the spatio-temporal identifications underwritten by sensory processes. Similarly, the sensing of features at a place-time is 'proto-predicative'. As will be seen, these function in ways strikingly similar to reference and predication in a natural language, but they lack some of the more sophisticated features.

I call this hypothesis 'feature-placing'. Sensory representation, when successful, proceeds by picking out place-times and characterizing qualities that appear at those place-times. In our schema

((cheep) (here)) ((cheep-cheep) (there))

the first part stands for the machinery yielding a feature, the second for machinery identifying the location at which the feature appears. Typically, when the identification succeeds, these places are physical places, physically in front of the sense organs. More precisely, they are place-times, in or around the body of the sentient organism. Visually the root form is something like

((red) (here)) ((green) (there)),

where the 'here' and 'there' pick out place-times somewhere in the line of sight, where the red and the green appear to be. For 'red' and 'green' substitute any of the visible qualities that can characterize such locales. In audition: 'here is a cheep, there is a honk', where 'here' might specify a direction overhead, and 'there' to your left. In bodily sensation we have 'here it tickles, there it hurts', where again the 'here' and 'there' latch onto particular bodily place-times, and the tickles and hurts can be supplanted by any of the somaesthetic qualities that might occupy such places. Crudely, when you have a pain in your foot, your state of sensing pain-in-the-foot picks out your foot (it identifies or selects that location, as opposed to any other one) and it attributes to it a particular somaesthetic quality (pain as opposed to ache, tickle, or chill).

I take the name 'feature-placing' from Sir Peter Strawson; his description of feature-placing languages (Strawson 1954, 1963, 1974) was something of an inspiration for this hypothesis (see Section 4.3). The results are also largely anticipated by Christopher Peacocke, with his work on 'scenarios' and the non-conceptual content of perceptual experience (see particularly Peacocke 1992*a,b*). A scenario is a way of filling out the space around a percipient; at every perceptible point in it we specify a value for each dimension of variation in phenomenal appearance that is perceptible at that point. The differences between feature-placing and scenarios are minor, and technical. It has been emboldening to note the similarities, since, as will be seen, the premisses leading to feature-placing are entirely independent of those which led Peacocke to scenarios.

Feature-placing imposes order on the blooming, buzzing, confusion in three modalities as follows:

((cheep) (here)) ((cheep-cheep) (there))
((red) (here)) ((green) (there))
((tickle) (here)) ((pain) (there)).

The qualities in first place in this scheme clearly vary from modality to modality. It is critical to understand that the capacities of spatio-temporal discrimination that serve to 'place' the given features also vary from modality to modality. The underlying mechanisms picking out 'here' and 'there' vary tremendously from audition to vision to touch, and so the homonyms above are almost guaranteed to cause misunderstanding. There is a visual manner of identification of place-times that is totally distinct from tactile or auditory manners. Their referents might in the end be identical (I so argue in Section 5.3), but the ways and means by which places are picked out vary enormously from modality to modality. They can also vary significantly from feature map to feature map *within* a given modality. As suggested in Section 2.2, egocentric and allocentric coordinates might both refer to the same place-time, but the two schemes pick out that same place-time in different ways. In short, the various 'heres' and 'theres' might differ from one another as much as colours do from tastes. The schema uses both qualitative and spatial place-holders. Feature-placing makes full use of both degrees of freedom.

It is vital also to emphasize that the use of English or any natural language to characterize the form or content of sensory states requires extraordinary caution. These formulations have a very narrow interpretation, which if ignored is apt to produce nothing but confusion. Sensory states are not sentences and do not resemble sentences in any natural language. They do not contain terms or expressions synonymous with any expressions in a natural language. The use of English words such as 'cheep', 'here', and 'there' should be understood schematically, as stand-ins for capacities that are far less sophisticated than those required to understand a natural language. Fundamentally the place-identifying terms in the schema reduce to capacities of spatio-temporal discrimination. It might be less confusing to replace the English with plastic wafers and arrows, but then this book would be difficult to print.

The feature-placing scheme of representation is pre-linguistic. Its architecture is common across vertebrates that can make simultaneous sensory and spatial discriminations. (It may be even more widely spread than that, but I do not know enough about invertebrate sensory systems to say.) Its blueprint may antedate the spine. Sentience is an ancient endowment, and in terms of its lineage the capacity to speak was acquired only moments ago. Think of the mind as a polyglot society, endowed with a babel of systems of representation and communication, of varying ages and propinquity. That noisome know-it-all up in the temporal neocortex is the greenest of newcomers. It is presumptuous to demand that all schemes of mental representation be translated into its terms. The task would be analogous to conveying a musical score by semaphore. Perhaps if the two parties could converse at length beforehand, some scheme could be devised, but sensing is mute, and no such conversation is possible. Many of the philosophical problems in understanding qualia indeed have an uncanny resemblance to the task of getting two different parts of the brain—two different systems of mental representation—to communicate with one another. The resemblance is reinforced when one realizes that one of the parts in question is pre-linguistic.

The sentence 'here it is red, there it is green' demonstratively identifies places and attributes features to those places. The *sensation* of a red triangle next to a green square does something analogous; it picks out place-times and attributes features to them. But the latter does not require or proceed in a natural language; any creature that can sense a red triangle next to a green square has the requisite representational capacity.

The feature term is replaced by some property of central states (probably some determinate value of an activation pattern) whose function is to represent a dimension of variation in phenomenal appearance—what I earlier analysed as a sensory quality. The demonstrative is replaced by some determinate value of activation patterns of mechanisms of spatio-temporal discrimination—the ones in the given modality responsible for tracking where the feature in question is to be found. Instead of 'here' or 'there', we have the activation of mechanisms of discrimination sufficient to pick out the *location* in question. They identify that place-time not with a word, but in the same way that a setter or bloodhound can point to the location of the fox or of the drug cache. Or, to vary the example, they pick out the location in the same way that a lioness crouching in the grass of the savannah tracks the location of a particular gazelle. Even though the lioness has no words, she definitely has something targeted, something in the cross-hairs, whose position and distance is gauged very carefully indeed. A philosopher set loose in the savannah would be unwise to think 'she cannot identify my location, since her lexicon lacks demonstrative terms'. The feature-placing content operative in the lioness might be something of the form 'prey there' (or perhaps '*food* there'). Instead of the demonstrative 'there' we have mechanisms of spatial discrimination, currently activated so as to track the location of that very same (and we hope tasty) academic, soon to be valued not for his insights, but for his protein content.

Feature-placing, as least so far as it is found in sensory representation, does not proceed in sentences. Probably it proceeds in *feature maps*. Here is a foretaste of details to come. When I talk about 'feature-placing' representation, I hope to be talking about the same thing that neuroscientists refer to as 'feature maps' in primary and secondary sensory areas of cortex. There we see the first stirrings of what one might be tempted to call sensory content. If with Dennett and Kinsbourne (1992) we think of 'content-fixations', proceeding massively and in parallel throughout the brain, at varying levels of sophistication and interconnection, the simplest and crudest kind of such content fixations probably occur in these feature maps. It is hard to get much simpler, but enough occurs in the primitive flash of feature-placing for us to allow that some minimal content has been fixed. Crude it is, but so is sensing. So I will stake my claim on the feature maps. The drama of sentience begins there.

Given a feature map, there are two distinct questions one can ask about any portion of it. (1) What territory (what spatial region) is *mapped by* this portion? and (2) what features does this portion of the map attribute to that territory? These are the proto-referential and proto-predicative components of the representation. The intrigue of their interactions will fill out this book.

But before the next act opens and the plot gets more complicated, it may be helpful to reprise the action thus far. Consider a humble animal whose consciousness stops at sentience. One imagines its mental life to consist of nothing but a flux of sensory qualities. In a widely repeated and ancient image, its stream of mental processes is filled by variegated qualia, which over time pop up, bob along, combine, recombine, and ultimately sink back down into the muck. A mental life of pure sensation would be nothing but a stream, a flux, a flow of such stuff. It could be described entirely in propositional logic, using different propositional variables for the different qualities. At one moment in its career it might be confronted with

> brown and wet and slippery and cold

and at a happier moment with

> green and dry and warm and sweet-smelling.

Perhaps we need conditionals, negation, and disjunction to characterize its learning, but the on-going flood of qualia is at any moment nothing but a conjunction of qualitative features.

But this picture, ancient and widely repeated as it is, radically underestimates the sophistication needed by even the simplest animal. An animal whose mental life is a pure flux of qualities could not solve the Many Properties problem. It could not distinguish matte red next to glossy green from matte green next to glossy red. Nor could such an animal experience two distinct simultaneous instances of the same quality:

> (cheep) & (cheep)

is, after all, equivalent to

> (cheep).

Think of the Many Properties problem as a psychological test.[8] It marks a significant threshold in the complexity of one's psychological organization. To pass it one needs somehow to focus the attribution of qualities, so that one can distinguish a scene containing a red square from one containing something that is red and something else that is square. Merely adding more qualities will not help; they will be lost in the flux with all the others. In a similar way, the ancient image of a thing as a bundle of such qualities—concretions settling out of the flux—smuggles in more organization than one might suppose. If the qualities are sticks, we need some distinct principle by which to bundle the sticks together. A piece of string serves admirably, but notice that it serves a rather different function than that served by additional sticks. Tossing in more sticks leaves one just as disorganized as before; they will soon be bobbing down the stream, undifferentiated from all the rest. Even special sticks, labelled 'spatial qualia', are soon lost. Results include the varieties of mental disorganization described above (Section 2.3). We require some distinct principle by which to create bundles. Lacking string, the simplest way to count our things—our piles and bundles—is by location. Here is one bundle, and there is another. This pile of acorns is mine. That one is yours. From there it is but a short step to property rights and the glories of civilized life.

I suggest that the threshold of the Many Properties problem is the point at which we add to the flux of sensory qualities a distinct capacity for sensory reference. Past that point the organization of sentience requires two kinds of terms: general terms and singular terms. Descriptions of the mental life of an animal who passes the Many Properties test cannot be cast in propositional logic alone, but require the resources of predicate logic, or at least of predicates and names: sensory qualities and sensory reference.

---

[8] Perhaps human olfaction fails this test; it may lack sufficient spatial character. Can one smell two distinct simultaneous instances of the same acrid odour? Can one distinguish a presentation in which something smells both acrid and musty from one in which something smells acrid and something *else* smells musty? If the modality lacks such spatial character, then one cannot solve that modality's variant of the Many Properties problem. In such a case the flux of odours present at a given time could indeed be adequately described with propositional logic alone.

3

Places Phenomenal and Real

SPATIAL discrimination, like space itself, has a curious invisibility. We have found a division in the organization of sentience between features and the placing of those features. The former are at least relatively familiar; they are our old friends the sensory qualities. But the latter capacities, although just as important for the success of the scheme as a whole, are relatively unexplored. Their work is vital. Matte red next to glossy green can be distinguished from glossy red next to matte green only if the scene is represented in something of the form

((glossy red) (here)) ((matte green) (there)),

where 'here' and 'there' serve as spatial identifiers, picking out place-times, focusing the attribution of features. The achievement is not feature conjunction, but rather joint predication: not just a listing of qualities, but an identification of that which they qualify.

But the work of these identifiers can seem invisible; it is, almost by definition, featureless. Some philosophers are likely to consider incoherent the suggestion that sensory processes 'pick out' or 'identify' anything. So this chapter is devoted to an initial scouting and defence of the very notion of sensory reference.

3.1 SPACE-TIME REGIONS

A good place to begin is with the suggestion (of Section 2.4) that we require an apparatus of identification within the content of sensation itself. Recall poor Otto, striving to sense a red square. Placing quantifiers, variables, and identity statements outside the context of what Otto senses fails to identify or distinguish what goes on within. Even though there exists a region x that Otto senses as red, and a region y that Otto senses as square, and x is identical to y, Otto may stubbornly, perversely, fail to sense anything as a red square. Beating him over the head with quantifiers will not help. He must sense the red region *as* the square region; the identification must be achieved within, by his sensory processes. The proposal is that we endow Otto's sensory processes with a content spelled out not only with sensory qualities but with other terms, analogous to singular terms, which serve to pick out their subject-matters. To get Otto to sense a red square we need something like the following:

> To Otto it appears that there exists a region x and a region y such that x is red, y is square, and x is identical to y.

This moves an apparatus of identification—quantifiers and variables—within the scope of 'it appears that . . .'. Of course that content might not be satisfied—perhaps there is no red square in the vicinity, and Otto, while at last successful, is still wrong—but at least the formulation captures what appears to Otto. If he senses in that way, he senses a red region as square.

Now while it is highly unlikely that sensory processes actually employ quantifiers and variables, the argument from the last chapter established that they do employ something formally analogous to singular terms. Variables in the schema above might have such sensory identifiers as substituends. But what shall we take to be the values of these variables? What do they range over? More simply, to specify the content of what Otto senses, we need something like a 'sensory name'. The question is: What do such names name?

The simplest hypothesis, which I will defend, is that such names name space-time regions of finite but definite extent. These regions are physical regions: the very same ones about which physics may have something useful to say. In fact the story typically begins with some sort of physical interaction between those regions and the sense organs. These are regions in or around the body of sentient organism. They must be within 'signal range' of the sense organs for physical changes within them to have physical effects on transducers. Such circumambient physical regions provide all the values we need for our variables. They are not locations within a phenomenal field, nor are they occupied by merely phenomenal individuals. Likewise these variables do not range over merely intentional objects. When sensory reference succeeds, it picks out physical regions in physical commerce with the sense organs.

So there is a two-part claim: that we do need a referential apparatus to describe the facts of sensible appearance, but our needs will be satisfied by one whose variables range over space-time regions of finite but definite extent, in or around the body of the sentient organism. The artificial language closest to feature-placing is not Carnap's point-event language, but his language IB:

Here the individuals are taken to be space-time regions of definite but finite extent; here, therefore, both things and thing slices count as individuals, but not space-time points. This language form is the most convenient when we are content to speak of small but definite space-time regions instead of space-time points, yet wish—here departing from IA—to distinguish between various instants of time. (Woodger's system belongs to this language form . . .) It is possible, within this language form, to represent space-time points as relations of individuals, viz. as sequences of regions converging to zero. (This representation is used e.g. by Whitehead in defining 'point events' as 'abstractive series' of 'events'. . .) (Carnap 1958: 159)

Type I languages in general are ones in which 'the individuals are taken to be space-time regions' (Carnap 1958: 159).

In Language IB our feature-placing 'here' and 'there' would be cast as singular terms naming finite space-time regions a and b, and 'red here, green there' would be just 'Ra & Gb'. While a and b are here physical regions literally in front of the eyes, in other modalities the regions are not invariably distal or even extra-dermal. The place identified by a sensation of pain in the knee is neither. Bodily regions qualify; they are well within range of the nociceptors. Furthermore, although these regions typically have some sort of physical interaction with transducers, they do not always lie literally in front of the sense organs. Audition may pick out locations between the two ears. When one listens to a stereo recording through headphones, the strings sound as if they occupy left temporal cortex, the horns fill regions right and rostral, and so on. Intracranial regions are within auditory range, as bone-conduction of one's own voice demonstrates.

It is best to think of the values of the variables in spatio-temporal terms, as place-times, rather than simply as places. But here our science diverges somewhat from the content available in our sensings. At the very least we need a temporal coordinate to take into account the time it takes for signals to propagate from the regions sensed. Transmission speeds of stimuli and of sensory systems vary enormously. Light travels roughly a million times faster than sound. Within the body of the sentient organism, the varying transmission speeds and synaptic delays in different sensory systems will spread arrival times in the cortex over 'many tens of milliseconds' (Simmons 1996: 223). Small-diameter unmyelinated axons transmit impulses at less than a metre per second, while large-diameter myelinated ones are up to a hundred times faster (Churchland and Sejnowski 1992: 52). This is like moving from an old 300 baud modem to a new 33k model. The differences have real effects; for example, visual reaction times are typically 30 to 40 milliseconds slower than auditory ones (see Pöppel 1988: 28–30). Cortical responses to stimulus onset in varying modalities are spread over a range of 50 to 100 milliseconds (Simmons 1996: 224). Dennett and Kinsbourne argued that the 'temporal smear' introduced by staggered arrival times at different cortical sites might be as much as several hundred milliseconds (Dennett and Kinsbourne 1992: 184). So if we ask, 'What exactly are the physical phenomena that you are sensing *now*?' the answers must sometimes be backdated, and backdated differently in different modalities. If you are now seeing a star that is 4.2 light-years distant, the place-time you see now is as of 4.2 years ago. Similarly, a high-altitude jet is seen at one place in the sky and heard at another, with the apparent auditory location dragging along behind the visible one. At a given moment the rumbling place-time identified by audition is older than the bright silent one that is seen.

Even somaesthesis shows the need to think four-dimensionally. Fast-pain alpha-fibre systems might enable you to jerk your foot away before it is entirely crushed by your heavy-footed neighbour. But there can follow a notable and philosophically interesting time lag while you wait word from the so-called 'slow pain', thinner, C-fibre system. It will fill you in on the details. Even though the bad news is delayed, it is still bad news about the same place-time. Eventually you learn more about what transpired then.

The need for these differing temporal coordinates is impressed upon us by our science, not by the content of any act of sense. Feature-placing seems to lack all tense distinctions. There is no sensory content to the effect: 'that *was* blue'. The feature map is simply activated or not; it cannot distinguish between activations caused by older signals and those caused by more recent ones.[1] Everything presented is presented *now*, but what is presented is not presented *as* the present (that would require tense distinctions): it is just presented. With such tenseless sensory systems one hears the high-altitude jet to be in one place at the same time one sees it to be in another, although in fact at no time is it in both places. The time of the representing is apt to be confused with the time represented. Those who long to live in the present moment are sometimes advised to still all thought and clear the mind of everything but sensory experience. Clearly this is bad advice. The varying sensory experiences happening at a given moment are of place-times with varying temporal coordinates. So there is no one 'present moment' but a simultaneous distribution of different ones. But let us not convict these sensory appearances of any intent to deceive. Their only pretence to be 'the present' is that they all happen to be present.

Why not allow variables to range over space-time points? This issue is apt

---

[1] Of course this temporal version of univariance does not imply that one cannot sense a difference between simultaneous and non-simultaneous events, or detect differences in temporal sequence (see Pöppel 1988). Temporal after-effects exist: a stimulus that *was* blue can affect how a different one looks now. The simple fact that information is often carried by the *rate* at which neurons fire implies that the system must integrate over time. Perhaps feature-placing maintains some temporal indicators, at least of relative positions within the two- to three-second temporal interval of working memory. How the nervous system tracks time is one of the most interesting problems in all of neuroscience. An adequate treatment is beyond the scope of this book.

to confuse, because it can be difficult to make out the distinction between points and space-time regions that are very, very tiny. In sensory terms the regions can be minuscule indeed. For example, in some places on the skin one can feel vibrations of just 100 nanometres, which is less than the wavelength of visible light. Humans can detect vibrations on the eardrum whose amplitude is one-hundredth of a nanometre, which is less than the diameter of the hydrogen atom (Milner 1970: 218). Indeed, there are reports that under optimal conditions some youngsters can *hear* Brownian motion—the pitter-patter of molecules on the membrane (R. F. Thompson 1967: 264). So even though these space-time regions are of finite extent, the extents might be measured in subatomic scales. The same is true for temporal extents: these 'slices' can become vanishingly thin. Clearly we need to pare them to less than a millisecond, even though that is about the minimum interval between neural spikes. Phenomena such as the auditory system's use of interaural temporal disparities (Section 2.1) show that the nervous system can register intervals that are much smaller. At optimal frequencies, the interaural time difference just noticeable by humans can be as low as six microseconds (Carlile 1996: 55). Range-finding in bats demonstrates resolution of temporal differences smaller than a microsecond (see Section 3.6.2). In short, the space-time regions might be breathtakingly small—a cube whose edges are measured in nanometres, lasting for nanoseconds.

Now if we insist that we require space-time points, we are insisting that those cubes are still too big—in fact, infinitely so. Points are needed only if there is no lower limit on the size of the region that the spatial content of sensation might need to identify. That is, no matter how small that region, a sensation that is qualitatively distinct can be generated by shifting things about in a smaller region. On this account, there is no minimum to the minimum visibile; it can shrink *infinitely*. A red patch contains an infinite number of them. The issue is connected to some classical debates; for example, Russell (1903: 144) argued, on somewhat similar grounds, that there must be an infinite number of different colours. Either conclusion immediately settles the question of whether our sensation of the red patch could be instantiated in a digital device: the answer is 'no', since no matter how many discrete states such a device has, it has infinitely too few. It may be considered boorish to ask how a finite number of neurons could instantiate such a content, or for that matter, why they should: the content of such discriminations could not be exhausted or expressed in any finite lifespan, including the entire life of the species.

Ultimately the issue is an empirical one: is there some limit below which spatial differences make no qualitative difference? It is hard to believe that even as we continue to finer and finer scales of spatial resolution, down to the level of neutrinos, say, differences at that scale can still make some difference to the spatial qualitative character of sensation. If there is no difference in the appearance of Mona Lisa with neutrino feature and Mona Lisa without, then we do not need our sensory identifiers to name neutrino features. Differences at that scale do not make a phenomenal difference, and hence we do not need to posit a qualitative difference to account for it. But this is just an introspective appeal, and such appeals are usually wrong. There is no compelling evidence for an absolute threshold, below which physical differences make no difference. Instead discriminations are typically modelled as continuous functions, and discriminability becomes a matter of the statistical discrimination of two distributions. Give me a large enough sample size, said Archimedes, and I shall move that neutrino. Perhaps the mere fact that we model discriminability in terms of continuous functions requires us already to endow these space-time regions with some robust form of continuity. But the clash between rival discrimination models is lively and on-going. Given the empirical and metaphysical uncertainties, this is another issue that I shall leave to one side. I propose to leave open the question of whether we must move to space-time points, or can make do with space-time regions that are very, very tiny. The two are often confused anyway.

Now the claim is that the facts of sensible appearance require an apparatus of identification, but that the only variables needed to capture its content are those that range over space-time regions of finite but definite extent (or perhaps, reluctantly, to points). The main rival to this account is one in which the act of sense identifies, not some physical place-time, physically in or around the body of the sentient organism, but rather a place found in some variety of phenomenal or sensory 'field'. For example, one might grant that seeing can identify the places seen, but then insist that such places are places within a 'visual field'. These might be related in some fashion to physical places in front of the eyes, but they are not identical to them. The items to which one refers when characterizing how things look are the occupants of these 'fields', and are likewise thought to be merely phenomenal items. They are objects as represented, or intentional objects, but not necessarily real ones. So, for example, Leeds (1993) suggests as a first approximation that a sensory impression is the tokening of a sentence in the language of thought: 'the most basic phenomenal sentences have a logical form like that of "*a* is red now," namely "*Ran*", where "*a*" can be thought of as a name for a portion of the visual field, and "*n*" names the present moment' (Leeds 1993: 316). As already noted, unless tense distinctions are possible, I doubt we need the perpetual redundancy of naming the present moment. But more important for my purposes is the notion of naming portions of the visual field. The proposal has a recognizable kinship to the feature-placing hypothesis. But I will show that the term 'visual field' is three-ways ambiguous, and that only under one of these interpretations is naming a portion of the visual field equivalent to identifying a place-time in front of the eyes. The other two interpretations, I will argue, name things that we do not need to name. We can (and should) avoid entering existence claims for the entities in those other varieties of visual field.

The goal of this chapter is to show that describing the facts of sensory appearance does not require us to quantify over places in a phenomenal field or over objects that are merely intentional. The places picked out by feature-placing are part of the same space-time in which we live and breathe. All the appearances of reference to entities in a visual field can be recast in such feature-placing terms.

3.2 THREE VARIETIES OF VISUAL FIELD

To this claim the counter-example is invariably: what about the locations of after-images? To describe the experience of such, don't we need to quantify over locations in a visual field—locations that are distinct from the space-time regions so far mentioned? Or consider mirror images or phantom pains: are not their locations something other than physical locations?

To justify a negative answer to these questions, and show how plain old place-times suffice, the first task is to clarify the sense in which locations in a visual field are or are not distinct from the space-time regions so far countenanced. A vivid formulation of the issues is found in a brief passage in an article by Paul Boghossian and David Velleman (1989). In that passage they argue that after-images and double images have locations distinct from those of the distal objects in front of the eyes, and that such locations oblige us to postulate a visual field in which those images can reside. Boghossian and Velleman ask that one consider an experience

in which an after-image appears to you *as* an after-image—say, as a red spot obscuring the face of a person who has just taken your photograph. Since you suffer no illusion about the nature of this spot, you do not see it as something actually existing in front of the photographer's face. In what sense, then, do you see it as occupying that location at all? The answer is that you see it as merely appearing in that location: you see it as a spot that appears in front of the photographer's face without actually being there. Now, in order for you to see the spot as appearing somewhere, it must certainly appear there. Yet it must appear there without appearing actually to be there, since you are not under the illusion that the spot actually occupies the space in question. The after-image must therefore be described as *appearing in* a location without *appearing to be in* that location. . . . The only way to describe the after-image as appearing in front of the photographer without appearing to be in front of the photographer is to talk about the location that it occupies in your visual field. In your visual field, we say, the after-image overlays the image of the photographer's face, but nothing is thereby represented as actually being over the photographer's face. The after-image is thus like a coffee-stain on a picture, a feature that occupies a location on the picture without representing anything as occupying that location. (Boghossian and Velleman 1989: 93)

Roughly this argument has the following form:

(1) We must describe a non-illusory after-image as appearing in a location without appearing to be in that location.
(2) The only way to describe an image as appearing in a location without appearing to be in that location is to talk about the location it occupies in a visual field.

Hence when we talk about the location of non-illusory after-images we are talking about locations in a visual field.

The argument is valid, and I propose to concede the first premiss to Boghossian and Velleman, even though one could raise difficulties with it. The more serious problems lie in understanding what the second premiss and the conclusion mean.

3.2.1 The Field of View

Let us start with the conclusion. What have we endorsed when we endorse the existence of a 'visual field'? Or, perhaps a better way to put this: when we commit ourselves to the existence of a visual field, what commitments have we *added* to those we already had?

This latter formulation is useful, since even before this particular dispute reaches any resolution, theorists will already have undertaken many ontological obligations. In particular, with the possible exception of subjective idealists, theorists will already have endorsed the existence of *distal stimuli*—of physical objects and stimuli occupying regions in front of the eyes. These are such things as photons which strike rods and cones, as surfaces which reflect light in the visible spectrum, as tables and chairs. They are objects and phenomena described by chemistry and physics, residing in their brute physical way out there in cold physical space. Quite apart from the demands of common sense, theorists need these things because without them the entire story psychologists and neurophysiologists tell of vision, starting at the retina, could not be told. We could not mention rods or cones, retinas or optic nerves, photons or electron shells. All those items are physical items housed in the physical world.

Typically we take ourselves to be seeing some of such things. I look out of the window and see a house and a tree. The house that I see is made of wood, a complex organic structure which came from other trees, and of brick, which contains considerable silicon. Such objects reside comfortably out there in the physical world, in that same space through which photons can pass. Not all things seen can be classified as physical *objects*; we also see the sky, the ground, lightning flashes, shadows, reflections, glares, and mists; but all such sights can be classed as physical phenomena located in regions around the sentient organism. For each of them physics can contribute something to the story of what one sees.

The ur-concept of a 'visual field' is that of a *sum of things seen*; all three of the varieties I shall describe can fit under this heading. They differ over what it means to 'see', and over what sorts of 'things' can or cannot be seen, but they agree that in some sense or other subjects see things, and allow a 'visual field' as a mereological sum of things seen at a given time.

Now suppose we admit that we are surrounded by physical phenomena and that in some sense we see some of those phenomena. This yields the first variety of visual field. Define the *field of view* at time t as the mereological sum— the scattered totality—of physical phenomena seen at time t. Summing the sights in such a fashion can yield a stupendous physical phenomenon. It might be miles or light-years deep. As argued above, the place-times seen at t can have temporal coordinates antedating t, so the field of view turns out to be four-dimensional. Its spatio-temporal size and shape is determined at time t by the physical position of the head and eyes. With one's head in a closet, the field of view dwindles considerably. Close the eyes and it dwindles to nothing. But as long as one is seeing something, there exists a 'field of view': a sum of things seen.

That sum is a physical phenomenon, not defined by one's psychological constitution. If the honeybee and I both see the same flower, there is something—that flower—that is literally in both our fields of view. This despite the fact that the honeybee and I do not see it in quite the same way! Furthermore, the flower itself turns out to be a latticework of organic molecules, or at a deeper level, a cloud of elementary particles, in mostly empty space. Occupants of the 'field of view' can include clouds of elementary particles.

Even in this relatively simple version there is scope for confusion. Rival coordinate schemes are used in different stages of vision: retinocentric, egocentric, allocentric.[2] Is retinocentric space the same space as allocentric

---

[2] For example, the visual perimetry assessment of a scotoma, or 'blind spot', in terms of degrees of azimuth and altitude within the 'visual field', is just measurement of the field of view, described in retinocentric terms. Those terms are useful for such purposes because they can help identify the location of damage within the visual system.

space? Although it is possible to construct psychological models under which these terms refer to distinct domains, it is not obligatory. I urge that we confine ourselves to the place-times found in the field of view. We do not need any others as values of our variables. Different stages of processing may yield differences in modes of access to such regions, or in the means by which they are identified. Such differences can be psychologically significant, and obviously it is important to discover how we come to identify places in our surroundings. But the shift from retinocentric to allocentric coordinate schemes does not yield a new domain, a new set of locales; instead it provides only a new way of organizing the same domain. The place-times are the same; what we gain is a new means of identifying them.

3.2.2 The Sum of Impressions

Now for variety 2. It is plain that when Boghossian and Velleman talk about the 'visual field' they are talking about something *distinct* from the field of view. The after-image, they say, does not appear to be located *between* you and the photographer, or *on* the photographer's face. It does not appear to be located anywhere among the physical phenomena in front of the eyes. But the after-image *does* appear in front of the photographer's face. Hence, they say, we must posit locations in a visual field, distinct from locations among the objects in front of the eyes.

So what is this second variety of visual field? In contemporary terms it is something closer to the sum of visual representings than to the sum of things seen. Version 1 is filled with the sights, version 2 with the seeings. In classic terms, one sees by having visual impressions, and those impressions bear spatial relations to one another. The version 2 visual field is the sum of such impressions; I shall call it the 'array of impressions'. The qualities of visual impression are dependent on the psychology of the host; the honeybee and I have distinct visual impressions, and perhaps there is no element that can be found in both (see E. Thompson *et al.* 1992). So even if we share the same field of view, we will not share the same array of impressions.

The classic idea is that visual impressions have properties that serve as natural signs or indicators of their distal causes. Sensations of red are arbitrarily associated with the physical properties that cause them; those same physical properties could just as well have caused sensations of green. But visual impressions represent spatial characteristics of the distal scene in a less arbitrary fashion. The spatial relations obtaining within the array of visual impressions serve as a *map* of distal causes; they resemble or model the spatial relations among distal things. Crudely, if you have a visual impression of a red triangle next to a green square, then your impression of the red triangle is next to your impression of the green square. The resulting array of impressions is the version 2 visual field; places in the visual field are places within it.

We can give this idea a more sophisticated gloss by invoking the Sellarsian device of counterpart properties (see Section 1.1; Sellars 1963: 193, 1968: 25–30). We need not claim that if one sees a red triangle to the left of a green square, one's impression of the red triangle is literally to the left of one's impression of the green square. Instead the spatial characteristics ascribed to visual impressions are analogous to or modelled on the spatial characteristics ascribed to physical things. As Sellars puts it, there is some counterpart relation, left*, such that the impression of the red triangle is to the left* of the impression of the green square. These counterpart relations have structural properties analogous to those of the spatial relations obtaining among physical things; but they are not the same relations.

Even this more sophisticated Sellarsian reading of 'locations within the visual field' is still within the tradition. It still proposes an array of impressions—a version 2 visual field. Since left* obtaining among the impressions is structurally analogous to 'left' obtaining among their causes, the array of impressions can still serve as a map of those causes. Furthermore, the structural similarities underwrite a glossy and sophisticated version of old-fashioned resemblance. Sensations of red do not resemble their causes, but spatial characteristics of our visual impressions resemble the spatial structure of their causes. So ideas of red are ideas of secondary qualities, while ideas of left or next-to are not. The Sellarsian amendment still preserves this central feature of the model.

For my purposes the defining characteristic of a version 2 visual field is that it is a sum of visual impressions, organized in such a way that spatial relations or counterparts to spatial relations obtaining among the impressions resemble the spatial relations among things. The 'visual field' is not a 'field' unless its elements bear something like spatial relations to one another. It must make sense to talk about locations *in* the visual field. Classically the visual field has a shape that does not change as one turns one's head; there is a place in it that is its centre; and a red patch in it might be *next to* a green patch. Boghossian and Velleman endorse a modern descendant of this view.

In this they are by no means alone. The version 2 visual field remains a popular posit. For example, O'Shaughnessy (1980: 167–210) gives a lengthy defence of the visual field, defined as 'a sense field, i.e. a two-dimensional psychological map wherein sensations stand to one another in merely two-dimensional relations like "adjacent-to-left" "less-adjacent-to-right" "above" "below" ' (O'Shaughnessy 1980: 176). He agrees that after-images must be located in such a 'psychological space': they occupy a two-dimensional region within such a field. As noted previously, these denizens of the visual field are also 'projected' outwards onto physical objects. An after-image is 'experienced *as* inhabiting something that lies without the mind of the experiencer'; specifically, it is 'projected onto whatever physical item occupies its sector of the visual field' (O'Shaughnessy 1980: 178). Baldwin (1992) points out that projectivist accounts do not all necessarily endorse what is here called a version 2 visual field, but this one certainly does, since in its terms 'our visual field is constituted by a two-dimensional array of visual sensations which the mind "projects" onto physical space in accordance with causal connections between the structure of physical space and the intrinsic spatial structure of the visual field' (Baldwin 1992: 183). If projection is defined as a relationship between two distinct spatial domains, one of those domains will be a version 2 visual field.

Here is one other diagnostic test that may help to determine whether a theorist has invoked the second variety of visual field. Most of those who talk of 'visual space', and all who distinguish it from 'physical space', have endorsed version 2. Consider the claim that visual space has a geometry that is distinct from the geometry obtaining among physical objects. Many exciting and confusing things have been said about this topic. Visual space is non-Euclidean! Perhaps it is spherical! Or hyperbolic! One interpretation that would make sense of these claims is that we have a domain of visual impressions, distinct from that of distal objects; that some family of relations obtains among those impressions, relations that are at least analogous to spatial relations among things; and that the geometry that describes those relations differs from the geometry describing physical things. As one proponent says:

our immediate visual awareness consists of a phenomenal field of colors, visual space, whose geometrical and qualitative features are determined by causal connections with the physical objects being 'seen' . . . it remains possible that both the topological and the metric structure of visual space is quite different from that of physical space. Thus, an attitudinal shift is required here away from direct realism, which numerically equates the two, to a more neutral attitude where a geometrical analysis can be made of our visual experience in and of itself. (French 1987: 115)

A variant is to claim that the projection rules that map the relations among impressions onto the spatial relations among things cannot be written in Euclidean form; the 'projective geometry' is non-Euclidean.[3] Both versions endorse the second variety of visual field. As intimated above, it is possible for a theorist to use the term 'visual space' without implying that it is distinct

---

[3] For example, for a painting to 'look like' a three-dimensional scene, perhaps the globs of paint cannot be laid on the canvas in accord with the rules of Euclidean projective geometry, but must follow the rules of spherical or hyperbolic geometry. This strategy is pursued by Heelan (1983), who argues that the projective rules are hyperbolic.

from 'physical space', but once one enters claims for a distinct 'visual geometry', that possibility is foreclosed.

Already it should be obvious that theorists who deny the existence of a version 2 visual field are not oppugning something standing out in plain view. They are not denying the existence of all those things that you see in front of your nose. They are denying that we need a *second* set of entities and locations, in addition to those in the field of view. Perhaps our visual representings of space do not use space as their representational medium. It is possible.

3.2.3 A Virtual World

On the feature-placing hypothesis, we need to admit the existence of a 'field of view'—which is always just some sum of space-time regions of finite extent—and of a perceiver, who sees things, or has 'visual representations'. We must acknowledge the existence of states within the perceiving organism that grant it the capacity to see things: its visual sensory states. Such states yield the division between those things that are and those that are not within the field of view of that organism at that time. Furthermore, the account to be given of after-images requires states within the perceiver that (in some sense) represent items in that field of view.[4]

But with that the admissions can stop. No further additions to our ontology are necessary. We do not need to add a version 2 visual field—a two-dimensional array of impressions—and there is no good reason to believe in the existence of such an entity, at least in any known species.

This line faces a simple, intuitive objection, which might be put as follows. When you hold a finger between your eyes and a page that you are reading, you *seem* to see *two* of *something*. These 'two somethings' that you seem to see cannot be identified with any one object in front of the eyes. And each distinctly seems to be *somewhere*. They do not seem to be at the *same* place, and there is a clear distinction between the places they seem to occupy and the places they do not. These places where the somethings seem to be cannot be identified with places in front of the eyes, so we must admit the existence of a second set of locales, where such somethings can be lodged. It hardly takes an argument. Can't you just *see* that there are two of them? And if you can see two, how can you deny that they occupy different places?

Here I think we have reached the primal intuitions howling for a visual field. It seems that you can just see its occupants! The intuitive force of this

---

[4] Gibson (1979: 111) defines the 'field of view' of an animal at a time as that portion of the ambient optic array that 'can be registered by its ocular system' at that time. This depends on the position of the head and eyes, but also on the capacities of states of the ocular system to 'register' events.

premiss should be granted. When you have the experience of a double image, you do seem to see two of something. The objection becomes even more seductive when couched in terms of *images*. Those dark blurry outlines that you seem to see are unlike other objects that you do see, so let us call them *images*. By stipulation, when you have the experience of a double image, you *see two images*. Such images do not occupy physical places in front of the eyes, and they are just the sort of entity that would find a happy home in a visual field. Indeed, these odd residents and that odd locale are perfectly suited to one another.

This notion of 'image' invokes the third and final variety of visual field— not the sum of things seen, or the sum of visual representings, but the sum of things *as* represented visually—the 'intentional content' of one's visual repre-sentations. To describe this third variety of visual field, describe the world as it is represented visually: what the world would be if it were just as it visually appears to be. This is a treacherous and complicated exercise, but it is often attempted. By stipulation, seeing a dark blurry translucent *image* is just a matter of *seeming* to see something that is dark, blurry, and translucent. The dark blurry translucent image is the 'intentional' object of one's visual repre-sentation; the third variety of visual field is filled with such entities.

If we have visual representations at all, then in some sense there is a version 3 visual field.[5] To describe the content of those visual representations, describe the world as it appears visually. We could then talk about the objects within that world and the relations they bear to one another. This would be a devious but understandable way of talking about visual appearances. The objects described would be 'virtual': objects *as* represented. Some of them would not exist.

Boghossian and Velleman claim that a descriptive vocabulary ranging over intentional objects is also inadequate to describe the experience of an after-image or a double image. After describing the furtive way an after-image appears in a location without appearing to be in that location, they go on to say:

this description is not within the capacity of any intentionalist theory. An intentional-ist theory will analyse the visual appearance of location as the attribution of location to something, in the intentional content of your visual experience. But the intentional content of your visual experience is that there is nothing at all between you and the photographer. (Boghossian and Velleman 1989: 93)

---

[5] If our visual representations are veridical, the world as represented visually is just: the world. So if visual representation never erred, the third variety of visual field would be the same as the first one. But if visual representation is non-veridical, the third variety of visual field describes a possible world *other than* our own. (See Sect. 3.4; Hintikka 1969, 1975; Kraut 1982; Lycan 1987: 88.)

An 'intentionalist' theory is one that confines itself to a version 3 visual field. Boghossian and Velleman insist that neither version 1 nor version 3 will do; we also need a version 2. I will examine this argument in the next section.

When we start talking about images as 'virtual' objects, or objects *as* represented, we are invoking this third variety of visual field. One relatively clear instance can be found in discussions of mirror images. When you look in a mirror, what do you see, and where is it located? C. D. Broad suggested that what you see is made up of sensa—mind-dependent visible entities similar to those seen elsewhere. The direction of the sensum is identified by moving your head until the sensum is in the centre of your visual field, and then following your nose. The distance to the sensum is the number of steps you would need to take to reach that source 'if, in fact, the medium were homogeneous' and the sensa 'were due to the transmission of light directly from this source' to your eye (Broad 1927: 324–5). This specifies a location *behind* the mirror. Broad says that that location is the location of the mirror-image; it is 'partially optically occupied' by the sensa that make up the image. The occupation is 'partial' because those sensa are not visible from all angles, but only from the front of the mirror (Broad 1927: 329). This view has some recent instantiations:

Mirror images provide a good analogy . . . We see them, yet they are nothing in the physical world. The mirror image of my face appears behind the mirror, yet there is nothing there but bricks. The mirror image is there because I see it there, and not the other way around, namely, that I see it there because it is there. No wonder then that no one else can see the *same* mirror image. (Vendler 1994: 322)

Vendler here endorses the claim that one sees something that is located behind the mirror. He defends the view that mirror images are nothing in the physical world, and that their existence consists in being perceived (see Vendler 1991).

Now it really is very odd to locate the mirror image behind the mirror, back there inside the bricks. The physical location identified by Broad's directions has no causal role at all in the viewer's visual experience, and it is similarly odd to place any mind-dependent entity back there. But one must acknowledge a sense in which objects reflected in a mirror look as if they are arrayed behind it. For example, in a minor outbreak of the Flopped Earth syndrome (Section 1.4.3), drivers in Britain and America face visual worlds that are in some respects mirror images of one another. In America the steering-wheel is on the left and one drives on the right; in Britain the wheel is on the right and one drives on the left. But drivers on both sides of the Atlantic can be reminded of how things look to their counterparts on the other side of the ocean by simply scanning their own rear-view mirrors. So in America one scans the mirror and sees a car that looks British, with the wheel on the right. Similarly, a British-made car seen in a British rear-view mirror looks American-made. But in either case, to use the mirror you must look at it. If, using the mirror, you see a car that is travelling twenty feet behind you, there is a sense in which that car appears twenty feet in front of you, off to one side. That is where your eyeballs are focused.[6] The car also looks as if it were manufactured by your counterparts on the other side of the Atlantic. You seem to see a transatlantic car, twenty feet in front of you, off to one side. I suggest that such locations can best be understood as 'virtual locations': as locations within our third variety of visual field. Visually you represent the world as if there were a transatlantic automobile hanging in space twenty feet in front of you, fifteen degrees to the side. That is the place where an automobile would be, if the world were as represented. In fact there is nothing visible to you at that location (the mirror occludes it), and there may be no imported vehicles in the neighbourhood, but you represent the world as if there were. We have a virtual object, located behind the mirror.[7]

This terminology is unobjectionable until, in the next breath, we forget how it was introduced and begin talking about the places where those somethings that we seem to see *are* located. Recall our earlier travails when trying to fashion quantifiers and operators so as to compel Otto to sense a red square. That some qualities appear at a place does not imply that there is a place at which those qualities appear. The context 'seeming to see *x*' is paradigmatically intensional; you seem to see a transatlantic car in front of you, but there is no such car in that vicinity. Talk of images makes it too easy to forget the confines of intensional contexts. For example, we might allow, as above, that the experience can be described as *seeing an image*. So by stipulation you see an image of a transatlantic car. But the imported vehicle you seem to see at that location *does not exist*. Clearly this terminology has its dangers. The logic and grammar of object-talk is so powerful that we readily forget that some of these objects are *merely* intentional ones. It is dangerous to speak of virtual objects as if they are real, but unfortunately that is the only way one can talk about virtual objects.

---

[6] 'An object seen by Reflexion or Refraction, appears in that place from whence the Rays after their last Reflexion or Refraction diverge in falling on the Spectator's Eye' (Newton 1952: bk. I, pt. I, ax. viii). Newton goes on to say: 'for these Rays do make the same picture in the bottom of the Eye as if they had come from the Object really placed' behind the mirror.

[7] This would account for many of the characteristics that Vendler ascribes to mirror images. Such (intentional) objects exist only in an 'analogous' sense, are not necessarily occupants of the physical world, and do not share a genus with physical substance. Their *esse* is strictly *esse pro*; their existence is exhausted in being perceived (represented). This perception is trans-world: you see, not yourself, but your enantiomorphic counterpart. Amusingly, in *Through the Looking Glass*, Tweedledum is a mirror image of Tweedledee (see Gardner 1965: 231).

One describes the world as represented visually; that 'virtual' world is the third variety of visual field. But 'adding' such a visual field does not add anything to one's ontological commitments. We can talk of the objects in that world—of their properties and relations—provided we remember that perhaps none of them exist. If by stipulation whenever you seem to see something, you are seeing an *image*, then the image would be a denizen of that world. Its location may be *mere* appearance. Thankfully, such images, like unicorns, fictional characters, and other things that do not exist, occupy no space at all, and there is no special problem in making room for them in our ontology. We no more need places for them than we need places for our fictional characters. Indeed, on this interpretation the visual field is the perfect place to house Tweedledum, Tweedledee, and all the other entities found through the looking-glass.

3.3 WHY I AM NOT AN ARRAY OF IMPRESSIONS

Boghossian and Velleman claim that we *do* need a richer ontology than feature-placing provides. Describing the facts of visual appearance requires a second domain of entities and locations: 'An adequate description of the after-image requires reference to two kinds of location—location as an intrinsic property of features in the visual field, and location as represented by the resulting visual experience' (Boghossian and Velleman 1989: 93). Why? The argument rests on their second premiss: 'The only way to describe the after-image as appearing in front of the photographer without appearing to be in front of the photographer is to talk about the location that it occupies in your visual field' (Boghossian and Velleman 1989: 93).

One way to show that their way is not the only way is to describe another way, which is at least equally plausible, and which mentions no locations other than those of physical phenomena. I believe this can be done. To account for after-images we need to mention retinal locations, and locations in the field of view, but not locations in some distinct 'visual field'. In this way I hope to show that the facts adduced by Boghossian and Velleman do not *oblige* us to posit a version 2 visual field.

Here is a second way to tell the story. Your eyes are fixated at a certain point when the flashbulb goes off, flooding your face with photons. The lenses of your eyes focus some of this flood onto parts of your retina, where the rods and cones are momentarily 'bleached' by the energetic onslaught. That is, those cells contain photopigments which isomerize when they absorb photons, and it takes time to replenish the stock. Typically your pupil has its diameter adjusted to the intensity of ambient illumination, so that only as much light is admitted as can comfortably be handled by the receptors below. But the flashbulb may increase the photon flux by several orders of magnitude, and your pupil cannot react quickly enough. In some of the affected receptors, most of the available photopigment molecules might be isomerized as they absorb photons. (Even that is not enough to stem the flood; many photons will bounce off the membrane behind the retina and re-emerge out of the eye, giving the classic 'red eye' look beloved by amateur photographers.[8]) Those receptors are 'bleached'. It takes some time before additional photopigment can be synthesized.

After the bulb goes off you shift your gaze to the photographer's face. The bleached receptors are temporarily useless; light falling upon them triggers no reaction, since there is no photopigment available to isomerize. They are, at least temporarily, out of commission. The portion of your field of view focused upon those receptors cannot be seen. To use Gibson's term (1979: 69), that portion is a 'visual solid angle': a conical region, with fixed angular coordinates given in retinocentric terms, extending out into space. The eye cannot register much, if any, information about things within that visual solid angle. That visual solid angle defines the outlines of the *after-image*. Within it you experience the characteristic phenomena: an initial blank spot, which changes hue and loses definition as the retina recovers from the overload.

Given its genesis, an after-image shifts whenever you shift your gaze. You cannot scrutinize it or scan it; you cannot look at it directly, since whenever you move your eyes to do so, it skitters away. So an after-image has a constant retinocentric location but inconstant distal ones. We feel little temptation to assign a distal location to the after-image, since it moves with your eyes, and distal objects do not.

What sort of location *is* ascribed to these furtive phenomena? Boghossian and Velleman say that an after-image appears at a location without appearing to be at that location. Do we need a second set of locales—an array of impressions—to house such things?

I think there are at least two alternatives. One is to admit, not a different set of locales, but different sets of coordinate schemes operating at different levels within vision. The after-image is, in effect, a two-and-a-half-dimensional phenomenon. It has a fixed visual solid angle, but no fixed depth. It

---

[8] After a bright burst of light the retina becomes more transparent to light of the wavelengths the photopigments absorb, since after the pigment molecules absorb as many photons as they can, the remainder more readily pass through. By carefully measuring the wavelengths of the initial burst and of the light reflected back out of the eye, one can estimate the absorption spectra of the photopigments. This technique was one of the first used to estimate those spectra (see Kaufman 1974: 87–9). Note that the effects of dazzling lights are somewhat special; most after-images and after-effects are not caused by bleaching of photopigments.

might appear on the nearby page or the more distant wall, both times with roughly the same shape, but of differing sizes. Nevertheless, we do not need a full third dimension to describe its spatial appearance. Each ordered pair of coordinates of azimuth and altitude—each ray bundled within the compass of that visual solid angle—need have only one depth coordinate associated with it. We do not need three fully independent dimensions. The entities described by such a '2½d sketch' (Marr 1982) are indeed awkward to place within our normal coordinate schemes of two or three dimensions. Thinking three-dimensionally, one might identify the location of the after-image with its entire visual solid angle. This is a large conical volume in the field of view, extending outward from the eye indefinitely. Thinking two-dimensionally—considering 'the after-image' to be the *patch* of illusory contrast that appears on varying surfaces as you shift your gaze—allows us to be a bit more definite. That illusory patch appears at the place where the fixed visual solid angle first intercepts an occluding surface. *If* you are seeing anything when you 'see' an after-image, that is where it appears to be. As Emmert noted in 1881, the apparent size of the patch is a function of the apparent depth of that surface.

A second possibility is that as we learn more about their genesis, we may simply retract the hypothesis that the having of an after-image is the seeing of anything. There appears to be a spot in front of the photographer's face, but there is not. Perhaps the experience of having an after-image is an experience of something *other than* seeing. Within the visual solid angle defined by the bleached receptors, one cannot see anything (initially, at least). At best the information you can pick up within that angle is information about the state of your retina, as the receptors recover from overload. Perhaps within that angle after-imaging *rather than* seeing is going on. Under this alternative, after-imaging is not a visual representing of anything, but is a disruption or hitch in vision. You merely *seem* to see something. Now we do need to explain *why* you seem to see a spot where you seem to see it, but in principle it seems possible to explain that fact without mentioning any locations other than those within the retina, the nervous system, or the field of view. The explanation would rely on the premiss that if some receptors are 'bleached', and light falling upon them has no effect, then at that time one cannot see anything within the visual solid angle of light falling upon those receptors. This premiss makes no illicit references to locations in a visual field, and it seems relatively unproblematic. Filled out with descriptions of the array of retinal receptors and the optics of the eye, it would allow us to explain why you seem to see a spot *where* you seem to see it. That is, we could explain the location of the visual solid angle within which nothing is seen.

Suppose we admit the existence of visual representations—or at least of states of the organism that are its seeings of things. We could form a mereo-logical sum of such seeings, and this would be another sum of physical states. But now it might seem that a version 2 visual field can re-enter the drama by the back door, so to speak. Recall that one characteristic of the array of impressions is that elements within it have locations distinct from those of their distal causes. If visual representations turn out to be brain states, then those states have such locations. Even more alarmingly, much of the visual system employs 'place-coding', or is roughly topographical, so that adjacent areas in the field of view affect adjacent areas of the retina, adjacent areas of the lateral geniculate nucleus, and even adjacent areas of striate cortex. As mentioned above (Section 2.2), in visual physiology we find a bewildering array of topographical 'feature maps'. Different maps respond to different features in the field of view: spatial frequencies, edges, local motion, colour, shape, and so on. The maps form tangled hierarchies, with primary visual cortex (area V1) at the bottom of most of the tangles. Are these maps visual fields? Might some expanse of cortex, in which we find such a feature map, turn out to house a version 2 visual field?

One immediate embarrassment is caused by the sheer number of different feature maps. As already noted, the macaque monkey has at least two dozen, and perhaps as many as thirty-two, distinct areas of cortex, devoted to distinct visual features (Felleman and Van Essen 1991). If each of these is a visual field, then the macaque has at least two dozen distinct visual fields. In which one of these should we locate *the* after-image? (Which one would you look at first?) The prospect of assigning it two dozen distinct locations palls. Nothing in the argument of Boghossian and Velleman provides the resources needed to carry out such a task.

Furthermore, cortical feature maps do not entirely preserve topology; they have tears and discontinuities, most prominently down the midline. Signals from the left hemi-field in both eyes travel to the right cortex. A light source travelling left to right in the field of view does not cause a continuous arc of excitation to travel across the cortex; when the light crosses the midline in the field of view, the neural locus of excitation will hop, in the reverse direction, across to the other cortex. One notes no phenomenological hitch or hiccup when this happens. Vision scientists sometimes say things like 'all the visual fields start at V1', but they are speaking of feature maps, not arrays of phenomenal items. Those feature maps, unlike phenomenal fields, have a prominent split down the midline.

Perhaps it is worth mentioning some of the other reasons why psycholo-gists, physiologists, and neuroscientists have all abandoned allegiance to a two-dimensional array of impressions. It has some glaring deficits as a construct in a psychological theory. For example, if we adopt

O'Shaughnessy's criterion for which items are present in a visual field, then such a field lasts only as long as a fixation without saccades, and it includes only what can be seen in a single fixation. Experiments will show this is not much. Details can be resolved in the two-degree foveal field, but not elsewhere. The simplest demonstration of how meagre are such visual findings is to focus your eyes on a single short word somewhere on a page of text, and then try, without shifting your gaze at all, to read the words immediately around it. You might be able to read the words immediately before and after, and short words above and below within a line or two, but nothing else. Imagine a circle drawn around those words you could read. In that small compass are crowded the objects immediately apprehended by one act of the visual organ.

Most theorists who maintain allegiance to the two-dimensional array of impressions think of it as something larger, more detailed, and more coherent. They are imagining something like a painting or photograph of the distal scene. Most such 'visual fields' are sufficiently compendious that one cannot take them in with a single glance; they require multiple fixations and saccades (see Mach 1890: 16). How are they constructed? One needs some coordinate scheme applying across fixations, so that the disparate bits of information gleaned from each glance can be patched together. That scheme cannot be retinocentric. A retinocentric map fails as soon as you want to shift your gaze. The two dimensions applicable to it cannot tell you where to point your eyes next; that direction lies in a different space—excuse me, a different coordinate scheme—altogether. A head-centred scheme would work: directions relative to the eye sockets could coordinate successive fixations. In fact the system directing saccades is a beautifully integrated system of ballistic navigation (see Mazzoni and Andersen 1995; Dominey and Arbib 1992).

Two dimensions do not suffice to describe the gamut of spatial variations in visual appearance. Glares, shadows, occluding edges, and reflections pose some obvious problems. If the visual field has but two dimensions, then no part of it can cast a shadow on another part, nor can one part block the view of another. Boghossian and Velleman acknowledge occlusion, with their somewhat awkward suggestion that the after-image is 'like a coffee-stain on a picture'. Perhaps the stain blocks your view of the visual field.

Accounts of coloured reflections are similarly awkward. Perhaps you see a green pine tree through the window and, overlapping it, a red reflection in the glass. How exactly do we describe this in a two-dimensional visual field? With three dimensions it is easy: the green appears at a different depth from the red. But it is hard to capture with the standard two-dimensional colour patches. Perhaps we get two distinct colours at the very same place. Perhaps even though you think that the red and green appear separately and simultaneously, they do not; only one characterizes the given place in the two-dimensional array at a given time. Or perhaps they fuse to white, and only falsely appear to be separately red and green. None of these descriptions match the appearances!

Shadows and reflections already show that two-dimensional description is inadequate even for monocular snapshot vision. But a second eye adds additional difficulty. It does not merely add a second two-dimensional field to the first. If you hold a hand up and blink your eyes successively you get two successive snapshot views. Parts are out of register, and shift as you blink. One eye sees more of one side of the thumb than the other. But with both eyes open these failures of registration and these misalignments are *not* seen as blurs. We do not simply add a second two-dimensional array to the first one; instead we get a single representation of three-dimensional space. You see a distinct, curved, three-dimensional thumb. So called 'cyclopean vision' is not just a sum of two two-dimensional representations; it yields a unified three-dimensional field.

Stereograms show this most vividly. Some pixels are out of register; in the two eyes their borders are found at distinct two-dimensional retinocentric coordinates. But you do not see a blurred or indistinct two-dimensional edge; instead you see a perfectly crisp edge *at a depth*. The processes that do this cannot do it by simply extending a two-dimensional field outwards.

Spatial variations in visual appearance cannot be described adequately in just two dimensions. Ergo a visual field organized two-dimensionally will fail to explain the facts of visual appearance. If one has to add a third dimension to the construct, it loses much of its allure. One might quite reasonably wonder why the three-dimensional structure of space outside the head has to be represented by constructing an isomorphic model of it inside the head. In short, it remains logically possible that there exist creatures endowed with version 2 visual fields, whose representings of space themselves rely on spatial relations or counterparts of spatial relations. But it turns out, empirically, that we are not such creatures. We do not visually represent spatial relations in that way.

3.4 WHY I AM NOT AN INTENTIONAL OBJECT

Even if we abandon the second variety of visual field, perhaps we need variables that range over objects found within the third variety: the world as represented visually. Indeed in a sense this is entirely unobjectionable. If we treat visual sensation as a variety of representation, which I urge as a reasonable hypothesis, then we can speak intelligibly about the world as represented visually, or what the world would be if our visual representations were veridical. When those representations are veridical, the third variety of visual field collapses into the first. The world as represented veridically just is the world. Likewise, when visual representations are veridical, the objects in the third variety of visual field are just the objects in the first: the space-time regions constituting the field of view.

Suppose a stop light heaves into the field of view, and it causes in me a feature-placing representation: ((red)(there)). Suppose that this visual representation is veridical: by some standard the thing I see as red *is* red. It is notoriously difficult to provide a philosophic elucidation of those standards, though a stab at it will be made in Chapter 6. But in practical terms, traffic signals are deliberately engineered so that the assessment is easy: the motoring public should be left in little doubt when the signal *is* red. In such a case the thing in my visual-world-as-represented, which I represent as red, is the thing in my field of view, which *is* red. It caused that very representation. Such objects are not merely intentional. They might play a role in real traffic violations.

When the field of view is represented veridically, it is the world as represented; the two worlds are one. In these happy circumstances we can identify the object of the experience with the referent of the representation: what the experience is about and what it refers to are the same. This yields an interesting technique for picking out the 'object of experience': identify its referent. Here is how Valberg picks out a direct object of experience:

> The first step is simply to pick out or focus on something present in my experience. So I will do that. I will focus on *this*. This what? At any other time I would have said 'this book', but I am not allowed to say that now. I can say that my eyes are directed toward the book, or that I am looking at the book, but I cannot say (or imply) that the book is present in my experience. Let us say simply that I am focused on whatever it is that is present now in my experience while I am looking at the book. Certainly there is, right now, *something* present in my experience. (Valberg 1992: 28–9)

If the experience is veridical then these instructions pick out a region of space-time. Similarly, Snowdon (1992: 56) identifies the objects of direct perception as 'what we can, in the course of and in virtue of our perceptual experience, demonstratively pick out'. If you think 'this is a page' you are thinking that 'amongst the items which your current visual experience puts in your demonstrative range, is a page' (Snowdon 1992: 57). The 'demonstrative range' of visual experience includes all those things it allows you to identify. I will argue (Section 3.5.2) that this 'demonstrative range' is the same as what I earlier called the 'signal range'. It extends to the sensory horizon. If the experience is veridical, these things are just things in the field of view. They could not be anywhere else.

But the two varieties fly apart when representations are less than veridical. Perhaps the thing I see as red is not red at all, as I am suffering temporarily from the effects of some experiment performed on my retina. Or perhaps I am suffering from a florid hallucination, and the experience I have as of something red (looming menacingly, gurgling) is not a visual experience *of* any object in my field of view. In these cases the intentional object and the referent fly apart. The world as represented contains a menacing red thing, but the representation either refers to something that is not red, or it refers to nothing at all in the actual world.

Do we need to quantify over such entities as the menacing red thing found in my hallucinations? I hope not. Or at least we need to quantify over such objects only if they are also the subject-matter of some other, veridical, representation. Otherwise we should explain the episodes in which such things appear as episodes of misrepresentation. I represent there to be a red thing looming menacingly, but there is no such thing. Such non-veridical representation needs explaining, but our ontology requires no additions to the place-times in the field of view and the states inside the sentient organism which represent (or misrepresent) them.

How might one explain the occasional non-veridical sensory representation? Feature-placing immediately yields at least three possibilities. The first is that reference succeeds but predication goes wrong: the experience misattributes a quality to a successfully identified place-time. We are led astray by a hitch or glitch in the proto-predicative parts of the mechanism. For example, something that is not red might in particular circumstances look red because in those circumstances it causes the same sort of visual state as something that is red (see Clark 1993*b*). The strategy works if we understand in detail how different sorts of stimuli can produce the same sort of visual state.

A fuller understanding of mechanisms of sensory reference would open a second option: perhaps the less than veridical representation is due to misreference. A hitch or glitch occurs in the proto-referential parts. There is nothing amiss with the characterization of place-times, but the place-times are misnamed. Placing mechanisms kick out a spatial identifier, and it refers, but it refers to the wrong place. Some examples will be given in Sections 5.2 and 5.5.

Thirdly, there is the theoretical possibility of generating a name that entirely lacks a referent. No place-time is identified. Any such episode would be non-veridical because, like a sentence without a truth value, correctness conditions would not apply to it.

The feature-placing hypothesis proposes that when sensory representation is veridical, the success can be captured by quantifying over space-time regions of finite extent; and that when it fails, we explain the failure in one or another of these ways. The third variety of visual field is distinct from the first one only in its treatment of these non-veridical episodes. More precisely, the two visual fields differ ontologically only if the proponent of the third variety quantifies over the intentional objects of visual misrepresentations. Those objects are intentional inexistents, objects that exist (at best) only in *other* possible worlds.

For example, Tye (1992) considers the case of Paul hallucinating a pink square object. Tye says that if Paul introspects his hallucination, what he is aware of is the *content* of the hallucinatory experience. 'Likewise when Paul hallucinates a pink square what he introspects, I maintain, is the content of his hallucinatory experience' (Tye 1992: 162). Paul might not realize that the pink square is a hallucination, so he must be allowed to become aware of the content of his hallucination without becoming aware of it as a hallucination. The problem is an interesting one. We cannot say that there is a pink square of which he is aware, because there is no pink square. We cannot say he is aware of his seeing the pink square, because he is not seeing such a thing. We cannot say (without reservations, anyway) that he is aware of his seeming to see a pink square, because that might imply he is aware of the fact that he is hallucinating. Tye suggests that the object of his awareness is the intentional object—the object as represented in the hallucination.

But consider two other options. Just to be definite, suppose one morning Paul opens the door of his freezer, and when looking in it has a visual experience as of something pink and square, in fact pink and cubical: in fact, a homogeneously pink ice cube. There is nothing pink and cubical in the freezer, so the representation is not veridical. Paul slams the door shut, trembling. One possibility is that there is something in the freezer that can be identified as the thing Paul saw *as* a homogeneously pink ice cube. Perhaps he keeps cans of concentrated pink grapefruit juice in the back, and the label on one of the cans momentarily, in that light, given Paul's state of mind, looked to Paul as if it were a homogeneous pink ice cube. He thinks a moment, reopens the door, and sees that it is just a product label. This gives a fairly clear alternative answer to the question of what Paul was aware of when he had his experience as of a pink ice cube: he was aware of that *place* in his freezer, but misrepresented it *as* a pink ice cube. That space-time region is the region he saw as a pink ice cube; his very ability to correct himself shows that even in the misrepresentation, sensory identification succeeds. He might think: 'I was mistaken; that's not a pink ice cube, it's a can of juice.'

This takes the 'object of experience' to be its *referent*; in this case a space-time region. Paul's visual experience characterizes an identifiable region of his freezer, but it characterizes it falsely. What makes it false is that there is no pink ice cube *at that place*. Paul detects the illusion when he looks again and sees that that very place is occupied by a can of juice.

The other possibility is that the hallucination is an episode of the third type: a sensory episode that lacks a referent. Certainly hallucinations are often assumed to be such (see Section 5.5). But without knowing more about their genesis this verdict may be premature. Clearly the demonstrative identification of an *object* will fail if it is based entirely on a hallucination. Macbeth's 'this' in 'Is this a dagger I see before me?' fails to refer to a dagger (see Shoemaker 1994*b*: 266–7). But his visual hallucination may successfully identify a region of empty air: the region that appears to be characterized by those glinting and bloodstained features. On this line, Macbeth's 'this' refers to that region, and the answer to his question is, simply, 'no'. His hallucination picks out a place-time but characterizes it falsely.

After-images provide a better example because we know more about how their placing goes awry. As two-and-a-half-dimensional phenomena, they are hard to place in the normally operative schemes of two or three dimensions. But, I allege, we can explain why they appear where they do, and how visual processes break down to yield that appearance. So it is very interesting to contrast this account with that of the clearest proponent of intentional inexistents: William Lycan. This time our subject is named Bertie:

Suppose Bertie experiences a pointy green after-image. There is a green spot in his visual field; if he denies it, he is a liar. He may sincerely believe that he is sensing and confronted by something green and pointy, but (we may suppose) there is no physical green thing in Bertie's line of sight, and certainly there is no green thing in his brain. It merely *seems* to Bertie that there is a pointy green individual before him; it is visually in his mind as if a pointy green object were before him. And this impression of his is simply mistaken. (Lycan 1996: 71)

The visual field about which Bertie is not allowed to lie is clearly some member of the third variety. It is filled with those things that Bertie visually represents to be around him, even if those representations are mistaken. In this visual field there is a green spot, even though there is nothing green in or around Bertie. To characterize this visual field we characterize how things look to Bertie: the totality of visual appearances presented to him, including illusory ones. The phenomenal individuals found within it are intentional objects. Some, like Bertie's green spot, are *merely* intentional, in the sense that they do not exist in this world.

Lycan thinks that adequate description of the facts of sensible appearance requires a rather robust referential apparatus, including quantification over apparent phenomenal individuals. The paradigm examples are red patches and pointy green spots. Adverbialism is a 'sham' (Lycan 1996: 180 n. 22) and is 'hopeless as a refuge from reference to phenomenal individuals' (Lycan

1996: 71). As already noted, I agree with the failure of adverbialism, and with the need to include an apparatus of identification within sentience itself. But it need not be extended to include merely intentional objects, such as the inexistent green spot in Bertie's third variety of visual field. The first variety of visual field offers a leaner universe, restricting the values of its variables to space-time regions here at home, or in the neighbourhood. Lycan allows them to range over objects in possible worlds other than our own: 'Apparent singular reference to phenomenal individuals, such as pointy light green spots in one's visual field, remains to be accounted for, and the obvious explanation is that the apparent singular reference is genuine' (Lycan 1996: 71). Whenever appearances are veridical, this has a straightforward interpretation. The 'visual field' is then the field of view: a sum of space-time regions of finite extent. The beloved patches and pointy spots that provide the paradigm examples of phenomenal individuals are just such regions. When Bertie is presented an appearance of a pointy green spot in his visual field, and it is not an illusion, then indeed the apparent singular reference is genuine: to that region Bertie sees as green. This is a space-time region lodged comfortably within his own world. It has to be in that world, and indeed within sight of Bertie, because in order to be sensed at all, that region must engage in an extended causal and informational commerce with Bertie's sensory nervous system.

The problem, if there is one, arises only in those cases in which Bertie suffers an illusion. In such a case is the apparent singular reference still genuine? Lycan suggests that it is:

In my view, the best going semantics for intentional inexistence is a possible-world semantics: The apparent mental references to phenomenal individuals are really to objects existing in or 'at' alternative worlds . . . it is important to see that the possible-world metaphysics is inessential to my more fundamental claim that apparent sense data are intentional objects. I happen to think that intentional inexistents are denizens of other possible worlds—or in some cases impossible worlds—but if you have a different metaphysic of intentional inexistents, apply it forthwith, and do not waste paper criticizing mine. (Lycan 1996: 72)

As noted, feature-placing allows us to distinguish at least three kinds of non-veridical appearance. In the first two we can still confine the values of our variables to space-time regions in this world. Perhaps Bertie's visual experience picks out a place-time but mischaracterizes it, or perhaps its non-veridical character arises from misreference. In either case there is some non-green region in Bertie's line of sight that Bertie experiences *as* being green. He visually represents ((green)(there)), and 'there' picks out a patch, surface, or volume in this world, but he is wrong about its features. His experience is wrong, but it is definitely wrong *about* some region in this world. The only kind of non-veridical appearance that might tempt us to stray into other possible worlds is the third kind. In it there would be *no* region in this world identifiable as the region that Bertie experiences as green. This is not a very plausible characterization of after-imaging, and so for now this third kind remains merely a theoretical possibility. But even if the characterization is true of some experiences, it need not force us into other possible worlds; we could simply accept the implication that such experiences identify *nothing* (see Elder 1998c). Further discussion is postponed until we take up the questions of misreference and missing referents (Section 5.5).

3.5 SENSORY IDENTIFICATION

With both version 2 and version 3 visual fields eliminated as candidates for values of our variables, we revert gratefully to the finite space-time regions that fill version 1. Adequate description of the facts of visual sensible appearance requires an apparatus of quantification over such regions, but no more. We do not need to quantify over sense-data, Meinongian objects, phenomenal individuals, or intentional objects, unless those various entities surprise their progenitors and reveal themselves to be identical to portions of physical space located in or around the body of the sentient organism. Visual representation when successful has mechanisms sufficient to identify such place-times. When sensory reference goes awry, it does not refer to objects in some other world, but simply misidentifies regions in this one.

This leaves the question of *how* such sensory identifications proceed. How do sensory mechanisms gain the wherewithal to identify place-times? For example, how does one's sensation of pain in the foot manage to pick out one's foot? One's first impulse is to point to a portion of a feature map in somatosensory cortex, and say, 'This portion of the feature map is about the left foot because the afferent neurons that connect to this portion originate in the left foot.' It is important to appreciate the inadequacies of this answer. Granted, the connections between those neurons and that region are important to the answer, but they are neither necessary nor sufficient. Thinking that the mere anatomical connection can do the job leads one headlong into the massed pikes of the brain–mind mysteries described in Section 2.2. Feature-placing can place features beyond the outermost end-points of one's afferent nerves, as when one hears the siren in the distance, or one feels the cold floor *underneath* one's feet. How would we manage to place features in regions not enervated with neural tissue? Furthermore, although one finds a mapping and regular causal connection between transducers located in the feet and portions of the feature map, one also finds such connections between neurons in later stages of sensory processing and the feature map. Such neurons, in the spinal cord, thalamus, or other subcortical way-stations, are closer to the cortical map, and show better correlations with its activity than do the more remote transducers. So why is not this portion of the feature map a map of events in one's own thalamus, and not of regions of the skin, much less regions beyond it?

The problem is to identify the appropriate territory—the target—and then explain why this portion of the feature map is a map *of* that portion of *that* territory. Much of this explanatory work is clearly work for the experimental psychologist. How do Otto and Bertie manage spatial discriminations of features in front of their eyes? Feature-placing refers to a psychological phenomenon, and the 'placing' portion of it is likewise a psychological phenomenon. The reason we can be confident that one does not need dendrites to dangle into every space-time region about which sensation can bring some news is simply that we can test the subject experimentally, and show that he or she can discriminate reliably among some of those remote events. We hope, for example, that Bertie can tell by looking whether the traffic signal ahead is red or green. In the lab such tests can become much more sophisticated and detailed. How much radiation of what spectral composition is required for a subject to detect a red spot against a background of such-and-such average intensity? What angular separation is needed for two lights in the signal to be seen as two? In a straightforward fashion we can test the parameters of variation to which the modality is sensitive, and determine spatial parameters of direction, angle, size, and distance.

While one does not need dendrites extending into every region that sensation can represent, one does require an information channel that reaches that far. There must be something going on in that region that can be detected reliably by sensory systems—some transmission from that region to transducers that can be registered in some regular fashion by subsequent sensory states. The traffic signal emits radiant energy that travels to the retina, and is absorbed and registered there. We find not only a causal chain extending beyond the outermost ends of the nervous system, but also an information channel, so that events in the visual system reliably register variations in the light from regions in front of the eyes. If we ever accept a ride from Bertie, we entrust our lives to the reliability of that channel.

3.5.1 Conditions on Placing

Since psychologists and neuroscientists will clearly be involved in finding the answer, I propose to divide the question 'How do sensory mechanisms gain the wherewithal to identify place-times?' into two:

1. How do mechanisms of spatial discrimination manage to satisfy conditions *C* (to be detailed)? and

2. How does the satisfaction of conditions C suffice to show that sensory mechanisms identify place-times?

The first of these is a more or less straightforward empirical question, to be handed over to the neurosciences as soon as conditions C are spelled out. To find conditions C, find the conditions under which sensory mechanisms work just as they should. These conditions delineate the prototypically successful sensory episode: conditions that the mechanisms of spatial discrimination satisfy when things are working well. Misfires, errors, and infelicities are certainly possible (see Section 5.5), but when sensory identification is successful, the structure of connections established between circumambient physical phenomena and the innards of nervous systems is a joy to behold. And to describe. These conditions on placing provide grounds for an argument, under the second heading, that sensory systems that do *that* do something that should be acknowledged as an act of identifying. The targets of these acts are place-times; if one is asked, 'What are sensory states *about*? What is the subject-matter of sensory representation?' the answer I suggest is, invariably, 'Space-time regions of finite but definite extent, in or around the body of the sentient organism'.

Suppose a modality presents the appearance of sensory qualities Q at region R. To introduce an example that will be elaborated in Section 5.1, suppose you have an itch on your foot. Hypothesis: σ, the sensory state that you endure, is a feature-placing representation. Its sensory characteristics can be partitioned into some set of dimensions $Q_1 \dots Q_n$ that enable you to discriminate an itch at that place from all the other somaesthetic qualities that might someday appear there, and a set $R_1 \dots R_m$ of dimensions of spatio-temporal discrimination, values of which enable you to discriminate that particular instance of itch on the foot from perhaps qualitatively identical itches elsewhere or subsequently. A fully determinate particular instance of a sensory episode in that modality, such as σ, includes an ordered n-tuple $(q_1 \dots q_n)$, with a particular value on each of the n qualitative dimensions. If spatio-temporal discriminations in that modality proceed in m dimensions $R_1 \dots R_m$, σ also includes a fully determinate instance of an m-tuple of values $(r_1 \dots r_m)$. I will sometimes abbreviate these as vectors $[q_n]$ and $[r_m]$ respectively. We shall place under the spotlight the collecting principles that tie together such fully determinate instances of qualities Q at regions R.

My goal is to persuade the reader that the place-time identified by $[r_m]$ is not just the place-time where the qualities presented by the sensory experience appear to be located, but also that it is the referent of the feature-placing representation. The sensation is a sensation *of* that region; that region is what the representation σ is *about*. In particular we need an argument for the claim that the collecting principles that apply to spatio-temporal and qualitative dimensions respectively are formally analogous to those that apply to singular terms and predicates. The key asymmetry found in the latter collecting principles was that general characteristics come in incompatibility groups, while particulars do not. Furthermore, while a particular instance of a singular term might collect many predicates, each particular instance of a predicate can collect but one singular term (see Section 2.5).

So much for preliminaries. The first condition to be listed in our set C emerges from a consideration of what is required to solve the Multiple Properties problem. Recall the special role that locations play in solving that puzzle (Section 2.5). To sense something as both matte and red, one must sense matte at the same place-time as red. The location of one feature must be identified with that of the other.[9] Such identities drive the bindings: to the matte feature are bound whatever other features are found at the same (spatio-temporal) region. But if this is so, identifiers of such regions collect features in somewhat the way that singular terms collect predicates. First, identity of such location underwrites the attribution of several features to one thing. We sense matte at location a and sense red at a, yielding a sensing as of something matte red at a. Distinctness of location likewise precludes attribution of both features to one thing. Suppose we sense matte at a and red at b. For this to be a sensing of something that is both matte and red requires an identification, partial or complete, of regions a and b. Partial identity (overlap) gives: some region of a = some region of b; full identity (coincidence) gives $a = b$. Either suffices to bind matte and red, so that the sensing is as of their co-instantiation. If the regions are entirely disjoint, then such sensing is the sensing of something that is matte and *something else* that is red.

Identities of place-times serve to collect features, while differences divide them. So each particular instance (or trope) of a feature, each particular attribution of a $[q_n]$, is tied uniquely to its place-time, in the same way that each particular smile of Socrates is tied uniquely to Socrates. Furthermore, the same place-time can collect multiple features. Socrates is not only smiling, but wise. In short, we get

1. *Collect the features.* A particular instance of qualitative feature q_i is tied uniquely to the place-time identified by $[r_m]$, but the place-time identified by $[r_m]$ may be characterized by multiple features.

This reflects the formal similarity in 'collecting principles' noted above. One senses qualities at a place-time. Spatio-temporal discrimination serves to pick out or identify such place-times. The qualities that appear at such regions *characterize* them.

---

[9] As noted in Sect. 2.5, I adopt the convention that 'location' and 'region' should be understood to include temporal coordinates: these are locations and regions of space-time.

(A technical note. With this development we can explain why the 'partitioning' of dimensions of variation in appearance mentioned in Section 2.4 satisfies the formal condition mentioned in 2.5. Suppose we have $n + m$ dimensions of variation in appearance, with an associated n-tuple of qualitative variations $(q_1 \ldots q_n)$ and m-tuple of spatio-temporal registrations $(r_1 \ldots r_m)$. The allocation of dimensions across this partition must be adjusted to satisfy the following condition: that for each unique m-tuple $[r_m]$ there can be no more than one n-tuple $[q_n]$. Why? Place-times collect features in this fashion. Suppose a particular instance of a qualitative property q_i represents a feature found at the place-time identified by $[r_m]$. Then q_i can be 'bound' to whatever features are found at the same location. That place will collect a value for each of the dimensions Q_1 to Q_n of qualitative variation. Since each dimension forms a range of contraries, that place will collect exactly one value from each (see Elder 1996*b,d*). Whereas features do not collect place-times in this way. With a successful partition, at a given visual place-time there is just one triplet of hue–saturation–brightness. But a particular colour can occur in many places simultaneously. Place-times can organize bindings while colours could not.)

Now consider a particular instance of such a representation, with each of the dimensions filled with a determinate value. A particular episode of itch-on-foot might have values $(q_1 \ldots q_n)$ on the dimensions of qualitative variation, describing the differences between itches-on-foot and all the other somaesthetic qualities-on-foot; and values $(r_1 \ldots r_m)$, activated in mechanisms of spatio-temporal discrimination, differentiating the apparent place-time of that itch from other places and times the same quality might appear to occupy. The having of σ thereby presents the appearance of qualities Q at region R. The following is then almost a truism:

2. *Apparent location.* The region identified by $[r_m]$ is where the itch appears to be. More generally, the place identified by $[r_m]$ is the place that qualities $(q_1 \ldots q_n)$ appear to characterize.

This makes the location of the itch (as well as the location of any bodily sensation) an intentional location, in the sense that the 'location of the itch' is the location the itch is represented as having. We pick it out by picking out which place is *represented* in σ by the activation of mechanisms of spatial discrimination. Condition 2 is almost but not quite a truism. It rests on the arguments in Chapter 2 over the apparent spatial character of sensory experience, and in particular on accepting the feature-placing resolution of those arguments.

What remain are various and more intricate connections between the sensory state σ and physical phenomena in the region that its qualities appear to characterize. The first is a generality, best expressed in common-sense terms:

3. *Stimulus location.* The place identified by $[r_m]$ is, when all goes well, the location of 'the cause' of—the stimulus for—σ.

We need scare quotes because any sensory state has multiple causes, and the first locution appeals to a common-sense understanding of what it is to identify 'the cause' of a sensation. Perhaps, for example, the itch was caused by an insect bite; the place identified by coordinates r is the place where the insect bit. The region where the brown of the brown table appears is occupied by a cloud of elementary particles which cause the visual sensation as of a brown surface. Such common-sense 'causes' are typically inconstant distal conditions, proximate to the sense organs, and at least partially determinative of the variations in the qualities sensed; but attempts to analyse this common-sense notion quickly become intricate (see Broad 1927; Dretske 1981, 1988; Mackie 1974; O'Shaughnessy 1980; Price 1932). Differences between these analyses are not essential to my purposes; the essential point is the existence of a causal relation, of an intricate character, whose intricacies shall remain hidden under scare quotes.

Psychologists call these causes 'stimuli'. For example, I am presented the appearance of a brown oblong filling a particular volume. Visual spatial discrimination allows me successfully to localize the stimulus that looks brown. (Recall that we are confining ourselves to successful episodes.) I perceive brown *there*, and 'there' can be unpacked to identify a place. When all goes well, the place where the brown appears to be is in fact the location of a stimulus that causes the sensation *of* brown. It is also the perfect spot for that table.

We can enlist the even more powerful terminology of information theory. In successful episodes, not only does the region identified by $[r_m]$ play a particular causal role in the genesis of σ; it also satisfies the relatively more intimate relations of dependency necessary and sufficient to posit an 'information channel' between the space-time region and the sensory state. 'Information' is here used in the strict Claude Shannon, information-theoretic sense, which can be unpacked in terms of conditional probabilities between ensembles at an input end and an output end. In particular, the qualitative variations presented by state σ form the output ensemble; they convey information about physical phenomena in the identified region:

4. *On-going channel.* There exists an on-going information channel between the region identified by $[r_m]$ and the differentiative properties $(q_1 \dots q_n)$ of σ.

Variations in qualitative states track variations in the properties of the stimuli that cause those states. The properties of this information channel or 'on-going information link' have been detailed by several authors (see Dretske

1981; G. Evans 1982; Clark 1993*b*). To revert to our homely example: that the foot feels specifically itchy, and not cold, or hot, or achy, or tingly, conveys some information about conditions in that region. At the very least, given that the foot feels itchy, the conditional probability that it has been affected by some classes of stimuli goes up, while the likelihood of its having been affected by other classes of stimuli goes down. Insect bites are more likely, ice water less. Such changes in conditional probability justify the application of information-theoretic terms.

All this machinery is helpful only if possessing state σ somehow helps the animal who has it. Even the most acute and informative discrimination of the location of the itch is barely half the battle; one hopes it also aids the project of scratching. We need some condition of the following form:

5. *Guide the host.* Coordinates $(r_1 \dots r_m)$ help guide σ's host; in particular they help it to localize the region in which the stimulus for σ lies; using them it can identify the subject-matter of the information it has received.

Here 'localize' means to help guide or direct behaviour involving the place-time in question. The behaviour might be to approach, to flee, to step around, or whatever; the paradigm I propose is the act of scratching. Coordinates $(r_1 \dots r_m)$ allow the sufferer to identify a bodily region, and, using that identification, scratch where it itches. We know that that region is the location of the cause of σ in part because scratching there makes the itch go away. More generally, manipulation of the region identified by $[r_m]$ can affect the course and character of the sensory state itself. We thereby receive efferent confirmation for the location of its cause.

And so we have the rudiments for a simple scheme of mental representation, with both sensory reference and predication. The referential apparatus is provided by spatio-temporal attributes of discrimination: structurally they are such that $[r_m]$ has something of the character of a singular term (condition 1). When all goes well, those coordinates serve to identify the place-time where the qualities presented by the experience appear to be located (condition 2); and in that region are located physical conditions that play a causal role in the genesis of the sensory state itself (condition 3). Qualitative variations in the state carry information about conditions in that region (condition 4) and that information helps guide the host in behaviours involving the cause of its sensations (condition 5).

This rather abstract set of conditions can be brought down to earth by considering the demands placed on a busy animal. Sentience is useful only when combined with motility and an uneven spatial distribution of positive or negative contingencies: food, poison, warmth, water, predators, mates, shelter, exposure, and so on. Even under those conditions sentience is useful only if it at least occasionally cuts the odds of encountering a negative contingency or improves the odds of a positive one. To change those odds, sentience must help guide movement through that spatial distribution, away from the nasty stuff and towards the good. (This movement need not be movement of the entire animal; it might consist of the flicking outward of a proboscis or the clamping shut of a shell of a creature wedded to a coral reef.) Success in such navigation requires a good sense of where things are. Only an evil deity would endow a creature with the capacity to detect the approach of noxious stimuli but without the capacity to wiggle away in the opposite direction. The mind likewise boggles at the prospect of a creature with the capacities to detect noxious stimuli and to wiggle away, but an incapacity to detect the direction whence the noxious stimuli come. Evolution is unlikely to cast its creatures into such perdition.

Suppose we have a successful instance of feature-placing, and the region identified by $(r_1 ... r_m)$ is the region where the qualities $(q_1 ... q_n)$ appear to be. Since the fundamental task facing our busy animal is navigation, these place-times cannot be *mere* appearance. A tiger located entirely in a phenomenal field can do no harm, nor can the mere appearance of bread sustain. The place-times identified by $[r_m]$ must have some connection with the good or bad contingencies that one might approach or avoid. And, one hopes, the qualities that appear at such places can help signal which way to go. A *merely* phenomenal visual field would not help guide you through the woods. You would be likely to bump into trees or trip over branches. But the dark blotches that the trunks present also appear to be in various locations, at various angles and depths. Those apparent places typically allow one to identify the physical cause of the sensation of dark blotch: they enable you to identify the location of the actual tree trunk. You can thereby cut the odds of tripping.

The machinery has been honed for hundreds of millions of years. Unlike errors in abstract reasoning, errors in these rather fundamental mechanisms tend to have costs both immediate and profound. It is thus not surprising that capacities to localize stimuli are in many modalities astoundingly acute and almost invariably reliable. With rare exceptions (see Section 5.5), spatial discrimination of region R enables the animal correctly to localize the *stimulus* that appears to be Q. That is, the spatial capacities not only present the creature with entertaining or distressing phenomena, but also allow it to localize the source of its joys or sorrows.

3.5.2 *The Sensory Horizon*

I have now detailed the contents of conditions C and argued that the question of how mechanisms of spatial discrimination satisfy conditions C is an empirical question, to be handed over forthwith to the neurosciences. The second part of the divided question is to argue that satisfaction of conditions *C* suffices to show that sensory systems identify place-times. Conditions *C* must be found sufficient to justify labelling these lowly mechanisms with terms out of the intentional lexicon: pick out, identify, refer, characterize, represent. This second task is much larger and occupies various portions of the remainder of the book. The overall strategy for such arguments is clear: show that sensory processes manifest enough of the features of genuine intentional states that the labels are not merely honorific. Those phenomena will in remaining chapters be seen to include such exemplars as opacity, ambiguity, misidentification, informative identities, and others.

That sensory experience has representational content is now widely acknowledged, and consideration of these phenomena may seem a waste of time. But the point is not simply to establish that sensory processes represent: it is to say something much more substantive about exactly *how* they represent. If we stop at the headlines we will be inclined to assimilate the intentionality of sensation to the intentionality of thought, to think of them as two variant dialects of the same lingua franca. That would be a mistake. A sensation of water and a thought of water are both about water; but they represent it in different ways. The 'ofness' of sensation is not the 'ofness' of thought. Perhaps these are species of the same family, but their differences are real. My use of the 'proto' prefix is an attempt to acknowledge those differences. Historically, many thinkers have accused sensation of 'pseudo-intentionality'; it apes some of the features of the intentionality of thought, but like 'ape language' turns out upon inspection to have few of the properties of the real thing.

The only way to untangle these issues is carefully to delineate how sensory processes proceed: how they pick out places and attribute qualities to those places, if that is what they do. Once all that untangling is done, and the various similarities and differences between these processes are displayed, then all the facts upon which a verdict depends will have been laid upon the table. Thereafter the question of where to draw the line between processes that manifest mere 'pseudo-intentionality' and those that demonstrate the real thing becomes purely verbal and (to this author) a matter of indifference. Provided one understands the ordering and the complex hierarchies of intentional capacities, one can attach the honorific at almost any point.

One prominent distinction between the intentionality of sensation and of thought can be flagged here: the sensory variety requires an on-going information link to the object in question (G. Evans 1982). Vision cannot veridically represent events outside the current field of view; somaesthesis cannot veridically represent events outside the body; hearing cannot veridically represent events beyond the range of audible compression waves in the atmosphere; and so on. These causal limits on the operations of the various modalities also limit the domain about which a given modality can proffer some news. With the raw materials of a sensory system it is hard to create a token that successfully picks out a place other than the place where the feature it represents appears to be. Unlike linguistic representation, the sensory variety lacks the wherewithal for reference that is assisted, deferred, or indirect.

A sensory system cannot refer to anything except those things to which it can refer directly, and such direct reference requires an on-going causal and informational link. So, for example, the visible horizon is also the limit of the subject-matter of visual sensation. That horizon is the limit of the 'signal range' (Section 3.1): the region within which a signal can travel to the transducers and have some detectable physical effect upon them. Whatever current visual sensation is about will be found somewhere within that region. At night the horizon extends to light-years, but the same idea applies. The subject-matter of auditory sensation is limited by a similar horizon: that range of things that can produce compression waves that are still audible when they reach you. So barring telephones and such the auditory sensations of someone in Connecticut cannot be about events in Oklahoma. No such limit bars Connecticut residents from *thinking* about Oklahoma. The subject-matter of bodily sensation is limited to those regions that can be registered by the somaesthetic nervous system. Bodily sensation cannot reveal anything about place-times that fail to impinge upon those nerves. (This is why phantom pain is considered to be less than veridical, and why exo-somaesthetic sensation—in which patients complain of feeling pains in other people's bodies—is considered a psychiatric syndrome.) The subject-matter of your tactile sensation is limited by your reach. And so on: that sensory reference is direct implies that sensory states can only be about regions within their various horizons. The 'horizon' in each case is defined causally.

But if this is so, then the way to understand how sensory states manage to refer is to study how the system manages spatio-temporal discrimination: how it can pick out and distinguish regions within the given horizon. Tell the story of how we manage visually to discriminate among space-time regions, and we will have told the story of how early vision picks out its subject-matter. Because it lacks the means to refer remotely or indirectly, visual reference proceeds in full daylight, so to speak, and its mechanisms are in this way open to view.

Sensory identification, unlike other kinds, reduces to spatio-temporal discrimination; the 'ofness' of sensation is just a matter of picking out *where* the qualities it presents appear to be. Sensory processes when successful 'pick out' or 'identify' those space-time regions where their qualities appear to be.

That is what they are about. The sensation of having a pain in your foot is about your foot because that is where the pain appears to be. The intentional character of the experience is nothing more or less than its spatial character. And the latter question is a tractable one. Understanding how we manage spatio-temporal discriminations in a given modality is a difficult empirical problem, but it is not conceptually problematic. Models of these capacities can be devised, tested, and revised by psychologists, psychophysiologists, and neuroscientists. As the models get better and better, so too will our understanding of how sensory identification proceeds.

3.6 SOME EXAMPLES OF SENSORY REFERENCE

Fortunately the story does not need to stop with schematic methodological arguments and grim generalizations. It can be fleshed out with many delightful examples of living, breathing sensory systems. In various modalities in various species we have glimmers of relatively complete understanding of the feature maps involved: not just of how activation patterns of populations of neurons represent features, but also of how a particular portion of a feature map picks out a particular portion of the territory in front of the sense organs. So in these examples we understand not only the sensory qualities but also the capacities of spatio-temporal discrimination yielding sensory reference, and so we have a relatively complete understanding of an entire system of sensory representation. Philosophers may be stunned to learn that one of the modalities in question is precisely the echolocation capacity of bats; it is one of the *best* understood of sensory systems (see Popper and Fay 1995: vii). But there are many examples, and an enormous literature, so here I can do no more than sample some of the delights. Perhaps thereby others can be lured into exploring these portions of neuroscience.

3.6.1 The Barn Owl

On a cloudy moonless night a mouse living in a barn might feel relatively confident in venturing out onto the floor. After all, a mouse can walk across a level surface without making much noise, and it cannot be seen in the dark. Nevertheless, such confidence is sadly misplaced if there is a member of the species *Tyto alba* in the vicinity. The night-hunting barn owl can intercept and pick a mouse off the floor in complete darkness, using only the auditory clues provided by the footfalls of the over-confident rodent. It can replicate the feat in controlled (even anechoic) conditions provided in a laboratory. (For a picture taken with an infra-red strobe light, see Konishi 1993: 67.) One would like somehow to warn the mouse that auditory localization in some species can be appallingly precise. Perhaps the mouse is making a philosophical mistake, assuming that the mechanisms of auditory localization must be introspectively accessible. Since it finds little of note within its own phenomenology, it proceeds blithely onto the floor, there to have its last mistake corrected.

Apart from its acuity, another aspect of the owl's behaviour makes it a perfect subject for the study of mechanisms of auditory localization. When the barn owl hears a sound of interest, it makes a ballistic head-turn towards the sound. It does this in the dark, with considerable precision, even if the sound is so brief that it is over before the head-turn begins (Takahashi 1989: 307). Fit the owl with some small electric coils, and place it in an electric field, and one can measure the azimuth and altitude of these head-turns. Happily, the owl responds ballistically even to ersatz mouse sounds presented through earphones. In this way various parameters of interaural difference can be controlled precisely, and the resulting head-turns measured. Two parameters of interaural difference prove to be predictive. Phase differences—the interaural time difference (ITD) between arrivals of the crest of the compression wave, as described in Section 2.1—yield a precise prediction of the azimuth of the head-turn. Intensity differences can also help, particularly in higher frequencies, which are not so readily diffracted around the large 'sound shadow' cast by the head. Interestingly, the barn owl has asymmetrically placed ears, with the left ear placed higher than the eyes and pointed down, while the right ear is lower than the eyes but pointed up. This would look odd in a human but it would yield definite advantages. With such asymmetric placement in the barn owl, differences in sound elevation create interaural intensity differences. A sound on the medial plane is louder to the right ear if it is above the ears, and louder to the left ear if below.

The two interaural differences yield unambiguous coordinates that predict the azimuth and altitude of the eventual head-turn (see Konishi 1993: 68). So the question becomes: how does the barn owl's auditory system discriminate interaural differences in timing and intensity?

One large problem in discriminating interaural time differences is that the intervals involved are several orders of magnitude smaller than any single neuron can register. The fastest neuron can spike about 1,000 times per second, or once per millisecond. Sound travels through air (at 15 degrees centigrade) at roughly 340 metres per second, and, with the owl's ears at most 6 centimetres apart, the distance from one ear to the other is traversed in no more than 180 microseconds—or roughly one-sixth the duration between the minimally separated spikes (Takahashi 1989: 308). Even that interval is the upper limit for ITD, as it would be produced by a low-frequency sound (one with a wavelength greater than the inter-ear distance) on the interaural axis, directly opposite one ear. Sounds presented closer to the midline, where spatial discrimination is actually best, typically involve time differences of less than 20 microseconds. Direct measurements show that a shift of 20 degrees off the midline changes ITD by 42 microseconds (Konishi 1993: 68); yet the owl can detect shifts in sound source location as small as 2 degrees. The problem gets worse at higher frequencies, since above 5,600 hertz the wavelength of sound is less than 6 centimetres. Several wave crests arrive in the time it takes the sound to travel from one ear to the other, and so it seems the system has to discriminate among events at an even finer level of temporal resolution.

Neurons are slow, but they have astounding capabilities when they are well organized. The trick is to shift the problem into a domain at which neurons excel: spreading the representation over space—over massed arrays of coincidence detectors, specifically—to make up for the inadequate temporal resolution. The first step is to get a reliable signal from each ear for the phase of the sound, and sure enough neurons in the magnocellular nucleus of the barn owl exhibit 'phase-locking': firing in synchrony with a given phase of the sound (at the crest of the wave or at the bottom of the trough, for example; the exact point in the cycle does not matter, as long as it is hit in each cycle). Once frequencies get above 1,000 hertz (which is just two octaves above middle C on a piano), even the fastest neuron will start missing beats, but the solution is easy: each neuron may spike only at every *n*th cycle, but it has neighbours that spike for the cycles it misses. The population as a whole shows phase-locking. Cells terminating in the magnocellular nucleus of the barn owl phase-lock up to 9,000 hertz (Albeck 1995: 892).

Suppose then that we have populations of neurons in left and right magnocellular nuclei showing phase locking for stimuli in left and right ears. How might one discriminate microsecond time differences between the two? A hypothesis put forth in 1948 by Lloyd Jeffress was on the right track. Even synaptic events require timescales of tens to hundreds of milliseconds (see Churchland and Sejnowski 1992: 175), but one cellular event that evolves on a microsecond scale is the movement of an action potential down a short length of axon. Perhaps one could register microseconds by registering differences in the *length* of axon down which a potential travelled. This is what the nervous system of the barn owl does, with 'delay lines' in its laminar nuclei. A phase-locked neuron from the right magnocellular nucleus sends an axon to the left laminar nucleus, and once there sprouts offshoots into it at regular spatial intervals. It takes microseconds for an action potential to travel the distance from one offshoot to the next: those constitute the 'delay'. A neuron from the left magnocellular nucleus does the same thing, but it enters the left laminar nucleus from the other side. Neurons in the laminar nucleus respond best when stimulated by offshoots from both the left and the right ear, firing simultaneously. With offshoots from left and right inter-digitated in this fashion, cells in one place in the laminar nucleus will fire if both ears are exactly in phase, but different cells will fire depending on the amount of delay needed in one or another ear to put them into phase. The place maximally active in the laminar nucleus hence registers microsecond differences in time.

An interaural time difference shows 'phase ambiguity'. That is, if a shift or delay of d will put two sounds of frequency f into phase, then so will a shift of $d + 1/f$, $1/f - d$, $d + 2/f$, $2/f - d$, and so on. (Instead of bumping the crest of one wave up to the nearest crest of the other, bump it to the cycle past that, or back to the previous one.) So even at a given frequency, multiple sites in the laminar nucleus will fire, corresponding to the multiple shifts that could bring the cycles into phase (see Takahashi 1989: 313). A related ambiguity: the same interaural time difference could be produced by stimuli at different azimuths, as long as we change their frequency.

The solution is elegant: just run the same delay line analysis for multiple frequencies, and then compare results. Since the auditory system is organized tonotopically, the laminar nucleus can be organized as multiple parallel banks of coincidence detectors, one bank for frequency f_1, one for f_2, and so on (see Albeck 1995: 892). Only one ITD will bring *all* the different frequencies into phase, and it will indicate auditory azimuth. Sure enough, at the next stage past the laminar nucleus, in the core of the inferior colliculus, results are summed across frequencies. The incorrect ITDs have periods that depend on frequency, and summing across frequencies cancels them. By the time signals reach the external nucleus of the inferior colliculus, the process is done. The one ITD that brings all the frequencies into phase emerges from the background noise like a mountain rising out of the clouds (see Albeck 1995: 894).

Knowing the mechanism, we can predict an auditory spatial illusion in the barn owl. If the barn owl is presented a tone of a single frequency—something like the sound produced by a tuning-fork—then disambiguating ITDs by summing over frequencies will fail, as there won't be enough frequencies over which to sum. To the owl the sound will appear to have multiple locations; the *reference* of states in its inferior colliculus will be ambiguous. 'When an owl attempts to localize a high-frequency tone burst, it behaves as though it perceives more than one source. If broad-band stimuli are presented, the owl's localization is precise' (Takahashi 1989: 312). One is hard-pressed to identify phenomenological grounds for such a phenomenological prediction; it derives instead from neuroscience. Knowing enough about how the system works, we can predict the conditions under which it will instantiate an ambiguous designator.

For our second spatial coordinate (auditory elevation), we need to register interaural intensity differences. This feature is processed in an entirely separate pathway. The auditory nerve bifurcates, with part going to the phase-locking ipsilateral magnocellular nucleus and the pathway already discussed. Another part goes to the ipsilateral angular nucleus, which does not show phase-locking, but instead registers auditory intensity, in maps organized (as always) tonotopically. The next way station is the posterior lateral lemniscal nucleus on the contralateral side of the brain. These two nuclei have direct connections to one another, and cells in them provide a feature map of intensity *differences* across the two ears.

Neurons at the bottom of the left nucleus respond maximally when sound is much louder in the left ear and . . . those at the top of the nucleus fire most strongly when sound is louder in the right ear. Similarly, neurons at the bottom of the right posterior nucleus respond most strongly when sound is much louder in the right ear, and those at the top of the nucleus prefer louder sound in the left ear. (Konishi 1993: 72)

The sharpening of intensity is not understood as well as the corresponding process in the timing channel; it seems to require far fewer steps. The separate pathways for interaural timing and intensity differences meet for the first time in the lateral shell of the inferior colliculus. Neurons in the lateral shell still show some phase ambiguity—multiple candidates with a periodicity of $1/f$—which may be eliminated by lateral inhibition (see Konishi 1993). But by the next synapse, in the external nucleus of the inferior colliculus (ICx), the channels have merged perfectly to produce a beautiful two-dimensional map of auditory space, organized by auditory azimuth and altitude. All the cells at zero degree azimuth are in one swath across the ICx, all those at ten degrees left are in the next swath, and so on. The differing auditory elevations are mapped in a regular fashion across each swath. Neurons at each point in this map are 'space-specific' in the sense that they will fire to any audible stimulus at the appropriate azimuth and altitude, regardless of frequency. Each such neuron has a receptive field, and just as in the visual system, those fields are smallest at the midline horizon (where discriminations are best) and grow as one moves further away.

The map so far is just two-dimensional, and leaves out auditory depth. Given its behavioural repertoire, perhaps the barn owl does not need particularly acute depth perception. If while flying about in the darkened barn, it hears a noise of interest, it will turn its head and start flying in that direction. If it hears a subsequent noise, it adjusts its path, and iteration of this strategy often results in interception. Generally a two-dimensional map will suffice if the animal can start *moving* in the appropriate direction, and adjust its path with subsequent 2d maps until interception. Depth unravels dynamically. In fact the need to use maps to adjust movement along the way has been offered as an explanation for why almost every bilateral vertebrate sensory system has contralateral projections. With sense organs on the right side projecting to the left side of the brain, activation by attractive stimuli on the right side can readily engage muscles on the left, slewing the animal round to the appropriately adjusted heading. Even in very simple creatures, this arrangement can generate the mid-course corrections often needed in the pursuit of happiness (see Braitenburg 1984). Of course it might be awkward always to crash into the target, and it would be handy if possible to anticipate interception. Even in the dark the barn owl makes anticipatory movements with its claws before it reaches its target. So it has some capacities to detect auditory depth, and these are unexplored and unknown.

Nevertheless, the success of the model for two dimensions of the barn owl's auditory space is quite impressive, and it illustrates the sort of answer that I think can be given to the question of how a particular sensory system manages to identify place-times. To revert to an earlier example: Suppose we hear a bird cheep out in the woods in a particular auditory direction—at a particular azimuth and altitude, overhead and to the left, say. Its distance might be more or less vaguely indicated. Simply saying that the auditory sensation refers to that space-time region does not constitute a theory of sensory identification. How does the auditory system manage to pick out that location? Phenomenally it may seem as if there is nothing to it, but that misimpression arises because the details of how the system works are not introspectively accessible. Audition just presents a ((cheep)(there)). Poking under the phenomenal surface, one finds an astoundingly complex and well-tuned mechanism for producing the simple impression as of (there). Humans are not barn owls, but there is no reason why we could not tell a similar type of story about human auditory localization as just told about the barn owl. If we did, I submit that we could answer the question of how audition picks out the region (there). In such fashion will neuroscience handle part of the job of explaining sensory reference.

3.6.2 *The Echolocating Bat*

Ironically, the modality from which we have derived our best understanding of auditory localization is one that some philosophers consider to be the very paradigm of inscrutability: the echolocation capabilities of chiroptera. Audition in bats is probably better understood than in any other order; in it, thanks to the work in the laboratories of Nobuo Suga, John Simmons, and others, we have a relatively complete inventory of the feature maps involved, including the mechanisms for range-finding. In the latter the bat puts even the barn owl to shame.

Biosonar allows the bat to discriminate among the many species of flying insects and select its targets. Such a feat is in itself incredible: such insects are at most a few centimetres long, yet their shapes, or perhaps some characteristic of their wing-flutter, are discriminated by audition alone—specifically by listening to the sounds *reflected* off of the body of the insect (Suga and Kanwal 1995: 344). To do this the moustached bat is equipped with a forbidding array of computational maps: azimuth, altitude, Doppler shift, velocity, auditory subtended angle, range, size, flutter, and perhaps other target characteristics. Many of the details of how these maps are organized have been worked out (see Suga and Kanwal 1995; Suga 1990).

Just as in the barn owl, the processing for several of the maps proceeds simultaneously, in parallel channels. The separation of the channels begins at the basilar membrane. As noted previously, different sound frequencies distort the basilar membrane maximally at different places, so a 'tonotopic' organization results from simple place-coding of the basilar membrane. The sound which the moustached bat produces in its echolocation efforts has eight distinct frequency components. Four are harmonics of a constant-frequency (CF) portion of each pulse, and four are found in the briefer frequency-modulated (FM) portion. The harmonics start at 30,000 hertz and run up to 120,000. Suga labels these CF_1 to CF_4 and FM_1 to FM_4. The second harmonic is the strongest component of the signal; its FM portion (FM_2) starts at 60 kilohertz and drops rapidly to 40 kilohertz. The FM portions become briefer as the bat approaches its target, and at the end may last only half a millisecond (Simmons 1996: 229). The eight different frequency components maximally stimulate different portions of the basilar membrane, so the separate channels producing the bat's auditory maps all commence at separate places on that membrane.

Some of the engineering to handle the CF components is relatively similar to that found in the barn owl. We find similar mechanisms to compute auditory azimuth and elevation. The fact that the bat can compare the outgoing sound to its echo allows it also to detect Doppler shift: the extent to which the returning echo shifts in frequency compared to the outgoing pulse. This shift can reveal the relative velocity of whatever reflected the echo. Since such information would be quite useful, it is not surprising to find that the bat extracts it, and has a portion of its cortex devoted to a CF–CF map. In it positive Doppler shifts (corresponding to an approaching target) are particularly well represented (Suga and Kanwal 1995: 345). In that region the variations in Doppler shift produced by the fluttering wings of the insect may also be registered.

The FM portion of the works adds something else that is new: *range-finding*.

Since the bat is both emitting a signal and detecting its echo, if the loop could be timed, the range to target could be extracted directly. For each millisecond added to that loop, add 17 centimetres to the distance, since in that millisecond sound can travel 17 centimetres and back. If one wants to detect insects as far away as 3 metres, one needs to measure echo delays of up to 18 milliseconds. (The duration of the delay sets the 'horizon' for this submodality.) The same mechanism used to detect interaural time differences can be pressed into service here: delay lines. These measure the delay between the onset of the burst heading out and the return of its echo, and the intervals are milliseconds, not microseconds.

For sonar, an FM signal works better than a CF signal. The broad-band character of the former can help resolve phase ambiguities, as noted above. It also allows the auditory system to exploit its tonotopic organization, and make multiple computations of range at different frequencies, further reducing ambiguity (see Suga and Kanwal 1995: 346). In fact range-finding in the moustached bat is exclusively a function of the FM portions of the bat's auditory system. Neurons in those channels can be tuned to respond only to FM signals, so that the CF signals do not interfere. Delay lines with the appropriate properties have been found within the FM_1 channel. Multiple delay lines (of up to 18 milliseconds) in FM_1 receive the outgoing signal, and wend their way to coincidence detectors in the medial geniculate body (MGB). FM_1 is the perfect channel to delay, since the bat hears it primarily by bone conduction, and very little FM_1 energy returns as an echo, so the delayed signal of the outgoing pulse is not confused with incoming echoes. Those echoes when they return to FM_2, FM_3, or FM_4 are fed without delay to the same coincidence detectors. They compare the delayed FM_1 signal to the undelayed FM_2, FM_3, or FM_4 signals of the echo. Such FM–FM neurons have been found. They will fire most vigorously for the delay line which best puts the two waveforms into register. The distance to the target is directly correlated to that delay, which has by this mechanism been registered by place-coding in the MGB.

How good is the range-finding acuity of this system? The mere fact that the bat can discriminate the shapes of different insects indicates that it must have pretty good temporal resolution: each millisecond is roughly 17 centimetres for this system, yet here it is detecting differences among the shapes of insects that might be just a centimetre long. We can ask a variant of the 'two point' threshold question for touch: how close must two points be before they cannot be discriminated as two? J. A. Simmons has investigated this question using several different tests. The basic experimental procedure for the tests has been increasingly refined since Simmons (1979). A bat is trained to stand on a platform in an anechoic chamber and emit shrieks into a microphone.[10] The sounds are digitized and filtered under computer control, delayed for a precise interval of a few milliseconds, then played back to the bat through one or another of a pair of ultrasonic speakers standing several metres in front of the bat. Needless to say, the bat is something of an audiophile, and so the speakers must be rather special ones, to handle frequencies up to 120,000 hertz. The delays are adjusted so that in each trial the sounds when they come out of the left speaker have one sort of delay characteristic, and when they come out of the right speaker they have a very slightly different one. For example, in one trial we might always present sounds through the left speaker with a constant delay of 3.67 milliseconds, so that to the bat it seems as if there is some object about 60 centimetres in front of it, producing the echo. (As with the barn owl, the bat is in effect responding to merely virtual auditory objects: to the appearances as of an object to the left, 60 centimetres away.) In the right speaker in that trial we might present the playback with a delay of 3.67 milliseconds, plus a second echo at 3.68 milliseconds. Or perhaps we present a single playback with a 3.66 millisecond delay. And so on. In a series of shaping trials the bat is taught which one of the two signals to identify as the target—the compound echo, the closer one, etc. Then in the experimental trials the location of the target is varied randomly from left to right. The bat's task is to indicate which of the two—left or right—is the target. The bat shrieks as many times as it wants in each direction, then indicates its choice by hopping to the left or right edge of the platform. If it identified the target correctly, it gets a mealworm; if not, more training trials.

The differences between the delay characteristics can be very precisely controlled over multiple parameters. We continue trials with the differences set at some level until the bat's performance reaches a plateau: it might be wrong in 10 per cent of the trials, but that error rate is constant, and shows no sign of decreasing further. At that point we decrease the differences between the two stimuli and try again. We keep doing this until the bat's error rate is 50 per cent, and it is doing no better than chance in its discriminations. With this basic design Simmons attacked the question: how small a difference, of what sorts, can the bat reliably detect? Various sorts of differences between delay characteristics could be explored.

The simplest is 'clutter interference', in which the bat is tested for its ability to discriminate between a presentation of a pair of stimuli *a* and *b*, and presentation of just *b* alone. In both cases *b* is presented with the same delay;

---

[10] It should be noted that Simmons and Suga studied different species of FM echolocating bats. Simmons studied brown bats, Suga moustached bats. Their echolocation capacities differ somewhat. Simmons notes that he retrieved many of his bats from attics of houses in Rhode Island and Massachusetts.

in the pair *a* precedes it by an interval δt. How close do *a* and *b* need to be before they cannot readily be discriminated from *b* alone? Simmons reports results in terms of the echo delay time separating the two points. Error rates in the discrimination rise to 25 per cent when the two are separated by intervals as small as ±350 microseconds. This interval

defines a region of time within which neural representations of echoes *a* and *b* must coexist in the same format so that the arrival of one echo obscures the presence of the other. In effect, waveforms of two echoes that arrive within about 350 μsec of each other are combined into a single compound echo, so that the presence of the second echo is masked by the first. In terms of the bat's sonar receiver, the width of this clutter-interference window is the integration time for echo reception (Simmons *et al.* 1989), but it also is about the duration of individual neural discharges within the bat's auditory system, which are several hundred microseconds wide. (Simmons 1996: 235)

In 350 microseconds sound travels about 12 centimetres, so this already is pretty accurate range-finding. But in fact it is the crudest of the discriminations; other tests reveal even better temporal resolution in the bat's auditory system. For example, an insect a few centimetres long will typically produce a double echo, as the sound reflects off different parts of its body, with a very small delay between the two echo components. Since the bat can discriminate among insects, perhaps it can discriminate among components of these closely spaced echoes. How far apart must double echoes be for the bat to detect that they are something other than a single echo? The answers range from 2 to 10 microseconds (Modgans and Schnitzler 1990; Simmons *et al.* 1989). In 10 microseconds sound travels barely 3.4 millimetres.

The test which reveals the best acuity is 'echo delay acuity', in which the bat is tested for its ability to discriminate between two stimuli, one of which is presented after a fixed delay *b*, and the other which alternates between two intervals, one of $b - \delta t/2$, and the other of $b + \delta t/2$. (So if *b* is 3.67 milliseconds, and in a given trial we have reached a δt of 10 microseconds, the target jitters between two echo components, one with a delay of 3.675 milliseconds and the other with a delay of 3.665.) The interval δt is centred on the fixed delay *b*. We gradually decrease δt until the bat cannot reliably discriminate between the stimulus with the fixed delay and the jittery pair. In this paradigm the interval δt between the two points can become unbelievably small. For example, if *b* is a fixed echo delay of 3 milliseconds, the bat can readily detect changes in echo delay of less than 0.5 microseconds—500 *nanoseconds*, or billionths of a second. Earlier experiments ran aground because the computers were not fast enough to time such intervals accurately. In one paradigm Simmons tested limiting acuity. Under optimal conditions the bat can make the discrimination successfully 75 per cent of the time with a δt of 10 to 15 nanoseconds. Even with noise introduced it can still perceive jitters as small as 40 nanoseconds (Simmons 1996: 233). This is the timescale on which we measure the speed of memory chips in a digital computer. In 10 nanoseconds a beam of light travels less than 10 metres; sound moves a few microns. Yet it seems the bat can discriminate two echoes as two if they have a difference in echo delay times as small as 15 nanoseconds.

From these results we can draw some strong inferences. If the FM–FM lines were used just for range-finding, there would be no need for such acuity. The bat typically uses its tail flap or a wing to scoop up its target, and for that task it does not need such fine spatial resolution. Yet it appears to possess auditory spatial acuity that can resolve distances of less than a millimetre. One hypothesis that could make sense of this endowment is that it is using this 'range-finding' also to discriminate among the *shapes* of the insects it pursues. Such shape discrimination would help the bat discriminate edible insects (or particularly tasty insects) from the others. That would require discriminations of less than a millimetre (Simmons *et al*. 1990*b*: 463). Insect body parts shaped differently and arrayed at different distances yield echoes with different components at different times. A particular insect has discrete reflecting points, or 'glints', along the target range. If those parts are spread out sufficiently, a sound wave striking them will produce a double echo that a bat might be able to discriminate from a single echo. Simmon's tests show that the bat can indeed make such discriminations, and that the 'spreading out' does not need to be extensive: an echo delay of 10 to 15 nanoseconds will do.

But this result leaves a large question unanswered. Fifteen nanoseconds is the delay between the beginning of the first echo and the beginning of the second, but of course the echoes overlap thereafter. Double echoes can be discriminated from single ones, but this discrimination might proceed on the basis of detection of the discrete onset times, or it might depend on the difference in 'spectral coloration' caused by the overlap of the two echoes (see Simmons 1996: 236). Can we distinguish between the two? That is '*Does the bat perceive the target as having components located at different ranges along a psychological scale of depth, or does the bat just perceive the echo as different in some spectral quality analogous to timbre?*' (Simmons and Chen 1989: 1348). Put 'in broader terms, what are the psychological dimensions of the images FM bats perceive?' (Simmons *et al*. 1990*b*: 450). This is a question of *how* the bat perceives the double echo: on what basis it discriminates double echoes from single ones. Has the bat 'perceived the filtered echoes as though the target contained two glints' (Simmons *et al*. 1990*b*: 468) or does it 'identify the shape from the spectral coloration of the double echo caused by interference . . . as an auditory quality of a more abstract nature (coloration or timbre)' (Simmons 1996: 236)?

About this question there is some debate. Earlier reports supported the hypothesis that double echoes were discriminable because of their differing 'spectral coloration'. For example, Menne *et al.* concluded, 'After analysing experiments of types 3 and 4, our conclusion was that bats perceive phase jitter as a separate quality independent of their range measurement system . . . perception of "phase" is qualitatively different from that of time delay' (Menne *et al.* 1989: 2649). Whereas Simmons (1996) and Simmons *et al.* (1990*b*) describe ingenious experiments yielding evidence for the rival hypothesis: that the double echoes are perceived as two glints, separated spatially. The system certainly has the temporal resolution needed to do this. The hypothesis is that

Eptesicus perceives images of complex sonar targets that explicitly represent the location and spacing of discrete glints located at different ranges. The bat perceives the target's structure in terms of its range profile along a psychological range axis . . . (Simmons *et al.* 1990*b*: 449)

A distinct glint is 'in effect, a separate object in the bat's perceptions' (Simmons 1996: 247). How does it perceive such glints?

Our working hypothesis is that the formation of acoustic images of targets takes place as a result of the convergence of information from frequency maps, which represent the spectrum of echoes using coordinates of frequency and amplitude, with information from range maps, which represent the delay of echoes using coordinates of time and amplitude. . . . We presume that the conversion of echo spectral information back into range information occurs because frequency maps can 'talk to' range maps, most likely at the level of the auditory cortex. (Simmons *et al.* 1990*b*: 464)

The result is that the bat 'ultimately expresses the acoustic image of the target along a single perceptual axis which corresponds directly to the natural spatial dimension of the distance or range over which the target is distributed' (Simmons *et al.* 1990*b*: 468).

We can draw one more strong inference. Although this theoretical dispute cannot be settled or even adequately described here, the citations are sufficient for us to notice something about the language in which it is cast. That language has moved overtly into the territory of phenomenology. It might be hard to notice this, because of the exertions needed to keep up with the new discipline. But we are indeed describing how the bat perceives these dimensions of variation: what it perceives them *as*. It perceives the echo as though it has glints at different distances. The separate echoes are perceived *as* separate objects in the image, not as a distinct auditory quality or as 'spectral coloration'. The bat represents the glints as at different depths. And remember that all of these 'objects' are, from the very beginning, phenomenal objects. The experiment does not put any real object 60 centimetres in front of the bat to produce an echo. It manipulates conditions to present to the bat an *appearance* as of an object 60 centimetres in front of it. Similarly, Konishi's barn owl is not presented with real mice, but with the appearances of such. It senses only ersatz mice. The 'discrimination task' in both cases is one of discriminating between appearances—appearances of objects that do not exist. Even in this new landscape we should recognize an old friend: phenomenology.

Not only is this phenomenology: it is objective phenomenology. We are describing what it is like to be a bat, but from the outside, in structural terms. The only mistake in Nagel's argument was to conclude that what it is like to be a bat can be known only by a bat (or something like a bat). There is indeed something it is like to be a bat—some way of perceiving, which is perhaps unique to the echolocation modality. But the structural features of that modality can be described, from the outside, even by creatures who do not possess it. They can be described, because *here they have been*. There is no need for a new discipline of objective phenomenology. We already have such a discipline. It is called psychophysics.

4

Sensing and Reference

IN one sense the claim that the sensory processes of pre-linguistic animals such as bats and barn owls refer to space-time regions is almost trivial, since it is a trivial consequence of the claims that those sensory processes represent features at place-times and that such representations are evaluable as true or false, or (at least) correct or incorrect. If a token is subject to semantic evaluation—if it can be assessed as true or false, correct or incorrect—then it must in this sense 'refer' to whatever needs to be identified in its truth conditions. Such reference is not an achievement, capacity, or ability, but a logical consequence of any claim to truth. If Bertie has a visual experience as of a pointy green spot in his visual field, and the experience is evaluable as correct or incorrect, then in this sense his experience refers to whatever regions in the field of view those correctness conditions mention.

But in another sense, 'identification' and 'reference' stand for capacities exercised by speakers and hearers in the course of their attempts to communicate. We talk of datable occasions of speakers referring and of hearers grasping the reference. Success in identifying happens some times and not other times. It depends on whether the users exercise their capacities, and sometimes the effort is half-hearted, or the work is skipped altogether. It may take a struggle to learn that by 'it' Bertie means his after-image, and sometimes the struggle is not worth it. Only in this sense, in which there can be varying capacities of identification, can there be *Varieties of Reference*, or ones that come graded in hierarchies of logico-linguistic types.

What makes the claim that sensation refers to space-time regions less than trivial is the less than trivial character of the claims that it is a system of representation and that those representations are semantically evaluable. The various considerations up to this point have yielded one strand of argument to the effect that sensory processes represent features of place-times identified in or around the body of the sentient organism. This chapter will present a second and entirely independent line of argument to the same conclusion. I will argue that this conclusion follows from other claims we accept already, or at least it does if we accept any sort of causal theory of the phenomena of 'direct reference'—most centrally the reference of demonstratives, but perhaps including

proper names and natural kind terms as well. Causal theories of direct reference require that sensory processes be endowed with specific capacities of
identification. Those capacities are akin to the ones granted to a user of a
simple language. In the course of the proceedings that language will be
described.

4.1 DIRECT REFERENCE

The argument starts from the fact that some simple varieties of reference in
natural language rely on the receipt of appropriate sensory experience; they
do not succeed unless one has immediate sensory contact with the object in
question. Consider, for example, demonstrative identification. Suppose we
want to learn the Oklahoma terms for native Oklahoma fauna, and to do so
we travel to the Oklahoma savannah—the tall grass prairie—and hire a guide.
As we sit, watching the tall grass waving in the endless wind, our guide
gestures and says 'That is a prairie dog.' A moment later, 'That is a prairie
chicken.' We want to walk away knowing what is a prairie dog and what is a
prairie chicken, and as you might guess, these are not peculiar varieties of
dogs or chickens that happen to live in Oklahoma. (A prairie dog is a species
of marmot—a member of the same genus as woodchucks—and a prairie
chicken is a species of grouse.) How might such demonstrative identifications
succeed?

   Everyone admits that one prominent route relies upon some variety of
direct sensory confrontation with the target. Sir Peter Strawson, for example,
says

A sufficient, but not necessary, condition of the full requirement's being satisfied is—
to state it loosely at first—that the hearer can pick out by sight or hearing or touch, or
can otherwise sensibly discriminate, the particular being referred to, knowing that it
is that particular. . . . I shall say, when this first condition for identification is satisfied,
that the hearer is able *directly to locate* the particular referred to. We may also speak
of these cases as cases of the *demonstrative identification* of particulars. (Strawson
1963: 6)

Strawson rightly presumed that a fuller characterization could someday be
given of the capacities of sensible discrimination and of 'direct location', and
that with it one could explain how those capacities secure the reference of the
demonstrative. Gareth Evans (1982) started the process of filling out this
characterization, suggesting that there must be an 'on-going information-link'
to the object in question, on the basis of which the hearer is able to locate it.
The literature burgeoned from there. Demonstratives provide the closest and
simplest connection between language and world, and that connection can be

secured through sensation. Instead of focusing on what such phenomena
show us about language, however, I propose to look in the opposite direction,
and focus on what they show us about sensory processes. The literature
burdens those processes with various tasks and responsibilities, and the occasional success of demonstrative identification implies that they have the
wherewithal to discharge them. So what do we require of sensation, if sensing can sometimes secure the reference of a demonstrative?

Our guide produced two tokens of the demonstrative pronoun 'that'. They
have differing reference—first to the prairie dog, then to the prairie chicken.
Your task as a tourist is to identify the two referents of the two tokens. Clearly
you could know all the linguistic rules governing the use of demonstrative
pronoun 'that' and still not be able to do this. Those linguistic rules presumably do not change between the first tokening and the second, yet the reference does.

These demonstratives secure reference only if they are accompanied with
what Kaplan calls an 'associated demonstration': 'typically, though not
invariably, a (visual) presentation of a local object discriminated by a pointing' (Kaplan 1989*a*: 490). Some indexical terms, like 'I' and 'now', do not
require anything over and above the context of their utterance to be assigned
a value. Kaplan calls these 'pure indexicals'. Others, like 'this' and 'that', and
directly referential uses of pronouns such as 'he' or 'she', can only be
assigned a referent if an extra-linguistic 'demonstration' accompanies the
utterance. 'Here' sometimes serves as a pure indexical, as in 'I am here now',
but in all our feature-placing examples ('here it tickles, there it hurts', etc.)
the demonstrative cannot be assigned a referent—a 'demonstratum'—without
an associated demonstration.

In Kaplan's original account, a demonstration has two components: some
variety of sensory presentation or appearance (visual, auditory, or whatever),
and some gesture or other aid to picking out or discriminating the referent of
the demonstrative from all the other items presented. The latter is abandoned
in the afterthoughts (Kaplan 1989*b*: 582) as having no special semantic
significance (though it is an aid to communication); whereas the former
remains essential. Interestingly, demonstrations seem invariably to rely on
phenomenal properties: how things appear, or what is presented. As a 'kind
of standard form for demonstrations' Kaplan (1989*a*: 526) suggests:

The individual that has appearance *A* from here now.

He says: 'A demonstration is a way of presenting an individual,' and continues that it is essential 'that it present its demonstrata from some perspective,
that is, as the individual that looks thusly *from here now*' (Kaplan 1989*a*:
525). We might pick out Hebb's barn as the one that looks red when viewed

from this ridge at sunset, even though it only looks red because of the character of the light at sunset—perhaps Hebb has not painted it in twenty years. Sometimes the picking-out or selecting of an individual from the panoply of appearance is a trivial matter. At rosy-fingered dawn we might hear a solitary bird commence to cheep. 'That's an Eastern Towhee' picks out the song (and thereby the bird) without any of the pointing or gesturing that will be required later, when the other birds wake up. But the demonstration *always* requires some sensory confrontation with the demonstratum. These 'perceptual demonstratives' (so labelled in Kaplan 1989*b*: 582) require that the demonstratum be perceived, and, if other items are perceived at the same time, that it be discriminated from those other items.

How do demonstrative identifications succeed? You need somehow to pick out the referent for 'that'. Evidently the identification relies on capacities that are extra-linguistic. The associated demonstration succeeds only if you *see*—or somehow perceive—*what* the guide is talking about. If you are blind, distracted, or looking in the wrong direction, for instance, the guide's utterances will be totally ineffectual. But even if you have normal vision, and you are looking attentively at the waving grasses, the identification still fails unless you can see *which* of the simultaneously visible items the guide is attempting to identify on your behalf. Prairie chickens in particular can be hard to spot. You might be looking straight at it but fail to discern it among the hummocks. A minimal condition for success at picking out the target is that you can discriminate or distinguish, among the simultaneously visible regions, some that are currently occupied by prairie chicken and some that are not. This condition does not necessarily require a sharp visible border between them, but if you cannot make any such distinction—any distinction between regions occupied by prairie chicken, and regions that are not—then clearly you have not picked out what the guide is trying to identify, and the demonstrative identification will fail. Seeing an undifferentiated blur of co-present items will not suffice. 'I do not see what you mean,' you might say. You must discriminate among those items, and see *which* one the guide means.

Not only are some such sensory processes necessary for the success of the demonstrative identification, but in some cases they are sufficient: they make the difference between success and failure. With all the other stage-setting fixed, these sensory processes can secure the identification. They assign the demonstrative a value. Suppose you are having trouble picking out the prairie chicken. The guide can of course provide descriptions that help you see what he means. He might say, 'Do you see the three hummocks with the rock on the left? Ten feet in front of them is something that looks like a shadow. That is a prairie chicken.' But this description does not itself provide you the wherewithal to use the term appropriately thereafter. It only works if it helps you to *see* which thing is the prairie chicken. If you see it, then and only then do you understand what the guide's demonstrative 'that' refers to, and only then do you learn the reference of the term 'prairie chicken'. So it is those visual processes—seeing *which* or seeing *what*—that make the difference. Your on-going sensory discrimination of the object secures the reference of the demonstrative.

But sensory processes can in this way secure an identification only if they themselves have some capacity to identify. If extra-linguistic processes can assign the demonstrative a value, they must have it within themselves to pick out that value, and hand it over. Ergo, these extra-linguistic systems have capacities of identification akin to those found in the referential apparatus of a language. In fact the referential character of some elements of the language—the perceptual demonstratives—depends upon those capacities.

One way to put this: the identification 'That is a prairie chicken' works only if we know what 'that' refers to. The latter shifts disconcertingly even while the rules of the language stay constant. So we hand over the question 'What does "that" refer to?' to some underlings—our sensory processes—and sometimes they come back with an answer. 'Here is the referent for that,' they might say—if they could talk. The route they provide to the identification is extra-linguistic: an 'alternative road to reference' (see Kaplan 1989*b*: 578). As Ruth Millikan puts it:

The pointing finger is understood only if what it points *at* is visible or otherwise independently identifiable. Or suppose it is the job of 'that' to point out a direction, 'that way'. . . . The interpreter must be able independently to *identify* that direction, not necessarily with a name ('east', 'west'), but, say, via an ability to track it, to know what it would be to continue following that selfsame direction, as opposed to turning away from it. To know what an indexical indexes, to identify the indexed, requires that one have a *second* route to thinking of it, a route other than the indexical token, and that one grasp this second route *as* one arriving at the same referent. (Millikan 1993*c*: 271)

The suggestion is that our sensory underlings cannot provide such a route unless they have the capacity to identify or at least contribute to identifying the target.

What this contribution might be will be detailed in the next section. But I should note immediately that the kinship between sensory reference and the linguistic varieties might be a distant one. The capacities of the underlings are similar to those of language-users who can refer to things, but perhaps minimally so. I think the required capacities might be as minimal as simply discriminating between differently occupied regions of space—between, for example, regions occupied by prairie chicken and regions that are not.

Typically, though, your success in such endeavours is rather more secure. Not only can you discriminate chicken-occupied regions from others, but you might see the outline of the animal, and discern its shape and size. Visual processes of edge detection, segmentation, grouping, and size and shape constancy all kick in; you see that region *as* a bounded volume having a particular shape and size. This is typical, and helpful, but not necessary: the identification can succeed even if one cannot pick out the precise borders of the target or discern its shape. The target may *lack* precise borders, size, or shape. Consider terms for mountain features such as 'col' and 'couloir', 'cirque' and 'cornice'. Such features have no edges and no particular shape or size. But you might hire a guide to go climbing and teach you how to recognize them. Success with 'That's a col' entails some minimal ability to discriminate regions that clearly are cols from regions that clearly are not. Notice this does not imply the existence of a sharp border. Such spatial discrimination is sensory, and it is sometimes sufficient to secure the identification. So it seems fair to speak of sensory identification.

Demonstrative identification is in some ways the simplest variety. But if you accept any version of a causal theory of reference, the moral of our story about spotting the prairie chicken can be generalized, perhaps alarmingly.

According to the causal theory, the reference of a designator is established by a causal connection between the term and the referent itself. The connection can become remote and indirect, as subsequent users of the term pick up its use and pass it on to others. But ultimately even such chains of assisted reference must be 'grounded' in the object itself. ('Grounding' is the term used by Devitt 1981.) It is very interesting to think about what has to happen for such a grounding to take place. The paradigm is a 'baptism', or an introduction of a new proper name in the presence of the person or thing named. Kaplan (1973, 1989*a*: 560) calls these 'dubbings', and notes that demonstratives are vital to the process. More broadly, for natural kind terms, reference is secured only if one can trace the reference back to some episode in which an instance of that kind is present and can be identified demonstratively. One might learn how to use a sortal by a demonstrative identification of an instance. In these cases of direct reference, as with perceptual demonstratives themselves, we trace the chain back to some direct face-to-face perceptual encounter with the referent of the designator. Something has to happen during that encounter sufficient to fix the reference of that designator to that referent. What has to happen? Here's what Devitt says:

In a grounding a person perceives an object, preferably face to face . . . The grounding consists in the person coming to have 'grounding thoughts' about that object as a result of the act of perceiving the object. A grounding thought about an object is one which a speaker of a public language would express using a demonstrative from that language . . . However, I see no reason to deny that beings which do not speak public languages could have grounding thoughts. If they do have them, then they must have appropriate mental representations. Call all these representations of the object in grounding beliefs 'demonstrative representations'. The act of perception leading to these representations defines a mode of presenting the object. It leads to an ability to designate made up of these grounding thoughts. (Devitt 1981: 133)

These 'demonstrative representations' are *required* for the grounding to succeed; without them the name fails to gain a reference. Devitt describes the naming of his cat Nana:

The chain underlying my first use of 'Nana' begins with Nana at her naming ceremony; it runs through my perception of that ceremony; from then on it is my ability thus gained to use 'Nana' to designate her. (Devitt 1981: 29)

The grounding 'runs through' the *perception* of the thing named. Suppose chains of indirect and assisted reference for proper names and natural kind terms are all ultimately grounded in face-to-face perceptual encounters with the objects designated, and those chains must 'run through' particular demonstrative representations caused in the language-user by those encounters. All subsequent reference depends upon those demonstrative representations. Their perception of the baptism gives attendees the power thereafter to use the new name to designate, and to pass that ability along to others.

But now it is hard to see how those grounding representations could do their job if they themselves failed to identify what is designated. And notice that these mental representations are by hypothesis extra-linguistic. It would be fatal to the theory if one had to know a language in order to have the requisite grounding representations. So on this account, direct reference ultimately relies upon some extra-linguistic capacities to pick out what is meant.

The ability to designate might be grounded minimally in the capacity to discriminate between regions occupied by the referent in question and others simultaneously present that are not so occupied. In short, the grounding might proceed through feature-placing. It probably requires nothing more than feature-placing for terms such as 'col', 'cornice', and 'couloir', or other terms for morphological or geographical features. Such spatio-temporal discrimination is sensory, and it is sometimes sufficient to secure the identification. What I have called sensory identification reduces to these capacities of spatio-temporal discrimination.

4.2 SENSATION AND DEMONSTRATIVES

I have yet to describe *how* sensory processes might secure, or contribute to securing, the reference of a demonstrative. Understanding the sensory end of a demonstrative identification will also help us understand the sense in which sensory processes are endowed with capacities to identify.

It bears emphasis that our quarry lies on the sensory side of these episodes, and so we will examine only those subsets of demonstratives and of episodes of demonstrative identification that cast light in the requisite direction. By no means should the discussion be interpreted as an attempt to provide a comprehensive analysis of demonstratives! Instead our brief could be limited to just one or two *particular* episodes of extra-linguistic demonstration. How do they help assign a demonstratum to a perceptual demonstrative?

Suppose the task is to identify which of the currently visible items is a prairie chicken and which is a prairie dog. What Gareth Evans (1982: 107) called a 'fundamental ground of difference' of an object at a time is that which distinguishes it from all other objects of the same kind at that time. A 'fundamental identification' or 'fundamental Idea' is one which correctly attributes a fundamental ground of difference to an object. Space-time location can provide one. To account for the productive character of thought about an object, Evans says,

an Idea of an object would need either to be a fundamental identification of that object, or to consist in a knowledge of what it is for an identity proposition involving a fundamental identification to be true. In the case of a spatio-temporal particular, this means that an adequate Idea of an object involves either a conception of it as the occupant of such-and-such a position (at such-and-such a time), or a knowledge of what it is for an object so identified to be the relevant object (or, equivalently, what it is for the relevant object to be at a particular position in space and time). (Evans 1982: 149)

Conceiving of the object as *the* occupant of such-and-such a space-time region can yield a fundamental identification of that object. A fundamental ground on which our tourist can differentiate the prairie chicken from the prairie dog and all other simultaneously visible items is that the prairie chicken is the occupant of one place-time, and the prairie dog the occupant of another.

Demonstrative identification could provide a 'fundamental identification' of an object by identifying a place-time such that the object in question is the only one of its kind to occupy that place-time. This is what 'direct location' of an object in Evans (and in Strawson) comes down to: individuation by location. Demonstrative identification requires perception of the object in question because, Evans says, it requires an 'on-going information-link' between the subject and the object in question. Furthermore 'in the standard cases, not only is there an information-link, but also the subject can, upon the basis of that link, *locate the object in space*' (Evans 1982: 150). With this my account so far is in complete agreement. Evans goes on to describe conditions sufficient to ascribe the ability to locate the object in space, and I agree too that those conditions are sufficient. But what work since his book has shown is that less may also suffice. In particular these 'abilities to locate' might be significantly more primitive than Evans suggested. There exists a capacity to locate features that can fairly be characterized as sensory. It does not rely on a 'cognitive map', on capacities to reason spatially, or on adequate Ideas of what it is to identify a place in egocentric space with a place in public space. It is prior to the locating of objects. In fact the sensory 'placing' of features must precede, and provide the wherewithal for, all these capacities.

Evans describes the ability to locate the object in space as a sophisticated cognitive achievement.

We now have to enquire what makes such Ideas of places in egocentric space adequate Ideas of positions in *public* space. Such an Idea, p, is adequate provided the subject can be credited with a knowledge of what it would be for $\lceil \pi = p \rceil$ to be true—where π is a stand-in for an arbitrary *fundamental*, and hence holistic, identification of a place. (Evans 1982: 162)

Shifting into this gear engages various high-level capacities. One must be able to find one's way about in the world, to discover where one is, and to engage in various kinds of reasoning in using a map.

It is, then, the capacity to find one's way about, and to discover, or to understand how to discover, where in the world one is, in which knowledge of what it is for identity propositions of the form $\lceil \pi = p \rceil$ to be true consists. (Evans 1982: 162)

The subject needs a 'cognitive map' of relations among places, and an understanding of what it is for a place in egocentric space to be a place in such a map. The map is accurately described as 'cognitive': it is independent of any sensory modality and any egocentric axes. Subjects must be able to locate themselves on such maps and reason spatially with them. They must be able to think of their spatial relations to objects as instances of the same relations that those objects bear to one another (Evans 1982: 163).

Clearly these conditions are sufficient to ascribe to the subject the requisite ability to locate the object in space, but perhaps they are more than sufficient. Less may suffice. The strategy is to exploit location in space as the fundamental ground of difference of an object. Strictly all that is required is a location that serves to individuate. If one manages to identify a place-time such that the object in question is *the* occupant of that place-time, then the demonstrative identification is secured. What I will argue can be readily anticipated: that sensory processes are perfectly fitted on their own to identify the requisite place-times.

First, it might be useful to give some examples of how demonstrative identification might succeed in a lower gear, in the absence of the rather sophisticated capacities that Evans describes.

(1) *The Arkansas funny house*. Suppose I recognize the name Webster Hubbell, but I have no idea what the man looks like. One day I get lost in a house of mirrors in a carnival in Arkansas. I am totally disoriented and don't know how to get out. Then in a mirror I see a face appear momentarily, and my companion says 'That's Webster Hubbell!' The miscreant ducks out of view. Neither of us knows exactly where in public space Mr Hubbell is standing, because of the confusing mirrors, but nevertheless after spotting his impassive visage I can thereafter identify the man when I see him standing outside the courthouse or being led away to jail.

(2) *Sortals in the funny house*. Same scene, but now I am presented such Arkansas items as armadillos, prairie dogs, prairie chicken, chicken fried steak, etc. My guide tells me what is what. Even though I do not have adequate Ideas of where these things are, I can learn the use of the terms. I might have no idea of where the armadillo is and where the prairie dog is, but I know that this one is the prairie dog and that that one is the armadillo.

(3) *Parietal damage*. Destruction of parietal cortex can lead to selective loss of abilities to orient and read maps, even though all sensory capacities seem untouched. This is one of the most astounding of neuropsychological syndromes (see Luria 1973; Kolb and Whishaw 1985). Suppose I lose that portion of my nervous system, and now get lost on the ward, lose my way when heading back to my bed, etc. I cannot draw a diagram of the room, use a map, or even read a clock. Nevertheless, I become quite good at identifying birds and trees out in the grounds of the institution.

(4) *The whisky drinker* (see Evans 1982: 161). Perhaps I know my bottle of whisky is *there* by the side of the bed, even though I don't know what room I am in, where the walls are, where *there* is relative to the door of the room, etc. But I can smell my bottle there and successfully reach out and grab it, even as the room keeps spinning.

(5) *The whisky drinker with parietal damage*. My career continues downhill. Now I lack the capacity ever to learn what are the spatial relations between the foot of the bed, the door of the room, the front of the house, etc. Nevertheless, I still know where my bottle is.

(6) *Creeping apraxia*. Due to brain damage my hand–eye coordination is now almost entirely destroyed. I cannot safely pour whisky into a glass, pick up a gun, etc. Dispositions to guide my behaviour visually are all awry, and perhaps I even stop trying. The attendants push me around in a wheelchair. Nevertheless, I can learn what an electroshock

machine is if someone points it out to me. This device, the one that I am now being strapped to, is an electroshock machine.

(7) *More dignified animals.* Barn owls or bats can identify the place of the prey even if they have no Thoughts, no reasoning, etc. Does the barn owl grasp the notion that it too is an object, located in and moving through the same space in which it hears the mouse? Must it formulate an adequate fundamental Idea before it can catch its dinner? I do not see why it must. (Of course if any spatial navigation ability counts as 'spatial reasoning', then the animals qualify as exemplary reasoners. The green sea turtle, who navigates across 3,000 miles of open sea, would be a master. But why call this reasoning?)

The last of these deserves elaboration. As seen above (Section 3.6), the bat has a truly astounding ability to identify the location of its targets, even if it does so entirely in egocentric terms. It might identify an auditory location as one that yields an FM–FM time lag of ρ, an intensity difference between the two ears of δ, and a phase difference of τ. Each of these differentiative properties is egocentric, making essential reference to the ears of the bat or to the delay lines with which it times phase differences and the receipt of echoes. Nevertheless, the triplet is true of just one place, one space-time region of finite extent, centred on a depth, elevation, and azimuth that yields the coordinates (ρ, δ, τ). That is the apparent source of the echo: the place-time whence it appears. (The temporal element is prominent. Presumably in its manœuvres the bat must take into account the fact that a place-time represented as further away is also older. In fact its tactics—and those of the moth as well—change as the distance narrows. See Fenton 1995; Simmons *et al.* 1995.) Perhaps the bat has *only* such egocentric specifications at hand. Perhaps it lacks the resources to conceive of allocentric space or to understand what it would mean for a place it identifies egocentrically to be identical to a place in such a space. But does this imply that the bat cannot identify place-times? Hardly. Or at least, if it does, it does so in a sense which offers no consolation to the moths in the vicinity.

If any of the examples succeed, they provide cases in which the subject lacks a cognitive map, lacks a unified notion of allocentric space, lacks an adequate Idea of what it is for $\lceil \pi = p \rceil$ to be true, or lacks the various reasoning capacities Evans suggests as necessary for demonstrating competence with a cognitive map, yet nevertheless succeeds in identifying the particular that the speaker has in mind. So perhaps less is required than Evans thought for a hearer to be able to 'locate an object in space'.

Here is how sensation-based identification might proceed. Demonstrative identification has two components, only one of which is strictly sensory. They are:

(*a*) the sensory identification of a place-time, and
(*b*) the individuation of the object in question on the basis of its occupation of that place-time.

All the sensory system does is pick out a place-time. That region need not be precisely coextensive with the object in question; it may include only a portion of it. But for the demonstrative identification to succeed, one must identify a place-time occupied by only one object of the kind in question. Sensation lacks sortals and count nouns, so it cannot attest to the satisfaction of the latter condition, but it is still a requirement. If our guide says 'That is Webster Hubbell' but two people are visible in the region indicated, then iden-tification fails. 'That is a prairie chicken' fails if there is more than one candi-date in the region specified. Securing (*a*) without (*b*) would pick out a place-time, but fail to individuate on its basis.

Many feature terms lack criteria of numeric identity and have only vague criteria of application. For such terms there is a range of instances to which the term definitely applies, and a range of instances to which it definitely does not apply, but in between it may be unclear what to say. Colours provide a prime example: some things we see are clearly red, and others clearly orange, but the exact border between the two is unclear. In between the paradigms we get increasing variability and inconstancy of judgements. Rosch (1973) suggested a basic scheme of paradigms and distance from paradigms that can accommodate such variability. Perhaps we have prominent landmarks or paradigm points in colour space, and a metric that orders the surrounding colours in terms of relative similarity. There is no sharp border between 'red' and 'orange', but as distance from the paradigm (or focal point) in colour space increases, eventually the probability of applying the term 'red' falls off, and the probability of applying other terms increases. One can find regions between foci about which a single respondent, queried repeatedly, will make contrary judgements. Sometimes it is called red, sometimes orange. But as one pulls out of these borderlands, the tug of attraction towards one or another paradigm increases, and variability drops.

I suggest that demonstrative identifications such as 'That is a col' or 'That is a knee' may succeed by referring to a region of space—the region occupied by col or knee respectively. The need to pick out a region explains why it is often so important for the speaker to look directly at the target and to point or otherwise gesture at it, and why the hearer must be able to determine the direction of gaze of the speaker or discern the target of the pointing. Now consider demonstratives for features that lack clear spatial boundaries:

That is a col; this is a cornice.
That is a knee; this is a shin.

Almost the same mechanism that works for colour terms could be applied to
these. That is, there are regions that are very definitely knee or very definitely
shin, surrounding regions that are highly likely to be considered knee or shin,
and finally more remote regions about which one is not sure what to say. With
colour terms we need a paradigm and an ordering of similarity in which
greater distance corresponds to greater dissimilarity. With terms such as 'col'
or 'knee' we have a physical focal point, and physical distance from it.
Perhaps the focal point for 'knee' is the centre of the axis of rotation. Regions
near it are definitely regions occupied by the knee. Surrounding bone and
cartilage are also pretty clearly identifiable as parts of the knee, but as one
moves to points further away or to regions around back it becomes less than
obvious whether the point in question is a point in the knee. The judgements
of respondents become increasingly variable and confused. Foils—or points
definitely not part of the knee—help, as they indicate increasing proximity to
other foci, such as those for shins or thigh. But beyond picking out the focus,
picking out some foils, and learning the probability distribution of judgements in between, there is nothing more exact to learn when one learns to
identify knees. Nevertheless, we all understand the sense of the term sufficiently to be able to evaluate the truth or falsity of claims such as 'He banged
his knee', 'He sat with his hands on his knees', 'No skirts above the knee',
and so on.

'Col' is similar. When one points and says 'That's the col' the region identified is best thought of in terms of a focal point, some foils, and a probability distribution in between. The distribution might be asymmetrical and
anisotropic; it describes probabilities that respondents who speak the
language will assent to the query 'Is this point a point in the col?' Yet for all
that, we can tell when we have reached the col, and when not. If the demonstrative identification 'That is a col' can succeed, then clearly enough sometimes the demonstrative does nothing more than pick out a region of space.

How might sensory identification of a place-time contribute to demonstrative identification? Here is one possibility. In famous demonstratives such as

This is a hand. That is an inkstand,

the underlying identification might be simply

Here is a hand. *There* is an inkstand,

where the 'here' and 'there' identify place-times. Identification of these
place-times proceeds by *sensory* means, relying on mechanisms of spatio-
temporal discrimination similar to those found in the barn owl or the bat. The

demonstrata are assigned by sensory systems. Such a means of identifying places is prior to and independent of the identification of material objects. It does not require facility with a cognitive map, spatial reasoning, or a conceptual scheme of material bodies, but instead the mere sensory capacities to make spatio-temporal discriminations. This would give the demonstrative the overall form

> This (place) is (occupied by) a hand.
> That (place) is (occupied by) an inkstand.

The sensory contribution lies in picking out or selecting space-time regions; as noted, the further condition—that just one object of the given kind occupy that place-time—is one to which they cannot attest.

Clearly the ability to discriminate among differently occupied portions of space is necessary for the successful use of perceptual demonstratives. To understand the demonstratives in the sentences above, the places indicated by 'here' and 'there' must be identified, and in many circumstances the only route available for securing such an identification is sensory. In such a case, understanding the thoughts—the contents—requires capacities of spatial discrimination.

Two minimal ones at least can be described. First, there must be some sensory capacity to identify space-time regions and discriminate among them. Suppose one lacked all such capacity, so that sensation in every modality lacked spatial character. This differs from Strawson's 'No-Space world': it is 'No-Space sensation'. In it one could not understand the difference between 'this' and 'that' or 'here' and 'there'. The demonstratives above would all fail. Secondly, not only must there be some sensory capacity to identify place-times, but in these sorts of cases the capacity must be exercised, so that one distinguishes between some regions that are *P* and some that are not. (This is the prairie chicken condition, generalized.) If in the particular case one could not pick out any such differently occupied regions, then again the demonstrative fails. We would be incapable of assigning a truth value to the sentences above. So understanding the *thoughts* expressed in the sentences

> Here is a hand. There is an inkstand

relies on the *sensory* capacities to pick out, and differentiate between, places 'here' and 'there'. One entombed in No-Space sensation could not grasp these contents. Such is the cost of relying on extra-linguistic mechanisms to secure reference: contents thereafter become vulnerable to extra-linguistic disruptions. As Kaplan (1997: 677–8) says of similar cases, 'linguistic competence is simply insufficient to determine completely the content of what is said'.

On this account, sometimes the work of identification required to secure the reference of a demonstrative can be discharged by sensory systems: the discrimination and picking-out of place-times. As the means are primitive, antedating the conceptual apparatus of reidentifiable material bodies, so the place-times identified are identified only crudely. They may be identified only egocentrically, and indeed only as the places specified by one feature map. This sensory identification of regions is prior to and independent of the conceptual apparatus needed to conceive of an object. If the latter is 'identification' proper, this is 'proto-identification'. But it can be vital to the task of securing the reference of a demonstrative.

Demonstratives seem a mix of more sophisticated components grafted onto a relatively primitive system of identification. The sensory identification of place-times is extra-linguistic, non-conceptual, pre-objective. It is proto-reference: the 'placing' portion of feature-placing. Its referential character is to be unpacked by describing capacities of spatio-temporal discrimination: how sensory mechanisms pick out place-times.

4.3 FEATURE-PLACING LANGUAGES

What Millikan (1984: 239–56) calls the 'act of identifying' can be an act of greater or lesser sophistication, depending on the representational resources wielded by the actor. To identify is in the first sense to pick out or select. The sophistication of the act of picking out or selecting depends on how one represents the range of alternatives and the selection from them. At its most sophisticated, such acts as the identification of the seventh planet, of gravity waves, or of the top quark clearly require that the thing identified be conceived in a particular way. In humbler settings, perhaps you and I both see the same crowd of people coming out of the hearing room, but only you can identify the major donors, the vice-chairman, and the former partner of the Rose law firm. With tutoring I might be able to learn to make such identifications, but a guide dog, even if it sees all the parties equally well, could not. It cannot grasp the concept of campaign contributions. In the mountains both the novice and the guide might have visual states that refer to the same features of the alpine terrain in front of them, but only the guide can identify the bergschrund, the cornice, and the seracs. Instruction would be futile if the novice could not see, and its point is precisely to enable the novice to identify such visible and hazardous features as cornices and crevasses. Finally, both the human and the bat can pick out a moth, but only the human can identify it as Lepidoptera.

The previous section suggested that there is a sensory level of identification of place-times that is more primitive than the identification of three-dimensional material objects. Below our conceptual scheme—underneath the streets, so to speak—we find evidence of this more primitive system. The sensory identification of place-times is independent of the identification of objects; one can place features even though one lacks the latter conceptual scheme. Sensory identifications may proceed entirely in egocentric terms and without the benefit of a natural language. Animals without language exploit them still. For example, as argued above, a bat can pick out the place of the moth using purely egocentric identifiers: as the echo-source yielding such-and-such differences in time lag, phase, and intensity at its two ears. Furthermore, the bat can coordinate its various feature maps in a way that allows it (and us) to identify targets in one map with targets in another. This is a second sense of 'identify': to identify the subject-matter of one representation with that of another. That thing that is fluttering in such a mouth-watering way (on my target identification map) is the very thing that is moving at such-and-such a velocity (on my Doppler shift map), and is found at such a depth (according to my delay map). That the bat turns and dives as it does demonstrates its grasp of these identities. Even if it lacks the wherewithal to think of its target as a reidentifiable material body travelling through the same objective three-dimensional space as it does, nevertheless something is picked out and identified; both we and it have enough to pick out the subject-matter of the representations, and to say that the subject-matter of this representation is the same as of that one.

What I mean by 'sensory identification' is exactly this identification of place-times, preceding independently of and prior to the apparatus of identification of objects. Sensory processes can pick out, select, or identify space-time regions of finite extent. If they could not, many of our demonstrative identifications would fail. Seeing which one, hearing which one, and so on all devolve upon capacities of spatio-temporal discrimination. Sensing sameness of location provides the primal form of identification. Language and world come closest to direct contact in the face-to-face encounters of demonstrative identification. That is also the venue where the rational soul and sensitive soul must meet. The demonstrative is a token of their intercourse.

Sadly, any such colloquy will be rather one-sided. One way to illustrate the primitive character of sensory identification of a place-time is to contrast it with natural language names for places—such as Hyde Park, South Pass, Niagara Falls. A bird flying over might have a visual state which momentarily refers to one of these very places. The referent of its visual state is the referent of our name. But the bird presumably lacks our conceptual scheme of enduring three-dimensional physical objects that stand in observer-independent spatial relations. We would not want to credit the bird with the thought 'There goes Niagara Falls'. The bird's visual system does not operate with identifiers equivalent to any of those names. It uses a simpler system. As Strawson, Evans, and others have argued, the linguistic identification of such places is parasitic on the identification of reidentifiable material particulars. The bird might pick out the very same place-time as 'Niagara Falls' whenever it flies over, but unless we could endow it with such concepts, we cannot equate such sensory identifications with the identification of Niagara Falls. Same reference, but a differing capacity to identify. The bird may lack any adequate Idea of such a place.

It is these capacities to identify that come graded in hierarchies of complexity. The sensory lexicon lacks the terms with which to formulate the notion of an unobserved particular, of numeric identity, of a difference between qualitative and numeric identity, of a space independent of any particular sensory modality, and so on. So sensory identifications will be correspondingly crude. The difficulty in clarifying this suggestion lies in clarifying the sense in which sensory identification is a more primitive and limited system than that found in a typical natural language: the sense in which having a pain in your foot does or does not 'identify' your foot.

One idea that helps tremendously to clarify these claims is Sir Peter Strawson's idea of a 'feature-placing language'. Strawson is well aware that the capacity to identify is not an all-or-none affair, but that it comes graded, in rather intricate hierarchies of levels of complexity. Recall his description of a hierarchy of language types in *Subject and Predicate in Logic and Grammar* (1974). Only at the very top do we have the full resources of the apparatus of individuation found in a human natural language. Nevertheless, in the middle portions of the hierarchy, and even lower, we find capacities and accomplishments that are clearly necessary for full-blown individuation, and in many ways resemble the most sophisticated versions, but which, just as clearly, lack some critical ingredients.

Of particular interest to those of us intrigued by the muck and goo of raw sentience is the language-type at the very bottom of all the hierarchies. This is what Strawson calls a 'feature-placing' language. (See Strawson 1954, 1963: chs. 6 and 7, 1974: 135–8.) Such a language has an extremely simple lexicon, as it includes only indexicals and deictical demonstratives, the present tense of the verb 'to be', and what Strawson calls 'feature' terms. Since the language makes no tense distinctions or distinctions between singular and plural, the verb is actually redundant. Some examples of feature-placing sentences are:

> This is coal. That's gold.
> Snow is falling.
> Now it is raining.
> There is water here.

These demonstratively identify a place, and ascribe to it a feature. Feature-placing sentences name no particulars, and often have the form of a subject-less Lichtenbergian proposition: 'It is raining. It is cold.'

The paradigm example of a feature term is one which names 'some general kind of stuff' (Strawson 1963: 208). Strawson is, famously, interested in the conditions governing the introduction of particulars: objects (of whatever sort) for which we have criteria of identification and (where applicable) reidentification. We can tell one apart from another, and distinguish 'the same one, again' from 'a different one'. Feature-placing languages are for Strawson languages that proceed prior to that introduction. So a feature term cannot identify or presuppose any kind of particular. This rules out all sortals (or count nouns), such as 'finger', 'knee', 'apple', and 'cat', since those terms require the identification and reidentification of particulars. Universals that must be construed as properties of particulars are also forbidden. Allowed are the prototypical mass terms, such as 'gold' and 'water'. Others (such as 'It is raining now' and 'It is cold here') are allowed as long as they presuppose no particulars. Their instances fill space in the way that stuff like water or snow fills space. Interestingly, since 'cold' qualifies (see Strawson 1974: 137), most sensory qualities will as well. None of the following presuppose particulars:

> Thermal perception: it is cold here, it is warm there.
> Texture perception: it is slippery here, it is dry there (icy, scratchy, wet, soft, smooth, etc.).
> Olfaction: it smells acrid here, musty there.
> Audition: it is loud here; it is quiet there.
> Vision: it is bright here, dark there.

Colours and other sensory qualities could be entered in the same list. White may characterize a region in just the same way as snow, cold, slippery, and bright. 'Red here, green there' should be understood, not as attributing properties to particulars, but in this 'primitive, pre-particular' fashion (Strawson 1963: 212).

It is startling to see how much introspective content can be cast in this form. We have not only the Lichtenbergian 'It thinks', but the colloquial 'It hurts' and 'It stinks'. Thanks to Sellars, we also have 'It pinks'. My 'red here, green there' is already in feature-placing form. The sentence demonstratively identifies places and attributes features to those places. The *sensation* of a red triangle next to a green square does something analogous; it picks out places and attributes features to them. But the latter does not require or proceed in a natural language; any creature that can sense a red triangle next to a green square has the requisite representational capacity.

The feature-placing idea is anticipated by several authors. For example, in *An Inquiry into Meaning and Truth* (1962) Russell said

I wish to suggest that 'this is red' is not a subject–predicate proposition, but is of the form 'redness is here'; that 'red' is a name, not a predicate; and that what would commonly be called a 'thing' is nothing but a bundle of coexisting qualities such as redness, hardness, etc. . . . wherever there is, for common sense, a 'thing' having the quality *C*, we should say instead, that *C* itself exists in that place, and that the 'thing' is to be replaced by the collection of qualities existing in the place in question. Thus '*C*' becomes a name, not a predicate. (Russell 1962: 92–3)

In his Carus lectures, Sellars explores in typically exuberant fashion an ontology based on feature-placing:

100 . . . expanses of red would be (to use a word coined by John Wisdom in the early 30s) *reddings*. Thus

> There is an expanse of red over there

would point to

> It reds over there

just as, according to the argument given in Section IV above,

> There is a C♯ing in the corner

points to

> It C♯'s in the corner.

101. Indeed

> There is a rectangular expanse of red over there

would point to

> It rectangularly reds (!) over there

for the former's (noun modifier)–(noun) structure is being construed as a transformation of a depth structure in which what is modified is the verb 'reds', and in which the modifier is, therefore, in the broad grammatical sense, an adverb.

102. We suddenly see that the world we have been constructing is one in which every basic state of affairs is expressed by the use of verbs and adverbs.

103. The idea has fascinating implications. Indeed, we have in barest outline a truly heracleitean ontology. . . . There are no *objects*. The world is an ongoing tissue of goings on. (Sellars 1981*a*: 56–7)

Akins (1996) and O'Leary-Hawthorne and Cortens (1995) would agree: the scheme is 'pre-ontological', in that it posits no objects.

Strawson says that the placing of a feature is the simplest possible analogue for the attribution of a property to an individual. It includes precursors of both reference (to a place) and predication (of a feature). He nowhere uses my 'proto' prefix, but at one point labels these capacities 'pre-referential' and 'pre-predicative' (Strawson 1986: 529). These languages are at the very bottom of the hierarchy of subject–predicate forms. Strawson says:

If any facts deserve, in terms of this picture, to be called ultimate or atomic facts, it is the facts stated by those propositions which demonstratively indicate the incidence of a general feature. These ultimate facts do not contain particulars as constituents but they provide the basis for the conceptual step to particulars. The propositions stating them are not subject–predicate propositions, but they provide the basis for the step to subject–predicate propositions. (Strawson 1963: 218)

Feature-placing sentences do not introduce particulars because they lack the wherewithal to distinguish between 'one' and 'another one' or between 'the same one again' and 'a different one'. They lack negation and all other truth-functional connectives. They make no tense distinctions. Similarly, according to Strawson, the features attributed to places are not properties. Two instances of the same feature are at best qualitatively identical—there is nothing that can distinguish them—but feature-placing languages lack the means to express the idea that there is anything strictly identical in the two instances. And, in any case, they cannot count to two—or to any number. As Strawson says, 'The idea of a property belongs to a level of logical complexity which we are trying to get below' (Strawson 1963: 209). For a civilized Oxbridge philosopher such downward movement—such shucking of complexity—is indeed a struggle, but Strawson has some success.

According to Strawson, these languages do not contain sufficient resources with which to frame notions either of reidentifiable particulars or of properties. They lack the means to introduce the notion of an individual. Feature-placing sentences 'provide [some of] the materials' for the introduction of particulars, but do not (and cannot) themselves make that introduction (Strawson 1954: 244). The difficulties are instructive. The closest we can get to an individual is a locus at which multiple features can be placed: 'The individual instance . . . emerges as a possible location-point for general things other than the feature of which it is primarily an instance' (Strawson 1954: 249–50). Similarly, distinctness of placing underwrites distinctness of instances: 'The considerations which determine multiplicity of placing become, when we introduce particulars, the criteria for distinguishing this *patch of* snow from that, or the first *fall of* snow from the second' (Strawson 1954: 245). Strictly speaking, feature-placing languages are devoid of expressions for the identity relation, but these passages indicate that, as in sensory feature-placing, there must be some capacity to identify places: to identify a locus *as* a common locus of multiple features.

A very similar story might be told about one of Quine's examples. Suppose one sees a white cat facing a dog, bristling. As Quine notes, to say 'white cat' is not just to say white and cat, since the latter conjunction might be satisfied by a white dog facing a bristling cat. Whiteness must characterize the same place-time as bristling felinity. As in our earlier example (Section 2.5), the features must 'coincide or at least amply overlap' (Quine 1992: 4). Conjunction is inadequate ('too loose'), since

It tells us only that the four things are going on in the same scene. We want them all in the same part of the scene, superimposed. It is this tightening that is achieved by subjecting the four-fold conjunction to existential quantification, thus: 'Something is catting and is white and is dog-facing and is bristling'. . . . An object has been posited, a cat. (Quine 1992: 29)

What underwrites this introduction of a particular—this x that is both white and a cat—is ultimately the overlap of features at a place. To use Strawson's memorable metaphor: you put pressure on the idea of a particular, trying to reduce it to its ultimate logical constituents—and at the limit of pressure, it unfolds into a feature-placing fact (Strawson 1963: 219).

But feature-placing languages do not themselves have the resources to formulate notions of reidentifiable particulars or their properties. They lack the wherewithal to introduce individuals. The formulation sounds familiar. In fact if sensory representation in general proceeds by characterizing space-time regions, then sensory representation fits into feature-placing language like a hand in a glove. There could be no more natural expression of how sentience represents. I can now give content to the suggestion that sensory identification is a simpler and cruder system: it has powers and limitations akin to those granted to a user of a feature-placing language. The sentences framed in such a language are generally either true or false, and so they refer, in the formal semantics sense, to whatever one must identify in stating their truth conditions. Feature-placing languages are, in full measure, semantically evaluable. Nevertheless, they grant their users only limited powers of identification.

In fact sensory identification is very close indeed to what could be achieved by the user of a feature-placing language. To frame a language for sensory representation, first restrict the features named to sensory qualities. Restrict the placing of features to those capacities we have for discriminating places. Then, my ancient hominid friend, you are ready to burst into speech.[1]

---

[1] Or at least, all that you lack is speech itself, understood broadly to include capacities to produce and recognize sequences of discrete elements of a combinatorial system. This is by no means a trivial acquisition! The discrete and combinatorial character of linguistic representation is a critical invention, distinguishing it from sensory varieties.

I think the congruence is exciting: working upwards from sensory capacities, and downwards from subject and predicate in logic and grammar, we meet at feature-placing. The representation of features in space is arguably the most sophisticated of sensory capacities. From my point of view, looking up from the muck and the goo of the simplest sentience, such spatial representation is a complex and sophisticated achievement. Yet here it is sitting just below the least sophisticated of linguistic capacities, those sufficient for a feature-placing language. And if we can make that one tiny step, sensation and thought can at last commune. They can share contents.

4.4 SENSE-DATA REVISITED

The sentences 'This is a hand' and 'That is an inkstand' are famous, if not infamous, since they served as something of a launching pad for the theory of sense-data. That theory proposed a very different account of those sentences from the one offered above, and a useful way to clarify some of the features of sensory identification is to contrast feature-placing and sense-data.

Both accounts agree on the need for an apparatus of referring terms when characterizing the facts of sensible appearance. The content of the act of sense requires it. The apparent reference of sensory episodes cannot be analysed away, adverbialized into oblivion, eliminated, or swept under the carpet. But the feature-placing account and the accounts of Moore and Russell differ over the answer to the question '*What* is identified in the act of sense?' I proposed that the demonstratives 'this' and 'that' on some occasions have their values assigned by the sensory picking-out of place-times. The identification is of 'here' and 'there': our familiar physical space-time regions.

Moore and Russell agreed that 'this' and 'that' in these constructions should be treated as referring terms and should not be treated as referring to ordinary material objects. Furthermore, in sentences such as 'That is an inkstand' or 'This is white', the reference of 'this' or 'that' is secured by sensory experience. Having the appropriate sort of experience allows one to pick out the subject-matter of each judgement. But Moore and Russell thought that the demonstrative terms referred to rather extraordinary kinds of objects known as 'sense-data'. For example, Moore said:

When I make such a judgment as 'this inkstand is a good big one'; what I am really judging is 'there is a thing which stands to *this* in a certain relation, and which is an inkstand, and that thing is a good big one'—where '*this*' stands for this presented object. I am referring to or identifying the thing which is this inkstand, if there be such a thing at all, only as the thing which stands to this sense-datum in a certain relation; and hence my judgment, though in one sense it may be said to be about the inkstand, is quite certainly also, in another sense, a judgment about this sense-datum. (Moore 1965*a*: 13)

'This' and 'inkstand' refer to two distinct things, the first being the 'presented object', or sense-datum. Similarly, 'the proposition "that is a penny" is a proposition which is "about" or "refers to" two objects at once, *not* only to one' (Moore 1965*b*: 132). He also calls the former the 'ultimate subject' of the judgement:

When I judge, as now, that That is an inkstand, I have no difficulty whatever in picking out, from what, if you like, you can call my total field of presentation at the moment, an object, which is undoubtedly, in a sense in which nothing else is, *the* object about which I am making this judgment; and yet it seems to me quite certain that of *this* object I am not judging that it is a whole inkstand. (Moore 1965*a*: 9)

Moore was steadfast in his belief that the sense-datum is an object that can be picked out, without difficulty, from the total field of presentation. That belief underlies his famous instructions for the demonstrative identification of a sense-datum. Schematizing slightly:

In order to point out to the reader what sort of things I mean by sense-data, I need only ask him to look at his own right hand. If he does this he will be able to pick out something (and, unless he is seeing double, *only* one thing) with regard to which *P*. Things *of the sort* (in a certain respect) of which this thing is . . . are what I mean by 'sense-data'. (Moore 1993*a*: 128–9)

You look at your hand and *pick out something* satisfying the characterization *P*, and that thing is the sense-datum. The characterization *P* became notorious; it read:

he will see that it is, at first sight, a natural view to take that that thing is identical, not, indeed, with his whole right hand, but with that part of its surface which he is actually seeing, but will also (on a little reflection) be able to see that it is doubtful whether it can be identical with the part of the surface of his hand in question. (Moore 1993*a*: 128)

Moore sincerely thought that this characterization would help the reader 'pick out' a sense-datum. In a similar fashion, a guide in the Oklahoma tall grass prairie might try to help a tourist pick out a prairie chicken (Section 4.1). Moore had no doubt that such sense-data exist; they can, after all, be seen and felt. Like prairie chickens they can occasionally be hard to spot, but the attentive observer will eventually be rewarded.

  Russell also endorsed a very strong account of what can be identified in the act of sense. The demonstratives 'this' and 'that' are not only names; they are the only names:

The only words one does use as names in the logical sense are words like 'this' or 'that'. One can use 'this' as a name to stand for a particular with which one is acquainted at the moment. We say 'This is white'. If you agree that 'This is white', meaning the 'this' that you see, you are using 'this' as a proper name. But if you try to apprehend the proposition that I am expressing when I say 'This is white', you cannot do it. If you mean this piece of chalk as a physical object, then you are not using a proper name. It is only when you use 'this' quite strictly, to stand for an actual object of sense, that it is really a proper name. (Russell 1985: 62)

The 'object of sense' is not a common-sense material object, but a sense-datum, private to one observer. Under the pressure of Russell's arguments, sense-data began to acquire extraordinary properties. They are particulars with which one is acquainted at a moment: 'When I speak of a "sense-datum", I do not mean the whole of what is given in sense at one time. I mean rather such a part of the whole as might be singled out by attention: particular patches of colour, particular noises, and so on' (Russell 1981: 109). These particulars are remarkably evanescent, as they do not retain numeric identity across a blink or a shift in gaze. Acquaintance with such particulars yields knowledge of all their properties. In fact such acquaintance is required to assign a value to any logically proper name, because, as Russell (1985: 62) says, 'you cannot name anything you are not acquainted with'. So demonstratives become the only logically proper names; all other reference is by description.

Moore and Russell (at least in these periods) would agree that in examples such as 'That is an inkstand' or 'This is white' the reference of the demonstrative is secured only if one has the appropriate sensory experience. The feature-placing reading is that in such examples we rely on the sensory identification of a place-time and the presumption that that place-time is occupied by the object or feature in question. For the sense-datum theorist, the demonstratives refer to objects (sense-data) that are present within sensory experience itself, and can be picked out from within the total 'field of presentation'. If one lacks sensory experience altogether, there are no such objects to be had. These objects of sense might be (and in some accounts definitely are) private to each observer. In sense-datum terms the tourists in the tall grass prairie will not know what a prairie chicken is until each is presented a sense-datum that is the referent of the demonstrative pronoun 'that' in a true sentence of the form 'That is a prairie chicken'. The guide's task is not so much to navigate the grasses as to acquaint each tourist with the appropriate sense-datum.

In some passages Moore directly embraces the notion that the reference of a demonstrative pronoun can be secured only if one has the appropriate sort of sensory experience, though his explanation of this connection differs from feature-placing:

Suppose I am seeing two coins, lying side by side, and am not perceiving them in any other way except by sight. It will be plain to everybody, I think, that, when I identify the one as 'This one' and the other as 'That one', I identify them only by reference to the two visual presented objects, which correspond respectively to the one and to the other. (Moore 1965*a*: 13)

Without vision the identification would fail. The reason given is that without vision one lacks the two 'visual presented objects'—the two sense-data. How does one identify the two visual presented objects? At this point we reach bedrock, and our spade is turned:

I can identify and distinguish the two sense-data *directly*, this as this one, and that as that one: I do not need to identify either as *the* thing which has this relation to this other thing. . . . I have not four things presented to me (1) *this* sense-datum, (2) *that* sense-datum, (3) *this* coin, and (4) *that* coin, but two only—*this* sense-datum and *that* sense-datum. When, therefore, I judge '*This* is a coin', my judgment is certainly a judgment about the one sense-datum. (Moore 1965*a*: 14)

If one asks a sense-datum theorist, 'How does acquaintance secure the reference of a logically proper name?' the only answer can be 'Directly.' Introspection cannot provide any answer, nor can analysis. I agree that we have reached rock-bottom here, at least in terms of the picks and shovels found in the tool kits of philosophers. If the episode is recognized as one that exploits the resources of sensory mechanisms, however, one opens the possibility of models that tunnel underneath the phenomenal surface, and unearth structures of sub-phenomenal details, using the drill bits and blasting caps of psychology and neuroscience. This is yet another reason why, as argued above, the question 'How does sensory identification proceed?' is one that may profitably be handed over to the psychologists.

  We can note other points on which the theories agree or disagree. One disagreement: according to feature-placing we need sensory experience in these cases because of the capacities it grants us to identify distal place-times; using it can help us pick out things in the world. Tasks of identification can sometimes be subcontracted to sensory mechanisms, with their ancient and well-honed systems of discrimination and differentiation. For the sense-datum theorist the sensory experience is itself made up of objects, and it is to those objects that the demonstratives refer.

  A point of agreement: When they first hear a feature-placing sentence such as 'Here it is red, there it is green', some auditors will object that it is grammatically or conceptually improper to ascribe a colour to a place. Offering parallel constructions such as 'Here it is slippery, there is dry ground' or 'Here it hurts, there it tickles' does not make the objection go away. Sometimes the objection is based on the misapprehension that such a sentence attempts to give a universal ('red') a particular location ('here'), when at most what is found in any instance is a trope or particularized nature. (For elaboration, see Section 6.6.) If 'red' is a name, as Russell urged above, then in each particular instance what it names is this particularized nature. Such things can be located. But to the grammatical or conceptual objection the only palliative is finally to cough up a noun phrase, some subject to which 'red' can without qualms be attributed. The obvious candidate is a *patch*. A 'patch' is a connected space-time region of finite but definite extent. Colour patches become the paradigm objects of sense. The visual field (version 2!) is a collection of contiguous patches. By 1952 Moore came to the view that visual sense-data consist exclusively of just such patches: 'I should now make, and have for many years made, a sharp distinction between what I have called the "patch", on the one hand, and the colour, size, and shape, *of* which it is, on the other; and should call, and have called, *only* the patch, *not* its colour, size, or shape, a "sense-datum" ' (Moore 1953: 30; see also 34). He notes that what he calls a 'patch' is of arbitrary extent; it might be a barely visible dot, a line, or something tomato-sized. Those who think a place cannot be red are somehow happy to be offered patches, even though the patch that is red is nothing but a place. Both the feature-placing and sense-data accounts agree that the subject term characterizes locations, that the apparatus of singular reference serves to identify patches or places, and that different subjects thereof are differentiated by spatial discrimination. But the sense-data account treats the subject terms as referring to private objects found within sensory experience, while for feature-placing the sensory experience contributes to the identification of a space-time region physically in or around the body of the sentient organism.

Moore at one point considered the possibility of identifying visual sense-data with the visible physical surfaces of objects. This is a neglected but very interesting period in the development of sense-data theory. If we could identify these 'patches' with physical space-time regions, then feature-placing sentences and sense-data sentences would have exactly the same subject-matter. Drop some of the epistemological baggage loaded onto the lowly sense-datum, and the resulting theory could be something very close indeed to feature-placing. In fact I think there is very little that is wrong with sense-data accounts up to the point where that identity is denied. So what were the arguments for denying it?

One argument rests on the different appearances that might be presented on two occasions of looking at the same surface. Suppose on these occasions it is also obvious that it is numerically the same surface, so that on that second occasion we can correctly judge that '*This* part of a surface is the *same* part of the surface of the same thing, as that which I was seeing (or perceiving by touch) just now' (Moore 1965*a*: 19). Sometimes we can make this judgement even if the appearances presented on the two occasions differ.

> If I am looking at it, with blue spectacles on, when formerly I had none, the later presented object seems to be perceptibly different in colour from the earlier one. If I am perceiving it by touch alone, whereas formerly I was perceiving it by sight alone, the later presented object seems to be perceptibly different from the earlier, in respect of the fact that it is not coloured at all, and whereas the earlier was, and that, on the other hand, it has certain tactual qualities, which the earlier had not got. (Moore 1965*a*: 21)

The 'presented objects' are perceptibly different even though one judges oneself to be perceiving the same surface on both occasions. The conclusion:

> It seems, therefore, to be absolutely impossible that the surface seen at the later time should be identical with the object presented then, and the surface seen at the earlier identical with the object presented then, for the simple reason that, whereas with regard to the later seen surface I am not prepared to judge that it is in any way perceptibly different from that seen earlier, it seems that with regard to the later sense-datum I cannot fail to judge that it *is* perceptibly different from the earlier one: the fact that they are perceptibly different simply stares me in the face. (Moore 1965*a*: 21)

In a variant of this argument, instead of using one surface perceived by one person at two different times, Moore uses the example of one surface (that of an envelope) perceived by many people at the same time, but from different angles. Since everyone sees the same envelope, but different people see different 'sense-given shapes', the sense-given shapes cannot be identified with that of the envelope (Moore 1953: 30–8). Even if they are qualitatively similar, they are numerically distinct.

   The feature-placing reading is that the 'presented object' in each of these various occasions is exactly the same place. It might look blue on the first occasion (when seen through blue spectacles) and white otherwise.[2] Or perhaps it looks rhomboidal from here, rectangular from there. Numerically the same place might appear differently at different times, from different vantage-points, to different perceivers. Moore's reading is that on the first occasion there is a presented object that *is* blue, and on the second occasion there is a presented object that *is* white. Or perhaps, in the second situation, the sense-given shape that you see is rhomboidal, and mine is rectangular. But only if there exist presented objects that actually *have* those properties does the argument succeed. They change qualitatively but the surface does not.

---

[2] Though the first claim must be handled with care. Thanks to colour constancy mechanisms, it is enormously unlikely that one would ever be fooled into thinking that a white object has changed its colour simply because one puts on blue spectacles. In this sense white objects still 'look white' even through blue spectacles.

Hence the surface and the presented object are numerically distinct. The argument tacitly presumes that both presentations are veridical.

But suppose that at least one of these appearances is counted as less than veridical. Perhaps on one occasion the presented object shows its true colours, and on the other it does not. For that matter, perhaps everyone is misled, to a greater or lesser degree; and the presented object shows its true colours on neither occasion. If sensory reference can succeed even while qualitative attributions fail, we can still allow that the presented object on one occasion is numerically identical to that object on the other occasion. Sensory mechanisms identify the same region on both occasions.

Strictly, all that we need to de-fang the argument is to insist that the various claims about appearances, entered as premises, are not contraries. It looked white then and looks blue now. Of course there are two occasions—two appearances—but perhaps numerically the same 'object' is presented on those two occasions. Similarly, perhaps one and the same envelope looks rhomboidal from here, rectangular from there. One route to eliminating contrariety is to add appropriate relational details to the correctness conditions: there is a sense, after all, in which 'rhomboidal' is exactly how a rectangle *would* look from here. Nevertheless, we resist the inference that there exists anything in the situation that *is* rhomboidal. Or we can eliminate contrariety if at least one of the appearances is non-veridical. If the real colour of the congregational church is white, then when it looks blue, it looks to be a colour it is not. On that occasion one suffers a non-veridical representation. No presented object—nothing in the line of sight, nothing in the vicinity—*is* blue, even though something out there looks blue.

Moore realizes that his argument requires the 'sense-datum inference' that on any occasion on which a surface looks blue, there is something (a sense-datum) that *is* blue (see Moore 1965*b*: 133, 1993*a*: 130). He considered the possibility of rejecting this assumption. Perhaps the sense-data only appear to change in colour, but do not really do so; perhaps 'the sense-datum presented to me when I have the blue spectacles on is not perceived to *be* different in colour from the one presented to me when I have not, but only to *seem* so' (Moore 1965*a*: 22). Moore worries that this supposition might be nonsensical, and unfortunately he was eventually convinced (by Russell) that it was nonsensical (see Moore 1965*b*: 136). But suppose the sense-datum in the passage above *is* the surface of the church. The passage then has a perfectly coherent interpretation. The surface of the church seen through blue spectacles is not perceived to *be* different in colour from the same surface seen without them. It only *seems* to be so. It is the same place even though its current appearance is misleading. You might be wrong about some of its qualities; there is no epistemic surety in the connection between a percipient and a place. With the benefits of hindsight we can see that the moment of Moore's conversion by Russell is the moment at which sense-data were shanghaied by acquaintance.

An account that identifies visual sense-data with visible facing surfaces is in many respects very close to feature-placing. Such an account would also abandon the metaphysical and epistemological peculiarities of private sensory objects. Some of the epistemological claims staked out for sense-data must simply be denied, but the genuine peculiarities that remain, and that continue to characterize some sensory episodes, can often be explained in terms of the referential peculiarities of sensory identification.[3] That is, the feature-placing account replaces an odd kind of object (the sense-datum) with an odd kind of reference: one based on sensory mechanisms. Instead of attributing metaphysical and epistemological peculiarities to the objects identified, we strive where possible to allocate those peculiarities to the mechanisms of identification.

4.5 DIVIDED REFERENCE, DIVIDED SPACE

One final link can be forged between sensory identification and the more sophisticated varieties. The task of identification is the task of answering the question 'Which one?' Success can be had if one sees which one, hears which one, or otherwise 'sensibly discriminates' the target from the simultaneously present background. Conditions on the adequacy of such sensory identifications are pretty minimal. To 'see which one', one must have some visual capacity to identify multiple simultaneous items, and it must be currently exercised, so that one distinguishes between regions occupied by the target and regions that are not. We can think of such capacities as the capacity to 'divide space'. It is worth considering further the role of this capacity in the ontogenesis of reference. What would happen if we lost it altogether?

Feature-placing is at the very bottom of the hierarchy of capacities to identify. To move up in the grades, the crux is the acquisition of 'divided reference'. As Strawson puts it: 'The decisive conceptual step to cat-particulars is taken when the case of "more cat" or "cat again" is subdivided into the case of "another cat" and the case of "the same cat again" ' (Strawson 1963: 214). For this one needs sortals, the identity predicate, counting and count nouns,

---

[3] Of course a friend of sense-data would complain that the proposed therapy does not merely remove some minor blemish from the otherwise fair face of sense-data, but instead excises all of their essential properties, leaving just disconnected scraps in the operating-room. Abandoning both the special objects introduced by the theory, and the epistemological principles that they serve, not much of real sense-data remain!

singular terms: a substantial portion of what Quine calls the 'apparatus of individuation'. Competence in dividing reference is yet another major hurdle separating merely sensory capacities ('early vision') from object-based cognition. But it is difficult to see how one could master these idioms of divided reference unless one has a prior capacity to discriminate among differently occupied regions of space. Without the capacities of spatial discrimination, one could not move to the higher grades. How could one learn—how would one have any use for—the apparatus of individuation?

As already noted, a feature-placing language cannot get us there. It lacks sortals, count nouns, identity, plurals. In sensory terms we could at best pony up some features corresponding to cats, but they provide a poor simulacrum of the real thing (see Ayer 1973: 91–2—yet another cat-lover who discussed this very question). Encounters with cats would be construed as encounters with the feline feature, that feature filling a scattered totality of space-time in the same way as does snow or water. But in sensory terms we cannot count discrete cats or express the content that this cat is the same one I saw yesterday. Additional encounters with cats are always just 'more cat'. We might get a qualitatively identical presentation of the same feline feature, but the 'vocabulary of sense' is incapable of expressing the content 'Lo, the same cat again'.

One simple way to make the point is to revisit the prospect of No-Space sensation (Section 4.2). Suppose you lost all spatial discrimination in all of your sensory modalities. Even the word 'claustrophobic' seems too expansive for the result. While normally one can detect the spatial relations between two simultaneous but qualitatively identical bird cheeps, in No-Space sensation there would be nothing to distinguish them. One would lose all capacity to detect auditory directions and depths. Even monaural hearing would remain a spatial sense if (for example) it remained possible to distinguish the sounds of two identical tuning-forks, struck simultaneously. If the sound of one appeared to be located to the right of the other, the modality would still be spatial. In No-Space sensation, you could no longer discriminate between the sound of the tuning-fork on your left side and the qualitatively identical sound on your right. You would then have no grounds for saying that you hear two distinct sounds of the same pitch at the same time. The *only* differences one could sense would be qualitative differences. If the sounds are qualitatively identical, they would fuse. Similarly, our qualitatively identical bird cheeps, from overhead and from the left, could not be discriminated as two. There would be no way to distinguish between distinct simultaneous instances of the same feature.

In No-Space there would be nothing to distinguish two qualitatively identical yellow patches as two. Of vision all that could remain would be one minimally visible point, which perhaps varies in colour over time. This point must also lack any apparent depth or visible direction. It could not be seen as surrounded by a background, any more than the visual field is seen surrounded by a background; here the totality of what one sees dwindles to a point. Similarly, auditory qualities must be confined to a single point, which lacks any particular auditory direction. Since the visual and auditory points cannot be distinct, standing in some spatial relation to one another, they must fuse to one. The other modalities collapse into the same point as well; there ceases to be any distinction between their subject-matters. In this world, ideas of vision and ideas of touch must be ideas of the same thing. At one moment one might sense 'red & C major & sweet & ticklish' and later 'blue & B flat minor & salty & cold'; the 'point' to which all the qualities are attributed ceases to have any spatial meaning, and is suddenly recognizable as nothing more than a point in time. One still senses something—No-Space sensation is distinct from the complete absence of sentience, envisioned in the Preface— but that something is, at any moment, just one thing: that moment itself.

Observations could be keyed to the combination of features present at one time, but all observational laws would be laws of association or succession. One could sense the differences between dry, calm, wet, and windy, and scientists in this world could form temporal generalizations to the effect that after the windy spells it often becomes wet. But at a given moment one could not sense the simultaneous presence of something that is wet and something else that is dry. Our scientists would be stumped whenever one item in the manifold is P and another is not.

In short, we would fail the Many Properties test, and get sent back a few grades (see Section 2.6). All the content of a given moment could be conveyed using just the truth functions and sentence letters, one per feature. One would have no need for quantifiers, variables, or predicates to express the sensory content of a given moment. Now it is calm and warm, later it is windy and wet. One could not be presented an occasion on which it is windy here but calm there; every weather map would shrink to a dot, labelled with some combination of features. (Of course any larger map could not be seen by denizens of No-Space anyway!) Quantifiers would be necessary only to talk about distinct times.

I mentioned earlier human olfaction as a possible example of a modality that lacks spatial character, and thereby fails the Many Properties test (Section 2.6). Two simultaneous presentations of an acrid odour fuse to one; and one cannot discriminate the presentation of something that is both acrid and musky from the simultaneous presentations of something acrid and something else that is musky. Of course one can still use one's nose to distinguish an acrid thing and a musty thing from an acrid musty thing, but it requires successive sniffs and a generalization over times. This is one reason why we would still need variables ranging over times, even though propositional logic suffices for the olfactory qualities presented at a given time. Similarly, the earlier example of following one's nose into the kitchen (Section 2.1) could be explained in terms of a temporal gradient: find the heading along which the intensity of that alluring odour increases most rapidly. That algorithm gets you into the kitchen quickest. Even the dog sniffing along a deer track occasionally stops, points its snout here and there, and takes sample sniffs on alternate headings. In a modality lacking all spatial character, one cannot pick out distinct places, so cannot focus the attributions of features, so cannot solve that modality's version of the Many Properties problem. In such a modality the only identifiers required are to distinct times. On the principle that sensing lacks tense distinctions, it is doubtful that the sensory system itself provides them. To get into the kitchen or down the track one must *remember* that the alluring odour was more intense that-a-way. So it is not as if a non-spatial modality is useless, but it requires supplementation by non-sensory resources to yield some of the skills granted directly by spatially organized sensing.

In No-Space one might still have occasion to use the one-word observation sentence 'Cat', but as far as I can see one would never have—and could never have—an experience that would oblige one to say, 'Not just one cat, but two'. One might count a *series* of cat cries, but not simultaneously sensible cats. One needs the capacity somehow to discriminate among distinct simultaneously present instances. Without it, experience might present episodes of 'more cat', but never force upon us a choice between one cat and another. Or consider how we can distinguish Quine's white, bristling, dog-facing cat from a cat facing a white, bristling, dog. In one scene we can see that the cat's place is the place that is white, and the canine features are not coincident with bristling. But if we lost all capacity for spatial discrimination then we could not experience such spatial coincidences and divisions of features. We would have four simultaneously present features, but no capacity to divide the scene among them. In such a world it is indeed hard to see how one could ever make the 'decisive step' to cat particulars.

To get divided reference we must reach the point where we can count separate instances of F, or distinguish something that is F and G from something that is F and something *else* that is G. At root this rests on the capacity to discern that both features are features of the same place, or at least of overlapping places. Particulars emerge as loci for overlapping features. It follows that one needs prior capacities of spatial discrimination to achieve divided reference. Without spatial discrimination one could not detect the overlap or division of features, and so one could not make the decisive step to the introduction of particulars. In brief: there is no divided reference without the dividing of space.

I hope the contrasts drawn in this chapter have clarified the scope and limits of sensory reference. The powers of identification it grants its host are akin to those given a user of a feature-placing language. Of course sentences in that language are semantically evaluable, have truth conditions, and so in the formal semantic sense 'refer' to whatever one must quantify over when stating those truth conditions. But the language grants its users only limited powers of identification. The user has no identity predicate, no count nouns, no tenses, no terms for numeric identity or reidentification. The language lacks the idioms to express the difference between 'the same one again' and 'a different one qualitatively the same'. So although in the formal semantics sense, the sentences of the language refer to whatever we must quantify over when stating their truth conditions, the users of the language may have very limited powers to identify the particulars to which their sentences refer.

Similarly, sensory representation refers to whatever space-time regions we must name in describing the correctness conditions for feature-placing, but it may provide its hosts such feeble powers of identification that one might hesitate to describe a sensory state as referring to anything. Feature-placing is in this sense a language without objects: a language without particulars, preceding reification. Ontological nihilists are understandably attracted to it; the scheme has been described as 'pre-ontological' (Akins 1996). It operates at a level of sophistication clearly below that of our scheme of enduring and reidentifiable material objects. If it sufficed as a medium of observation, feature-placing would thereby neatly illustrate Quine's thesis of the 'indifference of ontology' (1992: 31).

This simpler system is vital to our acquisition of an object-based conceptual scheme, as well as to the continuing success of varieties of direct reference. The latter continue to place demands on ancient systems of sensory discrimination, and by the character of the demands met we learn something of the capacities of those systems. To summarize: sometimes a demonstrative identification requires an on-going sensory link to the target, and it secures its reference only if something happens that might as well be called a 'sensory identification': one sees or hears or feels or (in general) senses *which* of the many currently sensible space-time regions is *the* region containing the target. You *see what* the guide is talking about. Conditions on the adequacy of these sensory identifications are minimal. Clearly there must be some underlying capacity to pick out or select space-time regions. If all such capacity disappears, we are banished to No-Space sensation, and in such banishment the deliverances of the moment could be conveyed without the use of variables or singular terms at all. Sentential logic would suffice. Quantifiers would be needed only to distinguish among moments. So in this rather fundamental way our scheme of reference requires capacities of spatial discrimination. Furthermore, sensory identification secures the reference of a demonstrative only if the ancient engines of spatial discrimination are set in motion by the on-going link. At the very least one must have activated some ability to differentiate between regions that manifest the feature and regions that do not. Identifications involving the simplest demonstratives may succeed on the basis of this bare capacity to discriminate differently occupied regions. So 'This is Vishnu schist' may succeed as an identification even if no exact border is identified between Vishnu schist and other rock, and even if the hearer cannot see any sharp borders in the vicinity, as long as the hearer can make some discrimination between regions occupied by Vishnu schist and regions not so occupied. If the goal is to identify a col or a cornice (or, for that matter, a knee or a shin), exact borders cannot be provided.

Unless one is already endowed with some capacity for sensory identification, it is very hard to see how one could acquire any more sophisticated kind. Its influence does not stop at demonstratives, but like a ground shock moving through bedrock communicates itself throughout all the phenomena of direct reference. Any term whose reference is ultimately secured by a 'grounding' in a face-to-face perceptual encounter owes its reference in part to sensory mechanisms, for all those groundings proceed through and only succeed if one has the appropriate sort of sensory representation. Finally, our apparatus of count nouns and predicates, singular terms and identity, could not be acquired or mastered unless one has some capacity to divide the sensibly present scene, and note the occurrence of a feature here and here, but not there. To make the prodigious leap from 'white and cat' to 'white cat' one must not only place the features, but identify the places. The place of the colour is also the place of the cat. Here we probably reach the upper limits of what mere sensation can achieve. Although sensory representation lacks an identity predicate, and does not strictly speaking name any place, one can sensibly discriminate the overlap of the places to which the features are ascribed. Such overlap provides the primordial locus for the positing of an object. Philosophers have written at length on the utility of reification. In sentience we find the mechanisms that make reification *possible*.

5

The Feature-Placing Hypothesis

IT might be useful to recap the argument briefly, in fast-forward, and then run it again, backwards, by speculating on what it would be like to have a completed theory of sentience for a particular modality. I hold that such an empirical theory could explain whatever needs to be explained about sensing, and that the appearances to the contrary are illusions—extraordinarily sophisticated illusions, but illusions none the less. Of them Wittgenstein's diagnosis rings true: our intellect is bewitched by language.

In fast-forward the first exciting scene was the one demonstrating the need to partition variation in phenomenal appearance into two components, qualitative and spatial. These correspond to the two place-holders in the schema

appearance *of* quality Q *at* region R.

Partition is forced upon us by something as simple as the experience of hearing two qualitatively identical bird cheeps simultaneously, in different places. The oddities of spatial qualia and of No-Space sensation served to reinforce the idea that there is a formal difference between the two categories of variation in phenomenal appearance. While the 'of Q' component of the schema above can be filled out with an account of sensory qualities—colours, odours, tastes, and so on—the 'at R' component requires something new. It is to be filled out with an account of the mechanisms of spatio-temporal discrimination operative in the modality in question. Features in a modality can be placed only as accurately as those mechanisms allow. For example, some pesky invertebrate might cause in you a sensation of a pinprick on your leg. 'Of pinprick' is the qualitative component; 'on the leg' the spatial. Clearly the place of the pinprick cannot be identified with a precision exceeding the two-point threshold. Within that radius two points cannot be discriminated as two; two touches appear as one, at the same place. These radii vary from place to place over the body. Only experiment can reveal how such spatial discriminations work; how a sensory system manages to pick out and discriminate among places is not accessible to introspection. The examples of bat and barn owl showed that results can be surprising.

So we set loose an army of psychologists, physiologists, neurobiologists, neuroethologists, and so on, who will in time work out how the various sensory systems manage discriminations among place-times. The heavy armour advancing behind the ranks is the claim that the accounts of spatial discrimination they eventually provide will also account for the intentionality of sensation. First we notice that the 'collecting principles' that tie together qualitative and spatial dimensions are formally akin to those that tie together predicates and subjects. A particular instance of a quality can be tied to just one place-time, and qualities, unlike place-times, come in incompatibility groups. The 'formal' difference between the 'of Q' and 'at R' components of variation in phenomenal appearance is that 'at R' picks out or identifies that which 'of Q' characterizes. What is lost in No-Space sensation is the capacity (and the need) to count distinct simultaneous instances of the same quality. Our two bird cheeps fuse into one. Different instances of the same quality must differ temporally, and demonstratives, in so far as they have any use, are useful only to divide time.

The hypothesis that this book offers is that sensation is feature-placing: a pre-linguistic system of mental representation. Mechanisms of spatio-temporal discrimination, which effect the 'at R' component of our schema, serve to pick out or identify the subject-matter of sensory representation. That subject- matter turns out invariably to be some place-time in or around the body of the sentient organism. So the having of a sensation of pinprick on the leg is the having of a central state that picks out or identifies a space-time region on the leg, and characterizes it qualitatively, as feeling like a pinprick. Certainly the fact that spatial dimensions of variation serve an individuative role could be neatly explained by this hypothesis, as could the formal differences noted in the partition argument. The various characteristics cited as reasons for thinking that sensation is intentional can also be explained on this hypothesis. The 'aboutness' of sensation reduces to its spatial character.

The notion that a central state somehow 'refers to' or is 'about' a portion of space-time might seem overly intellectual, abstract, and tenuous, so it is worth emphasizing that sensory reference, when successful, is physical, direct, and robust. When the system works as it should, the features one perceives as occupying a location in fact carry news about what is happening at that very location. Events at one end of the link show sufficient conditional dependency on events at the other that one can apply to the connection not just causal talk but the full terminology of information theory; we find an 'ongoing information link' between the physical conditions at region R and the features Q perceived to occupy that region. The connection is physical and direct; success requires some physical transmission from regions R to the appropriate transducers. Events there must somehow tickle your transducers: no tickle, no sensing. Furthermore, sensing lacks indirect reference and a past tense, so its reference cannot successfully extend to events that are spatially or temporally remote from the channel itself. If we think of a sensory horizon spatio-temporally, as extending backwards in time sufficiently to take into account transmission speeds, then it is fair to say that sensory reference is always to something present within the sensory horizon.

5.1 HOW TO ITCH

To run the argument backwards, to sketch what a completed theory of a sensory modality might look like, I need an example of a sensory modality. To find one it pays to look far afield: all the way to the Serengeti conservation areas in Tanzania.[1]

In the Ngorongoro crater of that country there lies a large, irregularly shaped, and multiply protuberant rock that guides refer to as 'the scratching rock'. The reason becomes apparent in the afternoon, when zebra visit. One side of the rock has an overhang at shoulder height, another a bump on the side a bit lower down, while in a third location there is a sharp edge. At each such protuberance will soon be found a zebra, hunched over and contorted in some bizarre fashion, rocking back and forth, or up and down, or in circle, using the rock to scratch some otherwise inaccessible itch. One zebra might crouch down and drop its left leg to use the overhang to scratch between its shoulder blades. Other zebra patiently wait in line while the process is under way. When one is finished the next zebra might step forward, twist its neck, and use the same overhang to scratch behind an ear. The animals learn which portion of the rock is the best one to aim for, to employ for the current itch, as they form distinct queues behind each of the available protuberances. Who says that tool use is confined to primates?

Those queues make one proud to be a mammal. The scratching is so deliberate and so energetic that one can only sympathize with what the zebra must have felt beforehand, as it waited so patiently in line. The somatosensory modality containing itches is one that humans clearly share with other species. It is the perfect example to use to sketch what a completed theory of a sensory modality might look like.

First it is important to be clear about the limits of the domain that even a completed theory of sentience would try to explain. The goal is an account of some modality of sensation: an account, for example, of how to itch. This account will *not* explain consciousness or the conscious mind (see Dennett 1991; Chalmers 1996). Raw sentience is typically placed at the bottom of the

---

[1] A nature broadcast from WGBH Boston in Nov. 1996 allowed me to do this.

hierarchies of complexity leading up the summit of conscious human mental states. We will stay down in the foothills, where the geography is more settled, less vertical, and better known. Still it would be nice to know how the nervous system of the zebra incorporates processes sufficient to instantiate an itch. Scratching comes later, as an additional complexity, beyond the scope of this book. Feature-placing serves humbly, as a prolegomenon to scratching.

The primitive skeleton of feature-placing can still be discerned under the variously alluring forms of bodily sensation. In pains, itches, tingles, twitches, tickles, aches, and so on, distinct sensory qualities appear to occupy parts of the body. Such episodes can be analysed as attributing somaesthetic features to regions of the body. If you are cursed with an ache in the back, you can be pleased at least that you are suffering a canonical appearance: of features Q at region R. The region happens to be within the skin, and the feature is characterizing something going on within, but that border has no special significance as far as feature-placing goes. Feature-placing lacks the vocabulary to draw a distinction between the subject of experience and the rest of the world. It has no personal pronouns. We have just places and features. Physical processes are going on here and there. Here it is raining, there it is aching. Ontologically, metaphysically, epistemologically, it is all on a level.

Feeling an itch on the foot is likewise on a par with hearing a cheep overhead or seeing a shimmering to the right. We get the same partition between qualitative character and its apparent place. Just as with visual fields, the only entities we need to quantify over to account for the apparent location of bodily sensations are space-time regions of finite extent. Those are the ones represented to be aching, itching, cheeping, shimmering, and so on.

The first step in filling out this account would be to apply the techniques analysed in Section 1.1 (and Clark 1993*b*) to somaesthetic phenomena, so as to get some account of how an itch differs from a tickle, a pinprick, a twinge, a tingle, and so on. What are these somaesthetic qualities, and how many dimensions of variation are required to account for their variegated character? Actually this is already something beyond the bounds of what is currently known, since the skin senses are a ragtag lot and probably constitute several distinct evolutionary acquisitions. We have distinct systems for slow pain, fast pain, light touch, deep touch, hot, and cold; as well as more integrated systems for 'dynamic' touch (see Akins 1996; Turvey 1996). But the philosophical job is to characterize how the various possible empirical results might fit together, and the omnivorous maw of multidimensional scaling can, I think, accommodate any possible result. That is, at a given bodily location one can discriminate among various somaesthetic qualities of pains, itches, tingles, tickles, and twinges; and given grants enough and time, our army of investigators is duty-bound to elucidate their differences to whatever degree of precision the grant-giving bodies are willing to fund. Of course one cannot *say* what the difference is between an itch and a tickle—the sensory system is pre-linguistic, and hence responds mulishly to peremptory verbal demands—but there is a tangible sensory difference between them, and this difference could eventually be identified as a distance within a multidimensional space of somaesthetic qualities.

The various qualities that appear to characterize parts of the body are bound together by similarities that are grist for the mills of multidimensional scaling. For example, an itch has some similarities to the aversive qualities of pain, and some to those of a tickle. A tingle could by insensible degrees turn into a tickle, or it could, by indiscriminably small steps heading off in a different direction within the quality space, transform itself into an itch. Our army would be given the mission of determining the number of dimensions necessary to represent these variations, and then of finding a metric such that relatively more similar somaesthetic qualities are relatively closer to one another in the resulting multidimensional space.

This approach can tackle the sensory qualities of pain, but perhaps not what makes pain aversive. That differing pains have differing sensory qualities can be seen by reflecting on the enormous vocabulary we have for the episodes: they are aching, throbbing, shooting, searing, burning, dull, leaden, heavy, sharp, stinging, crushing, and so on and on through a long and sorry litany. Differences between these are differences in the sensory qualities of the pain, and probably reflect differences in the activation patterns of slow pain or fast pain systems. But the sensory qualities of pain do not themselves account for what makes pain painful, or why one wants it to stop. That the painfulness of pain has to be distinguished from its sensory qualities seems pretty clear from the clinical literature (see Melzack 1973). Anaesthesia can allow experience of the sensory qualities of pain without its aversive qualities. Perhaps pain systems are wired so that the sensing of qualities in that modality causes an immediate and overriding desire that such sensing cease. Some anaesthetics short that wire. In any case, what makes a particular sensory quality aversive or desirable, painful or pleasant, is beyond the scope of this account, since it involves desires and appetites. We can analyse the sensory qualities that distinguish aching pains from throbbing pains, but I have nothing original to say about what makes both of them painful.

Our various names for bodily sensations correspond to landmarks—notable places—within the resulting somaesthetic quality space. Just as blue and green are notable and worthy of being named with basic colour terms, while many binary hues are not, so itches and tingles are landmarks within somaesthetic quality space, while the gamut in between can only be described in terms of relative similarity to those landmarks. Perhaps, oversimplifying greatly, the paradigm itch is located at coordinates (i, j, k) within a three-dimensional somaesthetic quality space. We can be fancy and assign a foil at radius r from the landmark; anything beyond that radius from (i, j, k) is not clearly worthy of the name 'itch'. Even fancier, assess 'clearly worthy' in probabilistic terms. We have a paradigm itch, a landmark within somaesthetic quality space, which forms the centre of a probability distribution. Grading away from it, in increasingly distant and dissimilar 3-tuples, we get sensations that are increasingly unlike the itch and unlikely to be dubbed itches, until finally the attraction of other landmarks begins to dominate, and we have sensations that fall within the orbit of other foci, and are clearly not itches.

The next speculative leap takes us even further beyond the bounds of what is currently known. Per hypothesis somaesthetic quality space has just three dimensions of variation in phenomenal appearance. It would follow that a fully determinate specification of the qualitative character of bodily sensation requires an ordered triplet of values in three independent dimensions of variation in qualitative character. Suppose we learn which axes the nervous system actually uses to make its discriminations, and how it registers variations along each of the three axes. This is the critical step to explaining how the nervous system physically instantiates the sensory quality. Prior to this all we have is a similarity space with a number of dimensions, but no fixed axes, and no physical interpretation for any of those dimensions. It takes neuroscience to tell us how the nervous system actually makes the discriminations that account for that structure of similarities. After this step, we can reinterpret the coordinates (i, j, k), providing them with a neural model—a psychophysical interpretation.

One model that could do the job—and remember that is all we are hunting for—is a neural network. The virtues of these models have been well described elsewhere (see Paul Churchland 1995; Patricia Churchland and Sejnowski 1992; Rumelhart and McClelland 1986). Representations are stochastic and distributed over the entire network. With enough hidden units these models can represent variations in an arbitrarily large number of dimensions. The phase space of the network can be multidimensional even though no single neuron in it does anything particularly taxing. The quality corresponding to coordinate (i, j, k) is represented by an activation pattern of the entire network; the varieties of possible activation patterns yield the entire multidimensional quality space. So we suppose this step is complete too, and what in purely psychometric terms is identified as coordinate (i, j, k) in a multidimensional order is implemented by an activation pattern $(\alpha_i, \alpha_j, \alpha_k)$ in a neural network. Then we know what an itch is neurally: to have an itch is to activate (α_i, α_j, α_k) in the appropriate network. Probably the appropriate network is found in one or another of the areas of somatosensory cortex.

Anything distinctive in the sensory quality of an itch will show up as some way it can be distinguished from neighbouring qualities; and these 'ways' in turn emerge as dimensions of the quality space. All the facts of relative similarity and of local and global discriminability are reflected in the number and values of coordinates (i, j, k) within the quality space. Those coordinates summarize what it is to be an itch: how feeling an itch feels distinctively different from feeling a tingle, a pain, a twinge, and so on. To feel an itch is to feel a quality at that place in the quality space. But with the neural identification completed we could describe how the nervous system implements that structure of relative similarities. We could identify the physical properties on which turn the discrimination of itches from tingles.

Even if developments proceed successfully to this point, still we will have explained only the structure of qualities manifest at an arbitrary but fixed bodily location. At best this explains how one might be presented the appearance of an itch, but not how one might feel an itch on the foot, as opposed to (say) the elbow. How does one handle the apparent locations of these qualities? In particular, how does the central representation of the quality (i, j, k)— that is, the activation of pattern (α_i, α_j, α_k)—manage to make the itchy quality appear on the foot, and not the elbow?

Now this question can seem profoundly mystifying, but with adequate ventilation the air of mystification surrounding it can be considerably dispelled. The first point to insist on is that these apparent locations are just as much features of the appearances presented by bodily sensation as are the qualities that appear to occupy them. As noted earlier, differences that are purely spatial tend to sink out of view when one surveys the qualities of sensation. But discrimination among the locations of itches or tingles is just as much a characteristic of the modality as is the qualitative variation. It too requires explanation.

When one feels an itch on the foot, the qualities in virtue of which the itch feels as it does appear to characterize a part of the body. One feels the itch at a particular place. In common-sense terms, the itch is out there on the foot, at the place where the victim points when asked, 'Where does it itch?' The answer will refer to the bodily locations at which the itchy qualities appear. Similarly, in common-sense terms pains are localized conditions of the body; they occur in feet and elbows, for example, not just in the head. Painful qualities appear to occupy (and characterize) places throughout the body. We might urge that itches and pains cannot literally be located out there in the tissues, joints, and cartilage, and that such bodily conditions are merely the stimuli for itches or pains respectively. On this line the itch or the pain strictly speaking is something central: a sensing of that bodily condition. But even so we need to explain what is the quality of sensation in virtue of which the itch appears to be located on the foot and not the elbow.

To characterize exactly where the itch appears to be—to fill out the sensory characterization of the location—we need to detail what sorts of spatial discriminations the victim can make. For example, even a punctate impression such as a pinprick cannot have its apparent location specified any more precisely than given by the two-point threshold. To the victim the pinprick appears *there*, but if the victim cannot discriminate between a pinprick *there* and another *here*, then the region to which the pinprick is attributed must include both. We will characterize the force of the identification of region R by detailing how well mechanisms of spatial discrimination can distinguish region R from its neighbours.

So we attack spatial discrimination. For this enterprise itches turn out to be a bad choice. Any qualitative difference between sensations makes them discriminable on grounds other than merely spatial ones, so in testing spatial discrimination we need to be able to present stimuli in distinct places that do not appear to differ in anything but their location. We do not know the physical characterization of stimuli for itches; various skin conditions might be responsible. Also it is difficult to present stimuli that reliably itch in the same way, or indeed that reliably itch at all when repeated. So a light touch or a pinprick is much easier to use in testing spatial discrimination. Weber used the point of a compass, touched so lightly to the skin that it was barely detectable (Section 2.2). One can then proceed to study how one discriminates two points of the compass as two.

Let us tell a speculative story about somatosensory spatial discrimination. To explain the apparent location of the itch we need to understand the range of possible apparent locations, and then understand how its particular location is selected from that range. The range of possible apparent locations is to be explored by detailing spatial discriminations: where one can perceive somaesthetic phenomena to be. One can detail the topology and metric of those apparent locations, noting that acuity is much better in some places than others. To select a location from this range we need states carrying information sufficient to pick out a particular location from the range possible.

The simplest possible mechanism is place-coding: *which* neuron fires carries the information as to where the disturbance causing that firing occurred. (Note that it does not 'tell you where'; it does not represent the location, but carries information sufficient to identify the location.) Place-coding exploits the topographical organization of vertebrate sensory systems. Somatosensory channels run more or less in dedicated lines from end-points in the skin to end-points in the somatosensory cortex. Adjacency relations are generally preserved, so that stimuli next to one another on the skin are likely to stimulate neurons next to one another in the spinal cord, areas next to one another in the thalamus, and columns relatively close to one another in the cortex. (The exceptions, as in vision, are wholesale discontinuities, so that the left side gets mapped to the right cortex, and vice versa.) Also as in vision, more sensitive areas have smaller receptive fields and hence consume a bigger portion of cortex. There is a built-in inefficiency to the design: elephants need to dedicate a larger portion of their total cortex to somatosensory systems, simply because they have a much larger surface area of skin sending dedicated lines upwards!

We might poll the nerves terminating in primary somatosensory cortex, and find that while many nerves share the same receptive field on the skin surface, there are 100,000 distinct receptive fields among the population as a whole. These receptive fields overlap considerably at the skin surface. But with this arrangement, which neurons fire carries the information as to where the stimulus occurred. Call all the neurons that have the same receptive field a 'pool', and number the pools by distinct receptive fields. That pool 101 is firing (and not 102) is in principle sufficient to carry the information that the disturbance causing the firing occurs within receptive field 101, not 102. With the overlap of receptive fields localization can be even more precise. Pool 101 fires most vigorously, as the stimulus is dead centre in its receptive field; but other pools whose fields overlap that location will fire as well. A system sensitive to the distribution of activity across several pools could localize the stimulus with greater acuity than provided by any single pool alone. In fact such 'hyperacuity' characterizes the skin senses just as it does vision.

Now per hypothesis we have already explained somaesthetic quality space. To have an itch is to have an activation pattern within radius r of the paradigm $(\alpha_i, \alpha_j, \alpha_k)$ in a vector processing system. Suppose any one of those 100,000 distinct pools can set off activation pattern $(\alpha_i, \alpha_j, \alpha_k)$. Then, I claim, we would have the wherewithal to feel an itch on the foot. Pool 101 has its receptive field in the foot, and some bodily condition there sets it firing in whatever way is necessary eventually to produce activation pattern $(\alpha_i, \alpha_j, \alpha_k)$. We need not postulate dedicated 'itch receptors', and the 'pool' is not just a neuron, so the coding necessary to set off that pattern could be of many different sorts (not just firing frequency). Activation pattern $(\alpha_i, \alpha_j, \alpha_k)$ is one relatively most similar to the paradigm we call an 'itch'. That it is pool 101 firing carries the information that the bodily disturbance occurred out in the foot. We explain both the quality of the somaesthetic experience and its apparent location. It may seem that there ought to be more substance to the explanation, but the key is to see that it has all that is required.

Ultimately, perhaps it is only because pool 101 is firing (and not 102) that the itch appears to characterize the foot and not the elbow. How so? Per hypothesis the system employs place-coding; it can pick up and register the information naturally contained in the fact that it is this neuron and not that one that is firing. There are consumers downstream who are sensitive to such things. How does one manage to discriminate itching on the foot from itching on the elbow? We catalogue the range of possible apparent locations and show how one in particular is identified. Explain how the downstream consumers can discriminate between foot-caused activations and elbow-caused activations. Then, if we have a foot-caused activation, and a system that is sensitive to the differences between foot-caused and elbow-caused activations, we have explained (*a*) how the system selects one from among the range of possible apparent locations, and *hence* (*b*) how the itch appears to characterize the foot, and not the elbow. We will have explained all there is to explain about the identification of the region in which the itch appears.

Any kind of coding scheme requires a system that picks up or 'consumes' the information naturally contained within the coding. These consumers can not just sit back and watch the meters. It takes some work to learn that the firing of neurons in pool 101 indicates some problem *here*, not there. Perhaps an irresistible impulse to scratch drives them out of the armchair into activity. Even thereafter they may require training, to get better at aiming their efforts, before they can be said to be sensitive to the information naturally contained in the firing of pool 101. Pool 101 does not *tell* us—or anyone—where its receptive field is located. Nowhere do we find an explicit representation *that* the receptive field of pool 101 is such-and-such a region of the foot. Nevertheless, that pool 101 is firing, and not 102, carries information sufficient to localize the stimulus; and consumer systems could exploit it to learn where to aim the scratching. One thinks of young zebra, marching to the scratching rock.

It might seem odd to say that the activation of pool 101 and not 102 is what makes the difference between the itch appearing on the foot and appearing on the elbow. But this is the same oddity as found in the claim that activation pattern $(\alpha_i, \alpha_j, \alpha_k)$ makes the difference between the foot feeling itchy and the foot feeling tingly. In isolation both identities seem extravagant and incredible. They gain intelligibility only when one remembers how the content of the sensory quality or the apparent location is unpacked. Just as the attributed quality is spelled out by detailing its place in quality space, so the content of 'appearing there' is spelled out by cataloguing the sensory capacities to detect differences between 'appearing there' and appearing (for example) 'here'. If we then discover that the capacities to detect such spatial differences are subserved physically by place-coding among active pools, the inexplicable character of the identity should go away. Recall the barn owls. How one manages to discriminate the directions of sounds is not introspectively accessible, and phase differences and timing circuits do not seem to have anything to do with the apparent locations of sounds. They do not seem to be appropriate materials with which to construct auditory phenomenology. Nevertheless, if you work through the entire somewhat complicated story, you come to see first that the identification of a particular apparent auditory direction is a matter of exercising capacities of spatial discrimination, and second that a system that picks up phase differences and times could make the requisite spatial discriminations. So, appearances to the contrary, the story about phase differences and timing circuits turns out to *be* the story about phenomenal locations. Such a surprising if unsatisfying climax is characteristic of attempts to explain the phenomenal in non-phenomenal terms. Each step of the account is intelligible, and at the end the identity is secured, but that identity will never seem introspectively obvious, since one side of it requires terms whose sense does not lie in the phenomenal domain at all. The intellect at least should be satisfied; remaining bewitchments may require the tender mercies of Wittgensteinian therapists.

5.2 THE SENSORY NAME

Sellars famously disputed the Thomistic position that sensation belongs to the intentional order, and, with typical panache, he phrased some objections using the Thomistic terminology of what 'mental words' are present in the 'act of sense':

What, then, are the distinctive features of the vocabulary of sense . . . ? . . .

  (*a*) The vocabulary of sense contains only such predicative words as stand for the proper sensibles.
  (*b*) The vocabulary of sense does not include abstract singular terms (formal universals), e.g. *triangularity*. The intellect somehow forms these words from their predicative counterparts.
  (*c*) The vocabulary of sense does not contain such mental words as *mental word* or *signifies*. Query: does *mental word* belong to the vocabulary of inner sense? of the reflexive awareness of intellective acts?

I postpone for the moment the question as to whether the vocabulary of sense contains such basic logical words as *and*, *or*, *not*, *if* . . . then . . .* And I mention, for future reference, that according to the Thomistic position although sense belongs to the intentional order, it does not judge, i.e. the 'language' of sense contains no statements or assertions. Apparently sense can signify *this white thing*, but not *this thing is white* nor *this white thing exists*. (Sellars 1963: 45)

The vocabulary as listed lacks any referring terms, though at the end we do manage to signify *this white thing*. ('Thing' is perhaps a misnomer, since none of the predicative words will be count nouns, and we lack criteria of numeric identity. Similarly—to venture an answer to the postponed question—sensory systems lack the asterisked logical words.) I propose to consider the character of the sensory *names* found in the vocabulary of sense. Perhaps 'sensory identifier' would be a better title, since sensory systems (and feature-placing languages) lack proper names, and as has been seen they work in rather a different way than do names in a natural language. But with these provisos I will in this section use the term 'sensory name', since it provides such a provocative way of thinking about the problem.

To continue the example from Section 5.1, suppose that the itchy quality corresponds to a particular place (i, j, k) in a three-dimensional somaesthetic quality space. Suppose one feels an itch at a particular place, which we dub region R. Now the question is: How might the act of sense name region R? Mere points on the closed surface of the skin could be identified with just two spatial coordinates, but some somaesthetic phenomena have an apparent depth or volume as well, and we will need at least three dimensions to describe stabbing sensations, shooting sensations, and the other voluminous occurrences catalogued by William James. Notice that stabbing and shooting also take time. Because the targets are, after all, place-times, the coordinates will include some indices of temporal position. They may indicate only relative position in a sequence within working memory, or they may be more elaborate. Let us schematize and suppose that such spatio-temporal discriminations require m dimensions to catalogue. Region R might have coordinates $(p_1 \ldots p_m)$.

Suppose the ability to localize is implemented by place-coding, and this particular itch is localized at R because it is pool 101, and not 102, that is firing. Place-coding seems much sparser than a description of m dimensions of spatio-temporal variation in appearance. A given pool, one might think, just names the place of its receptive field. Pool 101 names place 101, etc. Why should we trot out m dimensions to characterize such a simple list? The reason is that the list is not so simple; place-coding contains considerably more information than could be conveyed in one. Real systems use a distribution of activity over pools whose receptive fields overlap. Some pool is firing most vigorously, and others less so. Perhaps pool 101 is dead centre on the location of the itch: its receptive field is entirely within the region where the itch appears to be. We also have a radius r, outside which pools are not firing above base rate at all. Between them we have a more or less complicated distribution of activity in pools whose receptive fields neighbour that of 101. Describing the information carried by this distribution—the information on which localization is based—may well require m dimensions of variation in our data-points, $(p_1 \ldots p_m)$. So even place-coding can be thought of as a vector $[p_m]$. It must preserve the dimensionality of spatio-temporal discrimination.

Let us double-check our route. We moved from the common-sense description of

feeling of itch on foot

to a partitioning of dimensions of variation in phenomenal appearance

appearance of quality (i, j, k) at region R

and thence to the corresponding qualitative properties of sensation. The sensory state is construed to have components that pick out space-time region R and ascribe quality (i, j, k) to it. Once the mechanisms of qualitative and spatial discrimination are understood, we can provide the neural details on those components. At that point the path might lead us finally to the neural implementation

activation pattern $(\alpha_i, \alpha_j, \alpha_k)$ tied to place-code $[p_m]$.

The latter could be fleshed out with explanations of how one feels the somaesthetic qualities that one does, and how one feels them *where* one feels them. It provides the neural details on how the itchy quality is attributed to a location. Now if activation pattern $(\alpha_i, \alpha_j, \alpha_k)$ should be included in the vocabulary of sense as a predicate analogous to 'itchy', should we also include the place-coding pattern $[p_m]$ in the vocabulary of sense, as a sensory name? It names the place where the itch appears to be.

Suppose the cortical feature map is everywhere at baseline when one itches nowhere. Suddenly the locus of an unpleasant encounter with an invertebrate earlier in the day starts to itch. A particular portion of the feature map lights up, and it lights up in a particular way. Perhaps only some cortical columns shift from baseline, and to describe which ones do, and by how much, we need to specify a place-coding activation pattern $[p_m]$. That portion of the map maps the foot. Other punctate impressions provide similarly vivid sensory identifiers. At dawn in the woods the first bird cheep might be heard at a particular azimuth and elevation, discriminations of which are implemented neurally by signals of phase difference and intensity difference. It is because the matinal song produces those signals that it appears to be *where* it appears to be.

A latter-day Thomistic suggestion is to think of the signal $[p_m]$ as possessing the semantic character of a 'sensory name'. When all goes well it serves to identify the location of the quality. Of course it is not literally a name any more than activation pattern $(\alpha_i, \alpha_j, \alpha_k)$ is literally a predicate. Such activation patterns do not have lexemic boundaries, but merge continuously one into another; they are not composed from a finite, discrete, and digitally recognizable alphabet; and no variation is possible in their 'word' order. As already noted (Section 4.3), sensory systems of representation lack combinatorial systems of discrete elements. They lack words. Nevertheless, transient states of these mechanisms may have semantic features, and those semantic features may be structurally analogous to the semantic features of names and predicates. This is what the latter-day Thomist suggests: these states are sensory counterparts to names and predicates. Flag them, Sellars-style, with asterisks.

Invoking the semantic terminology is worth while only if it does some work for us; and one task for which it is useful in its home territory is the cataloguing, diagnosis, and correction of communicative misfires. If misrepresentation were impossible, there would be little need to invoke the terminology of representation (see Dretske 1986). It is the possibility of misidentification or misreference that gives the talk of reference and identification its point, its *raison d'être*. So one trial we propose for the latter-day Thomist is a simple one. To justify invoking semantic terminology in the sensory domain, produce some episodes of sensory misfires—sensory misrepresentations—and show that the terminology is useful in cataloguing and diagnosing them.

It is not difficult to produce episodes of sensory misrepresentation: illusions will serve admirably. Appearances are sometimes less than veridical. Things are not always as they seem. The distinction between veridical and non-veridical appearance itself provides grounds for holding that sensory states have semantic features. They have at least correctness conditions, which serve to distinguish illusions and other non-veridical appearances from those that are veridical.

Interestingly, many cases of manifest illusion require successful sensory reference. The appearance is false, illusory, or misleading precisely because the region that appears to manifest qualities Q in fact does not. This requires one successfully to identify the region that fails to manifest those features. For example, consider the spreading neon effect. A figure is composed entirely of solid pink or solid black lines on a constant white background. But in the region of the pink lines the background white squares also look pink. An example is found on the back cover of *Consciousness Explained* (see Dennett 1991). On the back cover one seems to see a ring of solid pink, with a white centre and a white surround. Only careful examination shows that there is no pink ring on the back cover at all, but merely pink lines, black lines, and solid white. The appearance is an illusion. The lines on the back cover cause sensory processes that successfully identify places on the cover, but mischaracterize them. Indeed, there is a distinct place on the cover where there appears to be a solid pink ring—you can point to the place you see *as* a pink ring—but of that place the appearance is false.

Such cases of non-veridical appearance can be assimilated to a case in which reference succeeds but the referent fails to satisfy the conditions ascribed to it. If in fact we can distinguish mechanisms of sensory reference from those of sensory attribution, then there ought to be a second kind of illusion: one in which the non-veridical appearance is attributed specifically to an error in mechanisms of sensory reference. This would be a case of misreference. There would be nothing wrong with the attribution of qualities to places, but they would be attributed to the *wrong* place.

Mechanisms of spatial discrimination are extraordinarily reliable, since they are rather fundamental, and competitive pressures have been honing them for such a long time. Nevertheless, we already have the makings for a real-life example of sensory misreference. Consider the delay line cell assemblies in the barn owl (Section 3.6). Recall that the critical task of those assemblies is to register the delay from the time an auditory wavefront hits one ear until it hits the other. Given the distance between the two ears and the speed of sound, that 'phase difference' carries information about the direction whence the waves are coming. The delay line assembly has increased activity at the places corresponding to the delay d that puts signals from the two ears into phase. But because one wavefront is followed at frequency f by another, one might match the signal from the left ear either to one preceding it from the right ear, or to one following it. The delay line assembly will also have increased activity at points corresponding to these alternative phase-shifts of $d + 1/f$, $1/f - d$, $d + 2/f$, $2/f - d$, and so on. These will yield correspondingly different auditory angles, with some to the left and some to the right of the one indicated by delay d. As described in Section 3.6, the only way to sort out these ambiguities is to run the same analysis on multiple frequencies, and find the delay value that best puts *all* the frequencies into phase.

Now suppose that we have a narrow-band signal, containing fewer frequencies than normal, and, by chance, more than the average amount of noise in firing rates of neurons in the cell assembly, so that the wrong peak happens to be bigger. The dearth of frequencies would make the sound hard to localize in any case, and this time sheer stochastic variation in firing rates happens to bump one distribution up over another. In fact the sound is coming from azimuth θ, which yields a phase difference d, but given the combination of low signal and high noise, the distribution at $d + 1/f$ happens to be bigger and wins the competition. Then the delay line assembly, working as it normally does, will pick the peak at $d + 1/f$, and pass along the wrong azimuth θ'. The click or cheep might be heard as on the left, in direction θ', as opposed to on the right. You hear it in the wrong place. We have a failure not in the discrimination of auditory qualities, but in the mechanisms that localize them. They are mislocalized, misplaced.

Two points about this example are worth emphasizing. First, activity in the delay line assembly is interpreted just as it always is. A peak at $d + 1/f$ normally indicates azimuth θ', and in this example the same rule applies. But the system happens to produce the wrong sensory identifier. In effect it says 'Bob' when it should have said 'Rob'. But once the token is produced, we interpret it in the normal way: it is referring to Bob. Here the system produces a spatial identifier 'hither' when it should have said 'thither', but whichever one is produced is interpreted in the normal way. The features are 'mislocalized' or 'misplaced' because the system has named (produced an identifier for) the wrong place. Sensory misreference does not require any sort of breakdown in the rules for interpreting the identifiers, but rather the opposite: the same rules for interpreting the identifiers apply. Nor is it obvious that there must be some sort of malfunction or breakdown in the delay line assembly. The neurons are working fine. This is a case of 'normal misperception' (Matthen 1988: 12), specifically in mechanisms of spatial discrimination, giving us a non-veridical appearance due to an error in the mechanisms of sensory reference. They named the wrong place.

Secondly, notice that when mechanisms of auditory localization name 'hither' instead of 'thither' as the source of the sound, the sound *appears* to be hither. A vivid example is provided by the auditory front–back reversals mentioned in Section 2.1. Directions fore and aft are particularly difficult to disambiguate. Recall the narrow-band telephone signal trilling from an open door down the hall. The busy day at the office produces a high level of noise both extracranial and intracranial, smothering various auditory cues and making it difficult to discriminate among distributions of internal activation that differ only slightly. You can hardly hear yourself think, as they say. When the telephone rings, your auditory delay line assemblies happen to plump for ((telephone)(that-a-way)), but in this case they literally mislead you. You rush to your door, only to discover *en route*, probably at the next ring, that it is coming from another direction.

The telephone sounds as if it is coming from your door, but the cause of the sensation lies in a totally different direction. Sound from azimuth θ causes an auditory sensation that refers to the wrong azimuth θ'. It does this by producing a token of the wrong spatial identifier: an activity peak corresponding to $d + 1/f$, which, interpreted normally, refers to θ'. If we head out on bearing θ', hunting for the cause of the sensation, we shall forever be disappointed. We will not find *any* causal or informational traffic from place-times in that direction to the sensation as of sound that-a-way. Like the phantom pain located in the limb that no longer exists, or the mirror image located several feet behind the glass, the location at which these sensory features appear has at the time no causal connection at all with the sensory system.

The example also provides a perfect instance of the mystery of 'projection'. How can the sound appear *there*, in a place which in fact is empty and silent, and has no causal connection at all with the sensation of the sound? Since it is not a function of anything going on at that place, it must depend on us. We simply 'project' those features there. They land there, like the mirror image rammed unceremoniously into brick and plaster. As the latter example shows, the landings might be more or less successful.

I think we can deem the latter-day Thomist to have passed the first trial. Perhaps developments to this point allow us also to resolve the projection problem. It is resolved by assimilating projection to reference. Trilling qualities appear to be located in a particular direction down the hall. The 'projection problem' was to explain how qualitative properties of sensation appear to be located in such places, so far from the states of mind that in fact they characterize and whose properties they are. The suggestion already mooted (Section 2.2) was that talk of 'projection' is a funny way of talking about representation: to say that auditory features are projected from states of mind out into empty space is to say that states of mind, which do the representing, characterize volumes of empty space in that fashion. This suggestion is not by itself sufficient to lay all the worries to rest. The specific worry about projection is: *how* are those trilling qualities projected from states of mind out into empty space? *How* do those qualities appear out there? Projection is a suggested mechanism, answering this question. The optical metaphor provides a model linking states of mind to the apparent locations of sensory qualities.

Developments in this section provide a second possible mechanism. Trilling qualities appear to characterize that particular location, because the nervous system of our office worker has produced a token of the sensory name $d + 1/f$, and in normal cases tokens of that name refer to the location in question. Pressed for details we can explain exactly how this works (Section 3.6)—or at least the neuroscientists can, since the problem is handed to them forthwith.

Projection is even easier to explain in cases of veridical appearance, since in them the reference is genuine. I 'project' pink out onto that book jacket in front of my eyes (and not to some other place) because I successfully *identify* that particular region of space-time, and characterize that region (or perhaps mischaracterize it) *as* pink. Successful projection is successful reference. The 'mystery' of projection is that the reference of sensory representations is often distal, to regions of space-time in front of the sense organs, where no dendrites dangle; it will be solved as we clarify *how* sensory systems identify such regions. In brief, from Sections 2.3, 2.5, 3.5, and this one, we have established a three-term equation:

> explaining where sensory qualities appear to be located
> = explaining sensory capacities for spatial discrimination
> = explaining the reference of sensory representation,

where for the latter we can also accept other equivalent intentional idioms: identifying the 'object' of experience, the subject-matter of the representation, the referent of the sensory name, and so on. To these three terms we can now add a fourth: explaining how sensory qualities are 'projected' onto physical places physically in front of the sense organs. The latter is no more (or less!) difficult than explaining the reference of the 'sensory name'.

5.3 SENSORY IDENTITIES

In a natural language, reference and the apparatus of individuation manifest themselves in various paradigmatic phenomena: ambiguous reference, informative identity statements, intensional contexts, misreference, names of non-existent objects, and so on. If sentience includes capacities to refer to place-times, then one ought to find analogues of these paradigmatic phenomena in sensation itself. Finding them would also provide some corroborative evidence for the hypothesis that the content of sensation is just another variety of intentional content.

Ambiguous sensory reference is in natural contexts rare. One context that many authors describe as possessing the requisite structure for ambiguous visual reference arises with artefacts: the perception of pictures. Perception of the surface of the picture has, perhaps, an ambiguous reference: to the surface of the picture itself, or to the surfaces pictured. You might note the arches receding in the distance, or the gloss or dust on the surface of the region of the picture representing those arches. Even Gibson describes pictures as yielding perceptions that are in this fashion ambiguous:

A picture is both a surface in its own right and a display of information about something else. The viewer cannot help but see both, yet this is a paradox, for the two kinds of awareness are discrepant. We distinguish between the surface *of* the picture and the surfaces *in* the picture. In such paintings as those of the impressionists, we can see the difference between the illumination *of* the picture and the illumination *in* the picture. The two sets of surfaces are not comparable, and the two kinds of illumination are not commensurable. (Gibson 1979: 282)

One might deny that one literally sees any surfaces 'in' the picture in the sense Gibson indicates. Often there do not exist *two* sets of surfaces, for example:

the arches pictured receding in the distance might not exist. Further, if I hold up a photograph of Winston Churchill, the witness who sees it cannot on that basis alone testify truthfully to seeing Winston Churchill. The witness must have had a prior visual experience, somewhat similar to the one in the courtroom, but caused by Churchill himself. Yet the cases are not entirely clear-cut; we do, for example, speak of seeing someone when in fact we saw only glowing phosphors on a television screen. Looking at a picture, one can have experiences that are very much like seeing Churchill. The picture can stimulate visual processes in a way very much like the real scene, and one can note depths and features of the pictured scene.

I once took a good, sharp photograph of a lawn with trees and a paved walk and had it enlarged about twenty times so that it could be mounted on a six-foot panel. The observer stood at a point where the visual angle of the picture at his eye was the same as the visual angle of the array admitted to the camera. He was told to estimate distances in terms of the number of paces needed. To the question 'How far away from you is the elm tree?' he would visualize himself walking up to it and reply, 'Thirty paces.' But to the question 'How far away from you is the picture?' he would pause and reply, 'Oh, that's four paces.' For the latter estimate he had to shift the operation of his visual system so as to pick up quite different invariants. (Gibson 1979: 282)

The subject in the experiment is not strictly speaking seeing any elm tree at all; perhaps the one pictured was cut down years ago. Nevertheless, the experiment shows that his visual system is stimulated in very much the way it would be if he were standing on the lawn in question. His ability to estimate distances 'in' the picture shows that his perception of the picture is more than the perception of a flat surface. Picture perception resembles indirect discourse. At least in this experiment it seems fair to say that visual sensory processes prompted by the picture have an ambiguous spatial reference. They are not unambiguously about nothing more than a flat piece of paper. They also have much of the character of seeing a lawn with elm trees.

The earlier example of front–back auditory reversals might also serve. Auditory directions fore and aft are likely to be confused. Interestingly, some theorists deny that there are any ambiguous names, preferring to save the phenomena by postulating different names that happen to be homonyms. Perhaps the sensory identifiers for those two directions are near homonyms, like 'Tom' and 'Thom'. The system settles on one of them—it identifies just one of the directions—but sometimes it settles on the wrong one. A simple head-turn or another moment of listening can provide enough clues to push the system into a new equilibrium. In effect it says 'Not Tom, Thom'.

Many 'spatial illusions' generated by looking at pictures are also instances of sensory misreference. The flat array of lines somehow causes the system to mislocate a feature: a bisector appears here, rather than there (where a ruler confirms it should be); or the lines look curved, instead of straight. Often the array that does this is cleverly designed to kick off three-dimensional descriptors for a two-dimensional page (see Gregory 1977: 150–60). A random-dot stereogram provides a dramatic example. As noted above, any impression of depth derived from looking at a flat picture is a variety of spatial misreference; in some sense you see the flat surface of the painting as a configuration of differently aligned surfaces at different depths. These impressions involve an odd kind of partial referential misfire: the visible point is at the given azimuth and altitude, but it appears at an incorrect depth. Many of the spatial illusions are similar: they generate appearances of a scene whose spatial and metrical relations do not match those of the stimulus. Often this is because the stimulus excites some three-dimensionally sensitive systems even though it manifestly resides on a flat surface. In this way the picture makes you misplace some of its components.

Examples of informative demonstrative identities are perhaps easier to find. Consider these cases.

(1) *The Home Mechanic*. You are assembling some large contraption. One part is a large piece of sheet metal with holes drilled through it. You are attempting to put a bolt through one particular hole, but because of your position you cannot see either hand. You have the bolt in your left hand and the nut in your right hand. You feel each hole in turn with the index finger of each hand, until finally you feel your two fingers touch. Eureka! That hole (the one I feel with my left hand) = that hole (the one I feel with my right). Even more simply, that = that: two demonstrative 'modes of presentation' of the same place.

To see that this case is less than trivial, just try to touch the tips of your two index fingers together without looking at your hands as they approach. If you start with your arms behind your head, at an angle off to one side, the mishits can be embarrassingly large. The two 'modes of presentation' fail to identify one point in space-time. Any bilateral sensory system can generate equivalent cases. For example:

(2) *Seeing Double*. As a child you notice that a finger held between your eyes and something you are looking at looks double. You notice that the doubling goes away when you shut one eye, and gradually you realize that the double image is a result of seeing the same finger with two eyes. So that finger = that finger. (Note that this is an empirical discovery!) At the sensory level, before one learns the concept of countable fingers, the empirical discovery is that this place (the one presented by the dark blurry translucent outline on the left) = that place (the one presented by the one on the right). We have two modes of presentation of the same place, one to each eye.

(3) *The Telescope*. You are looking with one eye through your telescope, keeping the other eye open so as to point the instrument. You might pick out the same licence plate through both eyes. There is a sense in which that licence plate 'looks bigger' through the telescope. Perhaps you can read the digits only through the telescope. But nevertheless, that licence plate (which I can read so distinctly through the telescope) = that licence plate (which just looks like a blur from here).

Each blurry image in the double image is a mode of presentation of the same finger. If you try to point to one of the two images, you find that you can point to both simultaneously, using just one finger of the other hand. You need to shut an eye to be sure you know which one you mean. But it is quite a childhood discovery when one discovers that what seem to be two fingers are one. In its own way it is analogous to the discovery that the Morning Star is the Evening Star. Bilateral vision also gives the lie to the old saw that one cannot see two colours at the same place and same time:

(4) *The Binocular Reduction Tube*. Roll up a piece of paper to serve as a 'reduction tube'. Look at a bright red book cover through the tube with one eye, keeping the other eye open. Focus both eyes on the same spot on the surface. Through the reduction tube the red will look more saturated than it does through the other eye. The reduction tube decreases inhibition from the bright surround, and so increases apparent saturation. You are presented an appearance of two colours at the same place. (And by the way, which one is the 'real colour' of that portion of the book cover? From that spot the same stimulation—modulo quantum variation—travels to both eyes; the tube merely blocks stimulation from *surrounding* regions.)

So far the modes of presentation have been within one bilateral sensory modality, but examples multiply when one considers identities across different sensory modalities:

(5) *The Home Mechanic, II*. Another part of the same contraption, but this time you can at least see one side of the piece of metal. You keep your eye on the target hole, as you try to insert the bolt through it using your unseen left hand. You miss several times. By touch alone you cannot hit *that* hole on the first trial. Finally you get it right. That hole (the one I am touching) = that hole (the one I am seeing).

One can agree with Berkeley that ideas of vision are not the same as ideas of touch, and agree also that one could not deduce from the evidence of sight alone that the features one sees are features of things that one can also touch. Nothing in the tactile mode of presentation or in the visual mode of presentation indicates that both modes of presentation present the same place. But in fact they do. These identities are not analytic, but empirical. The visual idea has as its referent the same place-time as does the tactile idea. The Berkeleian point stands as evidence of the need to distinguish sense and reference even in the sensory arena. We have differing ideas (visual and tactile) of the same place.

Feature-placing diverges most radically from Berkeley in its suggestion that not all the content of the act of sense is manifest to the sensing mind. The mechanisms of sensory reference are not necessarily transparent to their host; scrutinizing how things seem will not necessarily reveal that to which these episodes refer. If we dub that object the 'phenomenal object', then such episodes do not reveal all there is to know about their own phenomenal objects. The objects of ideas of vision can have qualities other than merely visual ones; furthermore, we might discover that those objects are in many ways *unlike* their visible qualities. How such 'cross-modal' identities can be established will be further explored in Section 5.6. In the meantime we must remain open to the possibility that the phenomenal object is not *merely* phenomenal.

5.4 FEATURE INTEGRATION

Cross-modal identities have been a subject of continuous theoretical interest at least since Berkeley's day. If anything the problem they pose is more acute today than it was then. With the discovery that distinct dimensions of variation in visual appearance are often served by distinct feature maps in distinct areas of cortex, and that one can suffer blindness in various distinct visual submodalities—binocular disparity, red–green discrimination, face recognition, and so on—the very concept of what constitutes 'a' sensory modality is put under stress. It turns out that the patch that to Berkeley looked both red and glossy poses a variant of the same problem as the coach that is both heard and seen to be rattling down the cobbled street.

In fact the features registered by different feature maps, even within one modality, are not all of a piece. They differ in complexity, with some being more basic and others more derived. If we think in terms of the space-time regions to which the features are ascribed, some require a rather more compendious and complex assessment of regions than others. Treisman (1988: 233) clarifies matters with her notion of a *feature hierarchy*. Features are of different orders of complexity. The simplest and bottom-level visual features are those that can be ascribed to points minimally visible against a background. These are colour and luminance: red–green, yellow–blue, white–black.[2] Slightly more complicated are features that can only be features of surfaces: connected sums of at least several such minimally visible points. Only at this level can we find such features as texture and size, both of which require relations among several points. My specular features (glossy v. matte) would be found here. Treisman also includes relative motion and depth (parallax and binocular disparity). Features of points can also characterize surfaces, so colour and luminance are included at the surface level as well. If these surfaces are surfaces represented by the 2½d sketch, as Treisman proposes, we could also include simple orientation features (vertical, horizontal, tilted) and perhaps some segment features (curvature, straightness, termination, etc.). The latter characterize edges or lines. But a third level of complexity in the hierarchy includes features that require shape or three-dimensional object description. Shape features, even if only two-dimensional (square v. triangle, for example), are logically more complex than segment features (straight v. curved edges) or point features (red v. green points on the edge). The relational properties in virtue of which something is a square are more complicated than those in virtue of which an edge of it is straight. Other features found only at the 'shape' or '3d object description' level include topological properties such as closure, and full three-dimensional descriptors of volumes, surfaces, or oriented lines. Ayer's cat patterns would be found here. Again, features of surfaces can also characterize three-dimensional shapes, so texture, depth, motion, size, etc., as well as colour and luminance, are also found at the third level.

Features at low levels in this hierarchy fully qualify as 'sensory features'—as features extracted by 'early vision'. They also qualify as Strawsonian features (Section 4.3). Colour, luminance, relative motion, size, texture, flicker, line orientation, and segment features pass all the tests (see Treisman 1988: 230; Mack and Rock 1998: 13). According to Treisman's feature integration model, these are extracted automatically, in parallel, by pre-attentive processes. The latter phrase means that no attention is required, and indeed, these features provide the later targets for attention. A stimulus that possesses a unique value of such a feature will 'pop out' from an array of distractors—it draws attention to itself. More precisely, such a stimulus can be picked out from an array of distractors in (more or less) constant time, no matter how many distractors are present. The distractors are all rejected in parallel, automatically. Whereas search tasks that require serial atten-

---

[2] If the arguments of Sect. 1.3 are sound, even these bottom-level features are not strictly features of solitary points. The background is needed. Perception of black requires a bright surround, and chromatic qualia are likewise relational. (It follows also that the human perception of black would not survive translation into No-Space sensation, since the latter lacks a background. See Sect. 4.5.)

tion—time spent on each item in turn—take longer as the number of distractors increases.

Matters are not so clear for features higher in the hierarchy. Shapes are clearly a more complicated affair than colours or textures. Squares and triangles, for example, can be counted, and so may already violate Strawsonian strictures. Peacocke (1992*a*: 119) was right to isolate a separate level for shape perception, and label it 'proto-propositional'. Clinical phenomena found in visual agnosias indicate the real-world need to treat perception of shapes as a separate level. A simultanagnosic may have clinically normal perception of every point in visual perimetry, yet have considerable difficulties perceiving the shapes of objects (see Farah 1990). Grouping processes in general and shape perception in particular may require attention (Rock *et al.* 1992; Mack and Rock 1998). The question of which features provide the 'elementary alphabet of visual building blocks or primitives' (Treisman 1988: 230) is still open and highly contentious. Perhaps shape perception lies in the interesting and contested transition zone between 'early vision' and 'visual perception' proper. To use the older terminology, shapes lie in the no-man's land between sensation and perception. Features in the more complicated layers of the hierarchy certainly begin to take on some of the characteristics of object-based perceptual categories. Feature-placing does not deny the existence or importance of the latter processes, but since the goal is simply to give an account of sensation, it can stay safely on the sensory side of that no-man's land.

The sensory side, then, is thought to commence with bottom-up, automatic, and parallel registration of multiple features, such as colour, luminance, size, texture, orientation, and relative motion. Some have been shown to have their own distinct feature maps. In contrast, attention, which selects bits here and there out of the torrent, is not fully bottom-up or automatic, and is thought to be a limited capacity serial channel. Unlike the parallel processing of sensory features, attention can do just one thing at a time. With these assumptions we can understand the key empirical finding that prompted the feature integration theory of attention. In searches in which the target is defined by a unique conjunction of features, search times increase linearly with the number of distractors (Treisman and Gelade 1980). If we have just one bar that is both short and green in a display of red bars and green bars that are short or long, then the time it takes to find that one bar increases linearly with the number of items in the display. It is as if each item must be examined in turn; the task engages a serial process. Treisman's hypothesis: that process is focal attention. 'When features must be located and conjoined to specify objects, attention is required' (Treisman 1988: 203, 1996: 172). Since the target is identified only by a unique conjunction of features, one must attend to each location in turn, to conjoin colour and size.

Treisman and Gelade (1980) call the act of identifying the subject-matters of two distinct feature maps 'feature integration'. It requires attention to be directed at stimulus locations. 'Any features which are present in the same central "fixation" of attention are combined to form a single object' (Treisman and Gelade 1980: 98). It is important not to get lost among the various locations found in this model. The features are 'present' in the same fixation in the sense that they are features of the same place-time, located distally, in the line of sight. But features of that location are registered in distinct portions of distinct feature maps, scattered across the cortex. Attention, on this model, cannot be focused on any one place inside the head. They use the metaphor of the 'spotlight' of attention, but there is no one place inside the head on which such a spotlight *could* be focused. The macaque monkey does not shine a spotlight or focus its attention on thirty-two distinct regions of its own cortex. Instead the one thing that could be in the spotlight, that deserves to be in the spotlight, is the location of the *stimulus*—the banana in front of the eyes, say. The 'focus of attention' is, then, the place *represented by* those various portions of distinct feature maps. And the thesis is that by focusing attention on that location, one 'integrates' the various features: one comes to represent one thing—their common subject-matter—as having all those features.

Part of the Treisman and Gelade (1980) model includes what they call a 'master map of locations', which has two distinct functions. One is that it defines the targets or salient regions that determine where attention is directed. Locations represented by the master map are locations to which one directs one's attention; attention selects a location among them. Crick and Koch put this idea as follows

the brain has some sort of topographic saliency map that codes for the conspicuous-ness of locations in the visual field in terms of generalized center–surround operations. This map would derive its input from the individual feature maps and give a very 'biased' view of the visual environment, emphasizing locations where objects differed in some perceptual dimension, i.e., color, motion, depth, from objects at neighboring locations. (Crick and Koch 1997: 286–7)

Information from separate feature maps about that location must somehow be coordinated, and this is the second function given to the 'master map'. It has the job of identifying the locations *mapped by* the various feature maps. That is, to coordinate that information, one needs some scheme for establishing that this portion of the F map maps the same territory as that portion of the G map. This job is also assigned to the master map.

Notice that this second function does not require us to posit one central map, much less one that is nothing but a map of locations—whatever that would be. Instead the need is to identify the location mapped by one map as one also mapped by another. The goal of 'binding' is to indicate that the two portions of the two maps both represent features *of* the same location. They both map the same territory.

Or at least so it is in lower levels of the feature hierarchy. Feature integration may proceed in different ways at higher levels. There may be 'object descriptors' or other principles upon which bindings at higher levels depend (Kanwisher and Driver 1992). Furthermore, different principles may apply to pairings across levels compared to pairings within levels (see Treisman 1988: 233). The squareness of the red square does not fill the space it occupies in the same way that the redness of it does. This is one reason I used 'matte red, glossy green' as my example of a (level two) property-binding in Section 2.5, rather than the traditional 'red square, green triangle' example discussed by Jackson and Sellars.

There is one last theoretical nugget to be extracted from property-binding. It will allow us to close the books on a set of issues that opened in Section 2.4 with the partition argument. The need to integrate distinct feature maps puts some constraints upon them. Suppose you are reviewing the efforts of the interior decorator. You see red above the mantle—a feature map represents that place as red—and you would like to check whether that place is, as per your specifications, also glossy. Given vertebrate sensory organization, you (or rather your sub-personal minions) need to consult a different feature map, and after that map is found, determine what portion of it maps the same place. You might ask, rhetorically,

> Where, my minions, is the portion of this map that maps the same place as does that portion of that map?

Only after they have succeeded in answering this question can identification proceed. One must identify the *referents* of the two portions of the two maps.

The need to answer this question puts some constraints on the organization of sensory representation. It must be possible to answer the question, and to answer it in real time. Suppose one could not readily determine whether the question had been successfully answered. Perhaps it is unclear what place the current portion of the map maps. Or perhaps information about a given region is scattered randomly about, so that each time you pick a new region you must search the entire map to garner the news about it. Clearly either alternative would make the map useless as a map. It only works as a map if, given any portion of the map, it is readily determinable what place that portion maps; and given any place, one can determine in relatively short order what portions of the map carry information about that place. A road map, for example, would be of little use as a map if in answer to the question 'Where are we?' one would sometimes need to point simultaneously to two distinct places. It would be similarly disorienting to come across a portion of the map such that in principle one *could not* determine what part of the territory that portion maps. The piece of paper might have other uses, but it would be frustrating to try to use it to navigate.

Now in fact we do solve the Many Properties problem—we can differentiate glossy red next to matte green from matte red next to glossy green—and we do it using distinct feature maps for colour and texture. Therefore, those feature maps must satisfy whatever constraints are necessary to solve the problem in real time. The argument suggests two such constraints. First, from map to world: given a portion P of a source map, one can readily determine what space-time region R it maps. Secondly, from world to map: given a region R and a second map, one can determine in relatively short order what portion P' of the second map, if any, represents other features of the same region R. Portions P and P' of the two maps are thereby shown to map different features of the same territory.

I suggest that these requirements account for the 'formal differences' between qualitative and spatial dimensions of variation in phenomenal appearance. We need some dimensions of variation that satisfy those constraints, as otherwise the task of identifying subject-matters of portions of distinct feature maps would be intractable. The spatial dimensions of appearance qualify. Earlier I argued that the spatial character of experience is formally distinct from other dimensions of variation in phenomenal appearance: spatial identification can serve to individuate. Place-times and features enter into 'collecting principles' in different ways. Finally, spatial identification can serve as a principle organizing identifications across feature maps. What we see now—the closure I promised—is that these three characteristics are interconnected. Any creature that manages more than one feature map must have some dimensions of variation in phenomenal appearance that satisfy the map–world and world–map constraints, as otherwise it could not manage the coordination of distinct features. This creature could therefore partition its dimensions of variation of appearance into those that do and those that do not satisfy those constraints. The former will have something of the character of singular terms; they are the 'sensory names' in its vocabulary of sense. The species may eventually discover the same connection as we have between space and reference. In its early epistemologies it might call those qualities 'primary'. The other phenomenal dimensions are multiply instantiable and 'secondary'; when language eventually evolves they get cast as predicates.

The various cortical sensory areas present a ployglot babble of differing qualitative features in different maps. Furthermore, different maps employ radically different means of identifying their targets. Nevertheless, because the different maps all pin their different features onto space-time regions, their very different stories can be coordinated and merged, into one unified story. Spatial character provides a common coin in which they can all trade.

5.5 ERRORS OF SENSE

Like business stories, the sometimes spectacular failures of sensory representation can make for more interesting reading than the quotidian successes. Although failures and malfunctions are unlikely to form natural kinds, they can provide useful clues to the conditions necessary for success. A brief tour through the menagerie of sensory slips, hitches, glitches, misfires, failures, and infirmities will prove entertaining and instructive.

The door into this domain has already been opened by the delay line example introduced in Section 5.2. In it auditory features are not so much misperceived as misplaced. Instead of a faulty characterization of a successfully identified place-time, we have one perhaps successfully characterized, but misidentified. The error lies specifically in mechanisms of sensory reference. Other phenomena qualify. Phantom limbs, for example, demonstrate a dramatic misplacing of somaesthetic features. The features placed outside the bodily borders include not only pain, but sometimes also kinaesthetic, tactile, and thermal ones. The phantom may appear still to be occupied by qualities of pressure, warmth, or cold; or to feel wet, ticklish, sweaty, prickly, or itchy (Melzack 1992: 120). Given our preoccupation with the latter quality, it is startling to note Melzack's report that an itch felt on a phantom limb can sometimes be relieved by scratching the *apparent* site of the itch (Melzack 1992: 120). Some amputees have the impression of retaining volitional control over the phantom, so that if they try to get out of bed, for example, it will feel to them as if the phantom is present, moving and bending appropriately. Occasionally the illusion is so strong that an amputee will indeed get out of bed upon waking up, only to fall over when weight is shifted to the absent leg (Melzack 1992; see also Katz and Melzack 1990; Melzack 1989; Ramachandran *et al.* 1996). Clearly these are cases of illusion, or non-veridical appearance; but in these cases we have a breakdown of a particular kind: a misfire in the ordinarily reliable mechanisms of spatial discrimination. The dramatic mislocation of a phantom is an error of a different order from the typical illusion.

Evidently we must recognize at least two distinct varieties of non-veridical sensory appearance. In one, sensory reference is secured, but one misperceives the features of that locale. In the other, sensory reference itself goes awry. Features are mislocated or misplaced. The system produces an identifier, and it refers as normal to a place-time, but it was the wrong identifier. It says 'hither' when it should have said 'thither'. So in a catalogue of errors our first two entries are:

1. *Faulty predication.* A successfully identified place-time causes a misattribution of sensory qualities.
2. *Misreference.* A feature is mislocated or misplaced; a place-time, perhaps correctly characterized, is misidentified.

To this we can add a third entry. Spatial discrimination is typically a multidimensional affair. For the bat to identify the whereabouts of the moth, it needs to discern location in three dimensions of range, elevation, and azimuth, for which it needs information from range-finding delay circuits, from intensity differences, and from interaural phase differences. Other sensory modalities similarly employ distinct mechanisms for distinct spatial coordinates. Since these separate mechanisms can go wrong independently, this organization opens up the possibility of what might be called 'partial' referential misfires, in which, for example, two out of three spatial dimensions are picked up correctly, but something goes awry with the third. In such a case the sensory identification is partly right and partly wrong. We get the possibility of what I will call

3. *Partial mislocation.* Some coordinates are correct, but some are not.

This is an odd hybrid, for which there are no linguistic counterparts. It provides the proper bin for the various 'spatial illusions' generated by flat pieces of paper (Section 5.3). But vision is replete with examples:

One may be utterly perplexed what a thing is just because one is seeing it as at a different distance from the right one, and hence as the wrong size. Or vice versa. I once opened my eyes and saw the black striking surface of a matchbox which was standing on one end; the other sides of the box were not visible. This was a few inches from my eye and I gazed at it in astonishment wondering what it could be. . . . I took it for three or four feet distant, and it looked, if anything, like a thick post, but I knew there could be no such thing in my bedroom. (Anscombe 1981: 16)

Her experience of the matchbox identifies its azimuth and elevation correctly, but goes wrong about depth. As noted before, at a given visual azimuth and altitude, one often needs to assign just one depth coordinate—the depth of the first occluding surface at that angle. Anscombe's visual system correctly identifies the visual solid angle of the matchbox, but misidentifies the depth within that cone at which the surface is found. One could argue that Anscombe sees the surface of the matchbox, but sees it *as* a thick post, three or four feet away.

Lycan (1996) describes the wonderful example of the Victorian 'peep box'. Viewed through the peephole, the interior of the box looks like a miniature

Victorian drawing room; but viewed from the top one sees that the impression is created by cleverly arranged bits of cloth and wood, held at various odd angles and distances by pieces of wire. One might see a small Ames chair next to the ostensible table.

When one innocently views the contents of a peep box through its peephole, does one see veridically? Here again I think a very proper answer is 'Yes and no'. Yes, because one does see shapes and textures that are physically real; there really is a dark red plushy object at two o'clock, for example, even though it is not the sort of object one supposes it is and it may be nearer or farther away from one's eye than one thinks, and one sees real edges, lines, and expanses. But also, no, because one sees a miniature Victorian drawing room that simply does not exist. (Lycan 1996: 150)

I agree with Lycan on the 'yes and no' answer, but would urge that this is precisely a case of partial referential misfire. (Lycan explains his 'yes and no' answer in terms of a hierarchical representation that has more than one truth value at once, but I think this particular example can be explained in an even simpler way.) Looking into the peep box (or at the Ames room, the Ames chair, Gregory's impossible triangle, and so on) you suffer an illusion about one of three spatial coordinates for a visible edge, line, or expanse (Gregory 1970: 55). You see 'shapes and textures that are physically real' in the sense that their visual azimuths and altitudes are identified correctly. As Lycan puts it, there really is a dark red plushy object at two o'clock; one 'sees real edges, lines, and expanses' in just this sense. But you go awry on the third dimension. You misrepresent depth, and consequently shape and size. You are presented with the visual solid angles that would be presented by a miniature Victorian drawing room, in a context that removes most depth cues, so that those visual solid angles are in fact filled with little bits of wood and cloth cunningly arranged.

On this line all the edges and lines one sees are actual physical edges and lines, found at the azimuths and altitudes identified by one's visual system, but located at different depths. In this way one can be both partly right and partly wrong about the location and shape of that dark red plushy expanse at two o'clock. Similarly, Miss Anscombe both did and did not correctly identify the location of the matchbox. It did indeed lie within that visual cone, but at a depth different from the one her visual system indicated. Indeed, it is only because the matchbox was correctly located at that azimuth and altitude that she could learn that she had misperceived its depth. If her sensory identification had failed completely, she could not learn at the next moment that she had misperceived the depth *of that thing.*

A similar moral applies to after-images. Recall the story of Bertie, who cannot tell a lie about the pointy green spot in his visual field (Section 3.4). While it is true that to Bertie it seems as if there is a green spot before him, nevertheless it is quite unlikely that Bertie would ever respond by pointing to a surface in front of him and saying, 'That green spot is growing tiresome.' As soon as Bertie moves his eyes, the after-image moves,[3] and this is not normally true of places identified visually. Nor does the character of the after-image carry much if any information about the surface on which it appears. Once we too realize that Bertie is suffering from an after-image, our means of identifying 'that spot' shift from an allocentric coordinate scheme to a retinocentric one. We might say, 'There's no green spot there, Bertie. You must be having an after-image. Just wait awhile and it will go away.' In such assurances 'it' might refer to almost any distal location; construed allocentri-cally the pronoun is effectively a free variable.

The interpretation best at assigning 'it' a value is, as suggested earlier, 2½- dimensional. The latter scheme can make sense of the idea that when Bertie shifts his gaze he is still seeing that same green spot, even though his eyes are now focused on totally different things, and that spot now appears both larger and at a different depth. In fact 'that spot' might refer to anything within the visual cone defined by the fixed azimuth and altitude of the area of affected retina. This is how we understand the reference of 'it' in claims like 'That spot gets bigger when you see it on a more distant wall' or 'Just wait awhile and it will go away'. Two out of three coordinates are as they would be if a green spot were there (on the wall), but one quickly learns that the experience does not pick out any particular depth or distal location, and so does not characterize any such allocentrically identifiable location as being green.[4] To say the after-image *is* green is just to say that *whatever* surface first intercepts that visual cone will *look* green.

So far we have three entries in our catalogue of errors. A fourth entry, if we make it, corresponds to the most spectacular variety of business failure, which has yet to be mentioned: those shocking occasions when long-suffering cred-itors show up at the address of record, with their writs and liens, and find *nothing* there. The owners and the assets have decamped, vanished, vamoosed. Might the mechanisms of sensory reference similarly fire away and fire away and produce—nothing? Might they produce an identifier that simply lacks a referent? This entry would read:

---

[3]   This is not true of all after-images. 'Bidwell's ghost' appears to be a surface colour, and like other surface colours, it does not move as one moves one's eyes. A half-white disc rotating at high speed has a slot behind which sits a red light. With appropriate illumination, the disc looks bluish-green: the after-image of the red light. (I thank C. L. Hardin for pointing out this example; see Hardin 1988: 93.)

[4]   Similarly, the doctor might say to you: 'Don't worry about those floating spots; they are *muscae volitantes*.' Perhaps demonstrative pronouns can have their values assigned by any of various levels of representation within sensory systems. 'It' need not refer to an object, but might have its value assigned by a 2d retinocentric scheme, by the 2½d sketch, by 3d egocen-tric identifiers, etc.

4. *No referent.* The sensory system produces an identifier that refers to nothing.

The phenomenon most often mentioned in this context is hallucination. Kaplan notes, for example, that a demonstration that is hallucinatory fails to assign the perceptual demonstrative a value. The associated demonstration, he says, has no demonstratum (see Kaplan 1989*a*: 490, 515, 1989*b*: 585, 586). Indeed it is clear that a perceptual demonstrative that requires an associated hallucinatory demonstration will typically fail to pick out any reidentifiable material object. Macbeth's use of 'this' in 'Is this a dagger I see before me?' cannot be assigned any such object. But (as suggested in Section 3.4) might he not succeed in picking out a place-time? Under this interpretation, 'This is a dagger' has an underlying identification of the form 'There is a dagger', and is simply and straightforwardly false. There is no dagger there.

In any case our question here is not whether or not we should assign a null referent to a word like 'this' or 'that', but whether sensory identifiers, visual or otherwise, might ever lack a referent. Perhaps even if the demonstratives employed during hallucinations have no referents, the sensory states involved—if they are sensory states—still do. The hallucinated dagger appears somewhere; and, no matter where the appearances point, at that place we cannot lack for place-times. There must be something at that address, if only a place-time. That at least cannot decamp.

Hallucinations turn out to weave a complicated web. To clarify matters it is helpful to shift to an auditory example, even though the use I make of it is not that of its author:

Helen and Ellen are very much alike. They can be as similar as you please in purely physical terms—atom-for-atom replicas, say—but for some small details. Their environments are very similar too: again, let them be atom-for-atom replicas, except for an important feature. The important feature is a horse (Cowdell). Helen's immediate environment contains Cowdell, Ellen's lacks him (and every other horse or similar object). The situations are much as described in §58. Each needs a horse to save her kingdom; each is hyper-sensitive; each seems to hear a clip-clopping behind; each consequently swings round exclaiming 'That is a horse'. But remember the difference. In Helen's case she really does hear Cowdell, despite her hypersensitivity, and so really does refer to him as she swings round. However, Ellen is not so lucky. The small physical quirk that distinguishes her from Helen happens to make her imagine a sound just like that which Cowdell produced behind Helen. But there is no horse or any other source of the imagined sound behind Ellen. As she swings around she refers to nothing. (McCulloch 1989: 208)

McCulloch's interest (like Kaplan's) focuses on the question of whether Ellen refers to anything with the *sentence* 'That is a horse', and he has an interesting discussion of Fregean and Russellian treatments of the sentence. I propose to extend the gambit a bit and consider Fregean and Russellian treatments of the auditory experience. As suggested earlier, the demonstrative in 'That is a horse' might have its reference secured by the auditory identification of a place-time. In Helen's case, the successful identification has the force of

That (auditorily identified region) is (occupied by) a horse.

We can explain how the demonstrative in the sentence is assigned a value: the hearer of the sentence can also hear the horse. That is, the hearer can auditorily pick out the source of the clip-clopping sounds. Helen's turning round might help to disambiguate, as gestures often do in demonstrative identification. She means something that-a-way. With this assistance the hearer is in a position to grasp the thought that Helen communicates with her sentence.[5] Speaker and hearer identification both succeed.

Corresponding failures in Ellen's speech act can also be understood. In her situation there is no sound, so the hearer cannot by auditory means identify any particular region as the source of the sound, and so cannot identify what Ellen means by 'that'. Parties privy to the episode could not pick out any particular region of space-time as being the one that Ellen said was occupied by a horse. Hearer identification fails, and in that sense Ellen 'refers to nothing'. We hearers would have no grounds for saying of any particular region that it was the region Ellen thought was occupied by a horse.

The intriguing question remains of whether Ellen's *sensory* processes can be assigned a referent. To Ellen it appears that there is a sound behind her, since that is why she turns round. Lacking the requisite auditory input, no interlocutor can understand her sentence; but perhaps Ellen has succeeded in picking out a target for the demonstrative: a place-time, at least, to which she intends to refer. Perhaps her auditory processes successfully identify the place-time where to her the horse appears to be. They also mischaracterize that region, as being occupied by clip-clopping sounds. Perhaps they both mischaracterize a region and misidentify it, indulging simultaneously in our first two categories of error. Or perhaps Ellen's auditory processes produce the analogue of a name without a referent. The token has all the appearances of a referring term—it seems to pick a particular place-time—but for reasons perhaps not introspectively accessible to Ellen, the reference fails. How do we decide between these alternatives? This question is distinct from the question

---

[5]   As suggested earlier, circumstances can make such gestures unnecessary. (We are trudging along silently, and all hear a solitary clip-clopping.) Such cases show that the gestures and other aids to discriminating are themselves of no special semantic significance, but simply assist communication (see Kaplan 1989*b*: 582). But the auditory presentation (the sensory element of the 'demonstration') is essential and irreplaceable: if we were both deaf, this perceptual demonstrative would fall flat.

of whether or not her use of the pronoun 'that' refers to anything. It is not settled by showing that hearers privy to the scene could not identify what she means. Here the identification if any proceeds sub-personally, and the success or failure of the identification must be weighed in terms of sub-personal details. The relevant consumers of the sensory identification are all found within Ellen's head.

I have argued that the question of how mechanisms of sensory identification do their job is an open empirical question, and one to which a priori methods are unsuited (Section 3.5). Even the exact job specifications are unknown. We do not know enough about how experiences such as Ellen's are generated to produce any clear verdict. But it is easy to see how the case could fall under our first category of error: successful sensory identification of a place-time, which is then mischaracterized. For example, perhaps what McCulloch means by 'hypersensitivity' is that Ellen has rather dramatically dropped her 'response criterion' and is responding, in effect, to random neural noise in her sensory systems. A blip that under a normal response criterion would be discarded as noise is treated as a sound of Cowdell. But this blip might engage her delay line assemblies, or whatever other mechanisms she uses to locate sounds, correctly. It produces therein some activation pattern $[p_m]$ which, interpreted in the normal way, picks out the direction whence the sounds of Cowdell appear to come. So she successfully identifies that direction, but mischaracterizes events therein. Perhaps her interlocutors, trudging along in silence, can confirm that there is no sound in that vicinity, since there are no sounds anywhere. They could inform her that what she says is, straightforwardly, false. There is no horse there. 'It's your imagination,' they might say, using 'it' in a sense similar to that used earlier to reassure the dazzled Bertie.

The case might commit the first two categories of error simultaneously. Perhaps the neural noise causes Ellen not only to mischaracterize the auditory features of a region, but also to settle on the wrong estimate of its phase difference. So she misidentifies the very region that she also mischaracterizes.

To find a sensory identifier that has *no* referent, we must find one that is uninterpretable, that fails to pick out any place-time. The case must somehow suspend the mapping rules by which an activation pattern $[p_m]$ in auditory systems gets mapped to an auditory direction. The system must be placed in some condition under which those mapping rules do not apply, so that the coordinates are uninterpretable.[6] Examples in which the activation patterns

---

[6] This may be difficult, particularly if those mapping rules are a function of the selective history of the species. Whatever we do today cannot alter that history, and hence cannot alter how activation patterns in the auditory system *ought* to be interpreted. See Elder (1994*a*, 1998*c*).

themselves are scrambled or malformed will not suffice, since such examples fail to provide well-formed tokens of sensory identifiers. We need a well-formed token that has no referent. Even hallucinations may not qualify. The latter may in fact engage mechanisms of spatial discrimination in ways that yield fully interpretable identifiers. Or perhaps we will eventually determine that even though hallucinations in some ways resemble sensory states, properly they belong to a different taxonomic class altogether. If we knew more about what was going on in both the qualitative and the spatial components of the sensory system in episodes such as Ellen's, we could give a better answer, but right now we cannot.

It is appropriate, therefore, to end the discussion of hallucinations with a puzzle. The auditory hallucinations of alcohol hallucinosis or schizophrenia are thankfully rare, but a similar phenomenon that occurs among normal people is the so-called 'hypnagogic imagery': imagery that occurs in the hypnagogic state between waking and sleep. The most common form of auditory hypnagogic imagery involves hearing (or, pardon me, seeming to hear) one's own name being called (Zusne and Jones 1982: 129). In one study almost two-thirds of students surveyed reported such imagery (McKellar 1957; Reed 1972: 37). The experience is often sufficiently vivid to rouse its victim to full wakefulness. Suppose that in your student days, for which we shall hold you blameless, you suffer well-localized hypnagogic imagery: a voice, emanating from empty space, calling your name. When this happens is the one who is calling—to wit, some sub-personal part of you—referring to you? It does this, the therapist tells you later, for reasons of its own, reasons that you may find alarming but must learn to accommodate. Or are you perhaps referring to yourself? Perhaps in this case you literally hear yourself thinking. But what is the appropriate form of address? In the mirror you might see someone whose trousers are on fire, and shout 'You there' to warn that person, only to recognize belatedly that yours are the trousers on fire, and 'You there' is in fact self-referential (see Kaplan 1989*a*: 533). Hearing voices allows even odder varieties of indirection. You recognize that your name refers to you—it gets your attention, after all—but you do not recognize that you are the one referring to yourself. You could grasp the thought 'I am the one speaking', but you would deny it. Similarly, if the voice said, 'I am here,' it would say something false.

5.6 ESCAPE FROM THE SENSORY FIELDS

Just as the features ascribed by later maps can grow increasingly complex and perception-like, so also the means by which later maps pick out place-times become increasingly sophisticated. Maps higher in the hierarchy employ different coordinate schemes—different mapping rules, associating sensory names with referents. At some point the two improvements combined will have sufficient impetus to launch us out of the sensory domain altogether, and this section provides our last chance to review the pre-launch checklist.

The limits of a retinocentric scheme are exposed the first time an animal wants to shift its gaze. If it is visually to relate what it sees now to what it will see next, it needs some coordinate scheme in which multiple fixation points can be related to one another, and (as noted in Section 3.3) a retinocentric map fails. The next fixation point might lie off the edge of the map, in *terra incognita*. The simplest scheme in which distinct fixation points can be related spatially to one another is organized egocentrically, with eyeball direction coded relative to the position of the eye sockets. In this scheme, direction (0,0) is the direction one looks when one's eyes are resting neutrally in their sockets. A twitch on any of the rectus muscles attaching the eyeball to the skull will sling the gaze round to a new direction. Gaze management (and the visual orienting reflex, or VOR) indeed use such a head-relative coordinate scheme in their maps. But even this system fails to account for the possibility that the animal might someday move its head. The amusing spectacle of a crowd watching a tennis game, with all the heads bobbing back and forth in unison, would literally make no sense, since to the spectators the ball would not appear to trace a continuous path back and forth over the net. We need to endow the spectators with a visual coordinate scheme in which even though the ball maintains a continuous socket-relative direction of (0,0), it can still appear to move. Such a scheme is clearly a more sophisticated endowment than the one that manages saccades. Difficulties multiply when one realizes that spectators might manage the 'same' head rotation by twisting the neck, the torso, the hips, or some idiosyncratic combination thereof. The 'placing' component of feature-placing is by no means trivial; our sub-personal minions must toil mightily to manage the various coordinate schemes and to translate from one into another (see Grush, forthcoming). And the work has to be done fast. A gazelle who catches a glimpse of a lion through the grass cannot afford to sit and ponder the appropriate direction of egress; the translations of coordinate schemes, as it lifts its head, turns the 'other way', and runs, must be immediate. Small wonder that the same feature (such as hue) is often represented in multiple feature maps. Those maps may differ in coordinate scheme: in the means by which they identify the place at which the hue is placed. Note well that we are not introducing new places into the universe, or new kinds of space, but merely new ways of identifying the same old places.

The upper limit of such coordinate systems is found in so-called 'allocentric' space, in which all of the coordinates of the coordinate system are independent of the body. This too is not a new kind of space but a new way of identifying occupants of the one and only. No essential reference is made to the body of the percipient; instead identification proceeds entirely in terms of the relations that the objects in front of the sense organs bear to one another. In such a scheme the body of the percipient has no special place, does not serve as origin or axes, and indeed can be located in the scheme just like any other object. John O'Keefe and co-workers have produced convincing evidence that some visual feature maps are organized allocentrically (O'Keefe 1993). The coordinate system used is entirely unintuitive, as it relies on determining the *centroid* of a cluster of visual features and their slope, and then relating one object to another by distances from the centroid and angles relative to that slope. Yet O'Keefe has provided some compelling evidence of neural mechanisms sensitive to centroid and slope.

At the upper reaches of the hierarchy of cortical feature maps, vision is often described as splitting into two channels: 'what' v. 'where' (Davidoff 1991: ch. 2). The 'what' channel ends at the temporal cortex, and includes feature maps for colour and fine spatial detail. The 'where' channel ends at the parietal cortex, has high contrast sensitivity, high speed, and few maps for colour or spatial detail. As other authors have noted (McCarthy 1993), it is probably best to think of the contrast between 'what' and 'where' channels as a contrast between types of coordinate scheme, with allocentric schemes found only in the 'where' channel. Otherwise the contrast is difficult to make. A map of nothing but locations would be of dubious value, and similarly a pure 'what' map, with information only about what features are present, and nothing about where they are, would not be a map. The contrast is rather that allocentric coordinate schemes are found only in the sequence of maps terminating in the parietal cortex—in the 'where' channel. In the interests of speed that channel ignores some features altogether. The spurned features are found only in maps that employ egocentric identifiers, in the 'what' channel terminating in the temporal cortex.

I earlier defined sensory processes as those up to and including tertiary association areas in the cortex. At the allocentrically organized end-points of the 'where' channel in the parietal cortex, we have reached the borderlands of our subject-matter. Another sign that these areas provide for us a terminus is that such tertiary feature maps are often cross-modal or 'polysensory'. They might, for example, translate between kinaesthetic locations (for the direction of the saccade, say) and visual ones. This is 'translation' in the sense of vector translation: transforming coordinates. Once we reach a level where the identification of a place can proceed indifferently in either visual or kinaesthetic terms, we leave what most people think of as the realm of 'early vision'. Such cross-modal identities also allow us at last to escape the limits of sensory fields. Our map is no longer purely a visual map, or purely a kinaesthetic map, but something of both. Independence from a single modality is one touchstone for perceptual processes, and here is sounded the first declaration of such independence.

It is not surprising to find that the same sorts of translations of coordinate schemes that occur across feature maps within a sensory modality also occur across modalities. In fact the most interesting variety of informative identity (Section 5.3) was the cross-modal one, where, for example, a visual identifier and a tactile one were found to identify the very same space-time region. You might see your fingers at the keyboard, feel the pressure on your fingertips as you push on the keys, and hear the little clicky noises as the switches close. The tactile feedback from your fingertips appears at the place where you see your fingers, which is also the place where the clicky noises seem to originate. You have something like a visual identifier of a place, a tactile identifier of a place, and an auditory one; and all three refer to (roughly) the same place. This is so even though neither the sound nor the touch can be located visually, neither the sight nor the sound can be located by touch, and neither the sight nor the touch can be located by hearing. Nevertheless, the translation from one scheme to the next is (for the adult) effortless. You might hunt for the tilde key on the keyboard, and when you see it (if you see it), strike it with your left pinkie. The visual location becomes the target—the intentional object—for motor systems as well. Somehow you can look and issue a command, which (translated from its sub-personal dialect) might be rendered as: 'Go *there*, pinkie'. Your muscles oblige. What a wonder this is.

The source of wonder is that visual and tactile locations seem immiscible, incommensurable; yet here the translation from one to the next is effortless. Given that not one tactile location can be identified visually, how can one so easily translate, wholesale, from a visual coordinate scheme to a tactile one? One principle which makes it possible rests on the convenient fact that we are embodied. Transducers of different sensory systems have different fixed physical locations on that body. Even though the spatial relations between tactile and visual transducers are not apparent to vision alone or to touch alone, the brute existence of those relations makes possible the translation from one scheme to another. For example, you look at the keyboard and the various keys occupy different visually identifiable locations. You can sense pressure in your fingertips, as well as the angles and position of joints in fingertips, wrist, elbow, shoulder, and neck. The position of the eyeball in its socket can also be described in that same haptic coordinate system. Since the physical position of the eyeball determines the physical position of visual transducers, we can translate from retinocentric locations into haptic ones.

This is possible even though the positions of visual transducers can be neither seen nor felt. The two sensory schemes are related by a fact that is not apparent to either one alone: the transducers from which both commence stand in physical relations to one another.

Suppose, for example, we represent the disposition of all the joints and muscles with a three-dimensional stick figure. It might have a finger cocked over the tilde key, the wrist bent, the head bowed, and so on. The eyeball is part of that same stick figure; at a given moment it is positioned among those joints and muscles in one specific orientation. But that same eyeball is also oriented uniquely with respect to retinocentric visual locations. It becomes our Rosetta stone, allowing translations back and forth from visual to haptic coordinate schemes. One can correlate positions in the field of view with eyeball directions, which in turn can be correlated with the position of the head and body. Visual locations can then be placed spatially in relation to haptic ones. It becomes possible, as in Home Mechanic II (Section 5.3), to see and feel the same place. While it remains difficult to find and put your finger on the tilde key, it is now at least possible.

We can translate from haptic to auditory coordinates using the same strategy. Head orientation relates auditory azimuths and altitudes to a three-dimensional physical object: the head itself. Using the principles described in Section 3.6, differences in phase and intensity serve physically to place auditory features relative to the two ears. Our haptic stick figure has the same two ears, and it can thereby be oriented relative to auditory locations. This can be done even though the ears themselves do not have audible locations. We have common origins and a capacity to translate from one set of coordinates to another. With that one can identify the same place by sight, touch, or hearing.

In general, cross-modal identities are made possible by the fact that transducers for the different modalities stand in physical relations to one another, spread out over the same body. The physical inter-digitation of transducers is not apparent to either sensory modality, but it suffices that such cross-correlations exist and can be learned. Invisibly and silently, they provide the principles on which cross-modal identifications proceed. In this way the body itself provides the translation key for sensory coordination: the frame that makes it possible to translate one sensory coordinate scheme into another. Places thereafter can be identified independently of any one sensory modality. In the hunt for the tilde key, the target eventually identified is no longer purely a place in the visual field. It might be identified in a visual way, but it could also be identified in other ways. We reach the threshold of a concept of space that is independent of any particular sensory modality.

The notion of an external 'cross-fix' can, finally, help to resolve the 'Unlabelled Meter Reading' dilemma from Section 2.2. The original dilemma was: you are a homunculus trapped in the post-central gyrus, faced with a million meters indicating voltage levels in the somatosensory neurons. Your job is to throw any number of the million levers found in the pre-central gyrus, to steer the vessel out of harm's way. But unfortunately all of the meters and all of the levers are unlabelled. The neuron itself cannot inform you of its distal causes or effects. So how do you decide which levers to throw? A slight modification connects with the concerns of this chapter. Perhaps you see some particular meters firing in pattern (α_i, α_j, α_k), indicative of an itch. Some meters are active and some are not; you wisely adopt a vector notation, and dub the configuration of currently active meters 'configuration [p_m]'. Labelling the active lines with this name still does not tell you *where* those lines come from or where their receptive fields are located. So you still do not know where the itch is located, or what levers to pull to scratch appropriately. If you could somehow discover that the active lines all convey news from the left foot, the problem could be solved; but since you are confined to the post-central gyrus, all the lines are unlabelled, and no peeking is allowed, there seems to be no way for you to find out. Your host suffers the itch while you sit and ponder.

The central mistake made in posing the problem in this fashion is the supposition that if the problem is soluble, then at some moment some sub-personal system must be in receipt of information sufficient to justify (specifically, deduce) a solution. That same supposition can be detected lurking behind many of the 'brain–mind' mysteries posed in Section 2.2. But perhaps no such internal justifications are possible. If the solution is anything like the translation of one sensory coordinate scheme into another, then it rests on correspondences outside the head, beyond the ken of any one sensory system. Perhaps none of your components are ever in receipt of information sufficient to justify a solution, but nevertheless the problem gets solved. Learning is the wild card; it can come to reflect such correspondences even if there is never sufficient evidence to justify a claim *that* such a correspondence exists. Cross-modal coordination must be learned, as must the coordination between hand and eye, or between itching and scratching. The random stumbling and crashing about which such learning involves, and which appears wasteful and aimless, might in fact be the key to the solution. The information generated by such stumbling makes it possible to *learn* a solution to the Unlabelled Meter Reading dilemma.

Here's how random crashing about could be the critical ingredient in the solution. The activation pattern (α_i, α_j, α_k) corresponding to the itch is at least mildly aversive; it causes a peremptory desire that such sensing cease. The infant blunders about more or less randomly, expressing its displeasure. It is vital that this host *not* suffer in silence. As it squirms and flails, it generates both efferent and afferent signals. The arm arcing through space generates kinaesthetic and somaesthetic impulses: volleys of information about joint and muscle movement, about air moving across skin, about textures and temperatures. When finally the hand collides with the leg, new tactile information is relayed from both the hand and the leg. The infant discovers the informative somaesthetic identity: that spot (felt on the left leg) = that spot (felt with the hand).

Learning these informative identities makes a solution possible. Most of the blunderings and flailings will fail. But if the infant eventually tumbles onto the right place, and a scratch makes the itch go away, the event will be memorable, as it satisfies the peremptory desire. It will be worth remembering the association between the particular pattern of sensory inputs corresponding to itch-on-foot and the particular pattern of efferent impulses that finally dispatched it. When scratching hand encounters itchy foot, we also get a new cross-fix of tactile locations. The location of the itch can be identified with that of the fingertip sensations (and associated kinaesthetic sensations) of the scratching hand. Our informative identity acquires a third term. So even though the solution could not be deduced beforehand by a homunculus located anywhere within the system, nevertheless random crashing about can eventually lead to the discovery that

> this spot (felt on the left foot)
> = that spot (felt with the right hand)
> = the place to which $[p_m]$ refers.

Sensory generalization helps speed this process. A subsequent nearby itch will fire off some of the same receptors, and yield some propensity to produce the same efferent trajectory. As this gets shaped by experience one could learn a mapping of haptic identifiers to efferent trajectories. Then the next itch that comes along can be dispatched more quickly.

It remains possible that some cross-modal and sensory-motor coordination is hard-wired; innate links if any would only speed the process. Many ungulates walk moments after birth. But generally cross-modal associations seem remarkably plastic, as experiments with distorting goggles reveal (Kohler 1964). The goggles change the external physical correspondence between visual and tactile stimuli, yet the system adapts. Even a minor change in an eyeglass prescription late in life entails some relearning of visual–tactile and hand–eye coordination.

Whatever their origin, as cross-modal and sensory-motor identifications accumulate, we gradually acquire capacities of full sentience. A creature so endowed can turn its head towards a sound, look for prey it hears, run away from predators, and scratch its itches. At its most sophisticated it might acquire maps that are independent of any one sensory modality, so that it can find its way back to the burrow or the nest using clues that are visual, olfactory, or tactile. The notion of a place identified by such a map ceases to be a notion dependent on any one sensory modality. The places identified are no longer merely places in a 'sensory field', but are something closer to what we think of as modality-independent objective particulars. That spot on the trail home can exist unseen, because the rock there has a particular texture that one can feel with one's paws, or vegetation marking the spot presents a characteristic odour to one's snout. It is a small step from these modality-independent places to our folk notion of objective three-dimensional physical objects. These are independent of observers, exist unperceived, and bear relations to one another in one unified spatio-temporal coordinate scheme. Such sensory precursors of elements of our conceptual scheme make the leap into speech somewhat less problematic, and they might provide content for some early communications. Rock here, woods there. Our hominid bursts into feature-placing speech.

The multimodal association areas mark the limits of the subject-matter of this book; past them we are clearly in the domain of perceptual and cognitive processing proper. That domain is organized in terms of objects and properties enduring at locations specified in observer-independent terms. While sensory systems are the paradigms of non-conceptual representation, once we broach a system characterizing numerically reidentifiable particulars in objective space, our 'features' have acquired essentially all of the characteristics of predicates. Reference to places in these maps no longer has anything 'proto' about it; it is reference proper.

True Theories, False Colours

THE distinction between referential and predicative components of sensory representation serves as the key opening some new logical vistas before our astounded if weary eyes. The entire landscape of sensory experience will take on a fresh appearance. With these alluring visions I hope to tempt the traveller over the last ridge to the conclusion.

6.1 REFERRING THROUGH FALSEHOOD

The first vision is of massive falsehood, piles and piles of false propositions, accreted over centuries, through which, nevertheless, reference succeeds. The causal theory of reference illustrates how this might happen. We might today successfully refer to Moses—the causal chain governing our use of the name terminates in that very man—even though by some quirk of history the preponderance of our contemporary beliefs about Moses turn out to be false. Perhaps those few that happen to be true are not true of just one man, so we cannot today formulate a description that Moses alone satisfies (see Kripke 1972: 66–7). Or, to take a slightly different case, J. J. Thomson not only discovered electrons, but successfully referred to them, even though the bulk of the theoretical propositions he advanced about electrons have since been abandoned (see Newton-Smith 1981: 161). To make sense of either case requires us to isolate reference from the enunciation of true descriptions, and the causal theory obliges by describing a series of causal conditions connecting the use of the designator to the referent. That causal chain can remain intact even if the speaker who uses the designator uses it, regrettably, to speak only falsehoods.

With a similar isolation of mechanisms of sensory reference from those allowing qualitative discriminations, the sensory analogue for this phenomenon would be a case in which sensory mechanisms manage to identify a place-time, but the qualities that appear to occupy that place-time turn out not to do so. Perhaps we are trapped behind the veil of ideas, and none of the ideas composing it are satisfied by materials beyond the veil. Even in such a case sensory reference might succeed. This is analogous to referring to Moses even though we cannot formulate a true description that identifies him.

For example, perhaps I both see and feel what appears to be a smooth, solid, brown, and hackneyed wooden table in front of me. There have been many arguments through the centuries that philosophers should not trust the evidence of the senses. I suggest that even if we are tempted to endorse the notion that these sensory appearances are not veridical, it does not follow that they fail to pick out something physically in front of the sense organs. At that very place where there appears to be a smooth, solid, brown table, there is indeed something, but perhaps it does not have the qualities that it appears to have. Conceivably it is not really solid, it is not really brown, it is not really smooth. Instead the thing sitting there causing our perceptions of a table is a cloud of quarks, swirling in quantum mechanical fashion, interacting with incident electromagnetic radiation in such a way as to cause on-looking humans to have their hackneyed sensations. But those sensations correctly identify the place-time of their original; that indeed is where the cloud is to be found. Although not strictly speaking brown, that cloud of quarks has the requisite properties to serve admirably as a *stimulus* for experiences of brown. Its properties are cited in explanations of the genesis of such experiences.

So opens a second route through the veil of ideas, which we can take even though the veil be constituted entirely of falsehoods. The traditional approach to identifying the object of experience, or that which is 'directly' perceived, is to identify something that satisfies the content attributed by sense. So if you have a sensation as of something smooth, solid, and brown, the thing directly perceived must be smooth, solid, and brown. One historically influential variant of the line is to argue that the 'directness' of the relation between percipient and object is epistemic: about the direct object of experience you cannot be wrong. Not only does the object of experience satisfy the attributions of sense; it cannot fail to do so. An unfortunate consequence of this traditional line is to push the object of experience right out of the physical world, as the physical entities in front of the sense organs often do not satisfy the attributions made by sense, and the relation between percipient and physical object, while relatively direct, is not immune from error. So the object of experience or the object directly perceived becomes an intentional object, a sense-datum, or an idea: a mind-dependent entity. Our third variety of visual field was filled with items that satisfy the content of visual representations. It may be that no such items exist in this world. So its occupants become virtual or merely intentional objects. Perhaps only such entities can satisfy the collective attributions made by sensory systems.

But one can identify the 'object of experience' as nothing more or less than that to which sensory experience refers. Sensory systems might successfully identify something even though they go wrong about its properties. On this line the things you see 'directly' are the ones to which your visual representations refer. Possibly nothing has all those properties that vision represents the external world as having, but nevertheless we can usually pick out *which* things are the things that vision misrepresents in this way. Just as we might refer to electrons through the haze of a mostly false theory, or to Moses through the mists of legend, so sensory states might manage to pick out physical locations physically in or around the body of the sentient organism, even though we decide, at the end of the day, that sensory states in many ways misrepresent those locations.

6.2 CHROMATIC ATOMISM

To evaluate the perhaps alarming possibilities just mentioned, we require some account of the correctness conditions for feature-placing representation. These will vary from modality to modality. The task requires us to focus on one particular modality at a finer level of detail than that of preceding developments: we require details on how feature-placing in that modality is implemented and interpreted by its host organism. As colour perception is the best understood, and is the subject of lively discussion, I shall focus on it. Per hypothesis our chromatic sensory states have correctness conditions that specify when those states are veridical and when not. But what exactly does sensing a surface to be green represent that surface to be? And how exactly can such sensory states go wrong? If the surface lacks the properties attributed to it when it is sensed as being green, then that sensing is a misrepresentation or illusion; but what are those properties?

Suppose Jack sees a green patch. For simplicity suppose the patch is all of a uniform shade of green. Per hypothesis Jack has a sensory state σ that is a feature-placing representation: it identifies some finite space-time region R, corresponding to the patch, and characterizes that region as presenting a particular chromatic appearance—that particular shade of green. To identify R we need determinate coordinates on some m spatio-temporal dimensions, and to specify the particular visual appearance it presents we need determinate values on at least the three chromatic dimensions of red–green, yellow–blue, and white–black, as well as on other dimensions if the patch is glossy, shadowed, etc. The state σ has a particular qualitative character Q_g in virtue of which it represents the patch out there as being that particular shade of green. (This qualitative character is also a vector quantity; it is some n-tuple of determinate values $(q_1 \dots q_n)$ on all the dimensions of qualitative variation in the given modality.)

How do we provide correctness conditions for sensory state σ? One naturally assumes that this question is to be answered by careful study of the conditions under which such sensory states are produced. Various and sundry episodes cause Jack to enter states with character Q_g, and we naturally assume that what Q_g says about those space-time regions in his line of sight can be ferreted out by careful study of those causes. I shall call models that follow this plan 'production models'. They assume that correctness conditions for sensations of colour can be derived from the conditions under which those sensations are produced.

One large class of production models—including most of those current in the literature—provides a particular form of correctness conditions for colour sensation, as follows. In virtue of its qualitative character Q_g, sensory state σ represents region R as being a particular shade of green. Examine carefully the conditions under which tokens of state σ are produced, and in particular the physical properties of the stimuli for σ. We hope to discover some physical property P in those stimuli, such that a tokening of σ is veridical if and only if region R is P. This physical property will provide our answer to the question of what chromatic sensory states represent. What state σ with its qualitative character Q_g says of region R is that it has physical property P. Tokenings of σ that identify a region R devoid of property P are misrepresentations, falsehoods, illusions.

To provide correctness conditions for the entire gamut of chromatic sensory states we need to identify a gamut of such physical properties P. The model assumes this can be done colour by colour. That is, the schema provides a correctness condition for perception of one particular shade of green, without mentioning any other colours. The idea is to march through colour space, and provide such correctness conditions, point by point. If colours are intrinsic monadic properties, as so many philosophers insist, then truth conditions for chromatic perception should take exactly this form. They should yield a large collection of logically independent point-to-point mapping rules, each of which takes us from a particular chromatic appearance to a particular physical property.

I will call theorists who expect correctness conditions for chromatic perception to take this form *chromatic atomists*. The term is meant to suggest an analogy to the approach taken by semantic atomists to the interpretation of predicates of a natural language. The semantic atomist assumes that for each such predicate we can define some 'punctate symbol/world relation, some relation that one thing could bear to the world even if nothing else did' (Fodor and Lepore 1992: 32). Whether that relation obtains determines whether a sentence using that predicate is true. Since the contents are punctate and logically independent, we can proceed to provide truth conditions predicate by predicate. Similarly, chromatic atomists assume that correctness conditions for a particular chromatic content are logically independent of correctness conditions for all the other ones. Those conditions take the form of a point-to-point relation from a particular chromatic appearance to a particular physical property. Qualitative character Q_g represents physical property P, and this fact is independent of the correctness conditions for every other chromatic sensory state.

One can also think of chromatic atomism as the 'colour patch' model for how to go about assigning correctness conditions to our sensations of colour. Count a colour patch as any continuous region of the visual field sensed to be all of the same colour. Treat the visual field as the sum of all such colour patches. To give content to chromatic sensation, proceed patch by patch. The sensation of this particular region R as being that particular shade of green is veridical just in case region R is P: it satisfies the correctness conditions associated with the particular qualitative content Q_g.

Those who insist that colours are intrinsic monadic properties must endorse some variant of chromatic atomism, since the correctness conditions for the ascription of any one intrinsic monadic property are logically independent of those for all the others. The label is also meant to remind the reader of an informative episode earlier this century, when an earlier atomism foundered on the rocks of colour exclusion. I hope to show that contemporary chromatic atomists fare no better; that whatever the details, this entire class of theories is unworkable. But first some preliminaries.

It is vital to keep clearly in mind that we are here attempting to provide correctness conditions for colour *sensation*, and not for colour words. The former project has nothing to do with the meaning of ordinary language words like 'red', 'green', or 'blue', and can proceed entirely independently of such analysis. One way to highlight the distinction is to note that our current colour vocabulary has roots that go back a few hundred years, our capacity to write down any words at all dates back just a few thousand years, and our species has sported language for at most one or two hundreds of thousands of years. Whereas systems of chromatic perception are hundreds of *millions* of years old. Their age should be compared, not to the oldest of old cities, but to the rock on which it is built. Sensations of orange were already on-site when that rock was but clay. One can imagine giving correctness conditions for the chromatic perceptions of our hominid ancestors prior to their acquiring any capacity of linguistic representation. In fact the analogous exercise is available today: I can now reveal that my subject Jack, introduced above as someone seeing a green patch, is in fact a macaque monkey. (How speciesist of you, Oh gentle reader, to assume that he must be a human being!) The normal macaque monkey has colour discriminations that are essentially isomorphic to those of the normal human being, and there is no good reason to think that their colour perception differs in any essential way from our own. So if the question of what Jack's perceptions of that particular shade of green represent is well formed for a human Jack, it can be posed as well for Jack the macaque monkey. But the latter question makes vivid the fact that we are asking for the content of a sensory representation, not for anything linguistic.

A second proviso is related to this point. Just as one requires distinct truth conditions for distinct predicates, so one requires distinct correctness conditions for distinct colour sensations. It follows that the targets at the receiving end of our efforts to provide correctness conditions should always be thought of as fully determinate chromatic sensory states. For example, if the target is the sensing of a surface colour, what I mean by providing a correctness condition for 'a colour sensation' is providing one for a particular triplet of hue, saturation, and brightness: for a particular *point* in the quality space for surface colours. For other modes of colour perception the same principle applies: a target for a correctness condition is adequately identified only when one specifies a determinate coordinate for each of the dimensions of qualitative variation of which that mode is capable. The reason we must go to fully determinate shades of colour when providing correctness conditions is simple. If we can discriminate two shades of colour from one another, then they have distinct coordinates in such a space. If we provide colours that have two distinct sets of coordinates in that space with the same correctness condition, we are treating two qualitatively distinct colour sensations as one. This mistake is often a consequence of confusing the semantics of colour perception with the semantics of our colour words. Words such as 'red', 'green', and 'blue' are applied to an astounding variety of different shades—to large volumes of colour quality space. In the sense operative here, many different colours are all called 'red'. It is indeed a challenge to explain why one applies the same term to that enormous, oddly shaped gamut of distinct colours. But that challenge is distinct from understanding what a particular chromatic appearance says of the surface presenting it.

Production models hope to derive the correctness conditions for chromatic sensory states from the conditions under which they are produced. The prima-facie difficulty faced by all such accounts is that the conditions that suffice to produce a particular colour sensation—even a sensation of a fully determinate triplet of hue, saturation, and brightness—are enormously variegated. To get a sense of the size of this initial difficulty, some of the variations are worth describing. To make it more challenging we can exclude all the obvious abnormal observers and abnormal conditions, and confine the discussion entirely to variations in chromatic perception found among humans with normal trichromatic colour vision on a normal sunny day. That is, we will exclude all dichromats and anomalous trichromats, and include only those humans who have no identifiable abnormality in their colour vision. They all test normal for trichromatic vision. And if you would like to confine ambient optic conditions in this thought experiment to those mimicking some day in the Pleistocene, in the savannah or the rainforest, we could do that too. It does not matter; the variability remaining in normal human colour vision on that normal sunny day is still staggering.

Suppose we return to Jack looking at the green patch. He has a sensory state with a particular qualitative character Q_g in virtue of which that patch presents a particular shade of green. What does Q_g represent? We hunt for some physical property P common to occasions that produce states with that qualitative character. Some of those occasions are presumably instances of misrepresentation, in which Jack is presented something that merely looks to be that shade of green, but is not; and we hope that in those cases, P is absent.

One relatively well-known barrier to identifying any such property P is the existence of metamers: physically distinct spectra that have identical effects on the retina of the perceiver. Two stimuli will be metamers for Jack if they each yield the same number of absorptions in the short, medium, and long wavelength cones in Jack's retina. A physically heterogeneous variety of stimuli can produce such absorptions. Jack is physically incapable of telling such metamers apart; since they have identical effects on his visual transducers, the remainder of his visual system is physically incapable of distinguishing them. To predict which stimuli—which occasions—are metameric for Jack, we need to predict the number of absorptions they will produce in his three cone systems, and that depends among other things on the number of cones he has of each of the three types. Metamers for Jack may be discriminable for someone whose retina contains differing proportions of short, medium, and long wavelength cones.

The initial difficulty posed by metamers is that they force one either to define the property P so as to include all and only the metamers for a given favoured stimulus, or they oblige one to conclude that sensations of those metamers that lack P are misrepresentations, even though they present exactly the same appearance as those that happen to have P. Suppose some stimulus with a candidate property P causes states in Jack with the qualitative character Q_g. If P is to be some monadic physical property of the stimulus, it will prove impossible to define P so as to include all and only the metamers of that stimulus for Jack. The only physical property that all and only those metamers share is that they have identical effects on the three classes of cones in Jack's retina at that time. So we get the classic difficulty posed by metamers: there seems to be no observer-independent or 'objective' physical property that obtains among all and only members of a set of metamers.

Instead the collecting principles are relational and must, implicitly or explicitly, refer to effects produced in the eye of the beholder. The striking resemblance of those metamers cannot be deduced from any monadic property they
share.

The alternative route round this initial difficulty is to accept that metamers
of non-illusory colours are not necessarily non-illusory. Perhaps even though
Jack is physically incapable of distinguishing two chromatic stimuli, his
perception of one of them is veridical while his perception of the other is not.
Put differently, Jack perceives the 'real' colour of one stimulus, and he
misperceives the colour of the other, even though the two colours match
exactly. This is the ingenious route that Dretske (1995: 92) takes, and while
initially counter-intuitive, it does get us around the first crux.

Metamers illustrate the possibility of swapping the physical properties filling region R without altering the apparent hue of that region. The second and
more serious kind of variability in the production of chromatic sensory states
includes a large class of manipulations that alter the apparent colour
presented by region R without touching region R itself. One might think that
colour ascription is a simple two-term relation: region R presents qualitative
character Q_g. But those pesky experimentalists have isolated other variables,
extraneous to region R, that dramatically affect how R appears. If we add
these other variables that play a role in the production of chromatic qualitative character, we arrive at a rather staggering eight-term relation: region R
presents quale Q_g for observer O under adaptation condition A and ambient
illumination I with surround S at angle α and angular subtense β. Change the
value of any one of the terms of this eight-term relationship, and one can
change the apparent colour of region R. Some of these terms themselves
require multivariate description, such as illumination I—a spectrum of
light—or surround S—the spectral reflectance of the surfaces surrounding the
stimulus. Angle α is the tilt of region R relative to the eye; subtense β is the
angle of the visual cone that it occupies.

Changing the ambient illumination or the surround of region R can dramatically change its apparent hue. Adaptation effects are similar: an observer
who is 'flooded' with a strong red light subsequently has the red vectors
decremented. At least for a few moments, greens will appear more saturated,
and reds less so; and the apparent hues of colour mixtures will all alter
accordingly. Most colour patches that matched in hue before the flooding will
continue to match after it. But even though they continue to match, both
patches momentarily acquire a new apparent hue. The preservation of matching under varying conditions of illumination, adaptation, and surround is
probably the best way to define 'colour constancy'. But in none of these cases
are matches entirely preserved; colour constancy is not perfect. It breaks

down most readily if we replace broad-band stimuli with those that have just a few sharply defined peaks in their spectral composition. Adaptation or changing illumination might knock out just one peak in one of the stimuli, and so affect the match. Sulphur arc street lights provide a nice example; they have sharply defined spectral emission lines. Colour samples that match under daylight often do not under such street lights.

Merely by changing the illumination, the surround, the viewing angle, or other terms in this eight-term relation, we can generate a plethora of differing perceptions of the hue of any object. Such shiftiness raises a difficulty for any production theory. Under different viewing conditions, region R presents different chromatic appearances. We can change its apparent hue without touching region R itself. If there is a distinction between veridical and non-veridical perceptions of the colour of region R, we ought to be able to sort through these varying appearances and pick out some as veridical, some as not. In some of those conditions region R presents its real colour. In the others it does not: it flies false ones. The task of the production theorist is to identify that subset of conditions under which the chromatic sensations of region R are veridical and the real colour of R is perceived. But even the most minute and careful examination of those conditions fails to reveal any distinctive mark that justifies selecting such a subset. All seem to have an equally good (or equally bad) claim to the title of 'conditions under which chromatic sensations of region R are veridical'.

Consider some brick building that you see every day. It does not take an artist to notice that the apparent hue of the brick changes depending on the quality of the daylight and the surroundings. (To play by the rules set out above, we restrict ourselves to variations in viewing conditions found on any normal sunny day.) Its hue is barely distinct from grey in the light before dawn, and it may initially look brighter than the flowers around its base; but as the sun comes up, and the yellow–blue process wakes up, those now obviously yellow flowers soon outshine it in brightness. It might look washed out in the direct sun of a winter's day, but vividly red when framed with green vegetation or when seen at sunset. Its apparent colour changes as the sun moves across the sky, as clouds roll in, or even as you stroll round the building, viewing it from different angles and distances. If you look at it while facing into the sun, you might be startled to see something *black*. The challenge is to pick out from this plethora of conditions the one set under which one sees the real colour of the brick. If there is some observer-independent property of the brick that is its colour, and we sometimes see that colour, then somewhere in that set of conditions is the set under which someone sees that colour. But all the apparent colours seem to have equally good credentials; no one of them leaps to prominence as the one that is real. Not only will the selection of one castigate all the other appearances as non-veridical, but there is no principle on which to make a selection. Any choice would be discriminatory, in the *bad* sense of the word.

This point is typically obscured by the confusion noted above between the content of colour sensations and the content of colour *words*. One might object that the example overstates the variability of colour perception. The brick building always looks the same colour, because it always looks *red*. So there is no need to select among the many various viewing conditions; if the appearance it presents in any of them is veridical, then they all are, since they all represent the building to be the same colour, namely red. Now of course it is true that our judgements of which colour words to apply to an object are relatively constant. From dawn to dusk through all the variations on that normal sunny day we will invariably *say* that the brick is (still) red. But this objection defines 'sameness in colour' by 'sameness in colour category', where the latter categories are provided by one's proclivities to ascribe colour *words*. Of course the project of understanding our system of colour words is an important one, but it is not the same project as understanding our system of colour sensation. The latter has an independent and far more determinate content. From dawn to dusk we invariably say the building is red, but only because the word 'red' applies to a large gamut of discriminably distinct colours.

The conditions under which chromatic perception is veridical are also conditions under which we see the 'real' colours of things. The problem can be posed as a challenge to colour realism: justify the selection of the one favoured set of conditions under which the perception of colour is deemed veridical. Why pick that set and not some other? Or it can be phrased as a premiss leading to colour subjectivism: in principle there is no good reason to select one set of conditions as *the* set of conditions under which the real colour of the object is perceived. Disjoint sets, yielding dramatically different chromatic appearances, have equally good claim to the title. We get what Hardin (1988) calls 'chromatic democracy': each of the appearances has equal claim to being the real colour of the object. The result casts grave doubts on the viability of any 'production' model of correctness conditions for chromatic appearance, since it denies that there is any principled way to identify which of those many and contrary appearances is the correct one. In effect the colour subjectivist is a sceptic about the project of the production theorist. Hunt as you like through the conditions producing colour sensations: you will not find grounds therein to distinguish veridical ones from illusions.

Even if we get past these first two difficulties, a third and even more serious category of variation in the conditions producing colour sensations awaits: variation across observers. Matches made by Jack might not be made by Jill. The extent of the variability across observers, even among those with 'normal' trichromatic vision, is inadequately appreciated. The variability is again masked by the vagueness of ordinary language colour terms—we all agree that the brick is 'red', for example—but can be revealed with some simple exercises. Pass round a book of Munsell colour chips, for example, and ask each person in the room to pick the chip that presents the appearance of a unitary green—a green that is not at all yellowish and not at all bluish. The results are instructive: a sizeable proportion will pick chips that to you look bluish, and another proportion votes for chips that look distinctly yellowish. The results cannot be explained by error in the application of the definition of 'unitary' green: over successive trials, subjects will reliably pick out the same Munsell patch as the patch that to them looks unitary green. But different members of the audience will reliably pick out different chips.

If we take this phenomenon into the laboratory we can confirm that there are consistent differences in the chromatic appearance that a particular physical stimulus presents to different observers, even if all those observers have colour vision in the normal range. The simplest possible stimulus is light all of one wavelength presented through an optical viewfinder. We set up such a device and ask a human Jack, eponym of our macaque, to adjust the knob on it (controlling the wavelength of the light) until the light appears to be unitary green. Jack may stop with the knob at 490 nanometres. Jill looks into the viewfinder and complains that Jack is wrong: that light is distinctly bluish. She makes her adjustments, declares herself satisfied, and leaves the knob at 510. Given a second chance, Jack in turn will be startled at Jill's misperception of the stimulus. That light to him looks quite yellow. He will, quite reliably, adjust the knob back to 490. This dispute will not end. The prospects of this couple ever achieving harmony, at least of the chromatic variety, are bleak. If they are trying to pick a unitary green wallpaper, for example, *no* sample will *ever* satisfy both of them.

So who is right? Marriage counsellors are advised to dodge this question. The differences are probably due to individual differences in the relative strengths of yellow–blue and red–green systems, which in turn may be due to differences in the relative numbers and proportions of short, middle, and long wavelength cones in the retina. Those knob adjustments are attempts to balance the yellow and the blue opponent processes; the point at which the knob is left is the point at which the opposing vectors in yellow–blue exactly cancel one another, leaving 'unitary' green. Perhaps Jill's retina is stronger in the short wavelengths, and she requires more long wavelength light to cancel her relatively strong blue opponent process. But if the balance of power shifts, then so do the apparent hues of all the stimuli in the vicinity, in a systematic fashion. All the stimuli on one side of the balance point look yellowish (to a greater and greater degree), and stimuli on the other side look bluish. Hence the demonstration that different people select different patches as unitary green implies that *all* of the patches on the page look different to the different observers. The differences are small (small enough to hide under the gamut of the word 'green') but consistent, systematic, and measurable.

Now suppose we want to define correctness conditions for Q_g. Whom shall we use as our 'standard' observer? If we use Jack, correctness conditions for unitary green will identify physical property P of light whose wavelength is 490 nm. Jill is presented unitary green in circumstances in which P is absent, so her tokenings of Q_g are misrepresentations. But there is equally good reason to use the equally normal Jill as our standard-bearer, and render false all of Jack's perceptions in that portion of the spectrum. The dilemma cannot be dodged by mentioning both 490 and 510 in the correctness conditions for Q_g, since both observers perceive a large chromatic difference between those two stimuli. Production models are driven into a box: one observer has correct perceptions of the colour of light of 490 nm if and only if the other is incorrect.

Compared to the chromatic discriminations that any normal observer can make, the differences across normal observers are enormous. In a sample of fifty, choices for the wavelength that presents unitary green range from 480 to 520 nm, with a mean of 503 (Hurvich 1981: 223). Every member of that sample will perceive a large gamut of different colours in the range from 480 to 520 nm. Perhaps we should use the mean among normals as our standard? Q_g is then correct if the region manifests P: light of 503 nm. That setting would look yellowish to Jack and bluish to Jill; by this standard *both* of them misperceive when they perceive something as unitary green. Marriage counsellors might be tempted by this solution, but they would then find themselves disputing the perceptions of the majority of their clients. That is, the average setting of 503 nm is chosen by a bare plurality, of fifteen out of fifty. If we define correctness conditions by the mean, then more than two-thirds of individuals in the sample are misperceiving whenever they perceive unitary green. Prima facie it is a bad strategy to tell the *majority* of your customers that they are wrong.

6.3 PRODUCING CHROMATIC STATES

To the bewildering variety of causes of colour sensation the chromatic atomist has a bewildering variety of responses. For any favoured property P that Q_g is purported to represent, it seems we can find conditions lacking P that nevertheless produce sensory states with that qualitative character. Many responses to this problem share the same basic strategy, but diverge markedly over tactics. The shared strategy is one of careful selection: picking and choosing among the conditions of production. We confine ourselves to conditions that meet some additional criterion or qualification K, and hope to find that causes of *that* kind instantiate the target property P. But responses that share this strategy differ over what to use for that additional criterion or qualification.

For example, production theories might try to use only those episodes that are 'typical' or statistically normal, though we have just seen how using the mean can frustrate the majority. We get the quixotic hunt for 'normal' observers and 'standard' conditions (see Hardin 1983). Perhaps one selects just those episodes that occur in some stage of development or learning. These are all variants of the basic tenet of the production model: that correctness conditions for sensations of green (for example) can be divined from the conditions under which those sensations are produced. They differ over the particular kind K of conditions under which we will find the property P. Other variants have recently been suggested. Perhaps for kind K we use 'optimal' conditions. For Tye

> S represents that P = df. If optimal conditions obtain, S is tokened in x if and only if P and because P. (Tye 1995: 101)

So we first define 'optimal conditions', and then in those situations in which they obtain, define the correctness conditions for S by finding the property P among conditions producing S. Or perhaps we restrict the hunt to conditions of the kind under which colour vision evolved. This is Dretske's response (1995: 89–93) to the problem of metamers. If we have a big disjunctive mess of different objective physical properties, any one of which can stimulate the quale red, then we cannot pick just one of them as the one that the quale red has the function of representing. Dretske agrees with Hilbert (1992: 363) that colour is 'whatever property it is the function of the color vision system to detect'. The conditions that help explain what it was selected for (and hence help determine what its function is) might help us identify the one property P out of that list of metamers that the quale red has the function of representing. So let us restrict the hunt to conditions current when colour vision evolved. Here too we find the property P under conditions of kind K, so this is still a species of production model. The kind K is identified by appeal to biological functions.[1]

---

[1] As will be seen, I agree that understanding its biological function plays an important role in interpreting colour vision; but it is not quite this role. To anticipate slightly: we should not assume that the function of colour vision is to *detect properties*. Perhaps it is not in that line of business.

The fundamental difficulty with the entire family of production models is that the conditions they cite as determinative of the semantics of colour sensation underdetermine those semantics. One can compose alternative semantics for colour sensations, equally in accord with all the data employed by production theories, but assigning radically different correctness conditions to the same sensory states. One can do this, because different theorists historically *have* done it. The problem is not that production models cannot cope with the variability among the causes of colour sensation, but that they can cope too well; we find a variety of different accounts that all seem equally good. Given the expressive power of the theories, we have too few constraints, too few data-points, to assign correctness conditions in anything but an arbitrary and stipulative fashion. There seem to be no decisive grounds for selecting among them. Consequently, the arguments about what sensations do or do not represent, or (equivalently) what is or is not a 'real' colour, acquire an oddly arbitrary and indecisive character. We have a surfeit of theories and a dearth of constraints.

The classic route to demonstrating such underdetermination is to provide some rival semantic interpretations, which have radically different assignments, but which are equally in accord with all the data-points we are allowed. Oddly enough this task is easier to complete with sensory systems than with linguistic ones. In the history of the subject one finds many different atomist proposals identifying what properties colours are and what properties sensations of colour represent. With a theory in hand, take chromatic sensory states one by one and ask of each: is this appearance of colour veridical, or not? Theories differ dramatically over their proclivities to say yea or nay; over the universe of episodes of chromatic appearance we will get very different patterns of assignments of truth values. The resulting patterns fall along a spectrum, on which four way stations can be labelled:

(1) Always True
(2) Mostly True
(3) Mostly False
(4) Always False.

That is, some historical instances of atomist theories assign to all representations of colour the truth value True. On these accounts sensations of colour never misrepresent. Other historical instances of such theories assign to all sensations of colour the truth value False. All colours are illusory; none are real. Between these end-points almost every intermediary position has been, is, or will be occupied by some theorist past, present, or future. And all of these rival accounts of correctness conditions are equally in accord with all the data-points we are allowed.

For example, Locke defends a theory that falls in the 'Always True' category:

> From what has been said concerning our simple ideas, I think it evident, that our simple ideas can none of them be false in respect of things existing without us. For the truth of these appearances or perceptions in our minds consisting, as has been said, only in their being answerable to the powers in external objects, to produce by our senses such appearances in us: and each of them being in the mind such as it is, suitable to the power that produced it, and which alone it represents, it cannot upon that account, or as referred to such a pattern, be false. Blue and yellow, bitter or sweet, can never be false ideas, these perceptions in the mind are just such as they are there, answering the powers appointed by God to produce them; and so are truly what they are, and are intended to be. (Locke 1975: II. xxxii. 16)

Locke suggests that the truth of these simple ideas consists in their 'answering to the powers that produced them', and once understood in this way it is difficult to see how anything in those ideas could fail to be 'suitable' to those powers. This suggestion is the root idea behind a variety of contemporary dispositional accounts, which also tend to cluster towards the 'Always True' end of our spectrum. The dispositionalist shares the assumption that when Jack sees a green patch he has a sensory state with a qualitative character in virtue of which he represents the region in front of his eyes as having a particular physical property. What is that property? According to the dispositionalist it is the power that objects have to affect percipients in such a way as to give them sensations of green. The sensation of green represents objects to have the power to give one sensations of green. This might seem thoroughly circular, but it can be given content in various ways. We might use a reference-fixing manœuvre. Find an object that yields a paradigm sensation of green, then identify the property P as the power to produce sensory experiences of *that* kind. An object that has it will look *like so*. We use the current exemplar to fix reference to a kind. The kind is the kind of experience one has when one sees something that is or looks green.

One can see how dispositionalist analyses would tend to make every chromatic appearance veridical. The quality Q_g of my chromatic experience represents things to have the power to give me experiences of just that sort. So no matter what sort of experience I have when looking at things, the thing I am looking at has the power in those circumstances to produce experiences with that character. To evade this implication one can hedge and qualify, duck and dodge, in gestures awkward or artful. The content common to episodes of seeing something that is green and of seeing something that merely looks green is that both episodes are episodes of representing the thing as having the property P. This content is endorsed when one sees something green, and hedged when one says the thing merely looks green. Perhaps being green is the power to give the normal observer sensations of green in normal circumstances. When something merely *looks* green I represent it as being green, but in fact it does not have the power to give normal observers those sensations in normal circumstances. It causes me to represent it in that way, but for reasons other than its possessing that power.

Locke's genius (and geniality) is such that his text can also be cited as a source for entirely contradictory theories: those yielding assignments at the 'Always False' end of our spectrum. On Locke's official account of how ideas represent, ideas of the secondary qualities all fail to resemble those qualities as they are in the bodies themselves. Colours as they are in the bodies themselves are nothing but insensible textures, or modifications of the bulk, figure, and motion of insensible parts which give the body the power to cause sensations of colour within us. Since our ideas of colour do not resemble such insensible textures, officially all our sensations of colour (indeed, all our ideas of secondary qualities) ought to be given the truth value False.

The subjectivism of C. L. Hardin (1988) is the most prominent example of a contemporary theory typically placed at the 'Always False' end of our spectrum. The placement may seem appropriate, since Hardin says outright that colours are illusions (Hardin 1988: 81, 95, 111) and that physical objects are not coloured (1988: 96, 109, 112). But the claim that 'colours are illusions' must be handled with care. It does not necessarily imply that all chromatic perceptions are misrepresentations. For example, I have already endorsed the subjectivist premiss called 'chromatic democracy': that there are no good grounds for picking any one octet of observer and viewing conditions as the octet under which 'the real colour' of an object is observed. Other conditions and observers, yielding other chromatic appearances, have an equally good claim to the title. By saying 'colours are illusions' one might mean simply that no object has a single determinate real colour. Its various distinct chromatic appearances all have equally good claim to the title. In fact this interpretation is explicit in Hardin (1990: 566).

Hardin's goal after all is not the elucidation of correctness conditions for chromatic perception, but the defeat of objectivist accounts of the nature of colour. The 'objectivist' or colour realist claim is a conjunction of two theses:

(*a*) When we perceive colours, we perceive properties *P*, and
(*b*) Properties *P* are (in some sense) 'objective' properties. They are mind-independent, observer-independent, or physically real properties.

The objectivist or colour realist must show that the conditions for identity and difference of the candidate properties *P* cohere with the conditions for identity and difference of what we perceive when we perceive colours. Each conjunct on its own is easy; it is the conjunction that is hard. For example, it is relatively easy to establish the objectivity of a property such as surface spectral reflectance. The difficult part is showing that spectral reflectances are sometimes perceived, and that when we perceive similarities and differences among colours, we are perceiving similarities and differences among surface spectral reflectances. Sameness and difference of the candidate property must at least partially cohere with our perceptions of similarity and difference of colours.

The subjectivist claims that *no* set of properties will satisfy the joint demands of (*a*) and (*b*). Of course there are distal physical phenomena that play a vital role in the causation of experiences of red, green, yellow, and blue; and in a typical case it is fair to say that one sees a particular colour because of the particular constellation of physical phenomena in front of the eyes. Those are the *stimuli* for colour, and the subjectivist has no wish to deny their mind-independence. Change some physical aspect of that stimulus and you will change its apparent colour. The subjectivist can also admit that in many instances these phenomena are precisely the phenomena seen when one sees an instance of a colour. But the problem lies in collecting all the instances together, to make a property, and particularly to make something that is an 'objective' property. Even though in instance *A* I see a physical phenomenon and, because of its physical characteristics, it looks red to me, and in instance *B* I see a physical phenomenon, and, because of its physical characteristics, it looks the same colour as *A* did to me, nevertheless the redness I see as characterizing both *A* and *B* might not characterize any objective physical similarity between the instances. The only physical similarity between them might be that they have an equivalent effect somewhere within the percipient's visual system: the 'collecting principles', in virtue of which *A* resembles *B*, are found within the head of that percipient. And resemblances that rest therein are deemed not to be sufficiently objective. Although the instances would both exist without the percipient, their similarity would not.

This provides a second interpretation for the subjectivist claim that 'colours are illusions': nothing satisfies the joint demands of (*a*) and (*b*). It is an illusion to suppose that we are perceiving some objective physical properties when we perceive colours. But notice that this illusion has a sophisticated character. On this reading, what is illusory about colour is that it appears to be an objective monadic physical property of regions in the line of sight. To fall prey to this illusion one must be able to formulate the idea of objective monadic properties of regions in the line of sight. Anyone who cannot be credited with this rather sophisticated content would also be immune to this illusion. Jack the macaque monkey cannot be fooled by colours in this way, and his episodes of seeing something green are not on this account invariably misrepresentations. Indeed, if chromatic systems themselves cannot represent their targets as being objective monadic physical properties, then this 'illusory' character of the 'world of colour' does not imply that any particular chromatic appearance is, in the terms of the interpretation proper to it, illusory.

The two views at the end-points of our spectrum face a common problem. If chromatic appearances are either Always True or Always False, assigning them correctness conditions becomes an empty gesture. It loses its point. We discovered this already in the trials of the latter-day Thomist (Section 5.2). As Dretske (1986) and others have observed, the power of representation is fundamentally the power to misrepresent. The hard part is to show that a system has the power to go wrong, to represent what is *not* the case. Only then can we be confident in summoning forth the heavy machinery of content, correctness conditions, and reference. The challenge, when one issues that incantation, is to justify satisfaction conditions that sometimes—but not always!—yield the truth value False.

So we are tossed back into the changeable seas of chromatic appearance, and asked to define correctness conditions which on some proportion of occasions endorse those appearances and on some do not. It is up to us to determine those conditions, determine those proportions, and determine those particular occasions on which to issue endorsements. Does an examination of the conditions under which sensations of colour are produced provide us with the wherewithal to complete these tasks?

The first category of variability was that of metamers: physical variations in region *R* which, nevertheless, have the same effect on the retina and so present the same chromatic appearance. Metamers make it difficult to identify any property as the property perceived when one perceives a colour. If we follow David Armstrong (1997: 15, 26–7), to commit ourselves to the reality of this or any other property is to commit ourselves to the claim that there is something strictly identical between any two instances. If the maple leaf and the ripe tomato are both red, and we are realists about the universal 'red', then the maple leaf has something—redness—that is strictly identical with something the ripe tomato has (Armstrong 1989: 5, 82).[2] Metamers seem to violate

---

[2] A terminological note: I use 'property' as synonymous with 'universal', even though Armstrong (1987: 9) and Lycan (1996: 73) posit properties that are not universals—in particular, properties that are disjunctive, and not strictly identical in their instances. Disjunctive properties, if we admit them, behave very differently than do universals. For example, resemblances among disjunctive properties are no longer internal relations (as are resemblances among universals) and so claiming two instances share such a property no longer explains why the two instances resemble one another. Yet in colour perception that is the very problem that these properties are invoked to explain. I find it is less confusing to describe disjunctive properties as sums of tropes (see Sect. 6.6).

this condition: there is no objective physical property P that is strictly identical in all the different metamers for a given point in colour quality space. Instead we have a disjunctive list of metameric spectra: for Jack the particular shade of green Q_g has as metamers spectra λ_1 or λ_2 or λ_3 . . . and so on. That which collects all those disjuncts—that in virtue of which those metamers resemble one another—is just that they have identical effects on the three classes of cones in Jack's retina.

The problem is not confined to our reluctance to accept disjunctive properties. One might identify that particular colour with the disjunctive list of spectra λ_1 or λ_2 or λ_3 . . . ; what is strictly identical in all the instances is that each one of them has the property of being λ_1 or λ_2 or λ_3 . . . and so on. These properties would be, as J. J. C. Smart (1975) put it, 'disjunctive, idiosyncratic, and gerrymandered properties'. The sort of 'property' that Lycan (1996) endorses as 'real physical greenness' turns out to be similarly ill behaved. Colours are 'woefully disjunctive', 'an unruly, rough, and ragged lot', which 'form no natural kind'; a particular colour is 'surely no "genuine universal," and, more to the point, it is of interest only because of its relation to the human visual system' (Lycan 1996: 73). Lycan goes on to say:

> my sort of property inheres in an object on its own, regardless of how it is picked out or identified by me or anyone else, regardless of its ever producing sensations in anyone (or being detected by any being at all), and surprisingly, regardless of its actually constituting a disposition to produce sensations in anything. . . . It is as it is, whether or not anyone identifies it or refers to it, whether or not it ever produces sensations of any sort, whether or not it constitutes any disposition, and even if none of these were true. (Lycan 1996: 73–4)

Now all these characterizations seem precisely true of the *stimuli* for colour, and the subjectivist has no desire at all to deny the objective and mind-independent status of such stimuli. But if the extra-dermal stimuli for colours form such an 'unruly, rough, and ragged lot', the civilizing principles, or that which imposes order on such a motley crew, must lie elsewhere. For certainly colours as we perceive them, in rainbows and such, are ordered. One does not perceive the metamers for a particular shade of red as being woefully disjunctive, unruly, rough, or ragged; what is notable about them is that they all look *exactly the same*. The subjectivist insists that the principles of order and resemblance lie within the head; they are not objective or mind-independent, but depend upon the discriminatory capacities of a visual nervous system. It is the mind-independence of the property that is attacked, not that of its instances.

It is possible though to take an entirely different tack on the problem of metamers. Suppose we have some instance of a candidate property P which by hypothesis chromatic appearance Q_g represents, but then we find physically distinct metamers for P that also produce states with the character Q_g. Responses thus far attempt to expand the definition of property P so as to include all those metamers. The alternative, proposed by Hilbert (1987) and elaborated by Hilbert (1992) and Dretske (1995), is to resist such expansion. If the colour of an object is its surface spectral reflectance, then distinct reflectances are distinct colours. It follows that metamers are distinct colours. Typically (but not invariably) there is some viewing condition under which two metamers will be discriminable; that they appear to be the same colour under other viewing conditions is counted an illusion. 'There are differences of colour that human beings are not able to detect in normal lighting conditions' (Hilbert 1987: 85); the differences among metamers are among these. On this account a particular chromatic appearance Q_g represents just one reflectance property P from among its many metamers. The similarity—in fact, exact resemblance—of the apparent colour of those metamers is an illusion. So even though P and a metamer present exactly the same chromatic character Q_g, and under the given viewing conditions one might be physically incapable of discriminating them, nevertheless one correctly perceives the colour of only one of them. The other matches its appearance but is misrepresented.

To make this work one must have some reason for thinking that the reflectance spectrum of one metamer is represented by Q_g, while the qualitatively identical but physically distinct spectra of all the others are not. One must also be able to pick out which one is the special one. As noted earlier, here Hilbert and Dretske hope that evolution can help us out, by giving evidence that the function of sensations of Q_g is to detect the reflectance profile P. Colours become whatever properties it is the function of colour vision to detect (Hilbert 1992: 362; Dretske 1995: 93).

A consequence of this line will be to push our assignments down to the Mostly False end of the spectrum. Any two surfaces that are discriminable under some viewing condition have distinct reflectances and hence distinct colours. Under this criterion most apparent similarities of colour will be illusions. If there is *a* viewing condition under which the apparently similar surfaces can be discriminated, then they have distinct colours. Furthermore, any chromatic appearance deriving from something other than a surface reflectance property will on this line be counted as a misperception: so all perception of coloured lights and volumes, of coloured shadows and reflections, of iridescences, diffraction gratings, and interference patterns will be counted as illusions. These include the colours of the sun, the sky, the sunset, the shadows on the lawn, the blue eyes of a friend, the reflections in the windows, the light in the kitchen, the soap bubbles in the sink, the glare on the floor, and so on and on. So, oddly enough, just like subjectivism this version of objectivism agrees that colour vision is subject to massive and systematic illusion. Many if not most perceptions of colour are misperceptions.

An alternative response to metameric variation is simply to accept that colours are relational and dispositional properties whose identification requires anthropocentric reference to the visual systems of human beings. There is no way to determine whether a candidate spectrum should or should not be included in that list of disjuncts other than by calculating whether or not it has the same effect on an observer's retina (in a given state of adaptation, viewing angle, and so on) as do the other members of the list. So the property cannot be identified without implicitly referring to the observer. In that sense it loses its observer-independence. It becomes relational, dispositional, and anthropocentric (Averill 1985, 1992).

This line has many independent attractions. A natural way to cope with some of the phenomena of chromatic variation mentioned in the last section is to allow relational and anthropocentric properties to enter our correctness conditions. Perhaps, as a relational property, 'the colour' of an object is underspecified unless all the terms of the eight-term relation are fixed. Consider an earlier example (Section 4.4). When Moore holds up his envelope, only that member of the audience whose line of sight is orthogonal to the surface of the envelope is presented a 'sense-given' rectangle; others, looking at the rectangular envelope, experience various species of rhombus. But there is something odd about claiming that all those non-orthogonal views are non-veridical. After all, 'as a rhombus' *correctly* describes how a rectangle looks from this angle. That is precisely how a rectangle *would* look, when viewed from here; the sense-given appearance of a rhombus is, given the situation, veridical. In effect we add some of the relational details of the perspective into the satisfaction conditions for the sense-given shapes, and thereby convert what were simple illusions into less simple truths. The question now is whether similar monkey business with the satisfaction conditions for colour perceptions will similarly transform our truth assignments. For example, if we take into account some of the relational details, why could not the same white surface both look white and look blue? Perhaps 'bluish' accurately characterizes how a white congregational church looks, when viewed through blue spectacles. Both colours are its real colours; they are its real colours in two different situations.

On this line there is no one 'real' colour of the brick building; instead there is a real colour for Jack at noon viewing it from such-and-such an angle and distance under such-and-such light; perhaps a different real colour for Jack if he moves a hundred feet closer; and of course different real colours for different observers, under either those same viewing conditions or different ones. The same building can then be grey-at-dawn and red-at-noon; or red-from-here and black-from-there. Even better, once we allow anthropocentric considerations into these correctness conditions, the same strategy can handle variation across observers. Since one of the terms in our eight-term relation refers to the observer, we allow for the possibility that what is unitary-green-for-Jack is at the same time bluish-green-for-Jill. So 490 nm light is correctly perceived by Jack as unitary-green-for-Jack, and correctly perceived by Jill as bluish-green-for-Jill. Both appearances are real, and all contrariety vanishes in a commodious eight-dimensional relativism.

In Akins's (1996) apt term, these relational qualities are 'narcissistic'; they make some essential reference to the perceiving organism. Typically these are a far cry from 'objective' physical properties. If we allow narcissistic satisfaction conditions, we gain a stunning capacity to save the sensory appearances. Akins, for example, considers the thermal illusion created when the same bowl of lukewarm water feels warm to a hand that had previously adapted to cold water, and cold to a hand that had previously adapted to hot water. Strictly there is no contradiction in these appearances, though since ancient times it has been difficult to find satisfaction conditions that render them both truthful. Akins shows how. The thermal quality should not be interpreted as a measure of temperature, or even of heat, but narcissistically, as an indicator of rate of change in body temperature. The previously cold hand is gaining heat and feels warm; the previously hot hand is losing heat and feels cold. Both appearances are veridical.

Correctness conditions containing relational, anthropocentric, and now narcissistic properties are so wonderfully expressive that adopting them exposes us again to the danger of rendering all sensory appearances veridical by default. If we elect relativism and narcissism as co-consuls, both Jack and Jill are proclaimed to be correct about the colours of both lights; all the apparent colours of the brick building are real; and contrast and adaptation effects are not illusions but simply the revelation of yet more real colours under different viewing conditions. Family counsellors will like this regime, since under it all conflict disappears: we can all express our feelings and all be correct. The challenge is to resist slipping all the way down to the 'Always True' end-point of our spectrum. Such a consequence might seem to be the best possible outcome for a system of representation, but as already noted, it serves instead to vitiate the grounds on which we claim to have representational content at all.

In the end what is startling about this catalogue of different accounts is that they can differ so dramatically in their assessments of correctness conditions for colour sensation, and thereby produce such dramatically different assignments

of truth values to chromatic sensory states, without suffering any ill consequences, or indeed, any consequences at all. One can, it seems, assign radically
different contents to chromatic sensory states, provide different accounts of
what a 'real' colour is, defend different correctness conditions for the states, and
derive different patterns of truth value assignment, without bumping into the
least sign of resistance from any facts. Plausible arguments can be given for any
of these accounts, and none of the considerations to which we can appeal seem
decisive. It seems that we can simply stipulate the correctness conditions as we
like and pay the costs of our arbitrariness, since those costs are always zero.

6.4 CONSUMING CHROMATIC STATES

At this juncture Ruth Millikan steps forth with a very sensible suggestion:
look to the *consumers* of the representation. We shall spin our wheels idly if
we confine attention to the conditions under which such tokens are produced.
Prospects of finding the difference between truth and falsehood by looking
there are not good. But such a strategy ignores half the data. We need also to
look at how those tokens are consumed; at the systems that use those tokens:

These representations must function as representations for the system itself. Let us
view the system, then, as divided into two parts or two aspects, one of which produces
representations for the other to consume. What we need to look at is the consumer
part, at what it is to use a thing *as* a representation. Indeed, a good look at the
consumer part of the system ought to be all that is needed to determine not only representational status but representational content . . . the part of the system which
consumes representations must understand the representations proffered to it.
(Millikan 1993*a*: 88)

Where previously assignments of a particular content to a particular token
seemed cost-free, now one must show that some other part of the system
'understands' that content, or uses the representation of *P as* a representation
of *P*. Suddenly the game is not such a free-for-all; we must fit solutions to
some added constraints.

   This idea has some close relatives in the literature. For example, Dretske
(1988: 79), citing Armstrong (1973) and Ramsey (1931), describes beliefs as
'maps by means of which we steer'. While attention focuses naturally on the
character of the map and its relation to the territory, the critical point noticed
by all three authors is that what makes a map into something used as a map
is that *steering* mechanisms rely on it in a certain way. One turns left at this
intersection, because if the world is as represented by these squiggles and
blotches, that is the way home. Success in steering requires a univocal way to
read the map, but more importantly the content ascribed to the map falls out

as a consequence of explanations of how consumers downstream—the steering mechanisms—succeed. Dretske (1995: 2) applies the moral generally: a state *S* represents *F* if and only if the function of *S* is to provide information about *F* in some domain. If *S* is a token within a natural system of representation, it can be granted this function only if evolution selected for the provision of that information; and this in turn requires that providing that information gave the host a selective advantage. So the information must somehow be of use to the host; providing it to effector or control mechanisms gives that host some advantage. Consumers of the information must do something worth while with it.

It is worth detailing how one might apply Millikan's biosemantics to systems of chromatic sensory states. The theory is well articulated and complex, but in outline that application would proceed through four main steps.

1. Identify *producer* mechanisms and one or more *consumer* mechanisms. Producer mechanisms generate sensory states in some regular fashion. A consumer mechanism might have various jobs or functions. What makes it a 'consumer' is that it requires sensory states as inputs if it is to carry out those jobs.

2. Identify at least one *proper function* of that consumer mechanism: one whose performance explains why, given its history, ancestors or precursors of the consumer were 'selected for' (Millikan 1993*a*: 86). For *m*'s doing *F* to be a proper function of *m*, there must have been selection for the doing of *F* among ancestors of *m*. On Millikan's account, the biological functions of the consumer mechanism provide the norms telling us what states of that system are supposed to mean.

3. Provide a *normal explanation* for that proper function, telling how that function was properly performed on those historical occasions on which it was properly performed. We pick occasions on which the ancestor of *m* successfully did its job, and from them describe the design specifications for successful performance. (A 'normal explanation' yields what engineers would think of as 'design specifications' for successful performance: the parameters upon which the system depends in order to do its job.)

4. Identify *mapping rules* in those design specifications. The proper function of the producer is to guide the consumer to success in its endeavours. To help guide the consumer, the tokens yielded by the producer must somehow map onto the world; similarly, to do its job, the consumer mechanism relies on the world being as mapped by those tokens. So among the normal conditions for the proper function of the consumer mechanism will be found mapping rules that detail the correspondence between the tokens and the world.

These last 'mapping rules' are the source of the truth conditions or correctness conditions for sensory states (Millikan 1993*d*: 78–9). For things to go off without a hitch the consumer mechanism relies on the world being as mapped by the state, in accord with that rule. 'That the environment corresponds to the icon in conformity with this mapping rule is presupposed for proper operation of the system containing the icon' (Millikan 1993*b*: 106). The mapping rules are univocal or constant; their constancy provides the norms under which even a misrepresentation can be assigned a content.

Representational content rests not on univocity of consumer function but on sameness of normal conditions for those functions. The same percept of the world may be used to guide any of very many and diverse activities, practical or theoretical. What stays the same is that the percept must correspond to environmental configurations in accordance with the same correspondence rules for each of those activities. (Millikan 1993*a*: 92)

Any explanation of how the consumer mechanism does what it is 'supposed' to do will rely on constant mapping rules: those by which it steers the host, given the inputs to which it is privy.

One distinctive and under-appreciated feature of this account is that content is not confined to proper functions attributed solely to the producers, but can be derived from the mapping rules presupposed as a condition for the proper function of the consumers:

the content of an intentional icon is neither a direct nor indirect function of the stimulations, empirical evidence, or prior thoughts that induce it. Its semantic value is determined by whatever mapping relation is in fact doing the work of successfully guiding the organism through its activities in its world when controlled by the representation. (Millikan 1993*b*: 108)

To show that the system is using the representation *as* a representation, to show that the particular content ascribed by the mapping rule is 'understood' by the system itself, show that it serves to *guide the host*. The queried content will fall out from explanations of the success of consumer mechanisms (see Elder 1998*b*, *c*). It follows that, contrary to all production models and chromatic atomist accounts, correctness conditions for sensations of colour will not be uncovered by even the most minute examination of the conditions under which they are produced. That a sensation 'represents green' is not, on this account, derived from the claim that it is caused by things that are physically green. Instead one must look to the consumers, to the uses that the system makes of those sensory states. In particular one hopes to find activities guided specifically by sensations of colour, and then constant rules on which the system depends whenever it achieves success in such endeavours.

Satisfaction of the four conditions above would certainly provide grounds for much greater confidence in the ascription of a particular content to a particular sensory state than does any production model. It would require us to show that the system uses the state in question as a representation. We must show that steering mechanisms are guided by that content: that consumers cannot do their jobs successfully if the world is not as therein represented. If we could satisfy these four conditions, debates about sensory content and colour realism would lose their arbitrary character. Have we any hopes of satisfying them?

They certainly impose a heavy empirical burden. Even to establish that ancestors of *m* were *selected for* their doing *A*, and not their doing *B*, takes extraordinary work, which has been completed only for a few systems *m*. Empirically it has proven difficult in all but a few cases to rule out the null hypothesis, which explains current phenotypic variation with the 'Cambrian explosion' followed by random genetic drift. So ascription even of proper functions for mechanisms *m* is at this point almost entirely speculative. Nevertheless, the theory shows how such speculations *could* be underwritten empirically; how, as we proceed speculatively through the four steps, the liens and obligations we assume could eventually be paid off.

The first steps are to identify the consumers of sensations of colour and to identify the jobs they perform for which such sensations are required. A very sensible way to approach this question is to ask exactly what one loses when one loses colour vision. The deficits will point to jobs left undone, functions that cannot be performed. Even more precise is to ask about the functional differences between trichromats and dichromats: what one loses when one loses just one of two opponent process systems. As is widely appreciated, those deficits are not dramatic, and in some cases are difficult even to detect. Mollon (1991) suggests three advantages to being trichromatic:

(1) Improved abilities to detect fruit or other targets in contexts of 'dappled and brindled' illumination, as provided for example by the patches of light and shadow in a forest.

(2) Improved abilities to segregate and segment partially occluded objects by their colour. Disparate and detached portions of the field of view that have similar hues can be more readily seen as portions of one connected surface, partially occluded by foreground objects.

(3) Improved abilities to identify biological kinds and states of individuals of those kinds. Colour patterns are useful in identifying particular species of trees and plants, conspecifics, and the sex of conspecifics. Colour discrimination aids in identifying well-hydrated vegetation, ripe fruits, healthy skin tones, and the emotional and sexual states of

conspecifics (blushing, blanching, pallid, livid, mottled, ruddy, sallow, wan, ashen, etc.).

The dappled and brindled illumination within a forest is a pattern of randomly varying brightness values. Under such illumination, dichromatism leads specifically to a decreased 'ability to detect' fruit or berries. They can eventually be detected by a dichromat by differences in shape and brightness, but a trichromat who can perceive the chromatic difference across randomly varying brightnesses can pick fruit and berries much more quickly. Mollon notes that many of the early observations on 'Daltonism' in the eighteenth century were of individuals who had difficulties picking fruits and berries or spotting game. These observations were much more prominent in a day when a larger proportion of the population lived on farms and had to carry out such tasks to survive. But there is a modern analogue. The 'pseudo-isochromatic plates' of Stilling and Ishihara, used to detect red–green colour blindness, employ dots of randomly varying lightness in such a way that the outline of the red or green numeral emerges from the background only if our subject can detect the reflectance differences. (The dots that make up the numeral have the same average lightness as the background.) Here the dots of randomly varying lightness correspond to the dappled and occluded lighting of jungle canopy or savannah grassland. Seeing the numerals or letters in those plates relies on segregation by chromatic differences independent of random variations in brightness.

One can describe many applications of the first set of abilities as *camouflage-breaking*: one can pick out the fruit or berry hiding in the leaves, or the lioness hiding in the grass. Likewise, the second set is often involved in *contour completion*, so that even though the lioness or the fruit are occluded by confusing vegetation, and hidden by dappled light and shadow, the visibly disconnected and shadowed yellow surfaces can all be picked out as the surface of one unfriendly or friendly thing. You see all those yellow surfaces as parts of the surface of a lioness, hiding in the grass.

Time for a speculative leap. Suppose that Mollon got it right: that these three functions are the functions served by consumers of chromatic states. How might a mechanism successfully perform these functions, and more particularly, on what sort of mapping rules must such a mechanism rely? (Note that, as promised, we are descending into implementation details, of how chromatic feature-placing might be engineered reliably.) Mollon points out that of these functions only some of those found in the third category require colour constancy. The first two require only the abilities to detect spectral differences, and to discriminate between spectral differences and brightness differences. It will be convenient first to consider the design specifications for a system that can detect chromatic differences. I will then argue that such a mechanism could also have a surprising capacity to identify biological kinds.

Consider the primal scene of hunting for a banana amongst the leaves. The optic environment has dappled light and shadow, and randomly varying brightness levels, so that those of our hominid ancestors who lack colour vision—specifically here the capacity to make spectral discriminations independent of brightness—are more likely to go hungry. Those who can detect the colour difference gain an advantage, or at least they gain some bananas. One might think that any mechanism that could help them along must do so by representing the colour of the banana, and representing the colour of the leaves, allowing the host to represent that there is a difference between the two. The chromatic atomist makes precisely this assumption, agreeing that a chromatic state about region R represents a property P of the occupant of that region. So we go from region to region, identifying the colour of each.

I will call this scheme an 'occupant-coding' scheme. A sensation of region R represents a property of the occupant of R. Under it a solid colour patch on a constant background might be represented as follows:

```
22222222222222222222222222222
22222222555555555555222222222
22222222555555555555222222222
22222222555555555555222222222
22222222555555555555222222222
22222222555555555555222222222
22222222222222222222222222222
```

The 2s and 5s represent values on some dimension of discriminability; if it is redness–greenness, for example, we might have a red patch (high in the redness dimension) standing out from relatively neutral surround. The qualitative state q_5, caused by the patch, represents the colour of that region—some physical property of the occupant. The qualitative state q_2, caused by the surround, represents a different colour. Each token representing a visible region (or visible part of a region) R represents a property of the occupant of that region.

Occupant-coding is relatively inefficient, since for each visible point one must explicitly represent all the visible properties of that point. If all we need detect are chromatic differences, one could do that job with 'difference-coding'. This simply codes the differences, if any, between each point and its neighbours. Numbers now represent, not the colour of a given point, but the difference in colour between neighbouring points. Applied to the colour patch above we get:

```
00000000000000000000000000000
00000000033333333333000000000
00000000030000000003000000000
00000000030000000003000000000
00000000030000000003000000000
00000000033333333333000000000
00000000000000000000000000000
```

In this representation the edge—the chromatic difference—becomes salient. We represent that difference without representing separately the minuend and subtrahend. Chromatic differences fall to zero within the patch itself, just as they do across the constant background. Difference-coding is efficient because it only codes for the places where things change, and in scenes containing swaths of constant hue this cuts out lots of redundant chatter.

Difference-coding yields mapping rules of a different form from those envisioned by the colour patch model. The targets of semantic interpretation in difference-coding are not the values filling each patch but just the edges between them. Difference-coding says nothing in particular about the particular properties occupying a given region. It does not tell you the minuends or subtrahends. We do not get any absolute values, but just differences; no monadic properties of regions, but just relations at the edges. All it says is that here, things change (and in what direction). If the map above is a redness–greenness difference map, the 3s mean 'here things get redder'.[3]

But such a coding scheme could guide the hand towards the banana hiding in the leaves. We do not need to identify properties of the target or of its surround, as long as we can detect some difference between them. The critical task is identifying an edge: a place where the surface properties *change*. Such edges, changes, or differences can be represented without identifying the properties on either side of the divide. Recall that conspicuous differences are the subject-matter of Crick and Koch's saliency map (Section 5.4); such differences grab attention. Difference-coding would suffice for camouflage-breaking. Similarly, contour completion requires the occluded and disconnected patches of the target object to somehow stand out from the foreground objects and the background. Chromatic differences can help this segmentation. The model does not eliminate all appeal to similarities; the disconnected spots are grouped together because they all have a similar hue. But the

---

[3] Chromatic systems are not heavily involved in *detecting* edges; luminance discrimination can usually do that more quickly. The edge detection modules may be largely colour-blind (see Davidoff 1991). But detecting colour differences can help identify what type of edge it is: as one where spectral properties change. This is why the suggested content of chromatic sensory states is something like 'here things get redder'.

suggestion is that this similarity need not be a similarity in the monadic properties of occupants, but is instead a similarity in the difference between each patch and its background. The scattered visible portions of the banana might 'pop out' from among the occluding leaves because they all differ from those leaves in a +3 direction (see Treisman 1988: 226). A target that differs from the background in some unique way can be picked out from that clutter in constant time.

At this point in the argument our goal is to write mapping rules upon which consumer mechanisms could depend in discharging the various functions of camouflage-breaking and contour completion. There is little question but that difference-coding works better. Occupant-coding will not yield workable mapping rules. We need some univocal norm for the interpretation of chromatic states—some constant mapping rule—and what the occupant scheme proposes is that Q_g be mapped to some physical property P. Here the sheer variability of causes of Q_g, and all our earlier problems with production models, come home to roost. One cannot write a univocal rule that takes us from that qualitative character to all the tropes of that particular shade of green. Any such projection is inconstant, mapping Q_g to different physical properties on different occasions.

One might propose to map Q_g to the disjunctive list of P and all its metamers, but this raises additional problems. Those reflectance profiles will present different chromatic appearances under different viewing conditions, and so would each need to be included in several such disjunctive lists. Notice that occupant-coding is a superset of difference-coding: it still requires differencing operations somewhere, if it is to identify chromatic differences across borders; but in addition it retains information about the minuends and subtrahends. One wonders why it needs to retain that information. It is admitted by all hands that in fact we detect similarities among reflectance spectra in a very crude way, subject to massive error. Trichromatic vision can be modelled as a bank of three low-pass filters: reflectance profiles that cannot be discriminated by those filters are accounted 'the same'. The information that there is a difference in reflectance spectra at a particular place, even so crudely identified, can be very useful: it helps with detection, segmentation, camouflage-breaking, contour completion, and so on. But once it is acknowledged that the minuends and subtrahends are multiply ambiguous, it follows that differences between such disjunctive lists are no less ambiguous than they are in difference-coding. In short, occupant-coding cannot do any better than difference-coding on the important jobs; and the extra information it retains seems useless.

It also bears mention that the mapping rules generated by chromatic atomism are, perforce, atomistic. Interpretation of any one chromatic state must be logically independent of the interpretation assigned to any others. But as argued previously (Section 1.3), to have a state with one qualitative character, one must have the capacity to have others. Colour representation is systemic (see Dretske 1995: 15), not punctate; acquisition of chromatic sensory states does not proceed one by one, state by state, but as a package deal. Recent advances in genetics have provided new confirmation of this truth. The chromatic dimensions of yellow–blue and red–green are well known to be independent: they can be separately lost. They were also probably separately gained. Mollon (1991) and Goldsmith (1990) review various lines of evidence indicating that the yellow–blue system is much older than the red–green one. The short wavelength photopigment, and the divergence between it and the ancestor of our middle wavelength pigment, are both extraordinarily ancient, dating back over 500 million years (Goldsmith 1990: 293). Mollon calls the yellow–blue system the 'primordial' system. Our ancestors in Palaeozoic and Mesozoic times who had just two cone pigments were at best dichromats. The divergence between our middle and long wavelength photopigments, and with it the addition of a red–green opponent system, only occurred within the last 65 million years, when opportunities opened up thanks to the extinction of the dinosaurs. Trichromatism in mammals is recent and rare. Most species—including the New World monkeys—remained dichromatic (Neumeyer 1991). Mammalian colour vision still shows the effects of æons of oppression by the reptiles.

Presumably one can tell some story about the selective advantage of dichromatism over monochromatic vision—a story whose climax came over 500 million years ago. One can tell another story about the advantage of trichromatic vision over dichromatic, which could explain evolutionary events of 65 million years ago. But there is no logical guarantee that these two stories will be the same. The two opponent processes are, in many ways, two distinct sensory submodalities: one for yellow–blue, and a much more recent one for red–green. Single points along either one of these axes do not provide fit targets for interpretation. Since that entire range must be granted in one fell swoop—one either has the capacity to discriminate along that dimension, or one does not—it is the entire opponent system, not particular states within it, that can be assigned a proper function. Chromatic states within a given opponent system—determinate values within the range of determinables—gain their functions systemically, in virtue of their place within that dimension of discriminability.

Looking at the blueprint of a difference-coding scheme, one might think, 'What a bizarre architecture. I must be looking at the design for the sensory system of some alien creature, some fantasy found only in a thought experiment.' But the mind it describes is our own. It is much more likely that our chromatic systems employ difference-coding than occupant-coding. Our colour perception is organized around meaningful edges, not meaningful interstices. The interpretable elements are differences, not similarities.

It is amusing to note that philosophers and phenomenologists classically describe the visual field as a tableau of colour patches—patches and swaths of constant hue, abutting one another. Psychologists describe the visual field as a lattice-work of edges: places where things change. The two representations are complementary—one is just the dual of the other—but nevertheless the psychologist's vision has been more fruitful.

Perhaps it is simply a mistake—a big, old mistake—to assume that sentience is organized around the detection of *similarities*. The psychologist's suggestion is that its job instead is the detection of differences: edges, changes, and discontinuities. The edges are critical, not the character of the surfaces on either side. Judgements of similarities and of stasis fall out as failures to detect differences. That the system seems to detect two instances of an identical property (redness, say) is a simple consequence of it therein failing to detect any differences. But we cannot infer that two points both on the red side of the edge have anything in common other than a propensity to affect the visual system in the same way. Indeed, what they 'have in common' must be described negatively: that the system cannot tell them apart. This makes the sensed similarities an almost inconsequential by-product of the real job, which is the detection of differences. The swaths and colour patches are spandrels. The lattice-work of edges carries the load.

6.5 THE FALSE-COLOUR MODEL

Difference detection opens the exhilarating possibility of fomenting a Gestalt shift in our perception of the visual field itself. From a tableau of colour patches it emerges, reconfigured and transformed, as a lattice-work of edges. I said that the latter model, which was empirically derived, is the more fruitful one. There are advantages to shifting our attention to the edges. Now it is time to detail them.

First, difference detection allows us, thankfully, to give up on the hopeless task of trying to describe what the appearance of this particular shade of green represents to us about the region in front of the eyes. The mapping rules will proceed differently. The informative or content-bearing elements are not the swaths of constant hue, but the edges, where things change. Instead of trying to assign an interpretation to colour similarities, we shall assign one to colour differences. Colour vision is relatively uninformative about the physical similarities that underlie swaths of surface all of the same hue. Much less problematic is its capacity to identify places where the colours change. Swaths all of the same hue convey little news. The action, biologically speaking, is at the edges.

Perceptions of sameness and difference of colour show a stunning asymmetry in this respect. Two surfaces that cause experiences of the same colour may share no property specifiable independently of the fact that those two surfaces happen to affect our sensory systems in the same way. But in most naturally illuminated scenes, the places where we see colour *borders* typically correspond to places where there is a real physical difference across the border. For example, under fixed conditions of illumination and retinal adaptation, places where you see differences in surface colour reliably correspond to places where the reflectance *changes*. Our perceptions of sameness do not reliably indicate objective similarities, but our perceptions of surface colour differences do reliably indicate physical differences. We should discount the pronouncements of our visual system about sameness, but pay careful heed wherever it finds differences.

Such selective attention may seem inconsistent, but it makes perfect sense whenever we know of biases in judgement. For example, someone who is 'bullish' about the equity markets will tend almost always to be optimistic, and pronouncements to that effect gradually lose their informative character. But when even the optimists predict a downturn, it is time to pay attention. Our chromatic systems are optimists about similarities. They find them over a vast range of changing reflectance conditions. But when they find a difference—an edge—it is time to pay attention.

Nervous systems in general seem much more keyed to spatial and temporal changes and discontinuities than to spatial or temporal similarities. To sameness the neurons in every modality eventually adapt, accommodate, and grow quiet; but hit an edge, or make a change, and the alarms go off. Spatial and temporal edges are enhanced in every modality. It makes sense. If you are lost in the grass of the savannah, you would be alarmed at first, but you would quickly learn that the grass itself will not kill you. The unchanging sight of all those waving stalks might then grow tedious. Nevertheless, it remains advantageous to notice any changes, or any edges between grass and nongrass, such as any edge between grass and lioness.

It helps to think of the 'edges' across which differences are detected as not only spatial but also temporal. 'Edge enhancement' mechanisms in the nervous system operate as well for such temporal edges as stimulus onsets, stimulus changes, and stimulus offsets. The sun emerging from behind the clouds can wake up someone napping outdoors; it provides a temporal edge, even though the consciousness dozing behind those closed eyelids cannot localize a spatial boundary. It is simplest to think of these borders spatio-temporally, as borders of space-times. With this conception in hand we can formulate a breathtakingly simple design principle for orienting and arousal reflexes: Since I am alive now, as things are now, I need to start worrying only if things *change*. So alert me if things change, but otherwise, hold your course, and let me nap. The sensory subsystems devote their efforts to the reliable detection of differences and of changes, since those are what worry the captain. Spatio-temporal edge detection emerges as the critical job for any mechanism that might lend a hand in the steerage. These proto-navigators can hold a steady course unless some dangerous change is signalled in regions ahead; when such threats loom, they require accurate information about the location of those hazards. They have no need for an additional rule assuring them that all regions *not* sensed to change share some self-same physical property.

Difference detection fits with what we know of early vision. Receptor activation is not linearly related to ambient energy, but rather varies roughly in proportion to the logarithm of such energy. Arithmetically, subtracting logarithms is equivalent to dividing: computing a ratio. So even Hartline's model of the eye of the horseshoe crab, which starts with receptor activations proportionate to the log of intensity, followed by subtraction (inhibition) among neighbours, thereby registers ratios of energy across edges (see Cornsweet 1970). The powers of systems that can register such ratios are considerable. For example, they can explain Wallach's results, noted in Section 1.3. As Rock puts it: 'the perceived shade of gray of a surface, its lightness, is governed primarily by the luminance of that surface relative to the luminance of neighboring surfaces, as Hering (1920) suggested and as Wallach (1948) elegantly demonstrated. There is now fairly considerable agreement among investigators on this general principle' (Rock 1983: 203). A given lightness value—a point in the grey scale—does not correspond to a particular *amount* of energy in the flux of light reflected from that spot. It corresponds more closely to a particular *ratio* between that energy and the energy of surrounding fluxes. Furthermore, it has been known for a long time that systems built on these principles would manifest many of the features described as 'lightness constancy' and 'colour constancy'. Change the total illumination across the field and the outputs of the system barely budge; the ratios across edges are constant. Our grey patch may now be reflecting a hundred thousand times more energy into the eyes, but so are its neighbours, and the ratio of one of the other is close to constant. Lightness becomes independent of flux.

We cannot write a rule that maps a mid-level grey onto any particular surface condition or any particular flux of energy reflected from that surface. A closer approximation to a univocal rule for our mid-level grey is one that maps it onto a constant *ratio* between the energy of the flux and the energy of neighbouring fluxes. The same is true of perceived colours. No univocal rule can relate a particular perceptible shade of green to a particular surface or a particular flux of energy reflected from that surface. Instead that shade of green maps univocally onto a particular set of *ratios*: ratios of the activation levels of the three cone systems.[4]

The priority of difference detection is confirmed by subsequent stages of processing beyond the retina. Those stages detect edges, identify each as a luminance edge or a reflectance edge (and more specifically as some type of occlusion edge, object boundary, surface change, shadow, etc.), assign each a three-dimensional location, and then and only then assess the colour of the swatches between connected edges. That the apparent depth of a surface can affect its apparent hue and lightness was shown by some beautiful experiments by Alan Gilchrist (1977, 1980, 1990). Gilchrist showed that changing the apparent depth of a surface (making it appear co-planar with one or another of two different surrounds) changed the apparent lightness of that surface. It seems one detects edges, identifies them as luminance edges or reflectance edges, and determines their relative depths, before assessing the lightness of the now-situated surface. The quality which a colour patch model puts first actually comes last.

Krauskopf (1963) provided a startling confirmation that the same holds true for chromatic colours. Krauskopf presented his subjects with a bright green patch surrounded by a ring of red. Without changing the stimulus flux presented by the centre or by the ring, Krauskopf found an independent way to obscure the detection of the edge between them: stabilize it on the retina. Devious arrangements of mirrors and lenses, some placed on the eyeball itself, can be used to counteract the effects of eye movements, so that the border is always projected to the same retinal receptors. In such a case those receptors soon adapt and the stabilized edge rapidly becomes invisible. What happens next defies all expectation: the colour difference also disappears. The green centre vanishes, and the entire stimulus takes on the appearance of a uniform shade of red. Without the border, the differences in the stimulus flux between centre and surround—which are unchanged—no longer produce a perception of colour difference. It seems that early vision identifies chromatic borders, assesses the ratios of difference across the border, and only then identifies the colour of the connecting patches. Eliminate the edges and you eliminate the colours too.

---

[4] Interestingly, although the architectures are otherwise very different, this is one point of agreement between opponent process theory and Land's retinex theory: that 'we process the entire image in terms of the ratios of luminances at closely adjacent points' (Land 1990: 55). Land has shown how extracting such ratios can yield colour constancy. His analogue for an activation level of a cone system is a 'scaled integrated reflectance'.

This result is predictable, given difference-coding. Within the patch itself, differences fall to zero; so if its border is eliminated, a difference-coding system will entirely lose sight of the patch. As Gilchrist puts it: 'The most straightforward interpretation of this experiment is that the eye sends the brain only information about changes in light across boundaries, with areas where no change is reported being filled in by the brain as homogeneous' (Gilchrist 1990: 64). Difference-coding systems can be fooled by the converse phenomenon as well. The 'Craik–O'Brien–Cornsweet effect' provides illusory clues of a luminance step—a change in lightness—between what are actually two physically identical surfaces. The result is that the two surfaces appear to be of different lightness (see Rock 1983: 205; Cornsweet 1970). Lightness values of patches are determined by ratios found at their edges. As Rock puts it, 'The perception of lightness (and chromatic color as well) is based upon information at the edges between regions of differing luminance (or hue). Homogeneous regions between edges then "take on" the lightness value indicated by these edges' (Rock 1983: 204). It seems that mere difference detection—registering ratios of lightness levels across borders—can provide the consumers of chromatic sensory states with all they need to do the jobs of camouflage-breaking and contour completion. A system built on such principles could detect fruit and berries in conditions of dappled and brindled illumination, and spot the lioness in the grass.

It remains only to consider whether the same principles could provide mapping rules for the third function Mollon assigned to colour vision: to help identify biological kinds. For example, the distinctive plumage on the wing of the male blackbird makes its species and sex more readily recognizable, both to conspecifics and to other birds. Patterns of coloration of flowers, fruits, and vegetables presumably help foraging animals and insects recognize favoured kinds of food, and help the plant spread its seeds. One might think that in these cases chromatic atomism at last comes into its own. Some patch of the fruit has a particular reflectance spectrum P, and the function of the chromatic sensory state σ in the foraging animal is to help it identify reflectance P. Such identification helps secure dinner.

But even here the chromatic atomist cannot write a univocal mapping rule. Reflectance P will under differing viewing conditions yield many chromatic states other than σ. With changes in illumination, surrounds, viewing angle, retinal adaptation, and so on, the stimuli produced by interacting with P will describe, not a point within quality space, but a volume or gamut. Perhaps all the chromatic states within that gamut—all those within the limits of varia- tion in the appearance of the fruit—are to be assigned the job of identifying the same reflectance P. This in turn requires that none of those states have the job of signalling any of the other reflectances that in other viewing conditions might produce them. So none of the other points within the gamut can be assigned the job of signalling any other biologically significant kinds. To get point-to-point mapping rules, we must dedicate entire portions of colour quality space to the sole job of signalling reflectance P. The zoning is single-use. While it is possible that this zoning strategy will work out happily, it seems unlikely. It wastes our resources of chromatic discrimination.

Difference detection offers an alternative and less wasteful scheme. There is something much more distinctive in the patterns of coloration found in plumage or flower than the reflectance of any particular patch within it: namely the pattern itself. That pattern defines an invariant, even across those episodes in which the reflectance presents different appearances. If we can proceed to a higher-level property—a property of the relations among the colours making up the pattern—we can write a mapping rule that could serve in all those circumstances to help identify the kind.

The solution requires a slight extension of Nelson Goodman's notion of a 'colour shape'. This is not a coloured shape, but a set of relations among the colours of an object. As Goodman notes (1977: 184–5), the shape of a thing is a pattern of relations among the places it occupies. (Such patterns can be complex, which is why shapes are high up in the feature hierarchy.) One can construct such 'shapes' not merely out of places, but out of other qualities. Suppose we have a flag with just three distinct shades of red, white, and blue. We could identify the hue, saturation, and brightness of each of the three different colours in the flag, and plot each point in colour quality space. The 'spatial' relations among those three points in colour quality space gives us the 'colour shape' of the flag: a particular triangle. Just as the shape of the flag is a set of relations among its places, the colour shape of the flag is a set of relations among its colours. Similarly, a temporal shape is a set of relations among times: a rhythm.

Goodman's colour shapes are indifferent to the size or spatial arrangement of the colours within the given pattern. A French tricolour and United States flag might have the same (triangular) colour shape. But the notion can readily be extended so as to yield distinct 'spatio-chromatic' shapes for the two flags (or for any two distinct colour patterns). The only difficulty is that extending it pushes us into six (or more) dimensions, and shapes within such a space are difficult to visualize. To simplify, suppose we have two pieces of cloth, cut to the same physical size and shape. One has a red circle with a blue surround, while the other has a blue circle and a red surround. Suppose also that these colours are 'isoluminant' colours: they are matched in lightness and saturation, and differ only in hue. With all our differences lying in just two spatial dimensions and one chromatic one, it becomes easy to visualize a spatio-chromatic shape. The centres and surrounds of the two pieces of cloth have different hue coordinates. Represent those hue differences by different heights. One spatio-chromatic shape is then a three-dimensional object whose centre is 'higher than' its surround, like a two-layer wedding cake. The other is a three-dimensional object with the centre pushed down into the surround, like an inverted top hat. The spatio-chromatic shapes—the colour patterns—are as distinctively recognizable as wedding cakes and top hats. Notice that our pieces of cloth have identical physical shapes, and also what one could call identical luminance shapes. Because the colours are isoluminant, to a monochromat the border between centre and surround would be invisible. Each piece of cloth would appear to be a solid grey (of a constant lightness level); the two pieces of cloth would be indistinguishable. In the moonlight no human could distinguish the two pieces of cloth.

Because colours can vary in saturation and lightness as well as hue, and we have a third spatial dimension to include, a full spatio-chromatic shape consists of a set of relations among points in a space of at least six dimensions. Nevertheless, these shapes would distinguish United States and French flags; any difference in colour patterns or arrangement yields differences in spatio-chromatic shape.

Now suppose we consider the distinctive mark of a colour pattern in plumage or in a flower to be its spatio-chromatic shape. This cannot be identified by a particular chromatic appearance of any particular part of it, any more than the difference between a French flag and a United States flag could be identified by differences in their reds. Instead the pattern is a higher-level relational property; it is a set of relations among the colours and places that make up the pattern. And that set of relations can be recognized across changes in illumination, viewing conditions, viewers, and surrounds. Changes in those conditions may change the particular relata (the particular qualitative character of the components of the pattern), but they will not destroy the recognizable pattern of relations in which they stand.

Consider our two isoluminant flags. Changes in illumination, viewing conditions, and so on will somewhat change the apparent hues of the centres and the surrounds, and so change the relative heights of the two planes, but they will not alter the fact that one has the centre sticking out prominently above the surround, and the other has it below. It is difficult to confuse wedding cakes with top hats, even as the lights dim. Furthermore, global changes in illumination affect all the objects in the optic environment, shrinking hue differences globally. A distinctive spatio-chromatic pattern will remain equally distinctive relative to the objects in its environment even as the lights go down. Of course since the pattern is constituted by differences in colour, a species unable to discriminate those differences will fail to detect the pattern. This is exactly what one finds: 'Flowers, which have evolved to attract insects, very often have patterns which are invisible for us but can be seen by the honeybee' (Neumeyer 1991: 302). Neumeyer mentions several examples, including colour patterns in the plumage of birds and the wings of butterflies. Like the isoluminant flags to a monochromat, these patterns are invisible to us but not to the birds or other animals that have some stake in identifying them.

In short, what is distinctive about the signal is the colour *pattern*; and colour patterns can be analysed in terms of relations among the colours and places making them up. We can write a constant mapping rule if we write it in terms of those relations. It could pick out the same species of bird or flower over a vastly wider range of viewing conditions. Whereas our atomist will be frustrated whenever it gets cloudy, the sun sets, or the bird or flower falls into shadow.

Difference detection is perfectly adequate to the job of detecting the relations among the colours making up a spatio-chromatic pattern. Instead of coding each colour patch absolutely, just code how colours change at each edge. One does not require any absolute identification of the relata as long as one identifies the relations between them. This scheme also helps account for what colour constancy we have: a given deviation-from-background will still be a deviation-from-background even as the illumination changes. Colour 'constancy' is not constancy in the identity of relata, but is closer to identity in the relations that a point bears to its surrounds and its background. Those relations are 'constant' even as the relata alter.

One might object that there seem to be some chromatic biological signals that do not employ any fixed colour pattern, but instead an episodic presentation of a particular colour quale Q, which means something particular. For example, blushing presumably means something. It can be significant to notice someone blushing, though what exactly it means is hard to say. Perhaps it has some particular non-verbalizable socio-sexual content S, familiar to those raised in the hothouse of a primate social order, but hard to put into words. You need monkey ancestry to understand it. In any case perhaps conspecifics can pick up S because blushing always presents a particular skin tone Q. That particular shade of red then means specifically: S. Thus we gain one instance, at least, of the sort of point-to-point mapping rule that an atomist would like. But this instance fails too. Skin colours vary. Blushing will not produce the same reflectance property on the skin of every member of the species. Better to think of the episodic signal as yielding a temporal edge: the blushing does not always yield the same end-product Q, but is in everyone the same kind of *change* from the baseline skin tone. The skin gets redder. In this change our species is one. Difference detection across a temporal edge can handle such episodic signals.

So, in short, we find that detection of differences or ratios across borders allows us to write univocal mapping rules under which the consumers of chromatic states can do their jobs: detect the fruit hiding in the leaves, spot the lion creeping through the grass, and identify other biological kinds, friendly or not. Whereas attempts to find point-to-point mappings from chromatic appearances to biologically significant reflectance properties fail. The sensory system is built to detect differences, not similarities. Sensory similarities mark our failures to find difference.

An apt analogy for this model is provided by satellite telemetry. The data are often presented in what are called 'false colour' photographs. Different colours are used to represent arbitrary physical differences in a scene. We might use red to represent reflection of radar waves in the *L* band, and green to represent reflection in the *C* band (see D. L. Evans *et al.* 1994). In such a photograph we all admit that the objects on the red side of the border are not really red, and that perhaps the *only* physical similarity that all the items on the red side of the border share is that they affect the detectors in the satellite in the same way. Nevertheless, the borders between colours represent real physical differences in the scene. They might show the outlines of ancient craters or where the crop lands stop.

I think that all colours are, in this sense, false colours. Colour similarities may not represent any resemblance of physical properties other than the propensity of disparate classes of objects to affect our receptors in the same way. Nevertheless, colour differences—borders—can be informative about real physical differences in the scene. So false colours can accurately represent the location of real borders.

Even though the colours in a false-colour photograph are, in a sense, misrepresentations—that portion of the earth is not 'really' red—such a photograph can convey considerable news about objective physical properties in the scene. The same is true of a chromatic feature-placing system. It can serve accurately to identify edges: places in the scene where there is a real physical difference across the border. Those edges and borders are accurately located and typed, even if the colours attributed to either side say nothing particularly informative about the properties of the abutting surfaces. In fact the seeming similarity of points on one side of the divide should be discounted; they may after all be metamers, and any such sensed similarity merely reflects our incapacity to detect differences. But if we shift attention, as recommended, from patches to edges, our assessment of the reality and truthfulness of the appearances is also likely to change. It is bound to improve. The borders are accurately localized, and those edges are real. Exceptions are found only in the relatively rare cases of failure in spatial discrimination (Section 5.5). Satisfaction conditions demanding accurate localization of the places where things change can hence find visual appearances to be largely veridical, even though the colours involved are all 'false colours'.

Finally, we can explain the systemic (or non-atomistic) character of chromatic sensory representation. What we gained when we gained the red–green opponent system is an entire family of chromatic sensory states subject to univocal interpretation. The mapping rule is constant: such states all mark differences along that newly discriminable dimension of phenomenal variation. When a species adds a new photopigment, with a spectral sensitivity that differs from those it already had, some previously undetectable differences in the spectral composition of stimuli can become detectable. First, some equally luminous wavelength distributions can be discriminated, because one looks yellower or bluer than the other. It is particularly handy to add receptor types that allow one to track changes in daylight illumination, since they markedly increase the capacity to make contrast discriminations at all times of day (Neumeyer 1991: 300; Shepard 1992, 1993). Adding a new differentially sensitive pigment adds to the differences in wavelength composition that the organism can detect. Metamers for the dichromat appear as different colours to the trichromat. The trichromat can thereby detect more differences among surface reflectance spectra. Theoretically there is no upper limit to this process: adding additional pigments could add to the discriminations one could make among wavelength distributions, until finally vision might achieve narrow band-pass filtering, and any difference in the wavelength composition of two stimuli would be detectable. Such a plenitude of differentially sensitive receptors could make vision resemble audition, in which, thanks to narrow band-pass filtering, almost any difference in auditory spectra is detectable. Metamers would more or less disappear. Perhaps then we could be said to perceive reflectance spectra.

Unfortunately in visual systems the addition of new differentially sensitive cone systems has a cost: loss of spatial resolution. At some point the costs of lost spatial sensitivity outweigh the benefits of additional spectral discrimination, and acquisitions stop at some small number of distinct receptor types. With them one can detect some differences among spectral distributions; those that cannot be discriminated are treated as the same. We get false colours but real borders.

6.6 THREE BOLD AND TERMINAL CONJECTURES

Feature-placing has a number of subterranean implications that could either be left alone, unmentioned, down in the basement, or boldly hauled out and exposed to the light of day. In the interests of aggressive house-cleaning, I conclude with three such implications, rendered, in Popperian spirit, as bold conjectures. The test is to see whether they can survive exposure to sunlight.

The first is that qualitative identity is naught but a global failure to discriminate. It is a limit notion, and it must be assessed in statistical terms. While this claim might not seem bold, or even particularly conjectural, its implications are startling.

Identity of phenomenal properties is defined in terms of an incapacity to discriminate. It is relatively easy to show that a creature can discriminate between two stimuli, but to show that it *cannot* discriminate them one must rule out the hypothesis that it has the capacity to register any difference. Qualitative identity is defined in terms of global indiscriminability: a global incapacity to discriminate. Since random noise can enter the process, and tilt the scales either way, these assessments become statistical: over a long sequence of trials are the creature's discriminations better than chance? Qualitative identity hence also becomes a statistical notion: the assessment is that at such-and-such a confidence level, the distribution of responses to one signal does not differ in a statistically significant way from that of another. The entry of statistical concerns into any discussion of identity is somewhat disconcerting. But such entry is an inevitable consequence of the fact that indiscriminability cannot be established by a single trial, but requires the assessment of a distribution of responses.

It is conceptually disorienting to think of qualitative identity as a global failure in capacities of discrimination, or as a relation to be assessed in statistical terms. It follows, for example, that stimuli that are indiscriminable at a given confidence level, given a particular sample size, might register a statistically significant difference if only one could carry on the experiment long enough. So qualitative identity becomes something one can approach only at the limit. Peirce perhaps anticipated this implication. He thought that while 'sinsigns' or 'legisigns' have definite identity, 'qualisigns' do not. Qualisigns are 'of the nature of an appearance' while legisigns are 'of the nature of a general type', such as, for example, word-types. Peirce says: 'A legisign has a definite identity. . . . The qualisign, on the other hand, has no identity. It is the mere quality of an appearance and is not exactly the same throughout a second. Instead of identity, it has *great similarity*, and cannot differ much without being called quite another qualisign' (Peirce 1958: 391). It may or may not help relieve the sense of disorientation to note that materialists are already committed to the view that qualitative identity is a statistical relation. The particular qualitative character of a particular sensation is, according to the materialist, a property of the nervous system. Surely it is not the property of a single neuron. The most plausible hypothesis is that such qualitative characteristics are identical to activation patterns of large populations of neurons. To shift a sensation from red to green, one must shift the activation pattern of a population of neurons. Such shifts, like shifts in voting patterns, must be characterized statistically.

But if a particular qualitative characteristic is a characteristic of a population of neurons, wherein lies the identity of such characteristics? It is identity of characteristics of two populations, and so we find ourselves swimming in statistical seas. Psychophysics has long since adopted this viewpoint, with 'signal detection theory'. There is always some random noise in aggregates of millions of neurons, and even presentation of two physically identical packets of ambient energy (if that were possible!) would not result in identical activation patterns across those millions of respondents. But the differences might not be statistically significant. We calculate carefully to see if above the noise there is detectable 'signal'.

With identity in such tatters, the properties in the domain are likely also to suffer depreciation. After all, numerical identity is not identity at a confidence level, and its assessment does not require large random samples. Suppose Jill looks at a red leaf and a ripe tomato, and they happen to be metamers. As noted earlier, if we are realists about universals, and think colours qualify, then the maple leaf has something—redness—that is strictly identical to something the ripe tomato has. What is that wherein the maple leaf and the tomato are the same? The reflectance spectra differ physically. Even if Jill is detecting the same colour, she is not detecting identity of reflectance spectra. The fact that both look red, and indeed the exact same shade of red, is difficult to put into register with any identity of properties of things in front of Jill's eyes. Here the distal stimuli differ physically, as do the wavelength spectra reflected towards Jill.

So we kick the problem indoors. Perhaps we could say that the two merely *look* red, and that this appearance is to be explained by a genuine qualitative identity. Both yield visual sensations in Jill, and there is something strictly identical in those two sensations. They have identical qualitative character. But here we face the implications of our first conjecture. Even indoors we cannot sustain a claim to numerical identity. We find ourselves instead polling populations of neurons, and assessing the probabilities that two populations differ at a confidence level. Qualitative identity is a poor cousin among identity relations; it does not possess the logical features of the numerical identity we seek. The latter does not require confidence intervals.

We might ask Jill to judge whether the colours of the two patches match. When she brings her eyes to bear on the task, her visual nervous system must register at least three dimensions of variation for each patch: the dimensions of white–black, red–green, and yellow–blue. Even the degree of redness or greenness of one point of the patch is presumably represented by some population of neurons, whose activation levels jointly represent the redness–greenness of that point. So the match requires a comparison of averages of activation levels of large populations of neurons. The patches match if the averages for white–black, for red–green, and for yellow–blue do not differ significantly. One can imagine a population of neurons *voting* on the redness–greenness value to assign to regions of the patch. All in favour of neutral grey, say aye. A second population votes on a similarly worded issue about the other patch. The two colours match on redness–greenness if the two votes are not significantly different. With a big enough sample size there is no limit to how small a difference might be statistically significant. So are the two patches qualitatively identical, or not? One longs to replace this talk of qualitative identity with a description of the behaviour of all the voters, and leave it at that.

Second bold conjecture: we should resuscitate resemblance nominalism for colours, if not for all sensory qualities. Note that our resuscitative efforts are circumscribed; for many properties the thesis of the resemblance nominalist remains implausible. Two protons do not both have a positive charge because they resemble one another; instead they resemble one another in that both have a positive charge. It strikes many as implausible to construct a genuine universal from a resemblance relationship; instead the two instances resemble because they share some joint property. But the nominalist thesis, implausible as it might be for genuine universals, captures an important truth about sensory qualities. It seems precisely wrong to say of our metamers that they resemble one another because they share some common property. It seems precisely right to say of them that they are instances of red only because they resemble one another. They 'resemble' one another in that they have similar effects on some stage of the visual system; they affect the mechanism of sensory discrimination in such a way that it loses the capacity to discriminate between them. In that way the 'unruly, rough, and ragged' lot of metamers come all to look the same. The colour property is constituted by the sensory resemblance, not the other way round. Or, taking into account the first conjecture: the colour property is in truth constituted by the *lack* of significant alarms from the difference detectors. Their silence constitutes the 'sensory resemblance'.

Think in terms of the priority of explanations: What are the primitive terms of colour science, and what terms do we explain on their basis? If colours were real properties, we would expect the primitive terms to be those naming the properties that all and only the stimuli for red (or green, or yellow, etc.) share. On that basis, we would explain the sensory resemblances of things. Why does the red leaf look like the ripe tomato? It is because they both have that self-same property: redness. But in fact the science proceeds in precisely the opposite direction. The primitive terms are all relational terms for similarities and differences: variants of discriminability and indiscriminability. The dominant enterprise is the construction of models of colour discrimination. Resemblance in this context is not an unanalysable relation, but is instead the target explanandum of the entire enterprise. Why does the red leaf look like the ripe tomato? It is not because those physically distinct reflectance spectra share any self-same property, but rather because, given the known powers of our mechanisms of chromatic discrimination, the two will have identical effects on such-and-such a stage of the mechanism, and thereafter cannot be told apart. Because they resemble one another in that now explicable fashion, those stimuli both 'look red', and are both fitting targets for the colour term.

The priorities in colour science are clear: resemblance comes first, and it does the heavy lifting. Colour categories come later. The thesis of the resemblance nominalist—that two stimuli are instances of red because they resemble one another, and not the other way round—states an important truth about colours, and perhaps about sensory qualities in general.

Resemblance nominalism is particularly potent when allied with 'particularized natures' or 'tropes' (see Armstrong 1989: 113–33). Treat the redness of the maple leaf as a particular—perhaps a particular reflectance spectrum. The redness of the tomato is another, different particular. We can also find instances of red that involve no reflectance spectra at all, as in red sunsets, soap bubbles, compact discs, or mists. It is impossible to find a property in one of these particularized natures that is strictly identical to a property found in all and only the others. In fact if one of them is red, it seems the only reason the other is also red is that it happens to have similar effects on a visual system. Given the eight-termed nature of the matching relation, these resemblances are not intrinsic to the stimuli; they depend explicitly on the visual systems of the observers. The similarity in apparent hues of two objects can be changed without altering the objects at all. So, unlike real properties, these particularized natures do not have the same red hue because they share a property. Instead they are both red only because they have effects that resemble one another. And that indeed is resemblance nominalism. With colours the resemblances come first, and the 'properties', if you want them, second.

At one point C. L. Hardin (1988: 112) declares, 'We are to be eliminativists with respect to color as a property of objects, but reductivists with respect to color experiences.' I agree on both counts, and suggest that one way to describe the subjectivists' longing to be eliminativists with respect to colour as a property of objects is to call it by its old name: resemblance nominalism. It yields a nice crisp formulation of subjectivist ontology. Recall that the subjectivist does not deny the existence of mind-independent stimuli for colour. There are indeed physical phenomena in front of Jill's eyes that cause various of Jill's impressions of red, and those phenomena could exist and could have all the properties that they have even if Jill and every other sentient organism ceased to exist. Those stimuli are exactly the particularized natures of the resemblance nominalist. They exist, and as particulars could exist independently of any other particular, including any that might happen to achieve sentience. The subjectivist and resemblance nominalist agree: those particularized natures, making up the stimuli for colour, could all exist on their own, without any percipients on the scene. What would be missing from that scene are precisely: the colour *properties*. There would indeed be no resemblance among the motley crew of metamers; without any civilizing principles on the scene, they would remain an unruly, rough, and ragged lot.

Resemblance nominalism puts considerable weight on the reality of resemblances. Two metamers for green are both green because they resemble one another. I urged that the latter is ultimately explained as a failure to detect difference: the two instances have a similar effect on some stage of the visual nervous system, and so that system loses the capacity to discriminate between them. Such sensory resemblance carries little positive news. Massed banks of difference detectors, organized in map after map, modality by modality, scrutinize the landscape ahead. Qualitative identity means simply that no significant differences are detected. No alarms are set off. The captain is allowed to continue with his nap.

Philosophers from the *Aufbau* and *The Structure of Appearance* onwards have constructed their systems using some relationship of similarity as the root primitive term. Here is bold conjecture number three: in sensory systems the root relation from which order derives is not similarity, but difference. Instead of qualitative identity as the primitive term, the neural reality would be better reflected by using discriminability: the detection of differences. In sensory terms, similarity is naught but a failure to discriminate. Discrimination carries the load. As its dual, similarity gets a free ride.

Locke noticed the duality. One can identify the blue things by picking a paradigm and some foils, and stipulating that the term 'blue' is to apply to those things relatively more similar to the paradigm than to the foils. The choice of foils is not trivial, but scaling theory demonstrates it always to be possible. Locke noticed that one can also identify those things in terms of differences: 'the name, *Blue*, notes properly nothing but that mark of distinction that is in a violet, discernible only by our eyes, whatever it consists in, that being beyond our capacities distinctly to know, and, perhaps, would be of less use to us, if we had faculties to discern' (Locke 1975: II. xxxii. 14). The intriguing suggestion is that a colour name denotes nothing but 'that mark of distinction, discernible only by the eyes, whatever it consists in'. We do not identify what property is strictly identical among all the blue things, or that wherein all the blue things are the same; but instead that which distinguishes blue from all the other colours. 'Blue' marks that set of *distinctions*. The dual of our similarity baptism runs as follows. Pick out a paradigm and some foils and say: 'Blue is nothing but that mark of distinction, whatever it consists in, that allows the visual discrimination of this thing from all those other things.' Again one needs to pick the foils carefully, so as to rule out discrimination by shape, size, and so on. You would want other flowers of similar shape, size, texture, etc., but different colours. The result identifies a fully determinate shade of colour—a colour of just one thing. What is notably absent from the formulation is any implication that two blue things share some self-same property.

One reason to load the weight onto the difference dual and leave similarity alone is that the latter relationship has been left in such tatters by our earlier attentions. As Peirce noted, with it we have no 'definite' identity, but merely degrees of greater and greater similarity. It is a limit notion; qualitative identity is ultimately replaced by a statistical characterization of populations of neurons. Whereas sensed differences generally correspond to real physical differences in or around the body of the sentient organism. The occasional neural signals of borders, change, or discontinuity are more trustworthy than the long swaths of similitude in between. Better to build a career on the more reliable of the signals.

A second reason to load the weight onto discriminability is that it generalizes well. It is a relation common to all sensibles. We do not need special versions of it for each variety of appearance; it can serve as the primitive term generating order in every one. Using difference as the root primitive term meshes neatly with the 'false colour' model. It yields a pleasing account of the satisfaction conditions for chromatic sensory appearance. In the false-colour photograph we should focus not on the hues of any given patch, but rather on the borders where they change; if all goes well, those borders are real, and their location is accurately represented. Similarly, satisfaction conditions for visual appearance should focus on the feature-placing capacity accurately to locate borders, changes, and discontinuities. When all goes well such chromatic borders among surface colours represent facts of the form 'reflectance changes here'. Those contents are largely satisfied: the differences are real, even if the apparent similarities are eventually explained away, as by-products of our limited capacities of discrimination. At the end we may discount the features but pay careful attention to the location of the border between them.

We might as well start at the place where sensory representations get things right. But those points do not lie within the typical colour patch, so to speak. They lie at the edges. On this reading, as on Locke's, colour perception does not provide much news about portions of a swath all of the same hue. Features attributed to points interior to such a swath say little about what property those points must share if they are all to be really red. Perhaps the only property they share is the disjunctive, anthropocentric, dispositional power to affect a human visual nervous system in the same way. But the places where colours change generate some hard news. They typically point to the locus of some objective physical change. The system thereby identifies that locus, without saying much about conditions on either side of it. Such seems an apt characterization of the content of colour vision.

Recall the primal challenge of spotting the banana in the leaves. Success does not require strict identification of a surface property of the banana or the leaf. One needs merely the capacity to discriminate between them. The challenge is to see *where* leaf ends and fruit begins; the reader by now is not surprised to notice that 'Here is foliage, there is fruit' is a feature-placing sentence. Accurately locating the places where reflectance changes could do the trick. One sees those yellow patches *as* parts of a connected surface, partially occluded by foliage, obscured by dappled light. They pop out from the green surround. That edge—that kind of difference—can help make the banana salient.

Differing modalities register differing *dimensions* of variation; 'is redder than' and 'is lighter than', for example, are specifically visual order-generating relations. But the particular dimensions of variation in particular modalities are all variations on the theme of detecting differences. They can be thought of as relatively recent morphemic variations on a primitive common root. That root is the detection of differences: the relationship 'is discriminable from'.

This root form serves an ancient need, as befits its lineage. An organism that could not improve its chances for absorbing energy or of evading predators by moving from one place to another would have scant need to detect the difference. But add even the simplest form of motility, and an uneven distribution of food or predators, and the capacity to discriminate features of one's surroundings becomes invaluable. As soon as some portions of the slime pool were better for our ancestors than others, it became advantageous to be able to detect the difference between bad places and good, and to wiggle purposefully from one to the other. The pursuit of happiness no doubt started in those pools. Since then our tastes may have grown more discriminating, the competition and the environment more complex; but the ancient, underlying principles remain the same.

And with that our job of work is done; the feature-placing hypothesis can sally forth to meet its fate. As with any hypothesis its true function is not to live a long life, not to be happy or prosperous, but immediately to start breeding better successors. The current generation could certainly use more sustenance. Parts are schematic, if not skeletal, and need more muscle. These last sections I hope give some sense of the work required to flesh out the semantics of feature-placing representation in one small but colourful capacity in one sensory modality. If one lifts one's gaze to the full panoply of vertebrate sentience, and imagines all the features and sensory identifiers of all the modalities therein, the work that awaits to fill out feature-placing accounts at a similar level of detail throughout is daunting—and exciting. The philosophical goal is to give some sense of how all those parts will hang together: a synoptic view, a conceptual road map, that guides us towards the exciting places, and helps us avoid the methodological potholes and conceptual swamps. But half the fun is that we do not know what is out there, and these conceptual maps themselves need to be redrawn periodically as we discover new features and new mysteries in regions yet to be charted.

APPENDIX

Closing the Explanatory Gap

FORMALIZING should help to flush out any obscurities in this project. The goal is to derive identities of the form

sensations of red = brain process b

or, if we are talking about sensations of a particular shade P_r,

sensations of P_r = brain process b.

Strictly the goal is to derive whatever 'bridge principles' connect qualitative terms to neurophysiological ones. These may not be identity statements, but could take whatever form suffices to yield a neurophysiological explanation of colour perception. But let us see if we could derive the identity statement.

The key idea is that the structure needed to do this is not found in causal roles that serve to individuate. Sensations of red are not associated with any particular causal niche. Instead sensations of red are associated with a particular *qualitative* niche. This coheres with the idea that qualitative terms, to the extent that they can be defined, can be defined only by their relations to one another. No stimuli can be mentioned. Sensations of red are picked out by their relations to sensations of green, sensations of yellow, etc.; not (directly) by a particular and unique causal role. To do this we follow the fourfold way sketched in Section 1.1.

STEP 1

Using relations of matching, indiscriminability, and relative similarity, construct an ordering of stimulus classes. A stimulus is an instance, a presentation; the terms of the matching relation are such stimuli. Indiscriminability, however, requires an assessment over repeated trials, and its terms are hence classes of stimuli. All the members of such a class M match one another and are mutually indiscriminable. In a very strict sense they all 'look the same'; they might all look the specific shade of red P_r, for instance.

One can label a point in quality space with such a class M, but one cannot *define* a place in the ordering of qualities with any such finite listing. Physically the same stimuli might under different conditions present a different quality (see Section 6.2). And whatever class of stimuli one uses to tag a place in the ordering is not projectible: it will include a motley bunch of metamers, for instance.

STEP 2

Use these stimulus classes to identify phenomenal properties. Each point in quality space is a particular phenomenal property: a property of appearance. It is the property that all the stimuli in class M present. Stimuli in the physically heterogeneous class M all cause sensations as of the same red. Those stimuli all look to be that particular shade P_r.

A place in quality space is a particular, fully determinate sensory quality, such as the one that every member of the class M presents. It is a phenomenal property: the property that all the sensations caused by those stimuli are sensations *of*. Relations of similarity, relative similarity, mixing, matching, complementarity, and so on, which obtain among places in the ordering of qualities, are relations among these qualities.

Now we cannot use any particular stimulus to identify such a property, since physically the same stimulus might present different qualities at different times. So we must use a structure description to identify the particular quality that all those stimuli present. The 'niche' for this particular P_r is identified by relational facts of the form 'the quality that stands in such-and-such relations to other qualities'. For example, red is the complement of green (where 'complement' is a two-term relation, Cxy), the quality that must be added to yellow to get orange (a three-term relation, $Mxyz$), the quality more similar to orange than to blue ($Rxyz$), and so on. It is simplest to let our variables range over particular instances or tropes of colours (see Section 6.6), so 'Red(x_1)' means: x_1 is a trope of red. Then x_1 is red if it is the complement of green, is such that when mixed with yellow gives orange, is more similar to orange than to blue, and so on. We get something like

$$\text{Red}(x_1) \equiv (\exists x_2)\,(\exists x_3)\,(\exists x_4)\,(\exists x_5)\,(Cx_1x_2\ \&\ \text{Green}(x_2)\ \&\ Mx_1x_3x_4\ \&\ \text{Yellow}(x_3)$$
$$\&\ \text{Orange}(x_4)\ \&\ Rx_1x_4x_5\ \&\ \text{Blue}(x_5)\ldots)$$

But if such an equivalence holds, then all the hue names on the right side can be eliminated, since they can all be identified in the same way. We can form a 'Ramsey sentence' for the entire relational structure. To do this: string all the claims about relations among those qualities together into one big conjunction. Replace all the names of qualities with variables. Prefix the result with as many existential quantifiers as needed (see Block 1980). We would get something like

$$(\exists x_1)\,(\exists x_2)\,(\exists x_3)\,(\exists x_4)\,(\exists x_5)\,(Cx_1x_2\ \&\ Mx_1x_3x_4\ \&\ Rx_1x_4x_5\ \&\ \ldots)$$

The phrase on the right must continue until it includes all the relations of qualitative similarity holding among qualities in this multidimensional order. To simplify the string of initial quantifiers, we can use the notation:

$$(\exists\,[x_n])\,(Cx_1x_2\ \&\ Mx_1x_3x_4\ \&\ Rx_1x_4x_5\ \&\ \ldots)$$

Then a 'Ramsey correlate' collects all the relational properties for a particular point in the space (the particular location of our phenomenal property P_r) by using a particular variable in this structure, as follows:

$$P_r(y) \equiv (\exists\,[x_n])\,((Cx_1x_2\ \&\ Mx_1x_3x_4\ \&\ Rx_1x_4x_5\ \&\ \ldots)\ \&\ y = x_1).$$

Interestingly, only such structure descriptions generalize across people and across viewing situations (see Section 1.2). There is no stimulus that looks unitary green to everybody, but for everybody (who is not colour-blind) there is some stimulus that looks unitary green; and it looks unitary green if and only if it satisfies a structural definite description of the form given above.

STEP 3

Make the dramatic step from phenomenal properties to qualitative ones. The idea is that distinct phenomenal properties require distinct qualitative characteristics: distinct properties of sensation. The step depends on an account of the notion of qualitative identity.

The stimuli in class M all look the same; each causes a sensation of exactly the same red. Now a sensation of x is qualitatively identical to a sensation of y if and only if x presents exactly the same qualities as y. The qualitative character of a sensation is that in virtue of which the stimulus causing that sensation presents the appearance that it does. If we can find that the stimuli in class M present exactly the same appearance, then we can infer that the sensations they cause are qualitatively identical to one another. Although the move requires care (see Clark 1993b: ch. 3), it gets us from the properties that stimuli appear to have to the qualitative properties of sensation.

Suppose y is the same place as before in the quality space. That relationally identified place can now serve to identify a particular qualitative character: the qualitative character that any visual sensation has if it is a sensation *of* that particular red. Stipulate

Q_r = the property of sensations in virtue of which they are sensations of P_r

and then a Ramsey correlate can be used to identify this particular qualitative character. Variables z will now range over properties of sensation, not tropes of colours. Corresponding to tropes x_1 and x_2 being complements of one another, we have a new relation $C^* z_1 z_2$, the 'counterpart' relation that holds between a sensation of x_1 and a sensation of x_2 if x_1 and x_2 are complements of one another. With the other relations of similarity holding among phenomenal properties we can likewise associate counterpart relations holding among the qualitative properties of sensation. To identify Q_r, we use:

$$Q_r(y) \equiv (\exists\, [z_n]) \, (\, (C^* z_1 z_2 \;\&\; M^* z_1 z_3 z_4 \;\&\; R^* z_1 z_4 z_5 \;\&\; \ldots) \;\&\; y = z_1).$$

Here we are identifying a particular qualitative property that various sensory episodes can share. It is the particular qualitative character in virtue of which they are all sensations of that same shade of red. So we have reached the point where we are talking about the qualitative character of sensations of red, as needed in the identity.

STEP 4

Find the unique neurophysiological realizations. It turns out that the structure of phenomenal properties detailed above is anisotropic, asymmetric, has bumps and irregularities. So if its counterpart has a neural realization at all, it will be a unique realization, as symbolized by $\exists!$:

$(\exists![z_n])\,(C^*z_1z_2\ \&\ M^*z_1z_3z_4\ \&\ R^*z_1z_4z_5\ \&\ \ldots).$

And suppose eventually we find brain states $b_1, b_2, \ldots b_n$ such that

$C^*b_1b_2\ \&\ M^*b_1b_3b_4\ \&\ R^*b_1b_4b_5\ \&\ \ldots$

But then, as in D. Lewis (1966, 1972), we could *derive* the identity between states with the qualitative character Q_r and the corresponding brain processes. Since we had

$Q_r(y) \equiv (\exists\,[z_n])\,(\,(C^*z_1z_2\ \&\ M^*z_1z_3z_4\ \&\ R^*z_1z_4z_5\ \&\ \ldots)\ \&\ y = z_1)$

it follows, from our having established a unique realization, that there is a realization; and that brain states $b_1 \ldots b_n$ are the states that stand to one another in the relations so specified. So

$z_1 = b_1,\ z_2 = b_2,\ z_3 = b_3,\ z_4 = b_4,\ z_5 = b_5 \ldots;$ and
$Q_r(y) \equiv (y = b_1).$

Hence the having of sensations with the particular qualitative character Q_r is just the having of brain process b_1. The target identity has been derived. The structure description is generated not by causal relations but by qualitative ones. That particular sensation of red need not have any particular and unique causal role, but it would not be the sensation that it is were it not related as it is to the other qualities of sense. The key to closing the gap is not a causal niche, but a qualitative one.

REFERENCES

ABRAMOV, ISRAEL, and GORDON, JAMES (1994). Color appearance: on seeing red—or yellow, or green, or blue. *Annual Review of Psychology*, 45: 451–85.

AKINS, KATHLEEN (1996). Of sensory systems and the 'aboutness' of mental states. *Journal of Philosophy*, 93: 337–72.

ALBECK, YEHUDA (1995). Sound localization and binaural processing. In Arbib (1995: 891–5).

ALMOG, J., PERRY, J., and WETTSTEIN, H. (eds.) (1989). *Themes from Kaplan*. New York: Oxford University Press.

ALPERN, M., KITAHARA, K., and KRANTZ, D. H. (1983). Perception of colour in unilateral tritanopia. *Journal of Physiology*, 335: 683–97.

ANGELL, R. B. (1974). The geometry of visibles. *Noûs*, 8: 87–117.

ANSCOMBE, G. E. M. (1981). The intentionality of sensation. In her *Metaphysics and the Philosophy of Mind: Collected Philosophical Papers*, ii. Minneapolis: University of Minnesota Press, 3–20. First pub. in R. J. Butler (ed.) (1965), *Analytical Philosophy*. 2nd ser. Oxford: Oxford University Press.

ARBIB, MICHAEL (1972). *The Metaphorical Brain*. New York: Wiley.

—— (1989). *The Metaphorical Brain 2: Neural Networks and Beyond*. New York: Wiley.

—— (ed.) (1995). *Handbook of Brain Theory and Neural Networks*. Cambridge, Mass.: MIT Press.

ARMSTRONG, D. M. (1968). *A Materialist Theory of the Mind*. London: Routledge & Kegan Paul.

—— (1969). Colour realism and the argument from microscopes. In R. Brown and C. D. Rollins (eds.), *Contemporary Philosophy in Australia*. London: George Allen & Unwin, 119–31. Repr. in Armstrong (1980: 104–18).

—— (1973). *Belief, Truth and Knowledge*. Cambridge: Cambridge University Press.

—— (1980). *The Nature of Mind and Other Essays*. Ithaca, NY: Cornell University Press.

—— (1987). Smart and the secondary qualities. In Philip Pettit, Richard Sylvan, and Jean Norman (eds.), *Metaphysics and Morality: Essays in Honour of J. J. C. Smart*. Oxford: Blackwell, 1–15.

—— (1989). *Universals: An Opinionated Introduction*. Boulder, Colo.: Westview Press.

—— (1997). *A World of States of Affairs*. Cambridge: Cambridge University Press.

AVERILL, E. W. (1985). Color and the anthropocentric problem. *Journal of Philosophy*, 82: 281–304.

—— (1992). The relational nature of color. *Philosophical Review*, 101: 551–88.

AYER, ALFRED J. (1973). *The Central Questions of Philosophy*. Harmondsworth: Penguin.

BAKER, GORDON, and MORRIS, KATHERINE J. (1996). *Descartes' Dualism*. London: Routledge.

BALDWIN, THOMAS (1992). The projective theory of sensory content. In Crane (1992*b*: 177–95).

BARLOW, H. B. (1972). Single units and sensation: a neuron doctrine for perceptual psychology? *Perception*, 1: 371–94.

BEAUVOIS, M.-F., and SAILLANT, B. (1985). Optic aphasia for colours and colour agnosia: a distinction between visual and visuo-verbal impairments in the processing of colors. *Cognitive Neuropsychology*, 2: 1–48.

BENNETT, JONATHAN (1968). Substance, reality, and primary qualities. In C. B. Martin and D. M. Armstrong (eds.), *Locke and Berkeley: A Collection of Critical Essays*. Garden City, NY: Anchor Books, 86–124.

—— (1971). *Locke, Berkeley, Hume: Central Themes*. Oxford: Clarendon Press.

BERMÚDEZ, J. L., MARCEL, A., and EILAN, N. (eds.) (1995). *The Body and the Self*. Cambridge, Mass.: MIT Press.

BLAKEMORE, COLIN (1975). Central visual processing. In Michael S. Gazzaniga and Colin Blakemore (eds.), *Handbook of Psychobiology*. New York: Academic Press, 241–68.

BLOCK, NED (1980). Troubles with functionalism. In Ned Block (ed.), *Readings in the Philosophy of Psychology*, i. Cambridge, Mass.: Harvard University Press, 268–305.

—— (1990). Inverted earth. In James E. Tomberlin (ed.), *Philosophical Perspectives*, iv: *Action Theory and Philosophy of Mind*. Atascadero, Calif.: Ridgeview Publishing, 53–79. Repr. in Block *et al*. (1997: 677–94).

—— (1995). On a confusion about a function of consciousness. *Behavioral and Brain Sciences*, 18: 227–88.

—— FLANAGAN, OWEN, and GÜZELDERE, GÜVEN (eds.) (1997). *The Nature of Consciousness: Philosophical Debates*. Cambridge, Mass.: MIT Press.

BOGHOSSIAN, PAUL A., and VELLEMAN, J. DAVID (1989). Colour as a secondary quality. *Mind*, 98: 81–103.

—— —— (1991). Physicalist theories of color. *Philosophical Review*, 100: 67–106.

BORING, EDWIN G. (1942). *Sensation and Perception in the History of Experimental Psychology*. New York: Appleton Century Crofts.

BOYNTON, ROBERT M. (1975). Color, hue, and wavelength. In E. C. Carterette and M. P. Friedman (eds.), *Handbook of Perception*, v: *Seeing*. New York, Academic Press, 302–47.

—— (1979). *Human Color Vision*. New York: Holt, Rinehart &Winston.

—— (1988). Color vision. *Annual Review of Psychology*, 39: 69–100.

BOZICKOVIC, VOJISLAV (1995). *Demonstrative Sense: An Essay on the Semantics of Perceptual Demonstratives*. Aldershot: Avebury.

BRAITENBERG, VALENTINO (1984). *Vehicles*. Cambridge, Mass.: MIT Press.

BREWER, BILL (1995). Bodily awareness and the self. In Bermúdez, *et al*. (1995: 291–310).

BROACKES, J. (1992). The autonomy of color. In D. Charles and K. Lennon (eds.), *Reduction, Explanation, and Realism*. Oxford: Clarendon Press, 421–65.

BROAD, C. D. (1927). *Scientific Thought*. London: Routledge &Kegan Paul.

—— (1965). Some elementary reflexions on sense-perception. In Swartz (1965: 29–48). First pub. in *Philosophy*, 27 (1952), 3–17.

BROWN, HAROLD I. (1987). *Observation and Objectivity*. New York: Oxford University Press.

BURGESS, JOHN P., and ROSEN, GIDEON (1997). *A Subject with No Object: Strategies for Nominalistic Interpretation of Mathematics*. Oxford: Clarendon Press.

BUSER, PIERRE, and IMBERT, MICHEL (1992). *Audition*. Tr. R. H. Kay. Cambridge, Mass.: MIT Press.

CAMPBELL, JOHN (1994). *Past, Space, and Self*. Cambridge, Mass.: MIT Press.

CARLILE, SIMON (1996). *Virtual Auditory Space: Generation and Applications*. New York: Chapman & Hall.

CARNAP, RUDOLF (1958). *Introduction to Symbolic Logic and its Applications*. New York: Dover.

—— (1967). *The Logical Structure of the World*. 2nd edn. Tr. Rolf A. George. Berkeley: University of California Press.

CARR, C. E., and KONISHI, M. (1990). A circuit for detection of interaural time differences in the brain stem of the barn owl. *Journal of Neuroscience*, 10: 3227–46.

CASTAÑEDA, HECTOR-NERI (1966). 'He': a study in the logic of self-consciousness. *Ratio*, 8: 130–57.

—— (1967). Indicators and quasi-indicators. *American Philosophical Quarterly*, 4: 85–100.

—— (1977). Perception, belief, and the structure of physical objects and consciousness. *Synthese*, 35: 285–351.

—— (1989). Direct reference, the semantics of thinking, and guise theory: constructive reflections on David Kaplan's theory of indexical reference. In Almog, *et al.* (1989: 105–44).

CHALMERS, DAVID J. (1996). *The Conscious Mind*. New York: Oxford University Press.

CHURCHLAND, PATRICIA S., and SEJNOWSKI, TERRENCE J. (1992). *The Computational Brain*. Cambridge, Mass.: MIT Press.

CHURCHLAND, PAUL M. (1986). Some reductive strategies in cognitive neurobiology. *Mind*, 95: 279–309.

—— (1989). *A Neurocomputational Perspective: The Nature of Mind and the Structure of Science*. Cambridge, Mass.: MIT Press.

—— (1995). *The Engine of Reason, the Seat of the Soul*. Cambridge, Mass.: MIT Press.

CLARK, AUSTEN (1980). *Psychological Models and Neural Mechanisms*. Oxford: Clarendon Press.

—— (1985a). A physicalist theory of qualia. *Monist*, 68: 491–506.

—— (1985b). Qualia and the psychophysiological explanation of color perception. *Synthese*, 65: 377–405.

—— (1985c). Spectrum inversion and the color solid. *Southern Journal of Philosophy*, 23: 431–43.

CLARK, AUSTEN (1986). Psychofunctionalism and chauvinism. *Philosophy of Science*, 53: 535–59.

—— (1989). The particulate instantiation of homogeneous pink. *Synthese* 80: 277–304.

—— (1993*a*). Mice, shrews, and misrepresentation. *Journal of Philosophy*, 90: 290–310.

—— (1993*b*). *Sensory Qualities*. Oxford: Clarendon Press.

—— (1994*a*). Beliefs and desires incorporated. *Journal of Philosophy*, 91: 404–25.

—— (1994*b*). Contemporary problems in the philosophy of perception. *American Journal of Psychology*, 107: 613–22.

—— (1996*a*). Three varieties of visual field. *Philosophical Psychology*, 9: 477–95.

—— (1996*b*). True theories, false colors. *Philosophy of Science*, PSA Suppl. 63: 143–50.

CORNSWEET, TOM (1970). *Visual Perception*. New York: Academic Press.

CRANE, TIM (1992*a*). The nonconceptual content of experience. In Crane (1992*b*: 136–57).

—— (ed.) (1992*b*). *The Contents of Experience: Essays on Perception*. Cambridge: Cambridge University Press.

CRICK F., and KOCH, C. (1990*a*). Some remarks on visual awareness. *The Brain: Cold Spring Harbor Symposia on Quantitative Biology*, 55: 953–62.

—— —— (1990*b*). Towards a neurobiological theory of consciousness. *Seminars in Neuroscience*, 2: 263–75.

—— —— (1997). Towards a neurobiological theory of consciousness. In Block *et al.* (1997: 277–92).

CUMMINS, ROBERT (1989). *Meaning and Mental Representation*. Cambridge, Mass.: MIT Press.

DAVIDOFF, JULES (1991). *Cognition through Color*. Cambridge, Mass.: MIT Press.

DAVIES, MARTIN, and HUMPHREYS, GORDON (eds.) (1993). *Consciousness*. Oxford: Blackwell.

DENNETT, D. C. (1988). Quining qualia. In A. Marcel and E. Bisiach (eds.), *Consciousness in Contemporary Science*. Oxford: Oxford University Press, 42–77.

—— (1991). *Consciousness Explained*. Boston: Little, Brown.

—— and KINSBOURNE, M. (1992). Time and the observer: the where and when of consciousness in the brain. *Behavioral and Brain Sciences*, 15: 183–247.

DESCARTES, RENÉ (1984). *Meditations on First Philosophy*. In *The Philosophical Writings of Descartes*, ii. Tr. John Cottingham, Robert Stoothoff, and Dugald Murdoch. Cambridge: Cambridge University Press.

DE VALOIS, R. L., and DE VALOIS, K. K. (1975). Neural coding of color. In E. C. Carterette and M. P. Friedman (eds.), *Handbook of Perception*, v: *Seeing*. New York: Academic Press, 117–66.

—— —— (1993). A multi-stage color model. *Vision Research*, 8: 1053–65.

DEVITT, MICHAEL (1981). *Designation*. New York: Columbia University Press.

DOMINEY, P. F., and ARBIB, M. A. (1992). A cortical–subcortical model for generation of spatially accurate sequential saccades. *Cerebral Cortex*, 2: 153–75.

DRETSKE, FRED (1981). *Knowledge and the Flow of Information.* Cambridge, Mass.: MIT Press.

—— (1986). Misrepresentation. In Radu J. Bogdan (ed.), *Belief.* Oxford: Oxford University Press, 17–36.

—— (1988). *Explaining Behavior: Reasons in a World of Causes.* Cambridge, Mass.: MIT Press.

—— (1995). *Naturalizing the Mind.* Cambridge, Mass.: MIT Press.

DUMMETT, MICHAEL (1981). *Frege: Philosophy of Language.* 2nd edn. Cambridge, Mass.: Harvard University Press.

EILAN, N., MCCARTHY, R., and BREWER, B. (eds.) (1993). *Spatial Representation: Problems in Philosophy and Psychology.* Oxford: Blackwell.

ELDER, CRAWFORD (1988). On the determinacy of reference. *Southern Journal of Philosophy*, 26: 48–97.

—— (1991). Antirealism and realist claims of invariance. *Southern Journal of Philosophy*, 29: 1–19.

—— (1994a). Proper functions defended. *Analysis*, 54: 167–70.

—— (1994b). Higher and lower essential natures. *American Philosophical Quarterly*, 31: 255–65.

—— (1995). A different kind of natural kind. *Australasian Journal of Philosophy*, 73: 516–31.

—— (1996a). Content and the subtle extensionality of '. . . explains . . .'. *Philosophical Quarterly*, 46: 320–32.

—— (1996b). Contrariety and 'carving up reality'. *American Philosophical Quarterly*, 33: 277–89.

—— (1996c). On the reality of medium-sized objects. *Philosophical Studies*, 83: 191–211.

—— (1996d). Realism and determinable properties. *Philosophy and Phenomenological Research*, 56: 149–59.

—— (1998a). Essential properties and coinciding objects. *Philosophy and Phenomenological Research*, 58: 317–31.

—— (1998b). What sensory signals are about. *Analysis*, 58: 273–6.

—— (1998c). What vs. how in naturally selected representations. *Mind*, 107: 349–63.

EVANS, D. L., STOFAN, E. R., JONES, T. D., and GODWIN, L. M. (1994). Earth from sky. *Scientific American*, 271 6: 70–5.

EVANS, GARETH (1982). *The Varieties of Reference.* Ed. John McDowell. Oxford: Clarendon Press.

—— (1985a). *Collected Papers.* Ed. Antonia Philips. Oxford: Oxford University Press.

—— (1985b). Molyneux's question. In Evans (1985a: 364–99).

—— (1985c). Things without the mind—a commentary upon chapter two of Strawson's *Individuals.* In Evans (1985a: 249–90). First pub. in Zak van Straaten (ed.) (1980), *Philosophical Subjects: Essays Presented to P. F. Strawson.* Oxford: Oxford University Press, 76–116.

EVANS, GARETH (1985*d*). Understanding demonstratives. In Evans (1985*a*: 291–321). First pub. in Herman Parret and Jacques Bouveresse (eds.) (1981), *Meaning and Understanding*. Berlin: de Gruyter, 280–303.

—— (1985*e*). Identity and predication. In Evans (1985*a*: 25–48). First pub. in *Journal of Philosophy*, 72 (1975), 343–63.

FARAH, MARTHA (1990). *Visual Agnosia: Disorders of Object Recognition and what they Tell us about Normal Vision*. Cambridge, Mass.: MIT Press.

FELLEMAN, D. J., and VAN ESSEN, D. C. (1991). Distributed hierarchical processing in the primate cerebral cortex. *Cerebral Cortex*, 1: 1–47.

FENTON, M. B. (1995). Natural history and biosonar signals. In Popper and Fay (1995: 37–86).

FODOR, JERRY (1990). *A Theory of Content and Other Essays*. Cambridge, Mass.: MIT Press.

—— and LEPORE, ERNEST (1992). *Holism: A Shopper's Guide*. Oxford: Blackwell.

FRENCH, ROBERT (1987). The geometry of visual space. *Noûs*, 21: 115–33.

FUKUZAWA, K., ITOH, M., SASANUMA, S., SUZUKI, T., and FUKUSAKO, Z. (1988). Internal representations and the conceptual operation of color in pure alexia with color naming defects. *Brain and Language*, 34: 98–126.

GARDNER, MARTIN (ed.) (1965). *The Annotated Alice*. New York: Penguin.

—— (1991). The Ozma problem and the fall of parity. In Van Cleve and Frederick (1991: 75–96).

GIBSON, JAMES J. (1979). *The Ecological Approach to Visual Perception*. Boston: Houghton Mifflin.

GILCHRIST, A. L. (1977). Perceived lightness depends on perceived spatial arrangement. *Science*, 195: 185–7.

—— (1980). When does perceived lightness depend on perceived spatial arrangement? *Perception and Psychophysics*, 28: 527–38.

—— (1990). The perception of surface blacks and whites. In Rock (1990: 63–78). First pub. in *Scientific American*, 240 3 (1979), 112–25.

—— DELMAN, S., and JACOBSEN, A. (1983). The classification and integration of edges as critical to the perception of reflectance and illumination. *Perception and Psychophysics*, 33: 425–36.

GOLDSMITH, T. H. (1990). Optimization, constraint, and history in the evolution of eyes. *Quarterly Review of Biology*, 65: 281–322.

GOODMAN, NELSON (1972). *Problems and Projects*. Indianapolis: Hackett.

—— (1976). *Languages of Art*. Indianapolis: Hackett.

—— (1977). *The Structure of Appearance*. 3rd edn. Boston: Reidel.

GRAHAM, C. H., SPERLING, H. G., HSIA, Y., and COULSON, A. H. (1961). The determination of some visual functions of a unilaterally color blind subject. *Journal of Psychology*, 51: 3–32.

GRAHEK, NIKOLA (1995). The sensory dimension of pain. *Philosophical Studies*, 79: 167–84.

GREGORY, R. L. (1970). *The Intelligent Eye*. New York: McGraw-Hill.

—— (1977). *Eye and Brain*. 3rd edn. London: Weidenfeld & Nicolson.

GRINNELL, ALAN D. (1995). Hearing in bats: an overview. In Popper and Fay (1995: 1–36).

GRUSH, RICK (1997). The architecture of representation. *Philosophical Psychology*, 10 1: 5–23.

—— (forthcoming). Self, World, and Space: On the meaning and mechanisms of ego- and allo-centric spatial representation. *Brain and Mind*, 1.

GULICK, W. L., GESCHEIDER, G. A., and FRISINA, R. D. (1989). *Hearing: Physiological Acoustics, Neural Coding, and Psychoacoustics*. Oxford: Oxford University Press.

HAMLYN, D. W. (1956). The visual field and perception. *Proceedings of the Aristotelian Society*, 31: 107–24.

HARDIN, C. L. (1983). Colors, normal observers, and standard conditions. *Journal of Philosophy*, 80: 806–13.

—— (1984). Are scientific objects coloured? *Mind*, 93: 491–500.

—— (1988). *Color for Philosophers: Unweaving the Rainbow*. Indianapolis: Hackett.

—— (1990). Color and illusion. In Lycan (1990: 555–67).

—— (1992). The virtues of illusion. *Philosophical Studies*, 68: 371–82.

HARMAN, GILBERT (1990). The intrinsic quality of experience. In James E. Tomberlin (ed.), *Philosophical Perspectives*, iv: *Action Theory and Philosophy of Mind*. Atascadero, Calif.: Ridgeview Publishing, 31–52.

HATFIELD, GARY (1990). *The Natural and the Normative: Theories of Spatial Perception from Kant to Helmholtz*. Cambridge, Masss.: MIT Press.

HEELAN, PATRICK A. (1983). *Space Perception and the Philosophy of Science*. Berkeley: University of California Press.

HERING, EWALD (1878). *Zur Lehre vom Lichtsinne*. Vienna: Gerolds Sohn, 78–80. Tr. Don Cantor. In Herrnstein and Boring (1965: 253–7).

—— (1920). *Grundzüge der Lehre vom Lichtsinn*. Berlin: Springer Verglag. *Outlines of a Theory of the Light Sense* by L. Hurvich and D. Jameson. Cambridge, Mass.: Harvard University Press, 1964.

HERRNSTEIN, RICHARD J., and BORING, EDWIN G. (eds.) (1965). *A Source Book in the History of Psychology*. Cambridge, Mass.: Harvard University Press.

HILBERT, D. R. (1987). *Color and Color Perception: A Study in Anthropocentric Realism*. Menlo Park, Calif.: Center for the Study of Language and Information.

—— (1992). What is color vision? *Philosophical Studies*, 68: 351–70.

HINTIKKA, K. J. J. (1969). On the logic of perception. In his *Models for Modalities: Selected Essays*. Dordrecht: Reidel, 151–83.

—— (1975). Information, causality, and the logic of perception. In his *The Intentions of Intentionality and Other New Models for Modalities*. Dordrecht: Reidel, 59–75.

HIRST, R. J. (1959). *The Problems of Perception*. London: George Allen & Unwin.

HUMPHREYS, GLYN W. (ed.) (1994). *Understanding Vision: An Interdisciplinary Perspective*. Oxford: Blackwell.

HURVICH, LEO M. (1972). Color vision deficiencies. In D. Jameson and L. M. Hurvich (eds.), *Handbook of Sensory Physiology*, vii/4. New York: Springer Verlag, 582–624.

HURVICH, LEO, M. (1981). *Color Vision.* Sunderland, Mass.: Sinauer Associates.

—— and JAMESON, DOROTHEA (1957). An opponent process theory of color vision. *Psychological Review*, 64: 384–404.

JACKSON, FRANK (1976). The existence of mental objects. *Philosophical Quarterly*, 13: 33–40.

—— (1977). *Perception: A Representative Theory.* Cambridge: Cambridge University Press.

—— (1986). What Mary didn't know. *Journal of Philosophy*, 83: 291–5.

JACKSON, REGINALD (1968). Locke's distinction between primary and secondary qualities. In C. B. Martin and D. M. Armstrong (eds.), *Locke and Berkeley: A Collection of Critical Essays.* Garden City, NY: Anchor Books, 53–77. First pub. in *Mind*, 38 (1929), 56–76.

JACOBS, G. H. (1993). The distribution and nature of colour vision among the mammals. *Biological Reviews*, 68: 413–71.

JAMES, WILLIAM (1890*a*). *The Principles of Psychology*, i. New York: Henry Holt. Repr. New York: Dover, 1950.

—— (1890*b*). *The Principles of Psychology*, ii. New York: Henry Holt. Repr. New York: Dover, 1950.

JAMESON, DOROTHEA, and HURVICH, LEO M. (1989). Essay concerning color constancy. *Annual Review of Psychology*, 40: 1–22.

JEFFRESS, LLOYD A. (1948). A place theory of sound localization. *Journal of Comparative and Physiological Psychology*, 41: 35–9.

KANWISHER, NANCY, and DRIVER, JON (1992). Objects, attributes, and visual attention: which, what, and where. *Current Directions in Psychological Science*, 1: 26–31.

KAPLAN, DAVID (1973). Bob and Carol and Ted and Alice. In J. Hintikka, J. M. E. Moravcsik, and P. Suppes (eds.), *Approaches to Natural Language.* Dordrecht: Reidel, 409–18.

—— (1989*a*). Demonstratives. In Almog *et al.* (1989: 482–563).

—— (1989*b*). Afterthoughts. In Almog *et al.* (1989: 565–614).

—— (1997). Dthat. In Peter Ludlow (ed.), *Readings in the Philosophy of Language.* Cambridge, Mass.: MIT Press, 669–92. First pub. in Peter Cole (ed.) (1978), *Syntax and Semantics*, ix, *Pragmatics.* New York: Academic Press, 221–43.

KATZ, J., and MELZACK, R. (1990). Pain 'memories' in phantom limbs: review and clinical observations. *Pain*, 43: 319–36.

KAUFMAN, LLOYD (1974). *Sight and Mind.* New York: Oxford University Press.

KENNY, ANTHONY (1968). *Descartes: A Study of his Philosophy.* New York: Random House.

KERTESZ, A. (1979). Visual agnosia: the dual deficit of perception and recognition. *Cortex*, 15: 403–19.

KINSBOURNE, M., and WARRINGTON, ELISABETH K. (1964). Observations of colour agnosia. *Journal of Neurology, Neurosurgery, and Psychiatry*, 27: 296–9.

KOCH, C., and ULLMAN, S. (1985). Shifts in selective visual attention: towards the underlying neural circuitry. *Human Neurobiology*, 4: 219–27.

KOHLER, I. (1964). The formation and transformation of the perceptual world. Tr. H. Fiss. *Psychological Issues*, 3: 1–173.

KOLB, BRYAN, and WHISHAW, IAN Q. (1985). *Fundamentals of Human Neuropsychology*. 2nd edn. New York: W. H. Freeman.

KONISHI, M. (1992). The neural algorithm for sound localization in the owl. *Harvey Lectures*, 86: 47–64.

—— (1993). Listening with two ears. *Scientific American*, 268 4: 66–73.

—— TAKAHASHI, T. T., WAGNER, H., SULLIVAN, W. E., and CARR, C. E. (1988). Neurophysiological and anatomical substrates of sound localization in the owl. In G. M. Edelman, W. E. Gall, and W. M. Cowan (eds.), *Auditory Function: Neurobiological Bases of Hearing*. New York: Wiley, 721–45.

KRAUSKOPF, J. (1963). Effect of retinal image stabilization on the appearance of hetero-chromatic targets. *Journal of the Optical Society of America*, 53: 741–4.

KRAUT, ROBERT (1982). Sensory states and sensory objects. *Noûs*, 16: 277–93.

KRIPKE, SAUL A. (1972). *Naming and Necessity*. Cambridge, Mass.: Harvard University Press.

LAND, E. H. (1990). The retinex theory of color vision. In Rock (1990: 39–62). First pub. in *Scientific American*, 237/6 (1977), 108–28.

—— HUBEL, D. H., LIVINGSTON, M. S., PERRY, S. H., and BURNS, M. M. (1983). Colour-generating interactions across the corpus callosum. *Nature*, 303: 616–18.

LANDAU, BARBARA (1994). What's what and what's where: the language of objects in space. *Lingua*, 92: 259–96.

LEEDS, STEPHEN (1993). Qualia, awareness, Sellars. *Noûs*, 27: 303–30.

LEVIN, MICHAEL (1975). Kripke's argument against the identity thesis. *Journal of Philosophy*, 72: 149–67.

LEVINE, JOSEPH (1993). On leaving out what it's like. In Davies and Humphreys (1993: 121–36).

—— (1995). Qualia: intrinsic, relational, or what? In Metzinger (1995: 277–92).

LEWIS, CLARENCE IRVING (1929). *Mind and the World Order*. New York: Charles Scribner's Sons.

LEWIS, DAVID (1966). An argument for the identity theory. *Journal of Philosophy*, 63: 17–25.

—— (1972). Psycho-physical and theoretical identifications. *Australasian Journal of Philosophy*, 50: 249–58.

—— (1990). What experience teaches. In Lycan (1990: 499–519).

LLINÁS, RODOLFO, and CHURCHLAND, PATRICIA S. (eds.) (1996). *The Mind-Brain Continuum: Sensory Processes*. Cambridge, Mass.: MIT Press.

LOCKE, JOHN (1975). *An Essay Concerning Human Understanding*. Ed. Peter H. Nidditch. Oxford: Clarendon Press. (References to this text are by book, chapter, and paragraph rather than by page number.)

LOTZE, RUDOLF HERMANN (1852). *Medizinische Psychologie, oder Physiologie der Seele*. Bk. II, ch. 4, sect. 28. Tr. Don Cantor. In Herrnstein and Boring (1965: 135–40).

LURIA, A. R. (1973). *The Working Brain*. Harmondsworth: Penguin.

LYCAN, WILLIAM G. (1987). *Consciousness*. Cambridge, Mass.: MIT Press.

—— (ed.) (1990). *Mind and Cognition: A Reader*. Oxford: Blackwell.

—— (1995). A limited defense of phenomenal information. In Metzinger (1995: 243–58).

—— (1996). *Consciousness and Experience*. Cambridge, Mass.: MIT Press.

LYTHGOE, J. N., and PARTRIDGE, J. C. (1989). Visual pigments and the acquisition of visual information. *Journal of Experimental Biology*, 146: 1–20.

MCCARTHY, ROSALEEN (1993). Assembling routines and addressing representations: an alternative conceptualization of 'what' and 'where' in the human brain. In Eilan *et al.* (1993: 373–99).

MCCULLOCH, GREGORY (1989). *The Game of the Name: Introducing Logic, Language, and Mind*. Oxford: Oxford University Press.

MCGILVRAY, JAMES (1994). Constant colors in the head. *Synthese*, 100: 197–239.

MCGINN, COLIN (1991). *The Problem of Consciousness*. Oxford: Blackwell.

MACH, ERNST (1890). *Contributions to the Analysis of the Sensations*. Tr. M. C. Williams. La Salle, Ill.: Open Court.

MACK, ARIEN, and ROCK, IRVIN (1998). *Inattentional Blindness*. Cambridge, Mass.: MIT Press.

MCKELLAR, P. (1957). *Imagination and Thinking*. London: Cohen &West.

MACKIE, J. L. (1974). *The Cement of the Universe*. Oxford: Clarendon Press.

MALONEY, L. T., and WANDELL, B. A. (1986). Color constancy: a method for recovering surface spectral reflectance. *Journal of the Optical Society of America A*, 3: 29–33.

MARR, DAVID (1982). *Vision*. San Francisco: W. H. Freeman.

MARTIN, MICHAEL (1992). Sight and touch. In Crane (1992*b*: 196–215).

MATSON, WALLACE I. (1976). *Sentience*. Berkeley: University of California Press.

MATTHEN, MOHAN (1988). Biological functions and perceptual content. *Journal of Philosophy*, 85: 5–27.

—— and LEVY, EDWIN (1984). Teleology, error, and the human immune system. *Journal of Philosophy*, 81: 351–72.

MAZZONI, PIETRO, and ANDERSEN, RICHARD A. (1995). Gaze coding in the posterior parietal cortex. In Arbib (1995: 423–26).

MELNYK, ANDREW (1995). Two cheers for reductionism: or, the dim prospects for non-reductive physicalism. *Philosophy of Science*, 62: 370–88.

MELZACK, R. (1973). *The Puzzle of Pain*. Harmondsworth: Penguin.

—— (1989). Phantom limbs, the self, and the brain: the D. O. Hebb memorial lecture. *Canadian Psychology*, 30: 1–16.

—— (1992). Phantom limbs. *Scientific American*, 266 4: 120–7.

MENNE, D., KAIPF, I., WAGNER, I., OSTWALD, J., and SCHNITZLER, H. U. (1989). Range estimation by echolocation in the bat *Eptesicus fuscus*: trading of phase versus time cues. *Journal of the Acoustical Society of America*, 85: 2642–50.

MERBS, S. L., and NATHANS, J. (1992). Absorption spectra of human cone pigments. *Nature*, 356: 433–5.

Metzinger, Thomas (ed.) (1995). *Conscious Experience*. Paderborn: Imprint Academic Schöningh; Lawrence, Kan.: Allen Press.

Millikan, Ruth (1984). *Language, Thought, and Other Biological Categories*. Cambridge, Mass.: MIT Press.

—— (1993*a*). Biosemantics. In Millikan (1993*e*: 83–102). First pub. in *Journal of Philosophy*, 86 (1989), 281–97.

—— (1993*b*). On mentalese orthography, i. In Millikan (1993*e*: 103–22). First pub. in Bo Dahlbom (ed.) (1993), *Dennett and his Critics*. Oxford: Blackwell, 97–123.

—— (1993*c*). The myth of the essential indexical. In Millikan (1993*e*: 265–77). First pub. in *Noûs*, 24 (1990), 723–34.

—— (1993*d*). Thoughts without laws. In Millikan (1993*e*: 51–82). First pub. in *Philosophical Review*, 95 (1986), 47–80.

—— (1993*e*). *White Queen Psychology and Other Essays for Alice*. Cambridge, Mass.: MIT Press.

Milner, Peter M. (1970). *Physiological Psychology*. London: Holt, Rinehart & Winston.

Mogdans, J., and Schnitzler, H. U. (1990). Range resolution and the possible use of spectral information in the echolocating bat *Eptesicus fuscus*. *Journal of the Acoustical Society of America*, 88: 754–7.

Mollon, J. D. (1989). 'Tho' she kneel'd in that place where they grew': the uses and origins of primate colour vision. *Journal of Experimental Biology*, 146: 21–38.

—— (1991). Uses and evolutionary origins of primate colour vision. In J. R. Cronly-Dillon and R. L. Gregory (eds.), *Evolution of the Eye and Visual System*. Boca Raton, Fla.: CRC Press, 306–19.

Moore, G. E. (1953). Sense-data. In his *Some Main Problems of Philosophy*. London: George Allen & Unwin, 28–40. Repr. in Moore (1993*b*: 45–58).

—— (1965*a*). Some judgments of perception. In Swartz (1965: 1–28). First pub. in *Proceedings of the Aristotelian Society*, 19 (1918), 1–29.

—— (1965*b*). Visual sense-data. In Swartz (1965: 130–7). First pub. in C. A. Mace (ed.), *British Philosophy in Mid-Century*. London: George Allen & Unwin, 1957, 205–11.

—— (1993*a*). A defence of common sense. In Moore (1993*b*: 106–33). First pub. in J. H. Muirhead (ed.) (1925), *Contemporary British Philosophy*. 2nd ser. London: George Allen & Unwin, 192–233.

—— (1993*b*). *G. E. Moore: Selected Writings*. Ed. Thomas Baldwin. London: Routledge.

Morgan, Michael (1979). The two spaces. In Neil Bolton (ed.), *Philosophical Problems in Psychology*. New York: Methuen, 66–88.

Murch, Gerald M. (1973). *Visual and Auditory Perception*. New York: Bobbs-Merrill.

Nagel, Thomas (1979). What is it like to be a bat? In his *Mortal Questions*. Cambridge: Cambridge University Press, 165–80. First pub. in *Philosophical Review*, 83 (1974), 435–50.

—— (1986). *The View from Nowhere*. Oxford: Oxford University Press.

NATHANS, J., PIANTANIDA, T., EDDY, R. L., SHOWS, T. B., and HOGNESS, D. S. (1986). Molecular genetics of inherited variation in human color vision. *Science*, 232: 203–32.

NEITZ, M., NEITZ, J., and JACOBS, G. H. (1991). Spectral tuning of pigments underlying red–green color vision. *Science*, 252: 971–4.

NEUMEYER, CHRISTA (1991). Evolution of colour vision. In J. R. Cronly-Dillon and R. L. Gregory (eds.), *Evolution of the Eye and Visual System*. Boca Raton, Fla.: CRC Press, 284–305.

NEWTON, ISAAC (1952). *Opticks*. New York: Dover.

NEWTON-SMITH, W. H. (1981). *The Rationality of Science*. London: Routledge & Kegan Paul.

O'KEEFE, JOHN (1993). Kant and the sea-horse: an essay on the neurophilosophy of space. In Eilan *et al.* (1993: 43–64).

O'LEARY-HAWTHORNE, J., and CORTENS, A. (1995). Towards ontological nihilism. *Philosophical Studies*, 79: 143–65.

OLSEN, J. F., and SUGA, N. (1991). Combination-sensitive neurons in the medial geniculate body of the mustached bat: encoding of target range information. *Journal of Neurophysiology*, 65: 1275–99.

O'SHAUGHNESSY, BRIAN (1980). *The Will: A Dual Aspect Theory*, i. Cambridge: Cambridge University Press.

PAILLARD, JACQUES (ed.) (1992). *Brain and Space*. Oxford: Oxford University Press.

PEACOCKE, CHRISTOPHER (1983). *Sense and Content: Experience, Thought, and their Relations*. Oxford: Clarendon Press.

—— (1992*a*). Scenarios, concepts, and perception. In Crane (1992*b*: 105–35).

—— (1992*b*). *A Study of Concepts*. Cambridge, Mass.: MIT Press.

PEIRCE, CHARLES S. (1958). *Values in a Universe of Chance: Selected Writings*. Ed. Philip P. Wiener. New York: Dover.

PERRY, JOHN (1977). Frege on demonstratives. *Philosophical Review*, 86: 474–97.

—— (1979). The problem of the essential indexical. *Noûs*, 13: 3–21.

PITCHER, GEORGE (1971). *A Theory of Perception*. Princeton, NJ: Princeton University Press.

PÖPPEL, ERNST (1988). *Mindworks: Time and Conscious Experience*. Tr. Tom Artin. Boston: Harcourt Brace Jovanovich.

POLLAK, G. D., and CASSEDAY, J. H. (1989). *The Neural Basis of Echolocation in Bats*. New York: Springer Verlag.

POPPER, ARTHUR N., and FAY, RICHARD R. (eds.) (1995). *Hearing by Bats. Springer Handbook of Auditory Research*, v. New York: Springer Verlag.

POSNER, M. I. (1978). *Chronometric Explorations of Mind*. Hillsdale, NJ: Lawrence Erlbaum.

—— and PETERSEN, S. E. (1990). The attention system of the human brain. *Annual Review of Neuroscience*, 13: 25–42.

PRICE, H. H. (1932). *Perception*. London: Methuen.

PRINZMETAL, W. (1995). Visual feature integration in a world of objects. *Current Directions in Psychological Science*, 4: 90–4.

QUINE, W. V. O. (1966). Variables explained away. In his *Selected Logic Papers*. New York: Random House, 227–35.

—— (1992). *Pursuit of Truth*. Rev. edn. Cambridge, Mass.: Harvard University Press.

RAMACHANDRAN, V. S., *et al.* (1996). Illusions of body image: what they reveal about human nature. In Llinás and Churchland (1996: 29–60).

RAMSEY, F. P. (1931). *The Foundations of Mathematics and Other Logical Essays*. London: Routledge & Kegan Paul.

RECANATI, FRANÇOIS (1993). *Direct Reference: From Language to Thought*. Oxford: Blackwell.

REED, GRAHAM (1972). *The Psychology of Anomalous Experience: A Cognitive Approach*. London: Hutchinson University Library.

REY, GEORGES (1993). Sensational sentences. In Davies and Humphreys (1993: 240–57).

—— (1995). Towards a projectivist account of conscious experience. In Metzinger (1995: 123–42).

ROCK, I. (1983). *The Logic of Perception*. Cambridge, Mass.: MIT Press.

—— (ed.) (1990). *The Perceptual World*. New York: W. H. Freeman.

—— LINNETT, C., GRANT, P., and MACK, A. (1992). Perception without attention: results of a new method. *Cognitive Psychology*, 24: 502–34.

ROSCH, ELEANOR H. (1973). Natural categories. *Cognitive Psychology*, 4: 328–50.

ROSENTHAL, DAVID (1986). Two concepts of consciousness. *Philosophical Studies*, 94: 329–59. Repr. in David Rosenthal (ed.), *The Nature of Mind*. New York: Oxford University Press, 462–77.

—— (1991). The independence of consciousness and sensory quality. In Enrique Villanueva (ed.), *Philosophical Issues*, i: *Consciousness*. Atascadero, Calif.: Ridgeview Publishing, 15–36.

—— (1997). A theory of consciousness. In Block *et al.* (1997: 729–53).

—— (forthcoming). *Mind and Consciousness*. Oxford: Clarendon Press.

RUMELHART, DAVID E., and MCCLELLAND, JAMES L. (1986). *Parallel Distributed Processing: Explorations in the Microstructure of Cognition*. Cambridge, Mass.: MIT Press.

RUSSELL, BERTRAND (1903). *The Principles of Mathematics*. London: W. W. Norton.

—— (1962). *An Inquiry into Meaning and Truth*. Baltimore: Penguin.

—— (1981). *Mysticism and Logic*. Totowa, NJ: Barnes & Noble. First pub. London: George Allen & Unwin, 1917.

—— (1985). *The Philosophy of Logical Atomism*. La Salle, Ill.: Open Court. First pub. in *Monist*, 28 (1918), 495–527; 29 (1919), 32–63, 190–222, 345–80.

SAILLANT, P. A., SIMMONS, J. A., DEAR, S. P., and MCMULLEN, T. A. (1993). A computational model of echo processing and acoustic imaging in frequency-modulated echolocating bats: the spectrogram correlation and transformation receiver. *Journal of the Acoustical Society of America*, 94: 2691–712.

SAJDA, PAUL, and FINKEL, LEIF H. (1995). Intermediate-level visual representations and the construction of surface perception. *Journal of Cognitive Neuroscience*, 7: 267–91.

SCHIFFMAN, HARVEY RICHARD (1982). *Sensation and Perception: An Integrated Approach*. 2nd edn. New York: Wiley.

SCHWARTZ, ROBERT (1994). *Vision: Variations on Some Berkeleian Themes*. Oxford: Blackwell.

SCHYNS, P. G., GOLDSTONE, R. L., and THIBAUT, J.-P. (1998). The development of features in object concepts. *Behavioral and Brain Sciences*, 21: 1–54.

SEARLE, JOHN (1983). *Intentionality: An Essay in Philosophy of Mind*. Cambridge: Cambridge University Press.

SELLARS, WILFRID (1963). *Science, Perception, and Reality*. London: Routledge & Kegan Paul.

—— (1968). *Science and Metaphysics: Variations on Kantian Themes*. London: Routledge & Kegan Paul.

—— (1981*a*). Naturalism and process. *Monist*, 64: 36–65.

—— (1981*b*). Is consciousness physical? *Monist*, 64: 66–90.

SHAMMA, SHIHAB A. (1995). Auditory cortex. In Arbib (1995: 110–15).

SHEPARD, R. N. (1992). The perception organization of colors: an adaptation to regularities of the terrestrial world? In J. H. Barkow, L. Cosmides, and J. Tooby (eds.), *The Adapted Mind: Evolutionary Psychology and the Generation of Culture*. Oxford: Oxford University Press, 495–532.

—— (1993). On the physical basis, linguistic representation, and conscious experience of colors. In Gilbert Harman (ed.), *Conceptions of the Human Mind: Essays in Honor of George A. Miller*. Hillsdale, NJ: Lawrence Erlbaum, 217–45.

SHOEMAKER, SYDNEY (1990). Qualities and qualia: what's in the mind? *Philosophy and Phenomenological Research*, Suppl., 50: 109–31.

—— (1991). Qualia and consciousness. *Mind*, 100: 507–24.

—— (1994*a*). Phenomenal character. *Noûs*, 28: 21–38.

—— (1994*b*). Self-knowledge and 'inner sense'. Josiah Royce Lectures. *Philosophy and Phenomenological Research*, 54: 249–311.

SIMMONS, J. A. (1979). Perception of echo phase information in bat sonar. *Science*, 207: 1336–8.

—— (1996). Formation of perceptual objects from the timing of neural responses: target-range images in bat sonar. In Llinás and Churchland (1996: 219–50).

—— and CHEN, L. (1989). The acoustic basis for target discrimination by FM echolocating bats. *Journal of the Acoustical Society of America*, 86: 1333–50.

—— FREEDMAN, E. G., STEVENSON, S. B., CHEN, L., and WOHLGENANT, T. J. (1989). Clutter interference and the integration time of echoes in the echolocating bat, *Eptesicus fuscus*. *Journal of the Acoustical Society of America*, 86: 1318–32.

—— FERRAGAMO, M. J., MOSS, C. F., STEVENSON, S. B., and ALTES, R. A. (1990*a*). Discrimination of jittered sonar echoes by the echolocating bat *Eptesicus fuscus*: the shape of target images in echolocation. *Journal of Comparative Physiology A*, 167: 589–616.

—— MOSS, C. F., and FERRAGAMO, M. J. (1990*b*). Convergence of temporal and spectral information into acoustic images of complex sonar targets perceived by the echolocating bat *Eptesicus fuscus. Journal of Comparative Physiology A*, 166: 449–70.

—— FERRAGAMO, M. J., SAILLANT, P. A., HARESIGN, T., WOTTON, J. M., DEAR, S. P., and LEE, D. N. (1995). Auditory dimensions of acoustic images in echolocation. In Popper and Fay (1995: 146–90).

SINGER, W. (1993). Synchronization of neural activity and its putative role in information processing and learning. *Annual Review of Physiology*, 55: 349–74.

—— (1996). Neuronal synchronization: a solution to the binding problem? In Llinás and Churchland (1996: 101–30).

—— and GRAY, C. M. (1995). Visual feature integration and the temporal correlation hypothesis. *Annual Review of Neuroscience*, 18: 555–86.

SMART, J. J. C. (1975). On some criticisms of a physicalist theory of colors. In Chung-Ying Cheng (ed.), *Philosophical Aspects of the Mind–Body Problem*. Honolulu: University of Hawaii Press, 54–63.

SNOWDON, PAUL (1992). How to interpret 'direct perception'. In Crane (1992*b*: 48–78).

STICH, STEPHEN, and WARFIELD, TED (eds.) (1994). *Mental Representation: A Reader*. Oxford: Blackwell.

STRAWSON, GALEN (1989). Red and 'red'. *Synthese*, 78: 193–232.

—— (1994). *Mental Reality*. Cambridge, Mass.: MIT Press.

STRAWSON, P. F. (1954). Particular and general. *Proceedings of the Aristotelian Society*, 54: 233–60.

—— (1963). *Individuals*. New York: Anchor Books.

—— (1974). *Subject and Predicate in Logic and Grammar*. London: Methuen.

—— (1986). Reference and its roots. In L. E. Hahn and P. A. Schilpp (eds.), *The Philosophy of W. V. Quine*. Library of Living Philosophers, xviii. La Salle, Ill.: Open Court Press, 519–32.

—— (1988). Perception and its objects. In Jonathan Dancy (ed.), *Perceptual Knowledge*. Oxford: Oxford University Press, 92–112. First pub. in G. MacDonald (ed.) (1979), *Perception and Identity: Essays Presented to A. J. Ayer*. London: Macmillan, 41–60.

—— (1997). *Entity and Identity and Other Essays*. Oxford: Clarendon Press.

SUGA, N. (1988). Auditory neuroethology and speech processing: complex sound processing by combination-sensitive neurons. In G. M. Edelman, W. E. Gall, and W. M. Cowan (eds.), *Functions of the Auditory System*. New York: Wiley, 679–720.

—— (1990). Cortical computation maps for auditory imaging. *Neural Networks*, 3: 3–21.

—— and KANWAL, J. S. (1995). Echolocation: creating computational maps. In Arbib (1995: 344–8).

—— OLSEN, J. F., and BUTMAN, J. A. (1990). Specialized subsystems for processing biologically important complex sounds: cross correlation analysis for ranging in the bat's brain. *The Brain: Cold Spring Harbor Symposia on Quantitative Biology*, 55: 585–97.

SWARTZ, ROBERT J. (ed.) (1965). *Perceiving, Sensing, and Knowing*. Garden City, NY: Anchor Books.

TAKAHASHI, TERRY T. (1989). The neural coding of auditory space. *Journal of Experimental Biology*, 146: 307–22.

TAYLOR, B. (1980). Truth theory for indexical languages. In M. Platts (ed.), *Reference, Truth, and Reality*. London: Routledge & Kegan Paul, 182–98.

TELLER, DAVIDA Y. (1984). Linking propositions. *Vision Research*, 24: 1233–46.

THOMASON, R. (1973). Perception and individuation. In M. Munitz (ed.), *Logic and Ontology*. New York: New York University Press, 261–86.

THOMPSON, E. (1995*a*). *Colour Vision*. London: Routledge.

—— (1995*b*). Colour vision, evolution, and perceptual content. *Synthese*, 104: 1–32.

—— PALACIOS, A., and VARELA, F. J. (1992). Ways of coloring: comparative color vision as a case study for cognitive science. *Behavioral and Brain Sciences*, 15: 1–74.

THOMPSON, RICHARD F. (1967). *Foundations of Physiological Psychology*. New York: Harper & Row.

TOUCHETTE, NANCY (1993). Mixed up genes cause off-color vision. *Journal of NIH Research*, 5: 34–7.

TREISMAN, A. (1985). Preattentive processing in vision. *Computer Vision and Graphics Image Processing*, 31: 156–77.

—— (1986). Features and objects in visual processing. *Scientific American*, 255 4: 114–27. Repr. in Rock (1990: 97–110).

—— (1988). Features and objects: the fourteenth annual Bartlett memorial lecture. *Quarterly Journal of Experimental Psychology A*, 40: 201–37.

—— (1993). The perception of features and objects. In A. Baddeley and L. Weiskrantz (eds.), *Attention: Selection, Awareness, and Control: A Tribute to Donald Broadbent*. Oxford: Clarendon Press, 5–35.

—— (1996). The binding problem. *Current Opinion in Neurobiology*, 6: 171–8.

—— and GEFFEN, GINA (1967). Selective attention: perception or response? *Quarterly Journal of Experimental Psychology*, 19: 1–17.

—— and GELADE, GARRY (1980). A feature-integration theory of attention. *Cognitive Psychology*, 12: 97–136.

TURVEY, MICHAEL T. (1996). Dynamic touch. *American Psychologist*, 51: 1134–52.

TYE, MICHAEL (1989). *The Metaphysics of Mind*. Cambridge: Cambridge University Press.

—— (1992). Visual qualia and visual content. In Crane (1992*b*: 158–76).

—— (1995). *Ten Problems of Consciousness: A Representational Theory of the Phenomenal Mind*. Cambridge, Mass.: MIT Press.

VALBERG, J. J. (1992). The puzzle of experience. In Crane (1992*b*: 18–47).

VAN CLEVE, JAMES, and FREDERICK, ROBERT E. (eds.) (1991). *The Philosophy of Right and Left*. Boston: Dordrecht.

VAN GULICK, ROBERT (1993). Understanding the phenomenal mind: are we all just armadillos? In Davies and Humphreys (1993: 137–54).

VENDLER, ZENO (1991). Epiphenomena. In A. P. Martinich and M. J. White (eds.),

Certainty and Surface in Epistemology and Philosophical Method: Essays in Honor of Avrum Stroll. Lewiston, Ut.: Edwin Mellen Press, 101–14.

—— (1994). The ineffable soul. In Warner and Szubka (1994: 317–28).

VON DER MALSBURG, C. (1996). The binding problem of neural networks. In Llinás and Churchland (1996: 131–46).

WALLACH, H. (1948). Brightness constancy and the nature of achromatic colors. *Journal of Experimental Psychology*, 38: 310–24.

WARNER, RICHARD, and SZUBKA, TADEUSZ (eds.) (1994). *The Mind–Body Problem: A Guide to the Current Debate*. Oxford: Blackwell.

WARREN, RICHARD M. (1982). *Auditory Perception: A New Synthesis*. New York: Pergamon.

YOURGRAU, P. (ed.) (1990). *Demonstratives*. Oxford: Oxford University Press.

ZUSNE, LEONARD, and JONES, WARREN H. (1982). *Anomalistic Psychology*. Hillsdale, NJ: Lawrence Erlbaum.

INDEX

Page references in boldface indicate the location of definitions.